The History Of The Post Office
From Its Establishment Down To 1836

by

Herbert Joyce

Double 9
BOOKS

The History Of The Post Office
From Its Establishment Down To 1836
by Herbert Joyce

ISBN: 978-93-62202-99-4

Published by

DOUBLE 9 BOOKS

2/13-B, Ansari Road
Daryaganj, New Delhi – 110002
info@double9books.com
www.double9books.com
Tel. 011-40042856

This book is under public domain

ABOUT THE AUTHOR

Herbert Joyce, a distinguished historian and author, presents his magnum opus "The History of the Post Office, from Its Establishment Down to 1836." This comprehensive work offers readers an in-depth exploration of the evolution and significance of postal services up to the year 1836. Drawing from extensive research and a deep understanding of the subject matter, Joyce meticulously chronicles the development of the postal system, from its humble beginnings to its pivotal role in communication and commerce. Through vivid storytelling and insightful analysis, Joyce sheds light on the social, economic, and political implications of the post office's establishment and expansion. From the establishment of early mail routes to the introduction of postage stamps and postal reforms, Joyce traces the milestones and challenges that shaped the postal service's growth and modernization. "The History of the Post Office" stands as a testament to Joyce's dedication to preserving and sharing the rich tapestry of postal history. With its meticulous attention to detail and engaging narrative style, Joyce's masterpiece offers readers a captivating journey through time, illuminating the enduring importance of the postal system in connecting people and facilitating the exchange of ideas and information.

CONTENTS

CHAPTER I
EARLY POSTS 1533-1609...7

CHAPTER II
THE BATTLE OF THE PATENTS 1609-1635 12

CHAPTER III
THOMAS WITHERINGS 1635—1644..17

CHAPTER IV
EDMUND PRIDEAUX AND CLEMENT
OXENBRIDGE 1644—1660 24

CHAPTER V
WILLIAM DOCKWRA 1660-1685 31

CHAPTER VI
COTTON AND FRANKLAND Inland Service 1685-1705 38

CHAPTER VII
COTTON AND FRANKLAND Packet Service 1686-1713 58

CHAPTER VIII
AMERICAN POSTS 1692-1707 86

CHAPTER IX
THE POST OFFICE ACT OF 1711 92

CHAPTER X
RALPH ALLEN 1720-1764 112

CHAPTER XI
LEGISLATION AND LITIGATION 1764-1782..................................141

CHAPTER XII
JOHN PALMER 1782-1792 156

CHAPTER XIII
    THE NINETIES: OR, ONE HUNDRED YEARS AGO 208

CHAPTER XIV
    FRANCIS FREELING 1798-1817...242

CHAPTER XV
    IRELAND 1801-1828...270

CHAPTER XVI
    THE BEGINNING OF THE END 1817-1836 291

APPENDIX...315

INDEX 324

FOOTNOTES:..379

CHAPTER I
EARLY POSTS 1533-1609

The early history of the posts is involved in some obscurity. What little is known on the subject is touched upon in the first Annual Report of the Post Office, the Report for 1854; but the historical summary there given is, as it purports to be, a summary only. The object of the following pages is nothing more than to fill up the gaps and to supply some particulars for which, though not perhaps without interest, an official report would be no fitting place. The origin and progress of an institution which has so interwoven itself with the social life of the people as to have become one of the most remarkable developments of modern civilisation can hardly, we think, be considered a subject unworthy of study.

It seems almost certain that until the reign of Henry the Eighth, or perhaps a little earlier, no regular system of posts existed in England, and that then and for some considerable time afterwards the few posts that were established were for the exclusive use of the Sovereign. "Sir," writes Sir Brian Tuke to Thomas Cromwell in 1533, "it may like you to understonde the Kinges Grace hathe no moo ordinary postes, ne of many days hathe had, but bitwene London and Calais ... and sens October last, the postes northewarde.... For, Sir, ye knowe well that, except the hakney horses bitwene Gravesende and Dovour, there is no suche usual conveyance in post for men in this realme as is in the accustumed places of France and other parties." Sir Brian Tuke held the appointment of Master of the Posts, and he had received the King's commands to set up posts "in al places most expedient."

Before Henry's reign the only letters of which any record exists, letters to or from the Court and on affairs of State, were sent by couriers employed for the particular occasion. These couriers, styled "Nuncii" and "Cursores," appear to have answered to the Queen's messengers of our own time, and, as is evident from records still extant and dating back to the reign of Henry the Third, must have formed an important branch of the royal establishment.

To establish posts and to control them when established was not all or nearly all that Brian Tuke had to do. He had also to see, even where no posts existed, that the royal couriers were not kept waiting for horses; and this probably was his original function. The horses were provided by the townships, and the townships were kept up to their duty by the Master of the Posts. In some cases, indeed, special provision appears to have been made. At Leicester,[1] for instance, the members of the Corporation bound themselves under penalty to keep four post-horses in constant readiness for their Sovereign's use; but this can hardly have been a common practice. Where horses were not provided voluntarily, the magistrates and constables had orders to seize them wherever they could be found.

The close connection between the posts and the Sovereign continued long after the reign of Henry the Eighth. In 1572 Thomas Randolph, Master of the posts to Queen Elizabeth, rendered an account of the charges to which he had been put in the execution of his trust during the preceding five years; and in this account, which is given in considerable detail, not a single post is mentioned without some qualification identifying it with the person of the Sovereign—a post daily serving Her Majesty, a post for Her Majesty's service and affairs, a post during the time of Her Majesty's progress, a post for the conveyance of Her Majesty's letters and those of her Council. As late as 1621 all the posts of the kingdom, which even then were only four in number, started from the Court. I. "The Courte to Barwicke," *i.e.* the post to Scotland. II. "The Courte to Beaumoris," *i.e.* the post to Ireland. III. "The Courte to Dover," *i.e.* the post to the Continent. IV. "The Courte to Plymouth," *i.e.* the post to the Royal Dockyard.

The setting up of a post for a particular purpose and letting it drop as soon as the purpose had been answered was another peculiarity of these early times. The post to Plymouth, ordained in 1621 to be one of the standing posts of the kingdom, had been dropped since 1611, having then been declared to be unnecessary except in time of war. Even the post to Ireland had at one time been dropped and was not revived until 1598. In the same year a second post to Ireland, Irish affairs being then considered to require "oftner dispatches and more expedition," was set up by way of Bristol, and this in its turn disappeared. Indeed, it would probably not be too much to say that at the beginning of the seventeenth century no post set up in England during a war had lasted longer than the war itself. This practice of dropping a post as soon as it had served its purpose, a practice which must almost necessarily have existed from the earliest times, would seem to explain Brian Tuke's meaning when, after stating that in 1533 except those he mentioned "the Kinges Grace hathe no moo ordinary postes," he adds, "ne of many days hathe had."

For the regulation of the posts the earliest instructions of which we have any record were issued by Queen Elizabeth. Every "post" was to keep and have constantly ready two horses at least, with suitable "furniture." He was to have at least two bags of leather well lined with baize or cotton, and a horn to blow "as oft as he meets company" or four times in every mile. He was, after receiving a packet, to start within fifteen minutes, and to run in summer at the rate of seven miles an hour and in winter at the rate of five. The address of the packet and the day and the hour at which he received it were to be carefully entered in a book to be kept for the purpose. But the packets which were thus to be treated were only such as should be on the Queen's affairs or the affairs of State. "All others" are dismissed in a word. These, the instructions state, are "to passe as by-letters." To pass as by-letters probably means that the letters were to go when and as best they might, but that the post was not to go for the purpose of taking them. This view is confirmed by an order of the subsequent reign, that "no pacquets or letters," except such as were on the King's affairs, should "binde any poste to ride therewith in post." But be the meaning what it may, the expression seems to shew that even in the reign of Elizabeth letters other than State letters had begun to be sent to the post-houses, and that such letters, if barely recognised, were yet not excluded.

But the conveyance of the Sovereign's letters was not the only purpose which the posts as originally established were designed to serve. Another and hardly less important purpose was that there should be stationed and in constant readiness, at given distances along the chief roads of the kingdom, a relay of horses by which persons travelling on their Sovereign's concerns, even though not the bearers of letters, might pass between one part of the country and another. Of this second purpose a few words implanted in the English language, such as post-horse, post-boy, and travelling-post, are all that we have now left to remind us. But long after the public had been admitted to the free use of the post, the two objects of providing for letters and providing for travellers continued to be treated as inseparable. Hence the history of the posts during the seventeenth century and far into the eighteenth becomes complicated with the history of travelling.[2]

Indeed, there can be little doubt that it was as a means of travelling and not as a means of correspondence that the post first came to be used by others than those employed on affairs of State. Writing, during the sixteenth century, was an accomplishment possessed by comparatively few, whereas any one might have occasion to travel; and the resources of travelling, so far as these partook of an organised system, were in the hands of the Sovereign. Wherever there were posts, it was at the Sovereign's charge and for the Sovereign's use that horses were maintained; and where there were no posts, it was only for the use of the Sovereign that the townships were under obligation to supply horses. The natural consequence followed.

People pretended to be travelling on their Sovereign's affairs who were really travelling on affairs of their own, and so procured the use of horses which would otherwise have been denied them. The horses, moreover, were overridden and overloaded, and the persons by whom they were hired not rarely forgot to pay for them.[3]

No sooner had James the First come to the throne than he issued a proclamation having for its object to check these abuses. Only those were to be deemed to be travelling on public affairs who held a special commission signed by one or more of the principal officers of State. No horse was to be ridden, in summer, above seven miles an hour, and in winter above six; nor yet, without the knowledge and consent of the owner, beyond the next stage. The load, besides the rider, was not to exceed thirty pounds in weight. Persons riding with special commission were to pay for each horse 2-1/2d. a mile, besides the guide's groats, and "others riding poste with horse and guide about their private businesses" were to make their own terms. In all cases payment was to be made in advance. The proclamation contained another and most important provision, the effects of which were felt far into the next century. This was that, wherever posts existed, those who had the horsing of the posts were also to have the exclusive letting of horses to travellers. If the post-houses could not supply horses enough, the local constables with the assistance of the magistrates were to make good the deficiency.

The proclamation of 1603 was soon followed by another, prohibiting all persons not being duly authorised by the Master of the Posts from being concerned in the collecting, carrying, or delivering of letters. The effect, therefore, of the two proclamations together was that, except by private hand, no letter and, except along the bye-roads where posts did not exist, no traveller could pass between one part of the kingdom and another without coming under the observation of the Government. It has been suggested that the State monopoly of letters had its origin in a desire on the part of the Sovereign to reserve to himself the revenue which the letters brought; but in 1609, when the monopoly was created, the posts were maintained at a clear loss to the crown of £3400 a year, and this loss, as matters then stood, the erection of every fresh post would serve to increase. However it may have been in after years, the original object of the monopoly, the object avowed indeed and proclaimed, was that the State might possess the means of detecting and defeating conspiracies against itself. A system such as this object implies is absolutely abhorrent to our present notions; and yet it is a fact beyond all question that the posts in their infancy were regarded and largely employed as an instrument of police. It was not until the reign of William the Third that they began to assume their present shape of a mere channel for the transmission of letters.

But we are anticipating. In 1609 the cloud which obscures the earlier history of the posts begins to break, and from that year it is possible to present a tolerably connected narrative of their progress.

CHAPTER II
THE BATTLE OF THE PATENTS 1609-1635

At the beginning of the seventeenth century the established posts were only four in number,—the post to Scotland, the post to Ireland, the post to Plymouth, and the post to Dover; and of these the most important by far, because the most used, was the last, the post through the county of Kent. It was through this county that the high-road to the Continent lay, and, while commercial relations as between one town and another within the kingdom were yet a thing of the future, the foreign trade of the country had already reached very considerable proportions. The persecutions in France and the Low Countries had driven a large number of foreigners to London, and here the Flemings introduced the manufacture of wool into cloth. In this commodity alone the exports from England to the Netherlands in the time of Philip the Second amounted to five millions of crowns annually.[4] In education no less than manufactures the Flemings were far in advance of our own countrymen. There was scarcely a peasant among them that could not both read and write. While, therefore, the other three posts of the kingdom were still being little used except for letters on affairs of State, the post to the Continent had already become matter of public concern.

This post had long been jealously watched, the foreign merchants in London claiming to send their letters by their own agents, and the Crown insisting that they should be sent only through the established channel. It was an old feud, extending far back into the sixteenth century. In 1591 a proclamation on the subject had been issued. This, in respect to the post through the county of Kent, established that State monopoly of letters which was not made general until eighteen years afterwards. It was to the protection of the same post that the proclamation of 1603 had been directed, the proclamation reserving to those who horsed the posts the exclusive right of letting horses to travellers. But these measures had been of little avail. The foreign merchants still employed their own agents to carry their letters, and these agents, instead of resorting to the post-houses, still procured horses where and as best they could.

Once more recourse was had to a proclamation, which differed little from others that had gone before except in one important particular. This was the open avowal that among the chief cares of the State it had been and continued to be by no means the least "to meete with the dangerous and secret intelligences of ill-affected persons, both at home and abroad, by the overgreat liberty taken both in writing and riding in poste, specially in and through our countie of Kent." The magistrates were enjoined to take care that horses were procured at the post-houses alone. No letters were to be sent except through the post, and notice to this effect was to be served upon all the merchants of the city of London, "both strangers and others." Unauthorised persons suspected of having letters upon them were, before entering or leaving the kingdom, to be searched. And any packets or letters found to be illicitly conveyed were to be sent up to the Privy Council, and the bearers of them to be apprehended and kept in safe custody pending the Council's orders.

At this time the office of Master of the Posts was held by Lord Stanhope of Harrington, and under Lord Stanhope, to superintend the foreign post, was employed a foreigner of the name of De Quester. This man, with the assistance of his son, appears to have discharged his duties efficiently. He made communication with the Continent both cheaper and more expeditious. His promptitude in forwarding the public despatches had attracted the attention of his Sovereign. In 1619, in recognition of these services, the King created the control of the foreign post into a separate appointment, independent of Lord Stanhope, and conferred it upon De Quester and his son, under the title of "Postmaster of England for Foreign parts out of the King's Dominions."

It is possible that De Quester's appointment, though ostensibly a reward for good service, was dictated in part by policy. But if designed to appease the foreign merchants, it signally failed of its object. The truth seems to be that they were animated by feelings of profound distrust. Many years later, when De Quester had retired, the English merchants, in a petition to the King, protested against the choice of a successor being left to the "strangers." This, they said, would be to their own great prejudice. Even the letters patent by which that successor was appointed give as a reason for not letting the strangers have a post of their own that thus the secrets of the realm would be disclosed to foreign nations. Such being the feelings on one side, it would be strange indeed if they had not also existed on the other.

De Quester's appointment, while displeasing to the foreign merchants, gave dire offence to Lord Stanhope. The letters patent by which this peer held his office had expressly declared that not only the internal posts of the kingdom were to be under his direction, but also those "beyond the seas within the King's dominions." This expression, repeated from former patents, applied, no doubt, to Calais. And yet, could it in reason be contended that his rights were not being infringed if the post through which all letters between London and the Continent passed were transferred to other hands? Except for the practice of granting offices in remainder, Stanhope's death at this time would have settled the difficulty. As a matter of fact, however, the difficulty had only begun. By a deed granted thirteen years before, his son and successor in the title succeeded also to the office of Master of the Posts, and it soon became evident that the younger Stanhope had no intention, without a struggle, of letting the grant to himself be whittled away by a subsequent grant to another. The Council, not composed of laymen alone, but comprising among its members Coventry, soon to become Lord Keeper, and Heath, the Solicitor-General, advised the King that "both grants might well stand together, being of distinct places." Stanhope rejoined that his was "an ancient office tyme out of minde," and that by prescription it carried with it the control of letters passing between England and the Continent as well as others. Again the Council reported against his claim. In support of it, they said, no patent or proofs had been adduced before them more ancient than the time of Henry the Eighth.

Stanhope, who remained unconvinced, now proceeded to assert his rights, or what he conceived to be his rights, with remarkable vigour. He caused De Quester to be molested in the discharge of his duties; he placarded the city of London, cautioning all persons against sending letters except by his own agents; he instituted proceedings in the Court of King's Bench; and he even stirred up the foreign merchants to make common cause with himself against the intruder.

The probable explanation of Stanhope's conduct is that De Quester's appointment touched him in that most sensitive part, the pocket. His salary as Master of the Posts was £66:13:4 a year, and this he would of course receive in any case; but on letters to the Continent there were certain fees to be paid, a fee of 8d. on each letter to or from Amsterdam, and a like sum between London and Antwerp or London and Hamburgh, and these, as seems to have been admitted in the suit at law, were the motive cause.

In vain the King proclaimed against Stanhope's proceedings. The Privy Council met to consider the question as between him and De Quester, and separated without coming to a conclusion. Four more meetings were held, and with an equally unsatisfactory result. Clearly there was a conflict of opinion at the Council Board. Meanwhile the decisions as regards the merchants were marked by extraordinary vacillation. First, the Merchant Adventurers were "to have a post of their owne choice" to the city of Hamburgh and town of Delph, "where the staples of cloth are now fetched or to such other place or places whither the same shall happen to be removed"; then they were summoned before the Council to shew cause why they also should not send their letters by De Quester; then the concession was not only confirmed in the case of the Merchant Adventurers, but extended to all other "Companies of Merchants"; and then in the case of these other companies the concession was withdrawn, but only, in the course of a few weeks, to be restored. Only few restrictions were imposed. No one carrying the merchants' letters was to "keepe any publick office," to "hange up any Tables," or to "weare any Badge"; nor was he to be employed until his name had been submitted to the Secretary of State for approval. It was also provided that in times of war or danger the Secretary of State, if he required it, was to be "made acquainted" with the letters and despatches which the messenger carried.

The final decision of the Council, which left the merchants in possession of a post of their own, practically superseded De Quester's appointment, and this drew forth an indignant protest from Sir John Coke. The two Secretaries of State, of whom Coke was one, had been specially charged with the protection of De Quester's office, and the decision had been arrived at in their absence. Meanwhile a broker, of the name of Billingsley, was carrying the merchants' letters, and the same man was being employed by Stanhope. Coke's indignation knew no bounds. "I confess," he said, "it troubleth me to see the audacity of men in these times, and that Billingsley, a broker by trade, should dare to attempt thus often to question the King's service, and to derive that power of foreign letters unto merchants which in all states is a branch of regal authority." Can any place in Christendom be named where merchants are allowed to send their letters except through the authorised post? It is true that, as an act of grace, the Merchant Adventurers here have been suffered to send and receive their letters by private hand; but such letters have been only to and from their own mart towns and concerning their private business. That this man of theirs should be suffered to carry any letters he please—letters from merchants in general, and even from ambassadors, is a thing that has never been heard of nor durst any attempt it before. "Indeed the merchants' purse hath swayed very much in other matters in former times, but I never heard that it encroached upon the King's prerogative until now." A pretty account will those who are charged with the peace of the realm be able to give in their places "of that which passeth by letters in or out of the land if every man may convey letters, under the covers of merchants', to whom and what place he pleaseth." Coke went so far as to suggest that advantage had been taken of a small attendance at the Council Table to extort the concession from the King upon wrong or imperfect information. Surely His Majesty cannot have been informed "how unfit a time this is to give liberty to every man to write and send what he list."

Nor did Coke's indignation confine itself to words, for it is impossible not to conclude that he was at the bottom of the high-handed proceeding that followed. Stanhope had gained his suit at law; yet the Council, far from revoking De Quester's patent, granted him an order consigning Billingsley to prison. It was not until he had been there for three months that Parliament, which had recently passed a vote against arbitrary imprisonments, petitioned the King for his release.

Of the final issue of the contest nothing is known. But it seems probable that the foreign merchants were not deterred by the treatment which Billingsley had received from keeping up a post of their own. Other and more serious matters were beginning to occupy the attention of the Court, and it may well be believed that irregularities which had been challenged before might now be allowed to pass unnoticed. Be that as it may, in 1632 De Quester, who had lost his son, and had become old and infirm, associated with himself in the execution of his office two men named Frizell and Witherings, and to these persons he shortly afterwards assigned his patent. Frizell appears to have been little more than a sleeping partner; but Witherings soon established a high character for ability and powers of organisation. The foreign post had not been under his charge for more than three years before the King commissioned him to examine also into the inland posts, and to put them on another and better footing.

CHAPTER III
THOMAS WITHERINGS 1635—1644

Armed with the King's commission, Witherings lost no time in applying himself to his task. And, indeed, the state of things which he found existing afforded ample scope for his energies. Except to Plymouth and through the county of Kent, posts existed rather in name than in reality. Nominally there was a post to Scotland, and this post James had busied himself in improving, in anticipation of his progress to London; but since then it had languished and died, or nearly died, of inanition. Between the kingdoms of England and Scotland there had, up to the date of Witherings's commission, as expressed in the commission itself, been no certain or constant intercourse. The only remaining post, the post to Ireland, was in an equally forlorn condition.

This decadence can only be attributed to two causes, the paucity of travellers and the necessities of the King. Had travellers been numerous, the posts would have been kept up for the sake of the profit to be derived from the letting of horses. In the absence of travellers, the keepers of the post-houses were dependent upon their established wages, and these had long remained unpaid. As far back as 1628 a petition on the subject had been presented to the Council. The "99 poore men," as the petitioners styled themselves, had received no wages for nearly seven years; the arrears then due to them amounted to £22,626; some of them were already in prison, and many more were threatened with arrest. In 1635, as a consequence, doubtless, of their necessitous condition, they had ceased to keep horses, and letters were being carried on foot. In this manner a distance of only sixteen to eighteen miles was accomplished in a day, and to obtain from Scotland or from Ireland a reply to a letter written in London took "full two monthes."

Witherings was not long in producing his plan. Within the city of London was to be appointed an office or counting-house for the receipt and despatch of letters, and thence were to be established trunk lines of post to the principal towns of the kingdom, with corresponding branch posts, either foot posts or horse posts, according to distance, to the smaller towns. The branch posts were to be so fitted to the main posts that there was to be no waiting on the part of either; and these latter were to start and return at stated times, and to run night and day so as to cover 120 miles in twenty-four hours. From London to Edinburgh the course of post which had been full two months was to be only six days; and to Holyhead or Plymouth and back the distance was to be accomplished in the same time. Even Witherings himself appears to have been carried away by the brilliancy of the prospect. "Anie fight at sea," he says, "anie distress of His Majestie's ships (which God forbid), anie wrong offered by anie other nation to anie of ye coastes of England or anie of His Majestie's forts ... the newes will come sooner than thought."

An example has been left us of the process to be followed. The letters for Scotland were to be put into a "portmantle" directed to Edinburgh, into which were also to be put small bags containing letters for towns on the same line of road. At Cambridge, for instance, as soon as the Portmantle arrived, the bag for that town was to be taken out, and a foot-post, "with a known badge of His Majestie's arms," was upon the market days to go to all towns within six, eight or ten miles, and there deliver the letters, at the same time receiving any that might be handed to him. These he was to bring back to Cambridge in time for the return-post from Scotland. The return was to be on a particular day, and at a particular hour, and the letters were to be ready without fail, "upon the verie instant comeing back of the portmantle." The same process was to be adopted at Huntingdon and all other towns on the road.

It was an essential part of Witherings's plan that the posts should be not only regular and certain but also self-supporting. During the earlier part of the century they had been maintained at a cost to the Crown of £3400 a year, and this was a burden which the Crown was no longer in a position to bear. That they should be made to pay their own way was, therefore, an indispensable condition. But how was this to be accomplished? Witherings's sagacity left him at no loss for a reply. He discerned that to carry a letter is to perform a service for which a payment may fairly be demanded in return; and that the demand would meet with a ready response must have been plain to him from what he saw going on in the west of England. In 1633, or two years before he produced his plan, the Mayor and Aldermen of Barnstaple had set up a post between their town and Exeter. This post was to leave Barnstaple every Tuesday at 7 o'clock in the morning, and to be in Exeter early on the following day, in time to catch the King's post on its way from Plymouth to London. The King's post was maintained at the expense of the King; but for the local service, as a means of defraying the cost, the Corporation imposed a small charge, a charge of 6d. for a single letter and of 8d. for a double one. Other towns in Devonshire had adopted a similar course. That Witherings was aware of the existence of these posts is evident from the special allusion that is made to them in the Proclamation which he prevailed upon the King to issue;[5] and it was their success, probably, which suggested his own undertaking. Concluding that what private enterprise was effecting on a small scale the State would be able to effect on a large one, he proposed—and the proposal received the royal sanction—that for every letter sent by post a "port" or charge for carriage should be levied after the following rates:—

	Single Letter.	Double letter.	"If bigger."
Under 80 miles	2d.	4d.	6d. an oz.
80 miles and not exceeding 140	4d.	8d.	9d. "
Above 140 miles	6d.	12d.	12d. "
To or from Scotland	8d.	?	?
To or from Ireland	9d.	After two ounces, 6d. the ounce.	

This was the introduction of postage. The object of the exceptional rate in the case of Ireland was to avoid interference with a Proclamation which had been recently issued by the Lord Deputy and Council there.

Henceforth the posts were to be equally open to all; all would be at liberty to use them; all would be welcome. Important as this provision was, it followed as a natural consequence from the imposition of postage. The carriage of the subjects' letters was now to be a matter of purchase, and, unless the purchasers were sufficiently numerous, the posts would not be self-supporting. The custom of the public, therefore, was a necessity of their very existence.

In other respects the regulations remained much as they had been, except that now there would be the means of enforcing them. Every postmaster was to have ready in his stable one or two horses, according as Witherings might direct, the charge to be for one horse 2-1/2d. a mile and for two horses 5d. This 5d., however, was to include the cost of a guide who was always to accompany the horses when two were taken. On the day the post was expected, the horses were not to be let out on any pretext whatever, this being the first indication on record of letters enjoying precedence over travellers. And finally, with certain specified exceptions, no letters were to be carried or delivered in any part where posts should be established except by such persons as Witherings might appoint. The letters excepted were those sent by a friend, by a particular messenger employed for the particular occasion, and by common known carrier. On the common carrier, however, restrictions were imposed. He was to confine himself to his ordinary known journey, and was not, for the sake of collecting or delivering letters, to lag behind or outstrip his cart or horse by more than eight hours.

The reason for this last exception is not far to seek. The established posts were few in number, and even where they existed in name they had fallen into disuse. The common carriers had thus become the chief carriers of letters, and Witherings, in the furtherance of his project, was anxious to disarm their opposition. This he had already attempted to effect by argument; and now, as a practical step in the same direction, he procured their exemption from the State monopoly. But what may have appeared and was probably intended to appear as a valuable concession was really no concession at all. The carrier took eight days to go 120 miles. By the posts the same distance was to be accomplished in a day and a night. The carrier's charge for a letter from Cambridge to London, a distance of about sixty miles, was 2d. A postage of 2d., according to Witherings's plan, was to a carry a letter for eighty miles. If the posts were to be both faster and cheaper than the common known carrier, it might safely be predicted that as a carrier of letters he could not long survive.

In October 1635 Witherings, having completed the necessary arrangements, proceeded to carry his plan into effect. The results he anticipated from it, as shewn in a memorandum which he delivered to the Secretary of State, were promotion of trade and intercourse and the cultivation of better relations with Scotland and Ireland. That the posts might one day be more than self-supporting, that they would become a source of revenue, does not appear to have entered into his calculations; or, if it did, his silence on the point would seem to shew that, as compared with the other advantages, he deemed it too insignificant to mention.

It was probably about this time that the practice of writing "Haste, post, haste" on the outside of letters began to be discontinued. The term "post," as here used, meant nothing more than the carrier or bearer of the letter; and an injunction to make the best speed he could, properly as it might be given to a messenger who had a particular letter to carry, would be altogether out of place if addressed to a general letter-carrier who was bound by his instructions not to exceed a given distance within a given time. "For thy life, for thy life" had sometimes been added, as in the case of Protector Somerset's letter to Lord Dacre. "To our very good Lord, the Lord Dacre, Warden of the West Marches, in haste; haste, post, haste, for thy life, for thy life, for thy life";[6] and it seems probable, if the barbarity of the punishments in those days is considered, that this was no empty threat. It was "on payn of lyfe" that, according to Sir Brian Tuke, all townships were to have horses ready for their Sovereign's service. Among the Ashburnham manuscripts is a letter from Sir Edward Nicholas to Sir John Hippisley, Lieutenant of Dover Castle, written in 1627 or eight years before the introduction of postage. This letter is endorsed by George Villiers, Duke of Buckingham, and the cover is inscribed "for His Majesty's special affairs; hast, hast, hast, post, hast, hast, hast, hast, with all possible speede." The absence of any threat in this instance may of course have been due to the individual character of the writer, but it is more agreeable to think of it as a sign of the advance of civilisation.

In 1637, Lord Stanhope having surrendered his patent, Witherings was appointed in his room, and thus became centred in one person the offices of postmaster for inland and for foreign letters. In the same year a letter office, the erection of which had formed an important part of Witherings's plan, was opened in the city of London, and nothing remained to hinder him from carrying his project into full effect. But, fair as everything promised, hardly three years had elapsed before Witherings met with the fate which has overtaken so many of his distinguished successors. In 1640, on a charge of divers abuses and misdemeanours in the execution of his office, this eminent man was deprived of his appointment. Whether the charge was well or ill founded we have no means of judging. Only the fact has come down to us that after this miserable fashion ended the career of one who had the sagacity to project and the energy to carry out a system, the main features of which endure to the present day.

Among those who had lent money to the King was Philip Burlamachi, a naturalised British subject, and one of the principal merchants of the city of London. He had advanced, on the security of the sugar duties, no less than £52,000, an immense sum in those days; and it was probably this fact rather than any special qualification on his part that pointed him out as Witherings's successor. Be that as it may, into Burlamachi's hands the office of Master of the Posts was sequestered, subject to the condition that he was to discharge the duties under the control of the Secretary of State. The sequestration was announced to the public by means of placards fixed up on the old Exchange, and Witherings lost no time in fixing up counter-placards by way of protest.

And now began an unseemly contention which, arising ostensibly out of the rights of individuals, went far to bring the two Houses of Parliament into collision. In 1642, after struggling for the best part of two years to maintain his position, Witherings assigned his patent to the Earl of Warwick, and, under the influence of this peer, both Houses declared the sequestration to be illegal and void. Meanwhile Burlamachi had fallen into the power of one in whose hands he was the merest puppet. This was Edmund Prideaux, afterwards one of the Commissioners of the Great Seal and Attorney-

General under the Commonwealth. At his instigation Burlamachi still kept possession of the letter office. In vain the Lords ordered him to give it up to Lord Warwick, and summoned him before them to explain his contumacy. It was true, he replied, that the office was still kept at his house, but this house and his servants had been hired by Mr. Prideaux, and it was he that disposed of the letters.

Incensed at such contempt of their orders, the Lords authorised Warwick to seize the mails. After one or two half-hearted attempts to carry this authority into effect, arrangements were made for a more strenuous effort. On the 19th of December two of Warwick's agents lay in wait at Barnet and there surprised the mail as it came from Chester. Seizing the letters and the man that carried them, they made the best of their way towards London, but had not proceeded further than the foot of the hill beyond Highgate when they were themselves surprised by five troopers "on great horses with pistols," who barred the road, and, in the name of the House of Commons, captured the captors.

Meanwhile a still more exciting scene was enacting before Warwick's office near the Royal Exchange. There two of his men kept watch for the mail from Plymouth, and, as it passed on its way to Burlamachi's house hard by, they dashed into the street and seized the letters. Their success was but for the moment. Before they could regain the office, Prideaux had swooped down upon them at the head of some half-dozen adherents, and with his own hands had torn the letters away. "An order of the House of Commons," cried one of the bystanders, "ought to be obeyed before an order of the House of Lords."

On these occurrences being reported to the Lords, Burlamachi and all others who had been concerned in them, Prideaux alone excepted, were ordered to prison. Among these was the man who had been captured at Barnet and afterwards rescued, one Hickes by name; and this fellow proved to be Prideaux's own servant. On the part of that wily politician one looks in vain for any effort to procure Burlamachi's release, or even for the slightest indication of concern that he had been arrested; but the arrest of his own servant, the servant of a member of the House of Commons, excited his keenest resentment. This, in Prideaux's view, was a clear breach of privilege, and the House was pleased to agree with him. No sooner, therefore, had Hickes been imprisoned by the Lords than he was released by the Commons, and no sooner had he been released by the Commons than the Lords ordered him to be imprisoned again.

Matters having come to this pass, the two Houses held a conference. The result might easily have been foreseen. The Lords yielded to the

Commons, and Burlamachi, on rendering an account which had long been called for, was released from custody together with the others who had been imprisoned at the same time. Concerning the next two years little is known; but it seems probable that Burlamachi, who in his petition praying for release had pleaded old age and infirmities, did not long survive the indignity to which he had been exposed. At all events, in 1644, either by death or resignation, the office of Master of the Posts had become vacant, and, as Burlamachi's successor, the House of Commons appointed Prideaux.

Thus ended the battle of the patents, which had raged more or less fiercely for more than twenty years. It was long indeed before Lords Warwick and Stanhope ceased urging their claims, Warwick as Witherings's assignee, and Stanhope on the allegation that at the Council Table the Lord Keeper Coventry had cajoled him into surrendering his patent; but after Prideaux's appointment there was no farther appeal to force.

CHAPTER IV
EDMUND PRIDEAUX AND CLEMENT OXENBRIDGE 1644–1660

Hardly had Prideaux assumed the direction of the letter office before he gave public notice that there would be a weekly conveyance of letters into all parts of the kingdom. There is reason to doubt, however, whether under his rule as much or nearly as much as this was accomplished. Next to Norwich, Yarmouth was then, as it is now, the chief town in the eastern counties; and yet it is certain that a post to Yarmouth was not established until after Prideaux's rule had ceased; and more than fifty years later we find his successors lamenting that, while Lincolnshire generally was ill provided with posts, there were several towns in that county which had no post at all.

But to whatever extent Prideaux's professions exceeded his performance, it is beyond question that he spared no effort to extend the posts, and that he is justly entitled to the credit, not indeed of improving upon Witherings's scheme, but of carrying that scheme into more general effect. Despite his exertions, however, he failed to keep pace with the wants of the time. Indeed, what facilities for intercourse had been given already seem to have created a demand for more. In 1649 the Common Council of the city of London, not content with a post only once a week to Scotland, established a post of their own. Along the whole line of road between London and Edinburgh they appointed their own postmasters and settled their own postage, and the same plan they proceeded to adopt in other parts. Prideaux, who to his office of Master of the Posts had recently added that of Attorney-General, was highly incensed. Only a few years before, the State monopoly of letters, when the State was represented by the Crown, had been the object of his fiercest denunciation, and now this same monopoly was a cherished possession to be defended at all hazards. First he remonstrated. Then he threatened. And neither threats nor remonstrances having any effect upon the city authorities, he reported their proceedings to the Council of State, and the Council of State reported them to Parliament. Parliament was in no mood for concession. The city posts were promptly suppressed, and more than thirty years elapsed before private enterprise again embarked upon a similar venture.

The report which Prideaux made to the Council of State had another result, which probably he little contemplated. In that report he had taken credit to himself that, although the charges of management had risen to £7000 a year, or about twice the amount they had been in Witherings's time, he had relieved the State from the whole of this burden. In other words, the posts had become self-supporting, but, so far as appeared from the report, were nothing more. The House of Commons was not satisfied. Accordingly the Council was instructed to examine and report whether the terms on which the letter office was held were the best that could be obtained. The investigation was soon made. Heretofore, in consideration of his defraying the charges, Prideaux had been allowed to receive the postage and make what he could out of it. For the future, besides defraying the charges, he was to pay to the State a fixed rent of £5000 a year. This was the introduction of the system of farming, a system which, as regards the posts generally, continued to nearly the end of the seventeenth and, as regards the by-posts, beyond the middle of the eighteenth century.

In 1653 Prideaux ceased to be Master of the Posts. Two years before he had been elected a member of the Council of State, and shortly after his election, and probably as a consequence of it, the arrangements for communicating with the army had reached a high state of perfection. Between the Council and the forces in Scotland messengers, we are told, were passing almost every hour. But, useful as he may have made himself, Prideaux seems to have been altogether wanting in those qualities which are calculated to inspire confidence. At the Treaty of Uxbridge, where he was one of the commissioners, even his own colleagues had regarded him as a spy. This feeling of distrust may possibly explain how it happened that, after the expulsion of the Long Parliament, he was forced to content himself with his appointment as Attorney-General. The Council of State, as then reconstructed, did not include him among its members, and one of the first acts of the new Council was to relieve him from the responsibilities of the letter office. Grasping as he was, it is impossible to suppose that this can have been done by his own wish, for the appointment of Master of the Posts, though weighted with a rent of £5000 a year, was still a very lucrative one. His successor paid a rent of double that amount, and is reputed to have derived from his farm an enormous profit.

After Prideaux's death in August 1659, it transpired that his interest in the letter office had not ceased when he ceased to administer it. What was the interest he retained we do not know; but the matter seems to have been considered sufficiently serious to call for parliamentary inquiry. In the following February the House of Commons ordered "that the whole business concerning the Post Office, and what has been received by Mr.

Prideaux, late Attorney-General, out of the same, and what account hath been made thereof he referred to a committee to examine, and to state matter of fact and report it to the Parliament and their opinion therein." To this order, however, no return appears to have been made. It is probable that at the Restoration the committee had not concluded its labours.

Oldmixon speaks of Prideaux as "a very fierce republican, who got a great estate by his zeal against the Church and Churchmen"; and it is certain that to that estate his zeal for the Post Office brought him no inconsiderable addition. Of the destination of a part of his wealth we are not left uninformed. Towards the close of the century a judge, before whose ferocity even Prideaux's pales, set out on a circuit, the infamy of which will endure to the end of time. Arrived in Somersetshire, he found residing at Ford Abbey, in the neighbourhood of Axminster, an inoffensive country squire, son of the former Master of the Posts, and named after him, Edmund Prideaux. From this gentleman, apparently because he was his father's son, and for no better reason, Jeffreys under threat of the gallows extorted £15,000, and he bought with the money an estate "to which," Lord Macaulay tells us, "the people gave the name of Aceldama, from that accursed field which was purchased with the price of innocent blood."

In 1653 the posts were farmed to Captain Manley at a rent of £10,000 a year; and in 1655, Manley's contract having expired, Cromwell on the advice of his Council placed them in the hands of Mr. Secretary Thurloe, on his giving security to the same amount. The change of management was followed two years later by an important step in advance. This was the passing of an Act of Parliament intituled an Act for settling the postage of England, Scotland, and Ireland. Legislative sanction was now given to what had hitherto rested on no better authority than Proclamation or Order in Council. A general office, to be called the Post Office of England, was to be established for the receipt and despatch of letters; and under the title of Postmaster-General and Comptroller of the Post Office an officer was to be appointed who was to have the exclusive right of carrying letters and of furnishing post-horses. At the Restoration the Act of 1657, the "pretended" Act as it was now called, could not of course be recognised as possessing any legal validity, and so it was replaced by another; but the later Act was little more than a re-enactment of the earlier one. Virtually, it is to the Act of 1657 that the General Post Office owes its origin, although the Act of 1660, as being unimpeachable, has been commonly called its charter.

Similar as the two Acts are in the main, there is one important difference between them. The Act of 1657 gives as a reason for making the posts the subject of parliamentary enactment that they are and have been "the best means of discovering and preventing many dangerous and wicked designs which have been and are daily contrived against the peace and welfare of this Commonwealth, the intelligence whereof cannot well be communicated but by letter of escript." To the odious practice here implied no countenance is given in the Act of 1660. But, indeed, it needed not this evidence to prove that during the Commonwealth the Post Office was largely used as an instrument of police. Thurloe's "intercepted" letters are matter of history; and the journals of the two Houses of Parliament shew that the foreign mails, both inward and outward, were stopped for whole weeks together, and committees appointed to open and read the letters. On one occasion the Venetian ambassador, whose letters had shared the same fate as the rest, entered an indignant protest. "He could not persuade himself," he said, "that the Government of England, so noble and generous, should have so inferior a mind as to open the letters of an ambassador, and by this means to violate the laws, and to give an example to the world so damnable, and of so little respect towards the minister of the Serenissima Respublica." Nor was his indignation appeased until four peers had waited upon him in the name of the House of Lords, and tendered an ample apology.

The rates of postage prescribed by the Act of 1657 were only slightly varied by the Act of 1660. As finally adjusted, they were as follows:—

	On Single Letter.	On Double Letter.	Per Ounce.
80 miles and under	2d.	4d.	8d.
Above 80 miles	3d.	6d.	12d.
To or from Berwick	3d.	6d.	18d.
From Berwick within Scotland—			
40 miles and under	2d.	4d.	8d.
Above 40 miles	4d.	8d.	12d.
To or from Dublin	6d.	12d.	24d.
From Dublin within Ireland—			
40 miles and under	2d.	4d.	8d.
Above 40 miles	4d.	8d.	12d.

How these rates compare with those which had gone before we have no means of judging. We only know that during Prideaux's management the postage on a single letter was 6d.; that at some time between 1655 and 1657 it was reduced to 3d.; and that the credit of this reduction was due to Clement Oxenbridge. Oxenbridge, after acting as deputy first to Prideaux and then to Manley, appears to have taken a farm under Thurloe; and, rightly or wrongly, he affirmed that, as soon as he had improved the posts at a cost to himself of more than £5000, and had made his farm profitable, he was turned adrift by Cromwell.

If the comparison be carried forward instead of backward, and the rates of 1660 be contrasted with those of later years, there is an important consideration which cannot be too carefully borne in mind. It is this, that in 1660 cross posts did not exist. Between two towns not being on the same post road, however near the towns might be, letters could circulate only through London; and the moment London was reached an additional rate was imposed. Hence the apparent charges, the charges as deduced from the table of rates, might be very different from the actual charges. Bristol and Exeter, for instance, are less than eighty miles apart; but in 1660 and for nearly forty years afterwards letters from one to the other passed through London, and would be charged, if single, not 2d. but 6d., and if double, not 4d. but 1s. That is to say, the postage[7] or portage, as it was then called, would consist of two rates, and each of these rates would be for a distance in excess of eighty miles. David Hume, writing more than a hundred years later, observes that before 1657 letters paid only about half as much postage as they did in his own time. This, no doubt, is true if rate be compared with rate according to the distance; but the fact we have mentioned very materially qualifies the force of the remark.

On foreign letters the rates ranged from 4d., the lowest rate for a single letter, to 2s., the highest rate for a double letter, and from 1s. 6d. to 4s. an ounce for letters of greater bulk. No provision was made for any charge except on letters from Europe. Letters came indeed from other parts; but as the Post Office did not bring them and paid nothing for their carriage, no postage was demanded. From India, for instance, a letter brought to England and posted there would pay only the home postage.

For post-horses the charge was fixed at 3d. a mile for each horse, besides 4d. to the guide of every stage. Two concessions were made to the public. Horses were no longer to be seized without the consent of the owners; and a traveller if kept waiting half an hour without being supplied might hire a horse wherever he could. That the seizure of horses had been a source of intense annoyance seems beyond question. In a Proclamation of 1603, as a reason for helping the postmasters to keep horses in sufficient number for the service of the posts, the townships are reminded of "the ease and quiet they reape thereby"; and long after the immunity from seizure had been granted, the allusions to the former practice leave no room for doubt that, though the sore was healed, the recollection of it still rankled.

According to Lord Macaulay, a part of the Post Office revenue was derived from post-horses.[8] With all deference to that eminent authority, and with all modesty we venture to think that such was not the case. The Proclamation of 1603, which was the origin of the monopoly, while giving to those who horsed the posts "the benefit and preheminence of letting horses" to all comers, expressly provided that, except for the service of the posts or for the use of persons travelling on affairs of State, no postmaster need keep horses unless he pleased, and that, if he did so, he should be at liberty to make his own terms. On this last point the words are, "But of all others riding Poste with horne and guide about their private businesses, the hire and prices are left to the parties discretions to agree and compound within themselves." Again, an account is still extant, dated 1623, or twenty years after the monopoly had been established, and giving in minute detail the particulars of the expenses of the posts as they then were; records also exist extending in almost unbroken succession over more than eighty years of the period during which the monopoly lasted, and dealing with every variety of Post Office question; and neither in the records nor the account is there the remotest allusion to the receipt of any sums on account of post-horses. Yet one reason more for the opinion we hold. About the middle of the eighteenth century, as the result of legislation which then took place, the roads were measured, and the measured mile proved to be shorter than the computed mile. As a consequence of this discovery the charge for post-horses was raised. A distance which had hitherto been reckoned as eight miles proved to be ten miles, and a charge as for ten instead of eight miles was made. Travellers were up in arms, and complained that the Post Office had raised its charges. The answer was that the Post Office had nothing to do with the matter; that the postmasters were entitled by law to so much a mile; and that the whole of the charge went into their own pockets. For these reasons we think that no part of the Post Office revenue was derived from the letting of post-horses. Indirectly, no doubt, the monopoly was a source of profit because, except for it, those who horsed the posts would not have been content with the wages they received. These, according to the account of 1623, ranged from 3s. a day to 6d. a day. To supplement the postmasters' pay without expense to the Crown was, we make bold to suggest, the object with which the monopoly was granted. And, of course, the better the object was secured, the more carefully would the monopoly be guarded.

In May 1660 Clement Oxenbridge, to whose exertions the Act of 1657 would seem to have been largely due, petitioned the Council of State to reimburse him the expenses to which he had been put in improving the posts, and the Council of State, after investigating the claim, reported the particulars to the House of Commons for directions. It was not, however, until after William and Mary had ascended the throne that any further step was taken. Oxenbridge, whose necessities had become greater as his age advanced, was then by the King's direction given an appointment under the Post Office of the annual value of £100; and this salary he continued to draw, although too old to discharge the duties for which it was paid, until his death in 1696.

CHAPTER V
WILLIAM DOCKWRA 1660-1685

At the Restoration the Post Office was leased to Henry Bishopp of Henfield in Sussex, for the term of seven years at a rent of £21,500 a year, or more than double the amount which had been paid by the previous farmer. Before three years had elapsed, however, Bishopp surrendered his lease, and was succeeded for the remainder of his term and at the same rent by Daniel O'Neile, Groom of the King's Bedchamber. O'Neile had loyally adhered to Charles during his exile, had attended his Sovereign on his visit to Scotland, had been banished that kingdom, and in connection with his banishment had achieved a singular distinction. He had given a written undertaking consenting to his own death if he ever returned.

Even at a rent of £21,500, as the Court had doubtless by this time learned, the Post Office was not a bad investment. O'Neile, like Bishopp, was to enjoy a monopoly of the carrying of letters, and to make what he could out of it; but he was rigidly to adhere to the rates of postage prescribed by the Act, charging neither more nor less. Old posts were not to be altered nor new posts erected, without the sanction of the Secretary of State; and the Secretary of State was to possess a veto on appointments and, as occasion might require, to "have the survey and inspection of all letters." To these conditions was afterwards added another. This was that no postmaster or other officer was to remain in the service who should not within six months obtain and forward to the postmaster-general a certificate, under the hand and seal of the Bishop of the diocese, to the effect that he was "conformable to the discipline of the Church of England."

In 1667, O'Neile's lease having expired, Lord Arlington, Secretary of State in the Cabinet known as the Cabal, was appointed postmaster-general; and, after a while, the office was again let out to farm, this time at a rent of £43,000 a year. Rapidly as the rent had grown, the public demands had grown more rapidly still, and little, if any, effort had been made to satisfy them. How inadequate the posts were, about this time, to meet the public requirements may be judged from a circumstance connected with Bishopp's appointment. The letters patent appointing him were to take effect from the 25th of June 1660, but their validity was to depend on an Act of Parliament, the Act reconstituting the General Post Office, which did not pass until some months afterwards. Meanwhile a whole crop of posts had sprung up between London and the country, which could not be suppressed until the Act was passed. As compensation for the loss he sustained by this encroachment on his monopoly between the 25th of June and the 29th of September Bishopp claimed and received no less than £500.

There is preserved in the Guildhall Library a letter from the Duke of Buckingham, to which the following note is appended:—"The great fire of London broke out on the 2nd of September 1666. It is seen by the date of this letter that the Duke of Buckingham, at that time in the highest position at Court and in the zenith of his power, was at Worthing, and did not receive intelligence of the awful calamity until after the city had been burning for five days." We do not know by what means the Duke was informed of the calamity, nor is it material to our present purpose that we should do so. All we desire now to observe is that if, as is not improbable, he was informed of it by letter, the letter—as we proceed to shew—reached him in due course of post. The fire broke out at midnight on the 2nd of September, and the 2nd of September was a Saturday, after which, except to the Downs and to places abroad, there was no post out of London until Tuesday the 5th, or rather, as the mails started after midnight, until early in the morning of Wednesday the 6th. Arundel was then the post-town for Worthing, and for the first part of the distance the course of post was, as it continued to be until the day of railways, through Tooting, Ewell, Epsom or Ebbesham as it was still called, Leatherhead, and Dorking. Continuing thence, not, as in later times, through Horsham, but through the hamlet of Coldharbour, the post-road skirted the foot of Leith Hill and passed through Stone Street, Billinghurst, and Amberley to Arundel, which would be reached late in the afternoon of Wednesday. Between Arundel and Worthing the distance is ten miles, and the postmaster would not, at the earliest, take out the letter for delivery until the morning of Thursday the 7th, or five days after the fire had broken out. Indeed, it may be permitted to us to doubt whether the letter, if letter there was, would have been delivered as early as the 7th, had it been for a less important personage.

Meagre as the means of communication were in those days, even such means as existed were not matter of common knowledge. The Post Office did not advertise its wares; and no newspapers then existed to do for the Post Office what the Post Office omitted to do for itself. What towns possessed post-houses of their own, and how these towns stood in relation to other towns which did not enjoy the same advantage, might well be considered essential information; yet even of this no public announcement was given. Blome, in his *Britannia*, printed in 1671, remarks upon this defect, and for the benefit of his readers proceeds to supply it. After commenting upon the convenience which the Post Office affords, and lamenting that this convenience is not more generally known, he gives a list of the post towns which each county possesses, and supplements it with a series of county maps, so that, as he explains, persons desirous of writing to any particular place may be able to find out for themselves where the nearest post-house stands. As late as the end of the seventeenth and beginning of the eighteenth centuries separate maps appear to have been published with the same object, as a matter of private enterprise. In these maps the post towns are indicated by a castle surmounted by the royal standard.

But it was within the metropolis itself that the public need was greatest. Between London and the country posts went at unequal intervals indeed, and at intervals in some cases unduly long, and yet with regularity. To Kent and the Downs there was a post daily; to other parts of England and to Scotland a post every other day; and to Wales and to Ireland a post twice a week. But between one part of London and another there was no post at all. A resident in London having a letter for delivery within the metropolitan area had only one choice, to take the letter himself or to send it by another. And let the bearer of a letter be who he might, there was an inconvenience to which he was constantly exposed. The houses were not numbered, and were mainly to be recognised by the signs they bore. Later on, men who delivered letters over the same ground day after day complained that it was not always easy to find the address. Without local knowledge it must have been sometimes impossible.

Happily, in England the spirit of enterprise is such that an acknowledged want affecting any considerable section of the public is seldom suffered to endure very long. And so it proved in the present instance. The man who now undertook to relieve the capital from the intolerable inconvenience under which it laboured was William Dockwra, a merchant of the city of London. Dockwra had been a sub-searcher in the Custom House, and through some little interest he possessed at Court had been allowed to dispose of his place. The idea of the penny post is said indeed to have originated with Robert Murray, an upholsterer in Paternoster Row; but, be that as it may, to Dockwra belongs the credit of giving it practical shape. A man of less resolution or less convinced of the inherent merits of his undertaking might well have been daunted by the difficulties he had to encounter. The undertaking had been conceived in so bold a spirit that to carry it out would involve an expense which Dockwra's unaided resources were altogether unable to bear. A difficulty still greater than the want of funds was the determined opposition of the Duke of York. In 1663 the profits of the Post Office had been settled on the Duke for his support and maintenance, and, with an eye ever intent on his own interests, he discerned or thought he discerned in the new project an infringement of his rights.

Undeterred by these difficulties, Dockwra persevered in the task he had taken in hand. At length the appointed day arrived. On the 1st of April 1680,[9] London, which had hitherto had no post at all, suddenly found itself in possession of one in comparison with which even the post of our own time is cast into the shade. For the purposes of the undertaking London and its suburbs were divided into seven districts with a sorting office in each. From Hackney in the north to Lambeth in the south, from Blackwall in the east to Westminster in the west, there was not a point within the bills of mortality which the new post did not reach. Between four and five hundred receiving offices were opened in a single morning. Placards were distributed and advertisements inserted in the public intelligences announcing where these offices were. Messengers called there for letters every hour. These, if for the country, were carried to the General Post Office, and if for the town, to the respective sorting offices. From the sorting offices, after being sorted and entered in books kept for the purpose, they were sent out for delivery, to the Inns of Court or places of business ten or twelve times a day, and to other places according to distance from four to eight times. Nor was the service confined to letters. It extended also to parcels, the only condition being that neither parcel nor letter should exceed one pound in weight,[10] or ten pounds in value. Subject to these limitations the charge between one part of London and another was one penny. An exception indeed was made in the case of Hackney, Islington, Newington Butts, and Lambeth, which were then separate towns. There one penny carried only to the receiving office, and for delivery at a private house the charge was one penny more. Delivery in the street was not allowed.

But it was not only in the matter of weight and frequency of delivery that the new undertaking was conceived in the most liberal spirit. Provided a letter or parcel was securely tied and sealed and its contents endorsed on the outside, the charge of one penny covered not only cost of conveyance but insurance as well, up to a limit of ten pounds. That is to say, subject to this limit, if a parcel or a letter or its contents were lost, Dockwra would, the conditions being observed, make the value good.

There is yet another novelty which Dockwra introduced. As a check upon his messengers he supplied the seven sorting offices with stamps bearing their own initial letters and denoting the several hours of the day. With one of these stamps all letters and parcels were impressed as they passed through the post, and if in the busy parts of the capital they were not delivered within little more than an hour from the time denoted by the impression, the public were encouraged to complain. The following are specimens of the stamps which Dockwra used:—

This was the introduction of postmarks. In the first and last impressions Mor. 8 signifies of course 8 o'clock in the morning, and Af. 4, 4 o'clock in the afternoon. In the second or middle impression the initial letter L signifies Lyme Street, where the principal office of the penny post was held at Dockwra's private dwelling-house, formerly the dwelling-house of Sir Robert Abdy.

The General Post Office, until lately in Bishopsgate Street, stood at this time in Lombard Street, where it occupied a site on part of which the branch office now stands. There the persons employed, all told, numbered 77. In the country and dependent on the chief office were 227 postmasters, viz. 182 in England and Scotland and 45 in Ireland. Twelve persons were also employed in the office in Dublin. Altogether and throughout the whole of the kingdom the General Post Office, in 1680, gave employment to 316 persons, a number very much less than that which Dockwra employed in London alone.

On Saturday nights the penny post closed, in winter at six, and in summer at seven. On other nights of the week, Sundays excepted, it must have remained open to at least 9 o'clock, for at that hour the country letters were collected from the receiving offices and carried to the General Post Office. Besides Sundays, there were eight days in the year on which the post did not go, viz. three days at Christmas, two days at Easter, two days at Whitsuntide, and also the 30th of January, the anniversary of the death of King Charles the First.

In spite of the enormous advantages it conferred, the penny post was not at first received with unqualified satisfaction. Some fanatics denounced it as a Popish contrivance; and Lord Macaulay tells us how the porters complained that their interests were attacked, and tore down the placards on which the scheme was announced to the public. Even unprejudiced persons and persons who had no interests to protect complained that a large number of things were posted and not delivered. This Dockwra himself admitted, explaining that it was due to the illegible writing of the address or to the omission of some important particular by which the persons addressed might be identified, the omission of their trade, or of the signs which their houses bore, or of some well-known place or object in their vicinity. The manifest utility of the enterprise, however, soon bore down all opposition; and in little more than a year from its introduction the penny post, though weighted with a scheme of insurance, was very nearly paying its own expenses.

The establishment of the penny post had one effect which had probably not been contemplated. It increased largely the number of letters for the country. Every man had now a post office at his own door. It is true that Dockwra's four or five hundred receiving offices were intended primarily for town letters; but country letters might be posted there, and, as we have seen, were collected at a stated hour every evening. Hitherto the case had been very different. Up to the 1st of April 1680, incredible as it may appear, the General Post Office in Lombard Street was the only receptacle for letters in the whole of London. There and nowhere else could letters be posted. Little wonder if, before 1680, persons whom the cost of postage might not deter from writing were yet deterred by their distance from the Post Office.

Dockwra might reasonably now expect to reap some of the rewards of success. A small band of citizens who had joined in the original venture had afterwards deserted him, and for six months he had carried it on at his sole charge. Others had then come to his aid, and a fresh partnership had been formed. The undertaking prospered, became self-supporting, and at length gave promise of large returns. This very promise excited the greed of the Duke of York. So long as the outgoings exceeded the receipts Dockwra remained unmolested; but no sooner had the balance turned than the Duke complained of his monopoly being infringed, and the Courts of Law decided in his favour. Not only was Dockwra cast in damages, but the undertaking which he had impoverished himself to establish was wrested out of his hands, and the penny post, in less than five years from its introduction, was incorporated into the General Post Office.[11]

Generosity formed no part of James's character, and, so long as he sat on the throne, Dockwra's services remained without the slightest recognition. In 1690, however, upon an address from the House of Commons, William and Mary granted him a pension of £500 for seven years, and in 1697 the grant was renewed for three years longer. In the same year as the renewal of the grant, but a little earlier, he was appointed comptroller of the penny post at a salary of £200, and this appointment he retained until 1700. Then, both appointment and grant came to an abrupt termination together, for, on charges brought against him by his own subordinates, Dockwra, like

Witherings, was dismissed. Such was the tribute paid to the man who had conferred on his country benefits which he never tired of predicting would endure to all posterity.

Of the charges against Dockwra two deserve special notice, as shewing that the penny post, after its acquisition by the State, continued to be conducted on the same principles as before. These two charges were—1st, that, contrary to his duty, he "forbids the taking in any band-boxes (except very small) and all parcels above a pound"; and 2nd, that he takes money out of letters and "makes the office pay for it," thereby clearly indicating that at that time the State carried on a parcel post and continued the practice of making losses good. A third charge, the truth of which it is more easy to credit, imputed to Dockwra that he spoke and acted as if his object were to get the penny post into his own hands again. It is worthy of remark, as characteristic of the times in which he lived, and may perhaps be regarded as affording some presumption of his innocence, that Dockwra appears to have been at less pains to refute the charges than to prove that he had taken the oath of supremacy, or the oath which had been recently substituted for it, and that he had received the Holy Sacrament.

We have said that to us who live at the end of the nineteenth century it may appear incredible that up to April 1680 the General Post Office in Lombard Street was the only receptacle for letters in the whole of London. But it is by no means certain that our descendants may not think it more incredible still that London, with all its boasted progress, has only now recovered a post which, in point of convenience and cheapness, at all approaches that which an enterprising citizen established more than two hundred years ago. When and under what circumstances this post lost its original features will have to be considered hereafter.

CHAPTER VI
COTTON AND FRANKLAND
Inland Service 1685-1705

In 1685, on the death of Charles the Second, the revenue of the Post Office was settled on James, his heirs and successors. Rochester, the High Treasurer, became postmaster-general; and for the actual discharge of the duties a deputy was appointed under the title of Governor.

Two years before, the panic caused by the discovery of the Rye-House Plot had led to the issue of a Proclamation which, if differing little from others that had gone before, acquires importance from the circumstances under which it appeared. Unauthorised posts had again sprung up in all directions, simply, no doubt, because there was a demand for the accommodation they afforded; but the Government, no less than the persons who denounced Dockwra's undertaking as a Popish contrivance, seem to have been possessed with the idea that these posts were mere vehicles for the propagation of treason. To prevent treasonable correspondence was the avowed object of the present Proclamation, and the means by which the object was sought to be attained was the suppression of private and irregular posts, for by these, the Proclamation went on to declare, the conspirators had been materially assisted in their designs. Mayors, sheriffs, justices of the peace, constables and others were enjoined to make diligent search for letters passing otherwise than through the regular post. Special officers were to be appointed for the same purpose. All such letters, wherever discovered, were to be deemed to be "of dangerous consequence"; and not only were they to be seized and carried to the Secretary of State or the Privy Council for the purpose of being opened and inspected, but both the bearers and senders of them were to be proceeded against at law.

On James's accession to the throne the Proclamation of 1683 was succeeded by another in almost identical terms; and it is certain that during his reign the liberties taken with post letters were hardly less than they had been in the worst days of the Commonwealth. Only a few months before Rochester's dismissal, for no better reason than to gratify curiosity, orders were given that the bags from Scotland should be transmitted to Whitehall, and during a whole week not a single private letter from beyond the Tweed was delivered in London. Happily, however, this state of things was soon to cease. After the Revolution the appointment of postmaster-general was conferred upon persons who were otherwise unconnected with affairs of State, and the effect of this change was, as William no doubt intended, at once to lift the Post Office out of the region of politics. In the eyes of the Rochesters, the Arlingtons, and the Thurloes, busied as they were in the detection of conspiracies against the State, the Post Office had been little else than an instrument which might be usefully employed as a means to that end. With plain citizens unversed in the ways of government, the only consideration was how best they could accomplish the object for which they had been appointed; and this object was so to manage and improve the posts of the country as to secure to their Sovereign the highest possible revenue.

But, before William could give effect to his views, there was an adherent to be provided for. This was Colonel John Wildman, who was appointed postmaster-general in July 1689. Of Wildman's career at the Post Office little is known, except that he was profuse in making promises which he never performed. He might, perhaps, himself have pleaded that he was not given time to perform them, for after eight months' tenure of the appointment he was dismissed for some reason which is, and will probably continue to be, a mystery. Far different is the record left behind them by Wildman's immediate successors. These were Sir Robert Cotton and Mr.—afterwards Sir Thomas—Frankland, who became joint postmasters-general in March 1690, and served in that capacity for nearly twenty years. They had sat in James's Parliament, the one for Cambridgeshire, and the other for the borough of Thirsk, and these seats they retained under William. From the writings they have left behind them we are able to see these two men not as a biographer might dress them up, but as they really were. Everything about them, their virtues, their foibles, their habits, their ailments, their devotion to duty, their unwillingness to believe evil of any one, their hatred of injustice or oppression, their unbounded credulity, their anxiety about their re-election, their gratitude for any little scrap of news which they might carry to Court, their fondness for a glass of port wine, their attacks of gout, their habit of taking snuff, even the hour of their going to bed—all this and more is there revealed, and makes up a record of simplicity and benevolence which it is a delight to read.

The establishment over which these two simple gentlemen were called upon to preside had recently received a considerable addition. Out of London, the Post Office servants remained much as they had been ten years before, at about 239 in number, of whom all but twelve were postmasters; but in London the force employed at the General Post Office had been raised from 77 to 185. The Penny Post Office, which had now been wrested out of Dockwra's hands, accounts for the greater part of the difference. This gave employment, exclusive of receivers, to 74 persons—a comptroller, an accomptant, and a collector, 14 sorters and 57 messengers—at a total charge for salaries of £2000 a year. Another part of the establishment, and by no means the least important or the least difficult to manage, consisted of the packet boats. These, in 1690, were eleven in number, viz.—two for France, two for Flanders, two for Holland, two for the Downs, and three for Ireland. Owing to the war, however, the boat-service to France was now in abeyance.

Little more than half a century had elapsed since the introduction of postage, and meanwhile the revenue had risen by strides which were for those times prodigious. In 1635 the posts were maintained at a cost to the Crown of £3400 a year. Within fifteen years not only had they become self-supporting, but a rent was paid for the privilege of farming them. This rent was, in 1650, £5000 a year; in 1653, £10,000; in 1660, £21,500; and some time before 1680, £43,000. In 1690 the net revenue was probably about £55,000. In 1694, according to a return made to the House of Commons two years later, it was £59,972.

The headquarters of the Post Office were at this time in Lombard Street. Here the postmasters-general resided; and here, far from shutting themselves up, they were to be found at all hours by any one who might wish to consult them on business connected with their office. Freedom of communication with those among whom they lived, and not inaccessibility, appears indeed to have been a part of their policy. With the foreign merchants especially they maintained the most friendly intercourse, and were wont to defer to their wishes and suggestions in the arrangement of the packets. Besides giving constant attendance during the day, the postmasters-general sat as a Board every morning and night. To these Board-meetings they attached the highest importance, especially on the nights of Tuesdays, Thursdays, and Saturdays, when mails were despatched into all parts of the country. These were known as the "Grand Post Nights," and the others as "Bye-Nights."

The Post Office building appears to have been not ill adapted to its purpose. A massive gate opened into a court of oblong shape. This court was paved from end to end for the merchants to walk in while waiting to receive their letters. On the right was the Board-room with the residence of the postmasters-general attached; on the left the office for foreign letters; and in front, immediately facing the entrance, was the sorting office. The office for the letter-carriers was in the basement. The rest of the building was devoted to the use of the Post Office servants, who, owing to their unseasonable hours of attendance, were required to live in the office itself or else in its immediate vicinity.

The machinery for the dispersion of letters was very simple. For Post Office purposes the kingdom was divided into six roads—the North Road, the Chester or Holyhead Road, the Western Road, the Kent Road, and the Roads to Bristol and to Yarmouth; and these roads were presided over by a corresponding number of clerks in London whose duty it was to sort the letters and to tax them with the proper amount of postage. At the present time, when, owing to the system of prepayment, there is comparatively little taxing to be done, no less than 2800 clerks and sorters are engaged every evening in despatching the letters into the country. Two hundred years ago the whole operation was performed, both sorting and taxing together, by the six clerks of the roads, and they had not even a sorter to assist them until 1697.

The letters, as soon as they had been sorted, were despatched into the country, the usual hour of despatch being shortly after midnight; but, of course, with a force to prepare them of only six persons, a rigid punctuality such as that which now distinguishes the operations of the Post Office could hardly be observed. An instance remains on record of the disturbance caused by any unusual pressure. The 25th of February 1696, we are told, was a foreign post night, and it happened that the letters for the country as well as abroad were more than ordinarily numerous. On this occasion the mails which should have gone out before three o'clock in the morning could not be despatched until between six and seven.

Once clear of London, the letters passed into the hands of the postmasters, who were alone concerned in their transmission and distribution. At the present time, multifarious as the duties of a postmaster are, it is not one of them to transport the mails from town to town. But such was not the case in 1690. The post roads were then divided into sections or, as they were commonly called, stages; and these stages were presided over by a corresponding number of postmasters, whose duty it was to carry the mails each over his own stage. This had been the original object of their appointment, the object for which they had been granted the monopoly of letting post-horses, and it still remained their primary duty, to which every other was subordinate. And yet traces of this original function were already beginning to disappear. The posts settled on the six main roads of the kingdom had not been long in extending themselves to other roads; and on these branch roads one postmaster would be charged with the carrying of the mails over two or more stages, leaving another without any transport duty at all. Kendal, for instance, lay on a branch road leaving the Holyhead Road at Chester; and from Wigan the letters for Kendal were fetched by the postmaster of Preston, who passed not only his own town but the town of Lancaster on his way.

In 1690 no provincial town had a letter-carrier of its own, as that term is now understood. Even at Bristol and at Norwich, which ranked next to the capital in size and importance, there was for all Post Office purposes one single agent, and that was the postmaster. Upon him and him alone devolved all the duties which now, at all but the smallest towns, a body of sorters and letter-carriers is maintained to perform. Whether out of London there was any settled mode of delivery is uncertain; but there seems little doubt that, soon after the establishment of the Post Office, to deliver letters in his own town had come to be a part, though a secondary part, of a postmaster's duty. At Maidstone, indeed, the delivery appears to have reached a high state of perfection. The postmaster there fetched the mails from Rochester and carried them to Ashford, dropping the letters for his own town as he passed through. These were at once taken out by two men of his own and delivered, so that, as he took pride in relating, a letter from London arriving by the morning post at noon could he answered by the return post, which left Maidstone at six o'clock in the evening.

But this must have been an exceptional case. Except perhaps at the largest towns, letters were yet too few to make such an arrangement necessary; and it seems probable that the hour at which the delivery was made and the area over which it extended were very much in the postmaster's discretion. One check there was, and, so far as appears, one only. This was the letter bill which accompanied the letters, and in which was inserted the postage which a postmaster had to collect and bring to account; but it frequently happened that he advanced the amount himself, and of course, where this was so, there was nothing to shew that any particular letter had been delivered, still less that it had been delivered within a particular time. Far more effective, it may well be believed, than any official check was the desire, the natural desire, to stand well with his neighbours; and the substantial marks of kindness which they seldom failed to bestow upon him whenever he was so unfortunate as to get into trouble, preclude the idea that, in the matter of delivery or otherwise, remissness or inattention can have been at all general.

In London, owing to recent malpractices there, attention had been directed to the salaries, and these had been improved. The six clerks of the roads received four of them £60 a year, one £50, and one as much as £100. The sorters received £40 a year, and the general post letter-carriers 11s. a week. The wages of the penny post letter-carriers or messengers, as for distinction's sake they were called, were 8s. In addition to their salaries the clerks of the roads enjoyed the privilege of franking newspapers or, as they were then called, gazettes. This privilege, which dated from the first establishment of the Post Office, had arrested the attention of James when Duke of York, and he had desired to take it away; but, on learning that compensation would have to be given, he decided to let it continue. By post the gazettes would have cost from 4d. to 6d. apiece. The clerks of the roads supplied them for 2d. The emoluments from this source kept steadily growing during William's reign. At first the longer and more frequent sessions of Parliament, and, later on, the war in which England was engaged, excited an appetite for news to which the two previous reigns afford no parallel. A statement which the postmasters-general made to the Treasury about this time, while evincing perhaps some little credulity, evinces also how keen, in the judgment of two shrewd and intelligent men, was the hunger after early intelligence. "In England," they say, "there are many postmasters, who some of them serve without salary, others for less than they would otherwise do, in consideration of their being allowed gazets by the office ffrank."

Another curious custom prevailed in 1690, and continued indeed for nearly a century afterwards. This was the distribution among the Post Office servants in London of a certain sum annually as "drink and feast money." The sum so distributed in 1685 had been no less than £60; and this was in addition to two "feasts" which were given them at the expense of the Crown, one at midsummer and the other at Christmas.

In the country, where there was no one to watch over the postmasters' interests, the salaries were merely nominal. The postmaster of Sudbury in Suffolk received a salary of £26 a year; and for this he had, three times a week, to carry the letters to Braintree and back, a distance of thirty-two miles, over a road that was barely passable. At Maidstone, in order to keep the delivery up to his own standard of excellence, the postmaster expended 2s. a day in what he called "horse-meate and man's-meate," yet his salary was only £5. Many postmasters received no salary at all. Even at Bristol, which stood next to London in population and wealth, the salary was only £60, having been recently raised to that amount from £50.

Nor was it only in the matter of salary that the postmasters were objects of compassion. The disturbed state of the country during the last few years had brought back old abuses. Officers of the army and others who had not the officers' excuse of urgency would override the post-horses, and when, as frequently happened, these were lamed or killed, no compensation appears to have been given. Another class of persons infested the roads, persons who, taking advantage of the general confusion, would hire post-horses and not return them. During the last twelve or thirteen years of the seventeenth century many postmasters were languishing in prison through inability to pay what they owed for postage; and among these there were few who did not trace their misfortunes to the fact that immediately before and after William's accession to the throne their horses had been killed or spoiled through reckless riding or else run away with.

But neither the loss of their horses nor the inadequacy of their remuneration was so galling to the postmasters as the liability to which they now became subject, of having soldiers quartered upon them. A standing army had been recently authorised, and there was little or no barrack accommodation. Hence a liability, which in our own time might be little more than nominal, was, in 1690, tantamount to a heavy tax. Under Charles and James[12] the postmasters had been exempt from this annoyance; but the exemption had been granted by virtue of the royal prerogative, and William could not be induced to continue it. In vain it was urged that, if a burden were cast upon them as novel as it was oppressive, justice demanded that their salaries should be increased. The King resolutely refused to make a distinction which the law did not recognise, and, except in a few isolated cases, the salaries remained unchanged.

Despite these drawbacks, there is no reason to think that the appointment of postmaster was not eagerly sought for, or that when obtained there was any general disposition to throw it up. The explanation is obvious. In the first place the appointment carried with it the exclusive right of letting post-horses. This monopoly, at all events on the more frequented roads, must have been remunerative; and it must have been especially remunerative where, as appears to have been generally the case, the postmaster was also innkeeper. Travellers were drawn to his house, for it was only there that they could procure horses to pursue their journey. He was, in a word, assured of custom. Other sources of emolument were—1st, gratuities, varying according to distance, from 1d. to 3d., on every letter he collected or delivered; and 2nd, what were technically called "Bye-letters." This term, whatever may have been the case a century before, had now a distinctive meaning. It meant letters which stopped short of London,[13] letters upon which at that time there was no check. In 1690 the postage on these letters was probably not large; but, large or small, the whole or all but the whole of it found its way into the pockets of the postmasters, and it was one of the first cares of the new postmasters-general to consider how the diversion might be stopped.

Such, in England, was the condition of the Post Office when Cotton and Frankland assumed the direction of it in the month of March 1690. In Scotland the posts were under separate direction, the direction of the Secretary of State for that part of the kingdom, and subject to the control of the Scotch Parliament. For purposes of convenience, however, an arrangement had been made between the two Post Offices. On letters between London and Edinburgh in both directions the English Post Office took not only its own share of the postage but the whole; and, in return, it paid the salaries of all the postmasters and defrayed the cost of all expresses between the Border town of Berwick-on-Tweed and Edinburgh. The correspondence at this time passing between the two capitals was of the slightest. It is true that for the three years ending March 1693 the amount due to the London office for postage on letters to Edinburgh was £1500, or at the rate of £500 a year; but the correspondence of the Secretary of State for Scotland, or "Black-box" as it was called, from the colour of the box in which it was carried, would probably account for nearly the whole. In 1707, which no doubt was a busy year in consequence of the Act of Union, the cost of carrying this box to and fro averaged £66 a month.

In Ireland the Post Office was managed by a deputy-postmaster, who was directly responsible to the postmasters-general in London. The method of business was the same as in England. Instead, however, of six "roads," there were only three—the Munster Road, the Ulster Road, and the Connaught Road. The Dublin establishment, clerks and letter-carriers included, consisted of twelve persons, of whom five received £20 a year, and no one, the deputy-postmaster excepted, more than £80. The deputy-postmaster himself received £400. Such at least was the normal establishment; but all was now confusion. The battle of the Boyne had not yet been fought, and Tyrconnel was still Lord Deputy. By his direction the Post Office servants in Dublin, down to the youngest letter-carrier, had been turned out of their appointments; and the mails from England, instead of being opened at the Post Office, were being carried to the castle and opened there.

The new postmasters-general had not long taken up their quarters in Lombard Street before they began to feel serious alarm for the revenue committed to their charge. It was in the matter of bye-letters that their apprehensions were first aroused. London, as the metropolis, sent and received more letters than any other town, more probably than all the other towns of the kingdom put together. Through London, too, as the centre of the Post Office system, many letters passed in those days which would not so pass now, because there were no cross-posts. Still there was a residue, a residue considerable in the aggregate, consisting of letters which did not touch London in any part of their course; and of these comparatively few were accounted for. Some thirty years later, after a check had been established, the revenue derived from bye-letters was only a little over £3000 a year. At the end of the seventeenth century it probably did not amount to as many hundreds.

It was, however, not the letters that fell into the post, but those that were kept out of it, the illicit traffic in fact, that caused the greatest concern. This traffic was assuming larger proportions every day. Under Charles and James searchers had been appointed, men who searched for letters as baggage is searched at the Custom House. No suspected person, no suspected vehicle, was safe from inspection. But there was no legal sanction for the practice, and it had ceased on William's accession. Early in the present reign it had been mooted whether a prosecution should not be undertaken, at all events against the principal offenders; but the King refused to consent to a step which he regarded as impolitic and calculated to excite discontent. License waxed bolder with impunity. Along the road from Bristol to Worcester and from Worcester to Shrewsbury men might be seen openly collecting and delivering letters in defiance of the law. Openly or clandestinely the same thing was being done in other parts. "Wherever," wrote the postmasters-general, "there are any townes which have commerce one with another so as to occasion a constant intercourse by carryer or tradesman, there we do find it a general practice to convey at the same time a considerable number of letters."

But the illicit traffic between one part of the country and another, large as were the dimensions it had assumed, was insignificant as compared with that which was taking place between the country and London. This was the natural result of the establishment of the penny post. At the first introduction of postage care had been taken so to fix the rates that for single letters the post should be cheaper than the common carrier. But the common carrier, in competition with the State, had one enormous advantage. He could reduce his terms at will. So long, therefore, as there was a profit to be made, the relative cheapness of the post had proved only an imperfect check.

A far more efficient check, in the case of the metropolis at least, had been the difficulty of dispersion. It was one thing to bring letters to London and another to deliver them. In a maze of streets consisting of houses which bore no numbers, a comparative stranger to the town attempting anything in the shape of a general delivery would have been simply bewildered. But all this was now altered. The penny post supplied the very machinery, the want of which had hitherto kept the illicit traffic within bounds. Once within the orbit of that post, a letter consigned to any one of Dockwra's four or five hundred receiving offices would be delivered in any part of what was then known as London for 1d., and in the suburbs for 2d. And these charges would carry up to one pound in weight; whereas a quarter of one pound by the general post, even from places no further distant from London than Croydon or Kingston, would be charged 2s. 8d.

Of course, under such conditions, to carry letters across the border-line, the line which separated the general post from the penny post, had soon become a regular traffic; and this traffic, in consequence of the impunity it enjoyed, was now being carried on with little concealment. No stage-coach entered London without the driver's pockets being stuffed with letters and packets, and he was moderate indeed if he had not a bagful besides. The waggoner outstripped his waggon and the carrier his pack-horse; and each brought his contribution. The higgler's wares were the merest pretext. It was to the letters and packets he carried that he looked for profit. So notorious had the abuse become that two private persons, unconnected with the Post Office, offered their services with a view to its correction. These persons were gentlemen by birth, and yet it is difficult to conceive an office more odious than the one which they were prepared to assume. They proposed to erect stands or barriers in Westminster, Southwark, and other places in the outskirts of London, and there to demand of suspected persons as they passed any letters they might have about them which did not concern their private business. They further proposed to deliver these letters by messengers of their own, and to collect the postage, and to proceed against the bearers of them for the recovery of the penalties. It is significant of the extent to which the traffic had grown, that in return for their services they asked no more than two-thirds of the postage they should collect, and even pleaded the heavy expenses to which they would be put as an apology for asking so much. The remaining third they would undertake to make over to the postmasters-general. They did not explain, however, how it was proposed to distinguish letters which concerned the private business of the bearers from those which did not, or how, while checking others, they were to be checked themselves. Nor indeed was any such explanation needed, for the postmasters-general very clearly discerned that the proposed remedy would be worse, far worse, than the disease.

Cotton and Frankland were sorely perplexed. They knew perfectly well that the true policy was to supplant and not to suppress; and experience had taught them that to facilitate correspondence was to increase it. These views they never ceased to inculcate; but their power of giving effect to them was extremely limited. They could not lower the rates of postage, for these were fixed by Act of Parliament. They could not set up a new post nor alter an old one without the King's permission. Neither was this permission so easy to obtain as it had been. The Post Office revenue was settled upon William just as it had been settled upon James; but while James kept the control in his own hands William left it to his ministers.[14] Constitutionally sound as the change of practice was, it had its drawback. James might care little for the convenience of trade and commerce; but self-interest would prompt him not to withhold facilities where these might be given at small cost and with the prospect of comparatively large returns. Ministers, on the contrary, even the most enlightened, concerned themselves mainly with the balance-sheet of the year, and no promise of future and remote profit would easily reconcile them to a diminution of present receipts. That the Post Office must sow before it can reap is a truism which those who hold the purse-strings have, at all times, found it hard to accept.

The ministers charged with the control of the Post Office were the Lords of the Treasury. How little the postmasters-general were left to act on their own responsibility will best be shewn by examples. Warwick, according to the computation of those days, was sixty-seven miles from London; but letters for that town passed through Coventry, thus traversing a distance of eighty miles. And not only was the route a circuitous one but it involved an additional charge for postage, the rates for a single letter being, for eighty miles, 3d., and for less than eighty, 2d. The postmasters-general desired to send the letters direct; but even so simple a matter as this they were not competent to decide for themselves. A change of route involved a reduction of charge; and a reduction of charge might affect the King's receipts. Before, therefore, the route could be altered, the King's assent had to be signified through his appointed ministers. In 1696 a post was established between Exeter and Bristol. This was the first cross-post set up by authority in the British Isles. It ran twice a week, leaving Exeter on Wednesdays and Saturdays at four in the afternoon, and arriving at Bristol at the same hour on the following days. From Bristol the return post, which went on Mondays and Fridays, started at ten in the morning. But in this case as in the other, the postmasters-general had not the power to act of their own motion. Hitherto letters between the two towns had passed through London, and so had been liable to a double rate of postage, to one rate of 3d. from Exeter to London, and to another rate of equal amount from London to Bristol, or 6d. altogether. For the future, the towns being less than eighty miles apart, the charge would be 2d. Large as this reduction was, the postmasters-general strongly advocated it. The existing post, they said, was both tedious and costly, and had been little used in consequence. A direct post, it was true, would require a small outlay to start it; but, this outlay notwithstanding, the post was certain to prove remunerative. Increase facilities for correspondence, and correspondence would assuredly follow. Besides, it would promote trade and be an inestimable boon to the public generally. To these representations the Treasury yielded; and before three years were over, the postmasters-general had the satisfaction of reporting that the new post was producing a clear profit of more than £250 a year. But complaisant as the Treasury had been on this occasion, their co-operation was fitful and uncertain. The Post Office could not advance a step without incurring some trifling expense; and the Treasury only too often acted as if to save expense, however trifling, were the highest proof of statesmanship.

The postmasters-general were indeed heavily handicapped. Even with a free hand their position would have been one of great embarrassment. But bound hand and foot as they were, what could they do? They did what was perhaps the very best thing that could have been done in the circumstances. They grouped large numbers of post offices together and let them out to farm. These groups, or branches as they were called, spread over a wide area. The Buckingham branch, for instance, not only included the county of Bucks but extended as far as Warwick. The Hungerford branch comprised sixteen post offices in the counties of Berks, Wilts, and Somerset. The Chichester branch covered a large part of Surrey as well as Sussex; and the six remaining branches, for eventually there were nine altogether, were equally extensive.

This, though by no means a perfect remedy for the existing evils, went far to mitigate them. The farmer, of course, could not alter the rates of postage; but with this single exception he was free from the restraints which hampered the postmasters-general. Within the area over which his farm extended he had only to consult his own interests; and, happily, his own interests and the interests of the public were identical. He improved and extended the posts, because to improve and extend the posts added to the number of letters and made his farm more profitable. He stopped the practice of levying gratuities on the delivery of letters, because this practice, by adding to the cost of the post, and so deterring persons from using it, diminished his own receipts. For the same reason he took good care that no agent of his own should omit to account for bye-letters, and, if other than his own agents continued to send letters by irregular means, that it should not be for want of facilities which he could himself supply.

To this community of interest as between himself and the public may be ascribed the exceptional feelings with which, at the close of the seventeenth and beginning of the eighteenth centuries, the Post Office farmer was regarded. The very name of farmer in connection with other branches of the revenue had become a by-word for all that was rapacious and extortionate. Only recently the farmer of the customs and the farmer of the hearth money had been stamped out as moral pests. The Post Office farmer, on the contrary, was welcomed wherever he came as a public benefactor. In his case outrages and exactions such as had disgraced the others were impossible. Before he could collect a single penny he had a service to perform; and according as this service was performed well or ill, he repelled or attracted custom.

The real secret of his welcome, however, was that he supplied an urgent demand; and how urgent this demand was may best be judged by the conditions on which he was glad to accept his farm. These conditions were a lease of no more than three years, and a rent equivalent to the highest amount which the post offices included in his farm had in any one year produced. For his profits he had nothing to look to but the increase of revenue resulting from his own management; and even of this he received the whole only in the first year, when he would, presumably, be establishing his plant. In subsequent years he received two-thirds, the remaining third going to the Post Office. If under such conditions as these it were possible to toil and grow rich, great indeed must have been the field of operation.

Among those who were commissioned to supply the accommodation which the postmasters-general were precluded from supplying themselves was one who deserves to be specially mentioned. This was Stephen Bigg of Winslow, in Buckinghamshire. Bigg farmed the Buckingham branch. He appears to have possessed and to have deserved the confidence of the postmasters-general. Of ample means, and endowed with no ordinary powers of organisation, he had probably embarked on his undertaking less with a view to profit than from a desire to improve the posts. Be that as it may, the same means which conduced to the one end conduced also to the other; and when the time arrived for him to render an account of his proceedings, he not only made over to the Post Office a handsome sum as one-third share of the profits, but had earned for himself the gratitude of the large district over which his farm extended.

His success in his own county encouraged him to enlarge the sphere of his operations. Passing through Lancashire in the last year of the century, he was struck with the wretched accommodation which the posts afforded. As compared with those under his own control, they were slow, irregular, and, owing to the system of gratuities, costly. On his return to London he offered to take in farm the post offices of the whole county. The offer was accepted, and a lease was signed fixing the rent, as ascertained in the usual manner, at £2826. The history of this farm is curious. Bigg had not long been engaged in his new undertaking before the cross-post which had some few years before been set up between Exeter and Bristol was extended to Chester. It is not very clear how this interfered with Bigg's proceedings; but, as a matter of fact, it appears to have tapped an important source of supply. On this being pointed out to the postmasters-general, they at once, with that high sense of justice which distinguished all their proceedings, released him from his engagement and cancelled the lease.

The next county to which Bigg turned his attention was Lincolnshire. If Lancashire had bad posts, Lincolnshire had next to none. Five post towns were all of which Lincolnshire could boast—Stamford and Witham and Grantham, Lincoln and Boston; and of these only two were off the great north road which ran through the extreme west of the county. It is true that other towns received letters; but they received them only by virtue of a private arrangement, and heavily had they to pay for the luxury. From Lincoln, for instance, the postmaster went twice a week to Gainsborough and to Brigg, to Horncastle, Louth, and Grimsby, charging as his own perquisite on each letter he collected or delivered the sum of 3d. over and above the postage; but, so far as depended on any official post, these and all the intervening towns were absolutely cut off from the rest of the world. [15] Bigg procured a farm of the district in favour of his son, and the lease was signed on the 4th of August 1705. On the 1st of October in the same year posts began to run, and gratuities on the delivery of letters had become a thing of the past. One penny on each letter collected was the only charge that remained over and above the postage.

It would be less than justice not to recognise the important part which about this period the farmer played in the history of the Post Office; nor is it possible not to admire the sagacity of those who, when they found the posts to be slipping through their fingers, summoned this extraneous agency to their aid. It was no mere venture which by a happy accident happened to turn out well. The postmasters-general had foreseen and foretold exactly what would be the result—that under a system of farming the public would be better served, letters would become more numerous, and the revenue, when it should revert to the Crown at the termination of the lease, would be higher than when the lease began.

Next to Lincolnshire in poverty of the means of correspondence stood Cornwall. Until 1704 the post to Falmouth, after leaving Exeter, ran through Ashburton to Plymouth and thence along the south coast. Of the towns in Mid Cornwall Launceston alone possessed a post office. At others, indeed, letters were delivered, but only by virtue of a private arrangement and on payment of a gratuity of 2d. apiece. No farmer, unfortunately, offered his services here. But, what was perhaps the next best thing, the gentry of the county, headed by Lord Granville, took the matter up. Thus supported, the postmasters-general proceeded to concert their arrangements. They desired the postmasters of Exeter, Plymouth, and Launceston to meet together and prepare some scheme for facilitating the correspondence of the midland towns. Such a scheme was soon submitted, and, although it involved a cost of £260 a year, authority for its adoption was not withheld. Henceforth the post for the extreme west of England was to go, not by way of Plymouth, but direct from Exeter to St. Columb, and thence through Truro to Falmouth. A single post through a wide extent of country might ill accord with our present views of what the public convenience requires; and yet at the beginning of the eighteenth century Mid Cornwall, by the mere alteration of the route for the Falmouth mails, obtained facilities for correspondence not inferior to those enjoyed by other parts of the country.

The speed at which the post travelled at the end of the seventeenth century only slightly exceeded four miles an hour. This slow rate of progress, added to the fact that, except to the Downs, the post left London only on alternate days, gave occasion for the not infrequent use of expresses. These were mounted messengers sent specially for the occasion. Whether for expresses there was any prescribed rate of speed is not known; but it seems probable that their instructions were to go as fast as they could. The charge for an express was 3d. a mile and 6d. a stage, a stage being on the average about twelve miles. The total sum which the Post Office received on this account during the half-year which ended the 29th of September 1685 was £337.

Occasionally several expresses would be required at one time. In 1696, on the discovery of Barclay's plot to assassinate the King, orders were given to close the ports; and these orders the postmasters-general sent, as they were instructed to do, by express. Some twenty years afterwards similar orders were given, and an account is still extant shewing how on the later, and probably the earlier, occasion they were carried into effect. The English ports were sixty-two in number; and to only ten of these were expresses sent direct from Lombard Street, the others being either taken by the way or reached by branch expresses furnished by the towns through which the expresses from London passed. Altogether the distance traversed was 2526 miles, the number of stages 202, and the sum which the Post Office received for the service from the Commissioners of Customs £36:12:6.

From expresses it seems almost natural to pass to flying packets, although between the two there is, so far as we are aware, no necessary connection. What was a flying packet? The term "flying," at the end of the seventeenth and beginning of the eighteenth centuries, was, no doubt, used in the sense of running. For this season, writes Lord Compton's private tutor to Lady Northampton, under date September 1734, "the coach has done flying." In like manner "flying post," a term as old as the Post Office itself,[16] meant nothing more than what in Scotland was called a runner. Possibly because the idea of expedition was conveyed by the term "flying," flying packet came to be regarded as synonymous with express. "I despatch this by a flying pacquett," writes Lord Townshend to the Duke of Argyll in 1715; and again, "My lord, after writing what is above, a flying packet brings letters from Edinburgh of the 12th." "By the flying pacquett which arrived last night," writes Secretary Stanhope about the same date, "I received the honour of your Grace's of the 21st inst." Here, by flying packet is obviously meant express. And yet, curiously enough, this is a sense in which the postmasters-general never employed the term. By them it was always designed to signify the thing transmitted, and not the means of transmission. What they called a flying packet might be sent by ordinary post no less than by express; and when sending one by express they never failed to state that it was being so sent. "You are therefore," they write in 1706, "on the receipt of the bag so delivered to your care [*i.e.* a small bag containing letters for the Court], to dispatch the same imediately by a flying packet from Harwich to this office, and to send a labil therewith expressing the precise time of the arrival and your having dispatched the same per express." On receipt of the Holland mail, they write again in the following year, "You are to take out the Court letters, and to forward the same express by a flying packet directed to Mr. Frankland at the Post Office at Newmarket." "The inclosed box being recommended to our care by His Grace the Duke of Queensberry, one of Her Majesty's principall Secretarys of State, we do send the same by a flying pacquet.... You are to send us advice by the first post of the safe comeing of this pacquet to your hands." In short, flying packet, in its original sense, appears to have meant simply a packet of which the enclosures were designed for some other person than the one whose address the packet bore. Within the Post Office it is occasionally necessary to employ technical terms which would not be intelligible to persons without; but this, so far as we are aware, is the only instance of the same term being used within and without in two totally different senses.

Of the state of the roads about this period the Highway Act 1691 affords, perhaps, not the least trustworthy evidence. To incidents which have resulted in nothing more than temporary inconvenience travellers are apt to give a touch of humorous exaggeration. An Act of Parliament, on the contrary, deals with facts as they are, and concerns itself not with imaginary ills. What, then, is to be thought of the condition of the roads when provisions such as these were necessary?—No causeway for horses was to be less than three feet in breadth, nor was the breadth of any cartway leading to a market town to be less than eight feet. In highways of less breadth than twenty feet no tree was to be permitted to grow, or stone, timber, or manure to be heaped up so as to obstruct progress; and hedges were to be kept trimmed, and boughs to be lopped off, so as to allow a free passage to travellers, and not to intercept the action of the sun and wind. Of any breach of these and other provisions the road-surveyor was, on the Sunday next after it became known to him, to give public notice in the parish church immediately after the conclusion of the sermon.

Long after the passing of the Act of 1691, and perhaps in consequence of it, the causeway formed an important feature of the roads. This causeway, or bridle-track, ran down the middle; while the margin on either side was little better than a ditch, and being lower than the adjoining soil, and at the same time soft and unmade, received and retained the sludge. But, in truth, the state of the roads concerned the Post Office far less at the close of the seventeenth century than it did at the close of the eighteenth. The mails were carried on horseback; and, even so, they were carried mainly over the six great roads of the kingdom. These roads, as compared with others, were good; and execrably bad as we might now think them, they were probably not altogether ill adapted to riding. The disasters which history refers to this period, as illustrating the difficulties of travelling, occurred generally on the cross-roads, and always with wheel traffic. For both wheel traffic and horse traffic the six great roads had, probably from the earliest times, been kept in some sort of repair. On the great Kent Road, nearly a hundred years before, a young Dane, with his attendants, had on horseback accomplished the distance between Dover and London in a single day.[17] In 1642 couriers had ridden from London to York and back, a distance of about 400 miles, in thirty-four hours,[18] a feat barely possible except on the assumption that the road was in tolerable order. Now and again, indeed, some postmaster, pleading for the remission of his debt to the Crown, would urge the losses he had sustained in horse-flesh by reason of the badness of the roads; but these roads were always cross-roads—roads along which, if he had delivered letters, he had delivered them on his own account. Of the six great roads as a means of transit for the mails there were no complaints.

It was when the Post Office required something to be done which involved transmission from place to place otherwise than on horseback that its troubles began. Such an event occurred in 1696. Sir Isaac Newton was then busy at the mint, devoting to the coinage those powers of intellect which were soon to astonish the world. The clipping of the coin had gone to such lengths that within the space of one year no less than four Acts of Parliament were passed with a view to abate the evil. Milled money was to take the place of hammered money. The clipped pieces had already been withdrawn from circulation, and now a date was fixed after which no broad pieces were to be received in payment of taxes except by weight. This date was the 18th of November, and collectors of the public revenue were allowed until the 18th of the following month to pay them over to the Exchequer. If not paid over by the 18th of December they were to be taken by weight and not by tale, and the collectors were to lose the difference.

Here was a clear month's grace, and the postmasters were under a strong inducement to see that the period was not exceeded. From Oxford the hammered money was sent by barge. No sooner had it started than a severe frost set in, and lasted for six weeks, the consequence being to delay the arrival in London until the 7th of January. To take the money by weight and not by tale would have been equivalent to a fine of about £23. From this, however, the postmaster was excused on the ground that the barge was the safest means of conveyance he could have employed. As a "flying coach"—a coach which travelled at the speed of about four miles an hour—had for many years been running between Oxford and London, it must be assumed either that it had stopped for the winter or else that for some cause or other, possibly on account of highwaymen, it was not considered safe. From Sandwich, in Kent, the hammered money was sent by hoy, which did not reach the Thames until the 20th of January. Again the postmasters-general urged that the delay might be overlooked on the ground that no earlier means of conveyance would have been safe. Altogether, when the 18th of December arrived, more than £1000 of hammered money was still outstanding in the postmasters' hands; and in every case the want of conveyance or the badness of the roads was assigned as the cause.

The penny post office, since it had passed into the hands of the Government, had undergone but little change. Its headquarters had been removed from Dockwra's house to seven rooms prepared for the purpose, not, indeed, at the Post Office in Lombard Street, where want of space was already beginning to be felt, but probably in the immediate neighbourhood. It had also, in the language of the time, been eased from a multitude of desperate debts. But the conditions on which it was conducted remained as they had been,—the same limit of weight, the same frequency of delivery, and the same rule as to compensation in case of loss. Dockwra, with the view, no doubt, of propitiating the authorities, had provided for the conveyance to Lombard Street of all general post letters left at his receiving offices; and this duty, when he was dispossessed, passed to the persons by whom those offices were kept. The result was not satisfactory. The receivers, in their desire to get the work done as cheaply as possible, employed to do it the most needy and most worthless persons, persons who could not get employment elsewhere. At length the miscarriages and losses became so frequent that the Post Office appointed its own messengers to go round and collect the letters. Nor is it by any means certain that the character of the receivers themselves was above suspicion. The plain truth is that they were, with few exceptions, keepers of public-houses. The collector who called there periodically to adjust accounts complained that often four and even five visits were necessary before he could obtain payment, and that the opportunity was taken to pass upon him bad money.

Times have changed indeed. With public-houses for receiving offices, with inn-keepers for postmasters, and with a considerable sum expended annually on drink and feast money, it can hardly be denied that the Post Office at the end of the seventeenth century was a good friend to the licensed victualler. At the present time no postmaster may keep an inn; no receiving office may be at a public-house; and not many years ago, when a hotel with its stock-in-trade was purchased with a view to the extension of the Post Office buildings in St. Martin's-le-Grand, some excellent persons were shocked because, under the sanction of the postmaster-general, were exposed for sale by auction some few dozen bottles of port.

Of the extent to which the penny post was used at this period we are not, so far as the suburbs are concerned, without some means of judging. According to the original plan, which had been adhered to in its integrity, one penny was to carry a letter within such parts of London as lay within the bills of mortality. Beyond these limits one penny more was charged; and this penny, which was technically called the second or deliver penny, constituted the messengers' remuneration. As this soon proved to be more than enough for its purpose, the messengers were put on fixed wages, and the second pennies were carried to the credit of the Post Office. Of the amounts derived from this source during the sixteen years from 1686 to 1702 a record is still extant. The lowest amount for any one year was £310, and the highest £377, the average being £336. It would hence appear that for such parts of London as lay outside the bills of mortality, for what in fact were at that time the suburbs, the number of letters at the end of the seventeenth century was about 80,640 a year, or, counting 306 working days to the year, about 263 a day.

On one point the postmasters-general were determined, that the penny post office should not be let out to farm. All overtures to this effect they resolutely declined. The penny post and the general post had become so interwoven, and, outside London, so short a distance separated the limits within which the one ceased and the other began to operate, that it was considered of the highest importance, both on the score of convenience and as a protection against fraud, that the two posts should not be under different management. The same considerations were not held to apply to Dublin. In Dublin, rapidly as that city was now growing in size[19] and population, a penny post, it was thought, could not possibly answer. Yet in 1703 a spirited lady sought permission to set one up. This was Elizabeth, Countess-Dowager of Thanet. A desire to supplement a jointure, originally slender and now reduced by the taxation consequent on the war, was the simple reason assigned for the enterprise, and yet with the highest professions of public spirit it might have been difficult to render to the community a more signal service. The Duke of Ormonde, who was then Lord Lieutenant, approved the proposal, and the postmasters-general had made preparations for carrying it into effect. The new post was to extend for ten or twelve miles in and around Dublin; no receiving office was to be within two miles of the first stage of the general post; the lease was to be for fourteen years; and one-tenth part of the clear profits was to go to the

Crown. At the last moment, however, the Treasury withheld their assent, and for no less than seventy years from this time Dublin remained without a penny post.

Of the internal affairs of the Post Office during the first fifteen years of Cotton and Frankland's administration of it little need be said. At first their only assistant was a clerk at £40 a year to copy their letters. In 1694 they procured a new appointment to be created, the appointment of Secretary to the Post Office. The Secretary to the Post Office at the present time has duties to discharge, of the variety and importance of which his mere title gives a very inadequate idea. In 1694 he was little more than a private secretary. One thing indeed he had to do, to which a private secretary of our own time might perhaps demur. During the night, if an express were wanted, he had to rise from his bed and prepare the necessary instructions. The salary of the appointment, originally £100, was raised to £200 in 1703. In this year a solicitor was appointed, also at a salary of £200.

Two years later a transaction was completed on which the postmasters-general had long set their hearts. This was the purchase of a part of the Post Office premises in Lombard Street. As far back as 1688 Sir Robert Viner, the owner, had offered the freehold for sale, but the Revolution had put a stop to further proceedings. In 1694, after Sir Robert's death, his nephew and executor again proposed to sell, and Sir Christopher Wren, on behalf of the Crown, surveyed the property with a view to its purchase. On examination, however, the title proved to be defective, and it was not until 1705, after the defect had been remedied by Act of Parliament, that the Crown secured the freehold for the sum of £6500. At the present time it matters not where Post Office servants reside, so long as they attend punctually. At the beginning of the eighteenth century it was considered important on account of the unseasonable hours of attendance that they should reside "in and about" the Post Office. The Post Office was, in effect, a barrack, and, except the premises in Lombard Street, there were none in the immediate neighbourhood that would well answer the purpose. Hence the anxiety to purchase the freehold; and the anxiety was all the greater because it had been threatened that if not purchased by the Crown the property would be sold to the speculative builder or, as he was then called, the projector.

CHAPTER VII
COTTON AND FRANKLAND
Packet Service 1686-1713

Of the packet service prior to 1686 we have no particulars; but that some such service had long existed, though probably on a very limited scale, hardly admits of a doubt. To Ireland, as to other parts of the kingdom, a regular post had been established in 1635; and it is difficult to suppose that a mail on arriving at Holyhead would be left to a chance vessel to carry it across the Channel. The probability of some organised means of transport is still stronger in the case of Dover. Dover was the town through which all letters for the Continent passed; and our trade with the Continent had for a century and more been considerable. Hence it was that the post through the county of Kent had been carefully nursed while as yet no other part of the country had any post at all. But if, as seems certain, both Dover and Holyhead were packet stations long prior to 1686, it is almost equally certain that these were the only two in the kingdom.

In that year the arrangements, whatever they were, for carrying the mails between England and France came to an end, and a new service was established between Dover and Calais and between Dover and Ostend or Nieuport. This was succeeded in the following year by a similar service between England and Holland. Both services were to be carried on by contract. In the one case the contractor was to receive £1170 a year, and also to have the management of the letter office at Dover. In the other the payment was to be £900 a year, for which sum three hoys were to be maintained, two of sixty and one of forty tons, and carrying six men each. For the service to Holland the packet stations were, on this side of the water, Harwich, and, on the other, the Brill.

To the letters which came to this country by regular packet must be added those that were technically termed ship letters—letters which were brought by ships arriving at uncertain times from any part of the world. These letters, according to the provisions of the Act of 1660, were to be given up to the postmaster at the port of arrival, so that they might be forwarded to London, and thence despatched to their destination after being charged with the proper amount of postage. In this particular, however, the Act proved of little effect. Masters of ships were offered no inducement to deliver the letters to the postmaster, and incurred no penalty for omitting to do so. The Post Office was then in farm; and desirous as the farmers were to make what they could out of their undertaking, they soon found that it would be well worth their while to incur some expense which should secure obedience to the law. Accordingly they undertook that for every letter which a shipmaster should bring to this country, and deliver to the postmaster at the port of arrival, he should receive the sum of one penny. This was the origin of ship letter money—a form of payment which has since received legal sanction, and exists at the present day.

It was into the port of London that ship letters chiefly came, and here the number which found their way to the Post Office in Lombard Street was seriously affected by the establishment of the penny post. That this was only natural will appear from a simple illustration. From Marseilles to London the postage was 1s. for a single letter. On one hundred such letters, therefore, the charge would be £5. But if, instead of taking these hundred letters to the General Post Office, a shipmaster on his arrival in the Pool dropped them into the penny post, they would all be delivered for 8s. 4d. It is true that he would thus lose his gratuity of one penny a letter; but the difference between the two rates of postage was such as to leave an ample margin of profit, even after making him full—and more than full—compensation for his loss. Indeed, if he had been bent on cheating his employer as well as the Post Office, he might with very little risk of detection have put the whole of the difference into his own pocket. In 1686 the number of ship letters accounted for to the Post Office was 60,447,[20] a number which, forming as it did the basis of a payment, may be taken as absolutely correct, because the Post Office would take good care not to pay more, and shipmasters not to receive less, than was absolutely due. It is to be regretted that no similar account is forthcoming for previous years, so that it might be seen what was the extent of the influence which the penny post exercised; but that this influence was considerable is certain from the continual references made to it by successive postmasters-general during a long series of years. It is to be observed, however, that they always speak of it as a thing that was past and gone, a thing baneful enough while it lasted, but as having been of only short duration. The explanation is no doubt to be found in the fact that in 1696 two officers were appointed, whose duty it was to collect letters from all vessels arriving in the port of London. The boat employed in this service had assigned to it special colours of its own, on which was depicted a man on horseback blowing a post horn.[21]

In 1689, on the breaking out of the war with France, the Dover boats ceased to run, and, in order to provide for the letters to Spain which had hitherto passed through that country, a service was established between Falmouth and the Groyne. On this service two boats were employed of two or three hundred tons each. They carried from eighty to ninety men besides twenty guns, and ran once a fortnight.

The Harwich boats were at the same time increased both in number and in strength. The three hoys were replaced by four boats—boats of force as they were called, carrying fifty men each. It may well be believed that, with so large a crew under his command, the captain of a well-armed vessel was loth to confine himself to the monotonous task of carrying the mails to and fro, and went in quest of adventure. But be that as it may, William, who since his accession to the throne had taken an extraordinary interest in the Harwich service, was not satisfied with the performances of these boats. It was his opinion that the first requisite in a mail packet was speed and not strength. Strength might indeed enable it to engage an enemy, but speed would enable it to avoid one. Accordingly, by the King's direction, the Post Office with the assistance of Edmund Dummer, the Surveyor of the Navy, built four small boats of its own—boats "of no force," but remarkable for their speed. The change was not carried out without much grumbling. The boats were low built, and, except in the calmest weather, shipped a good deal of water. The sailors complained that they seldom, from one end of the voyage to the other, had a dry coat to their backs. The absence of any armament was still more unpalatable to them. They dared not leave the harbour, at least so they said, when the enemy was to windward; and, as though to confirm their words, they sometimes after leaving returned. We shall probably do them no wrong if we distrust these excuses. No British sailor, or soldier either, cares to turn his back on the foe, and that this was expected of them, that they were required to run and not to fight, we suspect to have been the real grievance. Eventually, but not until some had refused to serve and others had deserted, matters quieted down. An increase of wages was given all round, raising the pay above that given in the Royal Navy, and, in order to compensate for the additional cost, the complement of the crew was reduced from thirty to twenty-one. It is a striking confirmation of the soundness of William's view that during the next twenty-four years, although no less than nineteen of them were years of war, only two of these boats were taken.

Until 1689 the Harwich packets had been self-supporting, the receipts from freight and passengers being enough to cover the cost. In that year, as a consequence of the war, the fares were raised. Passengers to Holland who had hitherto paid 12s. were now to pay 20s., and those who had paid 6s. were to pay 10s. Recruits and indigent persons passed free. In 1695 the carriage of goods and merchandise was prohibited. This prohibition afterwards became common in times of war, but in the present instance it was imposed in the vain hope of stopping the exportation of silver. In exchange for silver, gold had long been pouring into the country, as much as 200 ounces coming by a single packet; and advices had been received from Amsterdam and Rotterdam that future consignments would not be restricted even to that quantity. The reform of the currency, which alone could check this movement of the precious metals, was expeditiously accomplished; but the prohibition against the carriage of merchandise remained.

On the conclusion of peace in 1697 the service between Dover and Calais and between Dover and Ostend recommenced, but only to be discontinued again on the resumption of hostilities in 1702. During these five years the relations between the English and French Post Offices had at no time been friendly, and latterly had become very highly strained. Under the terms of a Treaty concluded with France in 1698, the mails, as soon as they arrived on this side at Dover and on the other at Calais, were to be forwarded to the respective capitals by express. England faithfully fulfilled her part of the engagement. By France the engagement was treated as a dead letter. The mails from England, on their arrival at Calais, instead of being forwarded to Paris by express, were kept back for the ordinary post; and this post went only once a day, leaving at three in the afternoon. If, therefore, the packet arrived at four or five o'clock, the letters were detained for the best part of twenty-four hours. At Lyons the letters between England and Italy were being treated after much the same fashion. On arrival in that town—such at least was the complaint in the city—instead of being forwarded with all despatch, they were forwarded seldom in due course and sometimes not at all.

M. Pajot was then director of the French posts; and in this capacity he had signed the Treaty. In vain Cotton and Frankland called his attention to the breach of its provisions. Their letter was not even acknowledged. For the transit of British mails across French territory England had agreed to pay to France the sum of 36,000 livres[22] a year, and a remittance in payment of the instalment due was sent to Paris; but not even of this could an acknowledgment be obtained. Let the nature of the communication to him be what it would, Pajot maintained an obstinate silence. When war broke out afresh, all intercourse between the two Post Offices had ceased for nearly three years, and the debt due to France had accumulated to the amount of 105,600 livres.

The cessation of the Dover packets in 1702 was soon followed by that of the packets between Falmouth and the Groyne, but the want of any regular means of communication with the Peninsular proved so inconvenient that, before many months had passed, the service was re-established in a slightly altered form. The boats, instead of stopping short at the Groyne, were to run on to Lisbon; and two years later their number was increased from two to five. This increase was due to political rather than commercial reasons. It is true that an important commercial treaty was about this time concluded with Portugal; but, what was considered of far greater moment, the Archduke Charles after passing through London had recently proceeded to that country in furtherance of his pretensions to the throne of Spain. It was at once resolved that communication with Lisbon should henceforth be weekly instead of only once a fortnight, and for this purpose less than five boats were deemed insufficient.

But of all the packet services in existence at the beginning of the eighteenth century none perhaps possesses more features of interest than the service to the West Indies. In James the Second's reign a Post Office had been established in Jamaica, and rates of postage had been settled not only within the island itself but between the island and the mother country. This was a new departure. In the original scheme of postage as propounded by Witherings no charge had been imposed except in return for some service. The same principle had been scrupulously adhered to in the Acts of 1657 and 1660. Under these Acts, except where a service was rendered or where payment for a service was made to another country, no charge was provided for. Yet between England and Jamaica, although the Crown was not at the cost of maintaining means of transport, postage rates were fixed of 6d. a single letter, 1s. a double letter, and 2s. an ounce. This was a pure tax, and the precedent, bad as it was and of questionable legality, was soon extended to the case of letters to America.

The war of 1702, while deranging other services, called the service to the West Indies into being. The West India merchants, a designation even then in vogue, were a large and important body, and, as opportunities of intercourse by private ship became rare and uncertain, a demand arose for some established means of communication. With the assistance of Dummer, Surveyor of the Navy, sloops were provided to carry mails to the Plantation Islands, and by way of helping to defray the cost, the postage rates were increased by about one-half. The vessels sailed at uncertain intervals, but otherwise the service was performed with regularity, the voyage out and home occupying from 90 to 116 days.

Dummer was so well satisfied with the result of his management that, rather than continue as mere agent for the postmasters-general, he desired to perform the service on his own account. For the sum of £12,500 a year he undertook to provide a monthly communication, and for this purpose to build and equip five boats of 140 tons each, and carrying twenty-six men and ten guns. These boats were to have two decks, and any of them that should be lost or taken by the enemy were to be replaced at his own cost. Of the £12,500 no more than £4500 was to be paid down. Freight, which was limited to five tons out and ten tons home, passenger fares, and postage were to go in part payment, and from these Dummer expected to make up the difference. Postage alone he set down at £6000; and that it might produce this sum he made it an express stipulation that the rates to the West Indies should be raised to the same level as those to Portugal, namely 1s. 3d. a single letter, 2s. 6d. a double letter, and 6s. an ounce. To double the postage, he took for granted, was to double the returns. Abler men than he and men living nearer to our own times have fallen into the same error; but seldom, probably, has it been sooner or more strikingly exposed.

The new rates came into operation in England in March, and in the West Indies in April. The effect of the alteration, as would now be predicted with confidence, was only slightly to increase the amount of postage and largely to reduce the number of letters. It is so seldom that in matters of this kind cause and effect are brought into such close approximation, that we offer no apology for giving the postage which the correspondence produced immediately before and immediately after the change:—

To the West Indies.

Date on which the Packet
sailed from England.

Date	Amount	of Postage.		
Jan. 25, 1705	£44	1	4	
Feb. 22 "	59	10	7	
Mar. 29 "	100	5	3	(New rates)
Apr. 26 "	129	2	6	
May 31 "	93	7	9	
June 28 "	75	19	3	
July 26 "	62	2	0	

From the West Indies.

Date on which the Packet
arrived in England.

Date	Amount	of	Postage.	
Feb. 10, 1705	£316	19		0

Apr. 18	"	622	11	6	(New rates)
Aug. 6	"	629	15	6	
Sept. 3	"	384	19	6	
Oct. 1	"	369	6	6	

Of course, the mails immediately after the change would carry what may be called surprised letters, letters which had been posted before the issue of the new regulations or before these regulations had become generally known; and the mail arriving in August would bring also the letters which had accumulated since the preceding April.

What at the present time is calculated to excite surprise is not that the aggregate amounts of postage should not have increased in proportion to the rates, but that these amounts should have been as high as they were. Trade with the West Indies was, no doubt, considerable. And yet, after making ample allowance on that score, of what sort can the correspondence have been to produce postage of between £300 and £400 by a single mail; and why should the amount in one direction have been nearly five times as heavy as the amount in the other? The answer, we think, is to be found in a letter which the postmasters-general wrote about this time. A small box for the Commissioners for the Sick and Wounded had come from Lisbon charged with postage of £26:2s. From this charge the Commissioners sought to be relieved on the ground that the box contained nothing but office accounts, which, besides being of no intrinsic value, were on Her Majesty's business. To such arguments, however, the postmasters-general turned a deaf ear. With the contents of the box they were not concerned. All they knew or cared to know was that it weighed eighty-seven ounces, and this weight, at the rate of 6s. an ounce, gave £26:2s. Forego the charge in the present instance, and how, they asked, could charges be any longer maintained on other packets not less on Her Majesty's business than this box, packets from the Prize Office, the Salt Office, the Customs and the Navy, and also, they added, on the large bundles of muster-rolls from the regiments stationed in the West Indies? In short, we entertain little doubt that the postage by the homeward mails was largely derived from official correspondence, correspondence which at the present time bears no postage at all.

The good fortune which had attended Dummer while acting as manager for the postmasters-general entirely deserted him as soon as the service came into his own hands. During the first twelve months the postage fell short of his expectations by about one-third; and freight and passengers, which he had estimated to produce £2000, produced little more than one-sixth of that amount. Nor was this the worst. The very first packet that sailed under his contract was taken by the enemy. Another, not many months later, was cast away on the rocks off the Island of Inagua; and a third fell into the hands of a privateer in the Channel. A series of disasters which would have daunted most men seems only to have inspired Dummer with fresh energy. Of the ultimate success of his undertaking he entertained no doubt. He held as strongly as we can hold at the present day, that trade and correspondence act and react upon each other; and that these should thrive he considered nothing more to be necessary than speed and regularity of communication. [23] With good heart, therefore, he applied himself to replace the boats which had been lost, fully determined that on his part no efforts should be wanting to supply the conditions on which alone he conceived success to depend.

The packet stations at this time were four in number. Dover was closed. Harwich and Falmouth were in full activity. Holyhead was a mere home station for the transmission of the Irish correspondence; and, the service being under contract, suffice it to say that the mails to Dublin went twice a week and were transported with marked regularity. Of the Harwich and Falmouth stations, managed as they were by the postmasters-general, we propose to give some account.

Each station was presided over by an agent, whose province it was to see that the packets were properly equipped and victualled, to arrange the order of sailing, to keep the captains to their duty, and generally to maintain order and regularity among the unruly spirits of which the establishment was composed. The outward mails, on their arrival from London, were to be despatched, if for Holland or for Portugal, immediately, and if for the West Indies, within two days; and, as soon as they were put on board, weights were to be attached to them so that they might be sunk at once if in danger of being taken by the enemy. So important was this precaution held to be that, although enjoined in the general instructions, it was continually insisted upon in particular cases. "Be sure," write the postmasters-general to one of their agents, "that before the captain sails, he prepares everything to sink the mail in case he shall be attacked by the enemy that he can't avoid being taken"; and to another, "We would have you take care to affix a sufficient weight to the mail so soon as 'tis on board"; and to a third, "We do not doubt but the mails will be ready slung with weights sufficient to sink them in case of danger of falling into the enemy's hands." Another rule to which the postmasters-general attached great importance was that more than two mails were not to go by the same boat. This rule, however, could not always be observed, for the boats had an awkward habit of finding themselves on the wrong side, and, by the time one had arrived, there was an accumulation of mails to be disposed of.

The inward mails, as soon as they reached the port of arrival, were forwarded to London by express. From Harwich the letters for the Court, or State letters,[24] as they were now beginning to be called, were sent in advance of the ordinary mail, arrangements having been made at the Brill to put these letters into a special bag by themselves. From Falmouth, where no provision had been made for distinguishing one class of correspondence from another, the same express carried the whole. When, as was sometimes the case, packets of documents reached the port unenclosed with the rest of the letters, these were to be chained to the "grand mail"; and on the label was always to be inserted the number of passengers that had arrived by the boat, so that the postmasters along the line of road might know for how many persons they had to provide horses. Between Falmouth and London the mails when sent express travelled at the rate of about five miles an hour; and this speed appears to have been regularly maintained. Expresses to carry a single letter or a message, or to overtake the Lisbon mail, were continually passing to and fro, and these of course went faster. From Harwich the mails would sometimes reach London in eleven hours, being at the rate of six and a half miles an hour; but on this line of road there was so much irregularity that the time ordinarily occupied in the journey cannot be stated with certainty.[25]

The seamen on board the packets were paid in no case more than 30s. a month and generally less; but the employment carried with it one great advantage. This was exemption from impressment. Even the carpenters hired to do odd jobs when the boats were in harbour were furnished with protection orders.[26] Partly on this ground, and partly, no doubt, on account of the gains to be derived from contraband traffic, admission to the packet service appears to have been eagerly sought. At one time, indeed, it threatened to become a matter of patronage; but the consequences of a first step in that direction effectually prevented another. The *Godolphin* packet had been taken and carried by the enemy into St. Malo. Her captain, a brave and experienced officer, did not hesitate to attribute the loss of his vessel to sheer cowardice on the part of the crew. One, at the first shot that was fired, had run down to the doctor and declared that he was wounded, whereas no sign of a wound was to be found upon him; another had taken shelter behind the mainmast; a third had been heard to declare that he would not hazard the loss of his little finger to save the packet. This conduct, as unprecedented as it was scandalous, led to a searching investigation, when it transpired that the so-called sailors were, many of them, no sailors at all, but mere landlubbers who had been taken on out of complaisance to the local gentry.

Each packet boat carried its own surgeon. A surgeon was also provided for the care of the sick on shore. This medical supervision was remunerated by means of a capitation allowance, an allowance of so much per head; but whereas it would now be in respect to all persons under the surgeon's charge, whether well or ill, it was then only in respect to those that were ill—1s. a day for each sick person and 6s. 8d. for each cure—a mode of payment which did not perhaps conduce to a speedy recovery. To provide for casualties, a fund was established, towards the support of which each seaman contributed 10d. a month out of his pay. If he were killed in action, provision was made for his widow, and, if he were wounded, he received a small annuity or, as it was called, Smart and Bounty money, the amount of which was nicely apportioned to the nature of his injury. Thus—

For each arm or leg amputated above the elbow or knee he would receive	£8	0	0	a year.
For each arm or leg amputated below the elbow or knee	6	13	4	"
For the loss of the sight of one eye	4	0	0	"
For the loss of the pupil of the eye	5	0	0	"
For the loss of the sight of both eyes	12	0	0	"
For the loss of the pupils of both eyes	14	0	0	"

It is a ghastly bill of fare; and yet the sailors laid great store by it. On one occasion, indeed, until assured that the transfer of a boat to Dummer's management would not affect their claim to these annuities, they absolutely refused to go to sea.

With few exceptions, no passenger was allowed on board a packet boat without a pass from the Secretary of State. The exceptions were shipwrecked seamen, recruits, and officers in charge of recruits. Shipwrecked seamen went free, free from any charge for passage-money or for maintenance. Recruits and officers in charge of recruits not being above the rank of lieutenant were charged for maintenance but not for passage-money. All others, though furnished with a passport, paid or were expected to pay for both.

Of these rules, however, there would seem to have been no public announcement, and this led to constant dispute and bickerings. An interesting event was expected in one of the many English families which at this time flocked to the Court of Portugal, and Dr. Crichton was despatched to Lisbon with a cow. Furnished with a pass by the Secretary of State he stoutly maintained his right to a free passage; and this right the postmaster-general as stoutly disputed. Nor, assuming the right to exist, could they conceal their surprise that under the circumstances it should have been claimed. To demur to a paltry charge of £4 indeed! Was it not notorious that for his mission to Portugal he was to receive £1000? Lord Charlemont with a number of attendants had crossed from Lisbon to Falmouth. The passage-money had been paid, and, pleased with his entertainment, he desired to gratify the captain. The captain's answer was to present a bill shewing what the entertainment had cost, and, on payment being refused, he detained some valuable silks which Lord Charlemont had consigned to his care. Lord Charlemont, on his arrival in London, at once proceeded to Lombard Street and complained of this treatment, when he learned for the first time that the passage-money, which he had supposed to cover everything, was simply the Queen's due, and that his entertainment had been provided at the captain's own cost.

Even the packet agents themselves appear to have been insufficiently instructed. On one occasion the Queen's domestic servants on their return from Lisbon, whither they had been despatched in attendance on the Archduke Charles, were allowed to pass free. On another, passage-money was omitted to be collected from some workmen who had been sent to Portugal by the Board of Ordnance. In both cases the act of their subordinate was repudiated by the postmasters-general. Proper as it might be that the Queen's domestic servants should have their passage provided—was this to be done at the expense of the Post Office? Forego payment in this instance, and where were they to stop? They must press their demand; and the demand was eventually satisfied. From the Board of Ordnance they did not even attempt to recover, aware probably of the futility of any such step; but the act of their agent in letting the workmen pass free evoked an earnest remonstrance. Does not the Board of Ordnance, they asked, charge us for the very powder we use; and yet, forsooth, you take upon yourself to give to their workmen a free passage. "Every office," they added—and the maxim might still, perhaps, be observed with advantage—"ought to keep its own accompt distinct."

But it was with officers of the army who were continually passing to and fro that the most frequent disputes arose. They apparently did not understand, and possibly the Post Office might have had some difficulty in explaining, why lieutenants in charge of recruits should be exempt from payment of fare and not officers of higher rank when employed on similar business; or why indeed officers engaged in fighting their country's battles should not have a free passage on board Her Majesty's packets. It had been the custom not to collect the fares until the end of the voyage; but it was found that, the voyage once accomplished, payment of the fares was not uncommonly refused. Accordingly it was determined that they should be collected beforehand, and that no officer not being a recruiting officer and producing a certificate to that effect should be received on board on trust. Recourse was thereupon had to every sort of artifice in order to evade payment. Officers above the rank of lieutenant would represent themselves as being of that rank, and they would even enrol their own servants as recruits to make it appear that they were engaged in recruiting business.

Through Harwich, now that Dover was closed, lay the only route to the Continent; and among the passengers frequenting this route were some to whom, for one reason or another, special attention was given. Baron Hompesch and Brigadier-General Cadogan are on their way to Holland. The packet is to be detained "till Thursday noon, at which time they think to reach Harwich." M. Rosenerantz, the Danish envoy, is returning to his own country. No passengers are to be admitted on board until he and his suite have been accommodated. A Queen's messenger is coming with "one Castello," who is in custody. This person is to be made over to the captain of the packet that sails next, and on arrival at the Brill is to be set on shore. Dirick Wolters is expected from Holland, if indeed he be not already arrived and secreted in Harwich. No pains are to be spared to discover and apprehend him, and to secure the sealed box he carries "directed to a person of note in London."

Goods, like passengers, were not allowed to be carried by the packets without the express permission of the Secretary of State; and this permission was seldom given except in the case of presents to royal personages and of articles for the use of persons of note residing abroad. Hence, such things as the following were being continually consigned to the care of the postmasters-general, with a request that they might be forwarded by the next boat:—

Fifteen couple of dogs for the King of the Romans.

Necessaries for Her Majesty the Queen-Dowager's service at Lisbon.

Three pounds of tea from Lady Arlington for the use of Her Majesty the Queen-Dowager of England.

Two cases of trimming for the King of Spain's liveries.

Two bales of stockings for the use of the Portuguese Ambassador.

Three suits of clothes for some nobleman's ladies at the Court of Portugal.

A box of medicines for the use of the Earl of Galway.

As the packets and everything on board of them were exempt from examination by the Customs authorities, there are no means of knowing how far a pass, where a pass had been obtained, was confined to its ostensible object. But it is impossible not to entertain suspicions on the subject. On one occasion the Portuguese envoy obtained permission to send by the packet six cases, which he certified to contain arms for the use of his Sovereign. The lightness of the packages when brought to the scale excited suspicion, and on examination they were found to contain not arms but dutiable goods. To a tradesman at Truro, in exception to rule, a pass had been granted which authorised him to send by the Lisbon packet ten tons of hats. Ten tons weight of hats, or what purported to be hats, had long been exported, and yet more and more hats were being regularly despatched by every packet.

But although without passes goods and passengers were prohibited on board the packets, it is certain that the prohibition was habitually infringed. The packet agents' instructions were to keep a record of the names and quality of all passengers, and to transmit a copy to London. Even if this were a complete and faithful record, the postmasters-general could not know that each passenger had produced his pass. The Secretaries of State, however, appear to have possessed some means of information unknown to the Post Office, and, in the matter of passengers, they were continually complaining of the regulations being broken. At one time it is Mr. Joseph Percival, a merchant of Lisbon, who comes over without a passport—which, from the tenor of Lord Sunderland's letter, the postmasters-general apprehend to be "an affair of moment." At another it is a Mr. Jackson who, also without a passport, crosses from Harwich to Holland. In this case Mr. Secretary Boyle affirms that the packet agent received a bribe of two guineas. To let passengers come by the Harwich packets without passports, he declares later on, has become a common practice.

In the matter of goods the evidence of irregularity is still stronger. Captain Culverden of the *Queen* packet boat brings into Falmouth thirty-six bags and seven baskets of salt, and there lands it clandestinely. Captain Rogers smuggles over twenty bags and one cask of the same material. Captain Urin from the West Indies makes Plymouth instead of Falmouth. Stress of weather is pleaded in excuse; but the postmasters-general feel sure that he might have made Falmouth, had he not "had private instructions otherwise." "We are uneasie," they say, "thus to find the West India boats for the most part driven to Plymouth, or to Liverpool or some port contrary to what is prescribed by our instructions."

But of all the captains there was none who in the audacity of his proceedings equalled Francis Clies. Clies had recently succeeded his father in the command of the *Expedition* packet boat. On his very first voyage home from Lisbon he was much behind time, having according to his own account been driven upon the coast of Ireland. On his second voyage he was later still. The time of his arrival at Falmouth had long passed, and serious apprehensions began to be entertained for his safety. At length a letter came from him dated at Kinsale, explaining that want of provisions had obliged him to put in there. "We have," wrote the postmasters-general, "very impatiently expected the arrival of the *Expedition*, which has been very long wanting, and are much concerned to find the second voyage even more tedious than the first; but are glad to find her at last safe arrived." "We would know," they added, "for how many days provisions had been put on board, and whether the *Expedition* sails not as well as formerly." Before a reply could be received to this pertinent inquiry, the Commissioners of Customs had lodged at the Post Office a formal complaint, in which Captain Clies was charged with bringing over from Ireland several bales of friezes and other woollen manufactures. The postmasters-general were deeply shocked. Not only was this a breach of the packet boat regulations, but to transport goods from what would now be one part of the United Kingdom to another was at that time prohibited by law under heavy penalties. If this charge be proved, they wrote to their packet agent at Falmouth, "we shall not be much to seek why the captain should be two succeeding voyages forced upon the coast of Ireland, when we have not had above one instance of that kind besides himself during this war." Narrow as was Clies's escape on this occasion, not four months elapsed before the postmasters-general were again condoling with him on another "very tedious voyage."

It may here be mentioned, as an instance of the inconsistency of human nature, that, although the packets were not provided with chaplains, there were two boats on board of which prayers were regularly said every morning and evening, and that of these two boats the *Expedition* was one.

Outwards as well as inwards the packet boats were, at the beginning of the eighteenth century, carrying goods in defiance of regulation and of law. Sir Paul Methuen, the author of the famous Commercial Treaty which bears his name, was at that time our ambassador to Portugal. His attention had been arrested by the large quantities of merchandise which the packet boats were continually bringing over from England, and in 1705 he made to the postmasters-general a formal representation on the subject. "In Lisbon," he stated, "there is a public market for English goods as often as the boats come in." Nor was the allegation denied by the persons implicated. They must, they said, live somehow. And this plea, generally the refuge of the idle and worthless, had in it in the present instance more force than might at first be supposed. The crews of the packets were paid only once in six months, and, as a check upon their conduct, six months' pay was always kept in arrear.

Thus, before receiving any pay at all they had to work twelve months, and even at the expiration of twelve months there was not always money at hand with which to pay them.

At Harwich, there can be no doubt, the same malpractices were going on as at Falmouth; but, owing to the almost unequalled facilities which the east coast affords for clandestine traffic, detection less speedily followed. In the movements of the packet boats there was much that was mysterious. Their frequent disappearance for long periods together when the wind was blowing from the quarter most favourable to their return, and their occasional punctuality when the wind was contrary and they were least expected, involved a contradiction which the postmasters-general found it hard to reconcile. "In our whole experience," they wrote to the packet agent on the 3rd of October 1704, "the passage of the mails was never so unconstant as it has been this last year." "You must be very sensible what reproach we have been brought under" in consequence. The ink was hardly dry on their pen before information reached them that on the 2nd of the month two packet boats had returned to Harwich, of which one had been gone since the 10th and the other since the 19th of September. Meanwhile the winds had been fair, and had carried out the men-of-war and transports from Spithead. "We have writ you so often," wrote the postmasters-general to the laggard captains, "upon these neglects of yours," and you have paid so little regard to our admonitions, that "you may expect to find when too late that we are not to be trifled with." The effect of this caution, if effect it had, was of short duration. "We are," they wrote only a few months later, "under a perpetual uneasiness and distrust," on account of the irregularity of the Harwich boats. "Our reputation has very much suffered in consequence, and we are looked upon at Court as remiss in our duty." Hitherto we have ever been ready to "take any appearance of reason or probability to excuse the commanders, but do now, having had these frequent provocations so often repeated, resolve to do justice to ourselves, and to have no other regard than the merit of the service." "Pray make inquiries," they say on another occasion, when no less than three boats are unaccountably behind time. It is of no use writing to Mr. Vanderpoel, "for he always favours the captains' pretences." Mr. Vanderpoel was packet agent at the Brill. He had stood high in William's favour, and was still drawing an allowance of £100 a year which, as an act of grace, that King had bestowed upon him in addition to his salary. "When we last waited on the Lord High Treasurer and Secretary of State," wrote the postmasters-general again on the 14th of June 1705, "we found them in their former opinion that there must be some secret more than ordinary that the boats should so frequently when least expected make their passage, and when the winds have in all appearance been most favourable, the mails then most delayed." A secret no doubt there was; but, profoundly dissatisfied as the postmasters-general were, no suspicion appears to have crossed their minds that the packet boats were engaged in other and more exciting pursuits than the transport of mails.

The captains of the packet boats were strictly forbidden to give chase. Their instructions were to fight, if fight they must, to avoid fighting wherever possible, and in no case to go in quest of adventure. In the case of the Falmouth boats, carrying as they did a considerable number of men and of guns, there can be little doubt that the prohibition was habitually infringed. Even Cotton and Frankland, with all their credulity, would seem to have entertained suspicions on the point; and yet when notice was given them that a fat prize had been captured, their instincts as Englishmen prevailed, and with a chuckle of satisfaction they would accept the result of their servants' prowess without too minutely inquiring into the circumstances under which that result had been achieved. "Well done," they would say in effect. "We heartily congratulate you. It has indeed been a tedious voyage; but of course you did not pursue. This, as you are aware, would be contrary to our instructions, which are to do nothing that might retard or endanger Her Majesty's mails. We shall make known your gallantry to the Lord High Treasurer, and move His Royal Highness the Prince to bestow on you some signal mark of favour." The Prince was at this time Lord High Admiral, and the captains of the packet boats having only sailing commissions, were not, like the captains in the Royal Navy and the commanders of letters of marque, entitled as of right to the prizes they took. These were the perquisites of the Lord High Admiral, and were by him resigned to the Queen.

When a prize was captured, it was seldom taken in tow. This would have retarded the progress of the mails. The practice was for the two captains, the victor and the vanquished, to agree upon the amount of ransom, and to give and receive bills for the amount, one or more hostages being taken as security for payment. The agreement was reduced to writing and made out in duplicate, so that each captain might have a copy, and it set forth where and to whom the money was to be paid. As a rule, the conditions appear to have been honourably observed. Some few exceptions, no doubt, there were. In 1708 the *James* packet was captured, and, after the amount of ransom had been inserted in the agreement, the French captain fraudulently altered the figures. A still worse case occurred on the English side. The *Prince* packet boat captured a vessel which was ransomed for 2500 pieces of eight.[27] This vessel, as it afterwards transpired, was plundered both before and after the ransom was agreed upon; and, more than this, the English captain refused or neglected to give her a protection order, the consequence being that, subsequently falling in with some merchant ships, she was taken and plundered again. But these were exceptions, and it is some satisfaction to know that the last-mentioned captain was soon driven out of the service.[28]

Pending payment of the ransom, the hostages were kept in prison. Ordinarily, their confinement was not of long duration; and if we cite an instance to the contrary, it is because it aptly illustrates the rough-and-ready sort of justice which was administered in those days. Clies, the captain of the *Expedition*, after many desperate engagements in which he had come off victorious, had been forced at last to strike his colours. Four French men-of-war had surrounded him, and having lost his masts, he had no choice but to yield. The ransom agreed upon was £550, and as security for payment of this amount the master of the *Expedition* and Clies's son, who was a midshipman on board the same vessel, were taken as hostages. This was in February, and they did not return to England until November. Meanwhile they had been imprisoned at Cadiz, where they endured the severest privations. Cold and damp and the want of the common necessaries of life, while affecting the health of both, had permanently disabled the master and brought him to the point of death. This appeared to the postmasters-general to be a case for compensation. And yet whence was compensation to come? They were not long in solving the question. It was a mere accident, they argued, that these particular hostages had been selected. The selection might have fallen upon any others of the ship's company. Yet these others had been receiving their pay and enjoying their liberty. Surely it was for them to compensate those at whose cost they had themselves escaped captivity and its attendant horrors. Accordingly the ship's company were mulcted in a whole month's pay, amounting to £118, of which sum the midshipman received £20 and the master £98; and the decision appears to have evoked neither murmur nor remonstrance.

In one respect the two packet stations were conducted on different principles. At Falmouth the agent was also victualler. At Harwich victuals and all other necessaries were provided by the Post Office. Neither plan was entirely free from objection. Where the agent was victualler, he naturally desired to make what he could out of his contract; and hence arose frequent complaints from the seamen as to both the quantity and quality of their food. Nor were such undertakings well adapted to those days of violent fluctuations of prices. The years 1709 and 1710 were years of scarcity, during which the cost of all provisions was nearly doubled. Fortunately, when the first of these years arrived, the packet agent's contract to victual for a daily allowance of 7d. a head had just expired, or the consequences to him or to the seamen must have been disastrous. But, from a public point of view, the chief drawback to the union of the offices of agent and victualler was that the victualling arrangements were apt to interfere with the movements of the boats. The *Prince* packet boat was due to start on a particular day, and to an inquiry whether she would not be ready, the answer which the postmasters-general received was, "No; our beer is not yet brewed."

At Harwich the inconvenience of a contrary system, a system under which the Post Office undertook its own victualling, was illustrated in a striking manner. There no bill for provisions represented what the provisions had really cost. To the actual cost was habitually added a further sum, which, under the name of percentages, went into the pockets of those by whom the order had been given. Of the extent to which these overcharges were carried we are not informed in the particular case of victuals; but other cases in which information is given will perhaps serve as a guide. Holland-duck for the use of the packet boats was brought over from Holland freight-free. Yet in Harwich the Post Office was charged for it 2s. 2d. a yard. In London a yard of the same material, freight included, cost 2s. In London the price of 1 cwt. of cordage was 30s.; in Harwich it was 40s. For piloting a packet boat from Harwich to the Downs the Post Office was charged £7. Inquiry at the Admiralty elicited that for ships of the same size belonging to the Royal Navy the charge never exceeded £3:15s. The plain truth seems to be that both at Harwich and at Falmouth the packet agents were in the power of the captains, and the captains in the power of the packet agents, and that they all combined to impose upon the postmasters-general.

Of the number of letters which the Harwich and Falmouth packets carried we know little or nothing. In the one case we have absolutely no information. In the other there remains on record a single letter-bill applicable to a particular voyage. Of this letter-bill we will only observe that, for reasons immaterial to the present purpose, it became the subject of a good deal of correspondence, and it is not unreasonable to suppose that, had the number of letters entered in it been much above or much below the average, the point could hardly have escaped remark. The document is as follows:—

28 April 1705.

Received on board the *Prince* Packet Boat the following Packets and letters.

Zech: Rogers ... Commander.

From my Lord Ambassador ... a Bag of Letters directed to Mr. Jones.[29]

Sixteen Packetts and letters for Her Majestie's Service.

From the King of Spain ... a very large Packett.
For London and Holland ... Double and Single letters ...
Two hundred and ninety six.

Thirteen Packetts Do.

Devonshire letters ... Double and Single ... Twenty nine ...
and three Packetts.
For Falmouth ... Double and Single letters ... six.
Two mails for London.

Outward-bound.

No Passengers.

Homeward-bound.

One English Merchant.

Three Dutch Gentlemen.

Four poor sailors discharged from Her Majestie's Ship *Antelope*
being incapable for the Service.

There were persons who thought that the packet boats might well
be employed to do something more than carry to and fro a mere handful
of letters. Among those who held this opinion was Colonel Stanwix. He
contended that the Lisbon packets should be required to carry not only the
mails, but recruits for the English forces in Portugal. By transport the fixed
charge for each recruit was £4. This expense would be saved to the public,
and the regiments would receive additions to their strength not fitfully, but
at regular intervals. Subject to certain conditions, the postmasters-general
resolved to give the plan a trial. The conditions were that not more than
fifty recruits should go in one boat, and that, instead of passing free, as
Colonel Stanwix had proposed, they should be charged £1 apiece—that
is, 10s. for victualling, and 10s. for freight. The experiment was attended
with deplorable results. It was midwinter. The recruits had been huddled
together in Pendennis Castle, under a strong guard, to prevent desertion.
Half-naked and only half-fed they were led or driven to the boat, and hardly
were they on board before the distemper broke out among them. Many fell
victims to it; many others, on arrival at Lisbon, were carried to the hospital,
and even the strongest among them were barely able to stagger ashore. The
return voyage was hardly less disastrous. The crew now took the disease,
and as they lay dying and dead upon the deck, a vessel of French build was
to be seen bearing down upon them. Resistance in the circumstances was

out of the question, and nothing remained but to save the guns. These, ten in number, were with difficulty thrown overboard, and no sooner was the task accomplished than the vessel, which had by this time come within speaking distance, proved to be Her Majesty's ship *Assurance*.

The liberty allowed to the Royal Navy to employ for its own purposes prizes taken at sea did not extend to the packet service. The Post Office was forbidden, under severe penalties, to use foreign bottoms. Often had convenience and economy to yield to the stern dictates of the law. Now it is a French shallop, admirably adapted for a packet boat, which has to be discarded simply because it is French; and now an express to Lisbon is on the point of being delayed because the regular packets are on the wrong side, and the only boat to be hired in Falmouth is not English built.

On the 20th of September 1707 the Queen, attended by her Court, set out for Newmarket. In this visit there was nothing unusual, but it will serve as well as any other to demonstrate that the close connection which had once subsisted between the posts and the Crown was not yet completely severed. In attendance upon his royal mistress was Court-post. This office, to which appointment was made by patent, had until lately been held by Sir Thomas Dereham. Court-post's duty was to carry letters between the Court and the nearest stage or post-town, a duty deemed so arduous that his stipend had been recently doubled, and now stood at £365 a year. At Newmarket and at Windsor, indeed, he had no long distance to traverse, these towns being post-towns; but when the Court was in London or at Hampton his journey was longer. In London he had to carry the letters between Kensington or Whitehall and Lombard Street; and when at Hampton, Hampton not being a post-town, he had to carry them to and from Kingston.

Besides Court-post there was now in the royal train the comptroller of the London sorting office, William Frankland, son of one of the postmasters-general. What Frankland's precise functions were we are not informed, but he was, in the language of the time, "in attendance on Her Majesty in the care of her letters." At Harwich, as soon as the mail arrived from Holland, the seals of the bags were to be broken, and the letters for the Court to be picked out and sent to Newmarket by express. This was, in effect, to establish a cross-post at a time when cross-posts did not exist. Moments, which would now be judged precious, appear to have been then of little account. Of the letters before they left Harwich the addresses were to be copied; and on arrival at Newmarket the express was to take them, not to the Palace, but to the Post Office, whither they were to be addressed under cover to Frankland. The Post Office once reached, how Frankland and Court-post were to adjust their respective duties is a point as obscure as it is, perhaps, unimportant. At the present day, when the palace possesses no postal facilities which are not enjoyed by the cottage, a single provision in the Statute-book is all that is left to remind us that at one time the posts were centred in the Sovereign. This provision, in exception to the practice which jealously excludes the Sovereign's name from all parts of an Act of Parliament except, indeed, the preamble, prescribes that the posts shall be settled, not as the Secretary of State or the Lords Commissioners of the Treasury may direct, but according to the directions of Her Majesty. To Her Majesty alone the law still leaves the supreme control over the posts, although it may well be believed that the ministers would claim to act on her behalf.[30]

After the battle of Ramillies, which put the Confederates in possession of Ostend, the packet service between England and Flanders, which had been suspended four years before, was re-established. The result disappointed expectations. The Government appear to have thought that it was only necessary to revive the service and the correspondence would at once resume its old proportions. But meanwhile the letters from Flanders to England had found a new channel. No sooner had Ostend been closed than they were diverted through Holland. To reverse this arrangement, involving as it would a readjustment of the internal posts, must, in any case, have been a work of time; and it was a work on which the Flemish authorities were little likely to embark so long as the neighbourhood of Ostend or any considerable portion of it remained in the enemy's hands. Of all this the postmasters-general were perfectly well aware, and they can have felt no disappointment that, on the first reopening of the Ostend route, the letters passing that way were extremely few; but the ministers, who had not the postmaster-generals' experience to guide them, grew impatient with a service which was maintained at heavy cost, and produced little or no return. Accordingly, having restored the service in June, they discontinued it in August; and no sooner were the boats dispersed than orders were given to restore it again.

This sudden change of purpose, we think there can be little doubt, was due to the influence of the Duke of Marlborough, who began about this time to take a lively interest in the postal communication with Flanders. Though not surprised at the meagreness of the correspondence, the postmasters-general were little prepared to find that, after the Confederates became masters of Ostend, the passage between that port and Dover would be even less safe than it had been before. Yet such was the case. The Flemish seamen, no longer able to obtain employment at home, flocked across the French border and joined with their foes of yesterday in preying upon the English shipping. As a consequence the Channel now swarmed with privateers. On the 25th of January a Dover packet, named *Ostend* after the port to which she ran, was taken by a Nieuport privateer of ten guns and eighty men.

The captain who brought this intelligence had himself had a narrow escape. Five privateers had extended themselves from Nieuport to Ostend in order to intercept him, and, after a sharp engagement, in which he was nearly captured, had forced him to make Harwich.

In this conjuncture the postmasters-general acted with remarkable energy, but with little regard to what would now be considered official propriety. Not content with making representations to the Secretary of State, they wrote direct to the English ambassador at the Hague, desiring him to urge upon the States of Flanders and Brabant the necessity of at once fitting out three or four ships of the Ostend squadron, with the twofold object of recalling the seamen to their duty and of clearing the coast. They at the same time waited upon M. Van Vrybergh, the envoy extraordinary from the States-General to the Court of St. James', and exacted from him a promise that he would exercise his influence in the same direction. But relief was soon to come, and from an unexpected quarter. Lewis the Fourteenth, by way of creating a diversion in the Netherlands, resolved to assist the Pretender in making a descent upon Scotland, and with this view he assembled a squadron before Dunkirk. England had no choice but to follow suit. Within an incredibly short space of time she equipped a fleet, and this fleet, under the command of Sir George Byng, left Deal for Dunkirk in the spring of 1708. How the Pretender evaded Byng, and how Byng pursued the Pretender and frustrated his object, are matters of history; but what concerns us at the present moment is that, before starting in pursuit, Byng detached a squadron for the purpose of bringing over some of the English troops which were about to be embarked at Ostend. It is probable that this squadron, after its immediate object had been accomplished, remained in or about the Channel, for after this time we hear no more of depredations on the Post Office packets.

Experience shews that there is a class, and not an inconsiderable class, of persons who, in time of war, find it hard to reconcile themselves to the pursuits of peace. John Macky, the packet agent at Dover, was one of these. The proximity of the battle-field, its easy access from Dover, and the stirring accounts arriving by every packet fired his imagination and filled him with martial ardour. Under the influence of this excitement he addressed a memorial to the postmasters-general, praying that he might be commissioned to go over to Flanders and settle posts for the army. This application he appears to have supported by the most unfortunate arguments. He urged not that it was a thing in itself reasonable and proper that the army should have posts of its own, and that his experience might be useful in establishing them, but that at Dover, though his salary was comparatively high, he had little or nothing to do, and that the commission for which he asked would give him employment more congenial to his tastes. The postmasters-general could not conceal their astonishment at the audacity of the proposal and the grounds on which it was based. "We were never before made sensible," they wrote, "that the business of the agent to the packet boats at Dover was so very inconsiderable as you have represented it to be, nor do we think that for so inconsiderable a business so high a salary can be needed." "We can only say," they added, "that if the present allowance be too much for the work, or if the employ be too mean for your expectations, we doubt not but that we shall be able to find those who will thankfully accept the post with an allowance that is much less."

But Macky's restlessness was not to be subdued by a mere admonition. As he could not prevail on the postmasters-general to send him to Flanders on official business, he asked to be allowed to go on his own account. This permission they readily gave, accompanying it, however, with a remarkable caution. "We must expect," they said, "that you do not intermeddle in any ways upon the business of the Flanders correspondence, or enter into any sort of treaty for the port of letters or jobbing of places which may bring us under any inconveniencys or our authority under any disreputation. We expect you take particular caution of these matters and wish you a good journey."

Within four months from the date of this caution Macky's relations to the Post Office had greatly altered. To the position of packet agent he now added that of contractor, having undertaken himself to provide for the Dover and Ostend service. For the sum of £2000 a year he was to supply four boats between twenty and thirty tons each, and to be at all risks from sea and enemy. One effect of this arrangement, by which Macky the contractor was to be controlled by Macky the packet agent, was to prolong his visit to Flanders. Under the pretext of keeping the captains to their duty he remained there until March or April 1708, when he returned to England, after an absence of eight or nine months. Meanwhile the packets to Ostend, like those to Holland and to Portugal, had been engaged in illicit practices. According to a complaint received from the Commissioners of Customs immediately before Macky's return, clandestine traffic was being systematically carried on, and the very last boat that had arrived had brought parcels of lace concealed in the flap of the mail. The postmasters-general were deeply annoyed. "Let this go on," they exclaimed, "and the mails themselves will be searched, to the great scandal of the office and of our management."

We have been thus particular in recording Macky's movements, because in connection with the service under his control an incident now occurred which brought the Post Office into serious discredit. The postmasters-general, in virtue of their office, which gave them control over the communications of the country, were in the habit of receiving priority of intelligence; and this at a time when intelligence travelled slowly and the means of disseminating it did not exist or existed only in the rudest form. Hence they acquired an importance which the mere office of postmaster-general, as that office is now understood, would not have conferred. An interest attached to them as to men who were reputed to possess exclusive information. They were welcome at Court, and not only welcome but often anxiously expected. Indeed, to act as purveyor of news to the Court had come to be regarded as one and by no means the least important of their duties; and with a view to its more effectual discharge their agents throughout the country had standing orders to send to headquarters the earliest intimation of any remarkable event that might happen in their locality. When any one of these persons was venturesome enough to send to his chiefs a present, the thanks he received were of the coldest,—"We thank you for the snuff," or, "We thank you for the port wine," and then was pretty sure to follow a sharp rebuke for some trifling irregularity, which, except for the present, would probably have passed unnoticed. But when a piece of news was sent, the thanks were warm and hearty; and woe betide the unfortunate agent who had news to send and omitted to send it. "We observe you give us no advice of the fleet under Sir George Byng being seen off Falmouth the 28th, tho' we saw letters from Falmouth which advised thereof. We are desirous to have the first advice of any remarkable news." "We received two Flanders mails on Sunday morning, and therewith your letter of the 5th advising of the Duke of Marlborough's being arrived at Flushing, for which account we thank you." "We do heartily congratulate your safe return, and do thank you for being so full and particular in the advices you have given us of what occurrences have come to your knowledge." "We are obliged to you for the news of the Nassau and Burford's prizes of which we had received advice before by some galleys from Gibraltar, and for your kind promise of communicating to us any considerable occurrences that may happen in your parts." "We thank you for sending us an account of all news and remarkable occurrences in your letters which we desire may be sent in the mails or annext to the labels." "We cannot but take very ill the captain's conduct on this occasion, for Mr. Bowen's intentions in sending his son over to bring so great a piece of news as that of the victory[31] to us ought to be esteemed as a great piece of civility, and, if the captain had not refused to sail when Mr. Bowen pressed him, we might have had the satisfaction of carrying the first account of that victory."

It was in the early summer of 1709, when this greed after news was at its height, that intelligence of vast import to the country was expected to arrive in London. Preliminaries of peace, after being arranged in Flanders, had been forwarded to Paris for confirmation. Would the King sign them? Or must the war which had already lasted more than six years be continued? A period of anxious suspense followed. The exhaustion of France, and the humiliating terms which were sought to be imposed upon her, made it certain that there would be neither ready acceptance nor ready rejection; and yet the latest date had passed on which a decision was expected and none had arrived. London was in a fever of expectation. Each mail from Ostend, as it reached the Post Office in Lombard Street, was eagerly seized and opened. The month of May was drawing to a close. On Saturday the 28th there was not only no news but no mail. Sunday came and, to the consternation of the postmasters-general, there was still no mail. The wind was in the right quarter. At Harwich the packets from Holland were arriving regularly. What could hinder the passage from Ostend? At length on Monday the 30th a mail arrived, and with it the news. The King had refused to sign the preliminaries of peace. Frankland and Evelyn[32] hurried off to the Lord Treasurer. Little were they prepared for the reception that awaited them. Godolphin's words have unfortunately not been preserved, but we know the substance of them. The news, he said, had reached the city the day before, having been conveyed there clandestinely. The packet agent or sub-agent at Ostend had sent it. Of this he held in his hand conclusive evidence. What means had been employed, and whether others were concerned in the nefarious transaction, it was for his hearers to ascertain; and the sooner they addressed themselves to the task the better. In short, the power of the purse had again prevailed, and the Post Office had been outwitted by the Stock Exchange.

It is difficult to suppose that the intelligence can have been conveyed from Ostend to London without Macky's connivance. And yet Frankland and Evelyn believed or affected to believe that he had had no hand in the business. Their position was, no doubt, one of embarrassment. Organised as the Post Office then was, they possessed no means of making an independent investigation. They contented themselves, therefore, with calling upon Macky to ascertain and report how it was that a letter from Ostend had reached London on Sunday, although on that day there had been no mail. The result might easily have been foreseen. Brown, the sub-agent at Ostend, whose letter it was, stood self-condemned, and Macky was required to dismiss him. And here the scandal ended. Macky's own character, with himself as reporter, may be presumed to have been cleared. At all events he appears to have been taken back into confidence, and, before many weeks were over, the postmasters-general had despatched him on an important mission.

This mission was no other than to lay down posts for the army in Flanders. The tardiness with which intelligence arrived from the seat of war had long been matter of complaint. In the city especially the dissatisfaction had been intense, and the recent scandal had not been calculated to allay it. With a view to remedy this state of things, Godolphin called upon the postmasters-general to devise some means for securing more rapid communication. The army was now in the neighbourhood of Lisle, and operations were about to begin anew. There was, therefore, no time to be lost. The postmasters-general had recourse to Macky, and in a few days he produced a plan with which Godolphin expressed himself highly pleased. Between Lisle and Ostend, and between Ostend and other places where the army might be, stages were to be settled; at each stage were to be relays of horses with postilions ready to start at any moment; responsible persons were to be appointed to collect and deliver the letters and to receive the postage; and the postage was to be regulated by distance and to be at the same rates as in England, and to go to the English Post Office.

Macky, to his extreme gratification, was commissioned to carry out his own plan. He was to repair at once to Flanders, to report himself to the Duke of Marlborough, and, having obtained his sanction, to proceed with the arrangement of details. Above all, he was to keep a close watch upon the sailing of the packets from Ostend, and to insist upon a rigid punctuality. From this time no more complaints were heard of the tardy arrival of intelligence from the seat of war. As postilions were employed on one side of the water, so expresses were employed on the other; and these, with punctual sailings between port and port, constituted a service which for those days might be considered excellent.

At first, indeed, the employment of expresses from Dover to London appears to have been a little overdone, and the postmasters-general, eager as they were to obtain early intelligence, found it necessary to regulate the practice. An express had arrived bringing a letter from Macky in Flanders. "Altho' we should be very well satisfied," they wrote to his deputy at Dover, "to receive an extraordinary piece of good news by a messenger hired for greater dispatch' sake, yet on ordinary occasions it might be more warrantable and make less noise and expectation to have the same sent by a flying pacquet under cover to us annext to the labell." This was written in August 1709, within six weeks of Macky's arrival in Flanders; and we know of no passage in the whole of the Post Office records which more forcibly brings home to us the difference between the London of to-day and the London of 180 years ago. Crowds no longer congregate at the doors of the Post Office eagerly waiting for news; nor is the neighbourhood of St. Martin's-le-Grand transported with excitement at the approach of a man on horseback.

On the cessation of hostilities at sea, which took place in the summer of 1712, although the Treaty of Utrecht was not signed until the following year, the postmasters-general proceeded to put the packets on a peace footing. The boats from Harwich to the Brill and from Dover to Ostend were reduced in number. The routes between Dover and Calais and between Dover and Dunkirk were reopened. The service between Falmouth and Lisbon, which during the war had been once a week, was now to be only once a fortnight; and the five boats engaged on this service, as carrying more hands than would any longer be necessary, were to be disposed of by public sale and their place to be taken by three of the largest from Harwich. The result of these several changes was to reduce the establishment, in point of numbers, by rather more than 120 men, and, in point of cost, from £21,960 to £15,632. As affecting the cost, hardly less important than the reduction of numbers was the permission now given to the packet boats to resume the carriage of merchandise. This was a source of profit to which the postmasters-general had long been looking as some set-off against the heavy expense.

Meanwhile Dummer's contract for the West India service had come to an abrupt termination. That contract had not been long in force before he began to realise how onerous was the condition that, out of a total sum of £12,500, he should receive only £4500 in money, and depend, for the difference on fares, freight, and postage. The postage, which from the first had fallen short of his expectations, did not increase; and the fact of his having, within a few months from the commencement of his undertaking, lost three of his boats, procured for him — what in the world of commerce is almost incompatible with success — the reputation of an unlucky man. The West India merchants enjoined their correspondents on no account to send goods by Dummer's boats. Thus the profits which he had expected to derive from freight had no more existence in fact than the profits from postage. Hoping against hope, Dummer struggled on; but ill-luck continued to pursue him. In little more than five years he lost no less than nine boats. In order to replace them he mortgaged his property to the full extent of its value and obtained advances on his quarterly allowance. This, of course, could not go on, and at length the crash came. The day had arrived for the West India mail to be despatched, and there was no boat to carry it. The whole of Dummer's property, boats included, had been seized for debt. The rest is soon told. The mortgagees, believing that they had the postmasters-general in a corner, refused to continue the service except at a preposterous charge, which Frankland and Evelyn declined to pay. Fortunately three private ships with consignments for the West Indies were then loading at Teignmouth and other ports in the south-west of England, and these relieved the Post Office from what might otherwise have been a serious dilemma.

Bankrupt and broken-hearted, Edmund Dummer died in April 1713, within eighteen months of the termination of his contract. It is his honourable distinction that he succeeded in all that he undertook for others, and that it was only in what he undertook for himself that he failed.

CHAPTER VIII
AMERICAN POSTS 1692-1707

American progress has long been the wonder of the world, and in nothing perhaps has it displayed itself more remarkably than in the matter of the posts. The figures which the United States Post Office presents to us year after year—figures as compared with which even those of the Post Office of Great Britain fall into insignificance—make it difficult to believe that only two hundred years ago an enterprising Englishman was struggling to erect a post between New York and Boston.

An Order in Council dated the 22nd of July 1688, after prescribing the rates of postage to be charged not only between England and the island of Jamaica, but within the island itself, ended with these words: "And His Majesty is also pleased to order that letter offices be settled in such other of His Majesty's plantations in America as shall by the said Earle of Rochester be found convenient for His Majesty's service, and the ease and benefit of his subjects, according to the method and rates herein settled for His Majesty's island of Jamaica."

Nearly four years later, namely, in February 1692, Thomas Neale obtained a grant from the Crown authorising him to set up posts in North America. The grant was secured by letters patent, which were to hold good for twenty-one years. Neale, who appears never to have set foot out of England, appointed as his representative in America Andrew Hamilton; or rather, as the patent required, Neale nominated and the postmasters-general appointed him. The patent also required that at the expiration of three years Neale should render an account showing his receipts and expenditure; but it was not until the year 1698 that this condition was fulfilled, and in the same year Hamilton came to England to report progress.

By this time a post, to run once a week, had been established along seven hundred miles of road, from Boston to New York, and from New York to Newcastle in Pennsylvania. What the postage rates were we do not know, except indeed that the charge on a letter between New York and Boston was 1s. On other points the account which Hamilton furnished on Neale's behalf gives full information. A salary of £20 a year is paid to

"Mr. Sharpus that keeps the letter office at New York." Mr. Sharpus also receives two allowances, one of £110 a year "for carrying the mail half-way to Boston," and another of £60 "for carrying the mail from New York to Philadelphia." Of the former allowance, Hamilton states that after the 4th of November 1696 he "retrenched" it from £110 to £90. There is also a salary of £10 "allowed to him that keeps the letter office at Philadelphia"; and "an allowance of £100 sterling per annum given by Mr. Neale himself to Peter Hayman, deputy-postmaster of Virginia and Maryland." Hamilton's own salary was £200, and his travelling expenses are thus stated in his account:—

To my expense of a journey from New York to Road Island, Boston, and eastward of it and back again, when I settled the Post Office there	£50	0	0
To my expense of a journey from New York to Maryland and Virginia and back again to settle the office there	50	0	0
To several other journeys and incident charges relating to the Post Office	16	18	0

In America as in England, from the first erection of the posts, the correspondence went on steadily increasing year after year. Thus, in the first year beginning the 1st of May 1693 the "New York Post" produced £61; in the second, £82; in the third, £93; and in the fourth year, ending the 1st of May 1697, it produced £122. The same progress is to be seen in what were called the "Boston, Road Island, Connecticut and Piscataway Posts." In the first two years beginning also in May 1693 these produced £296 or at the rate of £148 a year; in the third year they produced £227; and in the fourth, £298. The returns of the Philadelphia post also kept improving; but here Hamilton encountered difficulties of management, as will be seen by his own entries:—

By the produce of the Philadelphia post from the 22nd of August 1693 to the 23rd of April 1694, at which time I was forced to change the Postmaster	£10	9	6
By the produce of the same post from the 23rd of April 1694 to the 13th of February 1697, at which time I was forced to change the Postmaster again	105	3	7

The Virginia and Maryland posts were the single exception. Of these Hamilton records "The Virginia and Maryland posts never yielded anything, but cost Mr. Neale near £600." However much these posts might be improved, he dared not reckon upon the correspondence exceeding one hundred letters a year.

There is only one more entry which we will quote from Hamilton's account. It is this:—

By cash which the Postmaster of New York gathered

up upon the road in Connecticut for letters   £6   16   0

Promising as the prospect was on the whole, Neale's receipts from the posts fell far short of his expenses in erecting and maintaining them. His expenses up to May 1697 were £3817, and his receipts £1457, leaving him not only out of pocket to the amount of £2360, but with his means and his credit exhausted. It was admitted on all hands that the posts must before long become self-supporting, even if they should not prove remunerative. But meanwhile how were they to be carried on? Hamilton had his own plan to propose. This was first that within America the postage rates should be raised, and "that the post and his horse should go fferry-free"; and second, that between England and America rates should be settled, and that shipmasters should be required on the other as on this side of the Atlantic to take their letters at once to the Post Office of the port at which they first touched, and hand them to the postmaster, receiving as remuneration one penny a letter.

For inland letters the increased rates which Hamilton proposed were as follows, all but the first two entries being in his own words:—

	Pence.
Where the distance from New York does not exceed 80 miles	6
Where it exceeds 80, and does not exceed 150 miles	9
To and from Boston and New York, 300 miles	12
To and from Boston and Jersey, 370 miles	18
To and from Boston and Philadelphia, 390 miles	20
To and from Boston and Annapolis in Maryland, 550 miles	36
To and from Boston and James Towne in Virginia, 680 miles	42
To and from New York and Annapolis, 250 miles	24
To and from New York and James Towne, 380 miles, and many broad and dangerous bays and rivers to be ferryed over	30

It may surprise our readers to learn that between England and America there actually existed, 200 years ago, what now is little more than the dream of the postal reformer,—an ocean penny postage. Yet such is the fact. In 1698 it was the custom of the masters of ships bound for America to hang up bags in coffee-houses, and any letters that might be dropped into these bags they carried, and were glad to carry, over for one penny or twopence a letter, according as it was a single or a double one. This custom, as Hamilton pointed out, was liable to abuse. In the first place, any one who had put a letter into a coffee-house bag might, under pretence of wanting his own letter back, possess himself of the letter of somebody else. And secondly, on arrival in America, the shipmasters being under no obligation to make a prompt delivery, were apt to deliver the letters, not when they reached a port, but when they were on the point of leaving it, and after they had disposed of their lading. All this would be remedied if rates of postage were settled between England and America. The letters would then be in the custody of the Post Office until delivered to the shipmaster, and the shipmaster would be bound to restore them to the same custody as soon as he arrived at his destination.

But Hamilton's main argument in favour of establishing sea-rates of postage was the impossibility of things remaining as they were. Neale was without resources, and the posts were not self-supporting. Unless, therefore, some means should be devised for increasing the receipts, the posts must be given up. Let sea-rates be imposed, and the receipts would be increased at once, for all letters from Europe, which on arrival in America were now being delivered by private hand, would then fall into the post, and be forced to pay American postage. It was true that between the mother country and her colonies a packet service did not exist, and that to impose a charge where no service was rendered in return would be contrary to Post Office usage; but the object to be gained was too important to allow this consideration to prevail. Such were the arguments by which Hamilton supported his proposal that on letters between England and America postage should be charged—of 6d. for a single letter, 1s. for a double letter, and 1s. 6d. for "a packet."

There were one or two points on which Cotton and Frankland did not agree with Hamilton. Experience had taught them, as they stated on another occasion, that the way to improve the Post Office revenue was to "make the intercourse of letters easy to people." So now, in their representation to the Treasury, they condemned the inland rates which Hamilton proposed as altogether too high. They had been long enough at the Post Office, they said, to know that "the easy and cheap corresponding doth encourage people to write letters, and that this revenue was but little in proportion to what it is now till the postage of letters was reduced from 6d.[33] to 3d."

Hamilton had contemplated the passing of a fresh Act of Parliament in order to impose sea-rates and to oblige shipmasters to give up their letters as soon as they reached port. Cotton and Frankland were not satisfied that a fresh Act of Parliament was necessary; nor did they express any opinion as to the particular rates which should be imposed. They recommended, however, the appointment of an officer whose duty it should be "to take care of" all letters for America, and to put them into a special bag to be sealed with the office seal. Public notice should at the same time be given prohibiting the collection of such letters by other persons. To the shipmaster to whom the bag might be delivered the inducement to take it without delay to the Post Office of the port at which he should first arrive would be that he would there receive one penny for each letter the bag might contain. Hitherto, under the coffee-house arrangement, the penny had been paid in England; for the future, it would be paid in America. In other words, the shipmaster, instead of receiving his recompense in advance, would receive it after his work was done and only provided it was done properly.

On one point the postmasters-general held a decided opinion. Towards the support of the posts the Government of New York had made an annual contribution of £50, in consideration of which the Government letters appear to have been carried free; but otherwise Neale's undertaking had not received from the authorities that countenance and support which, in Cotton and Frankland's opinion, were essential to its success. They expressed themselves convinced that, for want of due encouragement, the posts would never prosper in private hands, and recommended that they should be transferred to the Crown.

Whether any, and if so, what action was taken upon the postmaster-general's representation we do not know. There is some reason to think that between England and America sea-rates of postage were settled, as had been done a few years before in the case of Jamaica; but we possess no certain information on the point. All we know is that, upon Neale being informed of the postmaster-general's opinion that the inland posts should be transferred to the Crown, he immediately offered to surrender his patent, and that the offer was not accepted. The payment he demanded was either a capital sum of £5000 or else £1000 a year for life or for the unexpired term of his grant.

Hamilton returned to America. The next we hear of him is in 1700. Neale was then dead, having shortly before his death assigned his interest in the posts as security for his debts. To Hamilton he owed £1100, and to an Englishman of the name of West he owed for money advanced £200; and into the hands of these two persons, in default of any one willing to act as Neale's executor or administrator, the posts now came. In April 1703 Hamilton also died; and for three or four years his widow carried on the posts at her own charge.

In 1706 Mrs. Hamilton and West urged that their patent, which had seven and a half years yet to run, might be enlarged for a further term of twenty-one years, and that they might have permission to set up packet boats between England and America. To this Cotton and Frankland were opposed, being still of opinion that the posts should not remain in private hands; and they recommended, as a more politic measure, that the patent should be purchased for £1664, a sum which the patentees had expressed themselves willing to accept. Whether this was the sum actually given we know not; but in the following year the patent was surrendered and the posts of America became vested in the Crown.

In connection with the transfer John Hamilton, Andrew's son, was appointed to his father's place of deputy postmaster-general, and this appointment he retained until 1722, when he resigned. It was then and not until then that the posts became self-supporting. "We have now," write the postmasters-general on the 10th of August in that year, "put the Post Office in North America and the West Indies upon such a foot that for the future, if it produce no profit to the revenue, it will no longer be a charge to it, but we have good reason to hope there will be some return rather from thence."

Such, hardly 200 years ago, were the humble beginnings of a Post Office with which, in the magnitude and diversity of its operations, no other in the world can now compare.

CHAPTER IX
THE POST OFFICE ACT OF 1711

In 1707, on the passing of the Act of Union between England and Scotland, the first step taken by the postmasters-general was to alter the colours of the packets. The cross of St. Andrew, with its blue ground, united with the red cross of St. George, now became the national ensign; and the packets no less than the ships of the Royal Navy were under obligation to carry it.

The Post Office in Scotland was at this time held in farm at a rent of £1194 a year. The lease expired on the 11th of November, and from that date the postmasters-general held themselves responsible for the Scotch no less than the English posts. They at once proceeded to frame an establishment. George Main, the farmer, was appointed deputy-postmaster of Edinburgh at a salary of £200, this being the amount which one year with another he had made out of his contract. Three persons were appointed to assist him, an accomptant and two clerks. These, with three letter-carriers at a crown a week each, and a postmaster at the foot of the Canongate, constituted the Edinburgh establishment.

In the country there were thirty-four postmasters, of whom only twelve were paid by salary, the remaining twenty-two receiving as their remuneration a certain proportion of the postage on inland letters. Thus, three had one-half of this postage, one had one-third, and eighteen had one-fourth. The highest salaries were given to the postmasters of Haddington and Cockburnspath, who received £50 apiece, the reason being no doubt that these two towns were on the direct line of road between Edinburgh and London. At Aberdeen, the postmaster's salary was £28; at Glasgow, £25; at Dundee, Montrose, and Inverness, £15; and at Dumfries and Ayr, £12. Runners[34] at a fixed charge were maintained between town and town— as, for instance, between Edinburgh and Aberdeen at £60 a year, between Aberdeen and Inverness at £30 a year, and between Inverness and Thurso at £18 a year: but except at Edinburgh there was no letter-carrier, and except between Edinburgh and Berwick there was no horse-post north of the Tweed. The establishment charges for the whole of Scotland, Edinburgh included, were less than £1000 a year.

But something more was necessary than to frame an establishment and to alter the colours of the packets. Serious doubts had arisen whether, as the law stood, the postmasters-general of England were competent to deal with the posts of Scotland; and, this vital consideration apart, between the two divisions of the kingdom certain inequalities existed which only fresh legislation could redress. Under the Scotch Act of 1695 the postage on a single letter between Edinburgh and Berwick was 2d. Under the English Act of 1660, 2d. would carry a single letter from Berwick northwards for only forty miles, and considerably more than forty miles separated Berwick from Edinburgh. This difference arose no doubt from mere inaccuracy of reckoning on the English side; and yet it was one which nothing less than a new Act, an Act by the united Parliament, would adjust.

It is the more singular that at this time the postmasters-general should not have taken steps to promote legislation, because, in connection with the English no less than the Scotch Post Office, there were several matters on which fresh legislation had become necessary. The statute on which the very existence of the Post Office itself depended had been found difficult to deal with, on account of its loose and ambiguous wording. The postage to America and the West Indies rested on no legal sanction. For the pence paid upon ship-letters the postmasters-general had no authority to produce, and the auditors had threatened to disallow, the payment. Even the penny post was of doubtful legality. The Courts had indeed decided that Dockwra's undertaking was an infraction of the rights of the Crown; but they had not decided, nor had they been called upon to decide, whether in the hands of the Crown the same undertaking would be legal. The law, as it stood, prescribed no postage lower than twopence. By the penny post the postage was one half of that amount.

With these and other matters requiring adjustment, it might well be supposed that the postmasters-general would have been glad of the opportunity which the Act of Union afforded to set their house in order. Yet, so far from taking any steps in that direction, they now remained perfectly passive. Of the reason for this inaction we are not informed; but we venture to suggest an explanation. Cotton and Frankland were advocates of cheap postage. Should fresh legislation be entered upon, what guarantee had they that postage would not be made dearer? So far, indeed, as they could judge, such was much more likely than not to be the case. As early as William's reign they had been asked to estimate how much an additional penny of postage would produce; and the necessities of the Civil List which had prompted the inquiry had since become more and more pressing.

It is not impossible that there was another, though subordinate, reason. Between Whitehall and Lombard Street communications had been passing from time to time, which might fairly raise the presumption that advantage would be taken of any fresh Act to insert a clause under which all Post Office servants, the postmasters-general included, would be disfranchised. Cotton and Frankland, who still retained their seats, the one for Cambridgeshire, and the other for the borough of Thirsk, were not the men to be deterred by personal considerations from doing what they conceived to be their duty; but if on principle they objected to an increase in the rates of postage, it was little calculated to reconcile them to a measure which they regarded as mischievous that, as a probable consequence of its introduction, they would lose their seats. But be the reason what it might, the fact remains that, whereas at one time they were continually suggesting the propriety of fresh legislation in order to clear up ambiguities in the existing statute, no such suggestion had been recently made, and they now remained perfectly silent.

Thus matters stood when, in October 1708, or a year and a half after the Act of Union had passed, an incident occurred which made silence no longer possible. Letters of Privy Seal had been issued granting salaries payable out of the revenue of the Scotch Post Office to certain professors of the Universities of Edinburgh and Glasgow, and warrants for payment of these salaries were sent to Lombard Street to be signed. The postmasters-general, being in doubt whether their signature would be valid, took the precaution of consulting the law officers. The law officers' opinion, which was not given until the end of December, must have struck dismay into the hearts of those who sought it. It was to the effect that the postmasters-general of England could not act as postmasters-general of Scotland until they had been to Edinburgh and taken the oaths prescribed by the Scotch law. A journey to Edinburgh in those days, especially in the depth of winter, was no light undertaking. But this was not all. And as soon—the opinion proceeded—as they have taken the oaths and qualified as postmasters-general of Scotland, they will cease to be postmasters-general of England.

The warrants were returned to the Treasury unsigned. And now that silence had once been broken, the postmasters-general offered suggestion after suggestion, each having for its object to remove the difficulty. Might not a clause be inserted in some bill now before Parliament, a clause under which they should be constituted postmasters-general of Great Britain, and be given jurisdiction over the Scotch as over the English Post Office? Would not the Scotch bill for drawbacks answer the purpose, or if that were likely to be displeasing to the North British members, some one of the many money-bills that were then pending? Would not the requirements of the law be satisfied if for the management of the Scotch Post Office some one were appointed by letters patent under the Privy Seal of Scotland, and placed under the orders of the postmasters-general of England? Or in view of a recent Act passed by the united Parliament, might not the English postmasters-general themselves be so appointed? To these suggestions, of which the first was made in December 1708, and the last in April 1710, the Lord Treasurer returned no reply. It was clear that Godolphin had other intentions.

Meanwhile events had taken place in London which must have gone far to convince the postmasters-general that, impolitic as an increase in the rates of postage might be, the need for fresh legislation was urgent. Charles Povey had set up a halfpenny post or, as he called it himself, a "half-penny carriage." For the sum of one halfpenny he undertook to do what Dockwra had done, and what the postmasters-general were now doing, for the sum of one penny. There were indeed points of difference. The penny post extended not only over the whole of London proper, but to the remote suburbs; the halfpenny post was confined to the busy parts of the metropolis, to the cities of London and Westminster and to the borough of Southwark. For the halfpenny post, again, letters were collected by the sound of bell. That is to say, Povey's men carried bells, which they rang as they passed along the streets, and so gave notice of their approach. This, though no doubt intended merely as an advertisement, possessed the merit of convenience. People had only to await the coming of one of these bell-ringers, and letters and parcels which they must otherwise have carried to the post themselves were carried for them.

Povey fancied himself a second Dockwra; but the two men were as unlike as the circumstances under which their undertakings were launched. Dockwra was gentle and conciliatory. Povey was violent and aggressive. Dockwra disclaimed all intention of transgressing the law. It was only necessary that his undertaking should become better known, and His Royal Highness, he felt sure, would withdraw his opposition. Povey expressed the utmost indifference whether his undertaking was legal or illegal, and defied the law to do its worst. Dockwra was a pioneer. When he established his penny post, there was nothing in existence at all resembling it, nothing with which it competed, and by supplying an acknowledged want he conferred an inestimable boon upon the community. Povey, on the contrary, was a mere adventurer. His halfpenny carriage was in direct opposition to an institution already existing and in full activity, an institution which supplied every reasonable want, and which it was the sole purpose of his enterprise to supplant for his own advantage.

So impudent an infringement of the rights of the Crown could not, of course, be tolerated, and the postmasters-general called upon Povey to desist from his undertaking. Povey's reply must have extinguished any hope they may have entertained of avoiding an appeal to the Courts. He should certainly not, he said, be so unjust to himself as to lay down his undertaking at their demand. If they were resolved on trying the matter at law, he was quite content. And happily, he added, we live not under such a constitution as Dockwra lived, a constitution made up of an arbitrary government and bribed judges. Thus defied, the postmasters-general had only one course to pursue, and that was to bring an action. As a preliminary step Povey and the keepers of the shops at which he had opened offices were served with notices setting forth the illegality of their proceedings. The shopkeepers closed their offices at once, and Povey was left alone with his bell-ringers.

The man now revealed himself in his true character. When first informed that an information would be filed against him, he published a pamphlet in which, after loading the postmasters-general with ridicule and abuse, he dared them to proceed to trial, declaring that a trial in the Court of Exchequer was the very thing he desired; but as time drew on and he found them to be in earnest, he became alarmed and desired to effect a compromise. With this object he attended at the Post Office and pleaded his cause in person. If only his bell-ringers might continue to collect letters for the general post and "such as pass between man and man," he would pay to the Crown one-tenth more than had yet been received from the penny post. Or let him take the penny post to farm, and he would pay double what that post had ever produced. Or was it to his bells that exception was taken? If so, and if only proceedings were stayed, his bells should cease to-morrow. But even if at one time such overtures could have been listened to, it was now too late, and the postmasters-general so informed him. At this announcement, and while they were still speaking, Povey bounced from his chair and flung himself out of the room. The case came on for hearing in Easter term 1710, and Povey was fined £100.

It may here be mentioned that the practice of collecting letters by the sound of bell did not cease with the halfpenny carriage. It was adopted by the Post Office, became general throughout the kingdom, and continued down to a time well within the recollection of persons still living.[35]

Although the postmasters-general had won their suit, they were not altogether satisfied. What Povey had done might be done by others, and his proceedings, they did not attempt to conceal, had caused them great annoyance. As soon as he found them bent on suppressing his undertaking, he had had recourse to artifice. In order that his bell-ringers might escape molestation, he had changed them about from place to place and made them assume fictitious names, so that the man who appeared in Holborn to-day under one name might appear in Westminster to-morrow under another. The task of fixing evidence had thus been made extremely difficult, and the postmasters-general had at one time almost given it up in despair. They also bitterly complained of the law's delays. For no less than seven months—from the 4th of October 1709 to the 4th of May 1710—the halfpenny post had been in full activity, to the serious injury of the penny post. Must the institution which had been committed to their charge remain, for periods of longer or shorter duration, at the mercy of any unscrupulous person who might choose to follow Povey's example? Or against future assaults of the same kind was it not possible to provide themselves with some less cumbrous weapon than they had now to their hands?

Whether the Act which subsequently passed conferred upon the postmasters-general all the powers they desired may be open to question, but there can be no doubt that, after the experience of the past few months, the prospect of fresh legislation, if not actually welcome, had lost half its terrors. For fresh legislation, however, the time had not even yet arrived. It is true that Povey's case, pending the consideration of which nothing of course could be done, had been heard and determined; but now political difficulties arose. Godolphin, the Lord Treasurer, gave way to Harley; and Harley's advent to power was followed by a general election. It was not until the beginning of November, or three weeks before the Houses met, that a decision was at last announced. Subject to the consent of Parliament, the rates of postage were to be increased, and a bill to carry out the object was to be prepared at once.

The office of Secretary to the Treasury was at this time held by William Lowndes, member of Parliament for the borough of Seaford. Lowndes had written a silly book on the currency, a book in which he endeavoured to prove that an Act of Parliament, by calling a sixpence a shilling, can double its purchasing power. He had seriously believed, when the postmasters-general recommended that the course of post to Warwick should be direct instead of by way of Coventry, that the recommendation was due to a bribe. When the postmasters-general were at their wits' end to put a stop to the illicit traffic in letters, he had suggested—and it was the only consolation which he had had to offer them—that in order to defray the expenses of the Civil List every letter passing through the post should be charged with an additional rate of 1d. Such was the man to whom was now entrusted the oversight of the Post Office bill. If confidence in the merits of the measure which the bill was designed to promote were any recommendation, a better selection could not have been made. Lowndes had long advocated an increase in the rates of postage. He had, there can be little doubt, brought Godolphin over to his views, and now, under Godolphin's successor, he obtained permission to carry them into effect.

At the Post Office, unfortunately, there was at this time no one to sound a note of alarm. Cotton was no more. Evelyn, Cotton's successor, was new to his duties. Frankland was old and gouty. Between Frankland and Lowndes, moreover, relations we suspect were somewhat strained. At all events, the fact remains that the postmasters-general, who never tired of inculcating as the result of experience that low postage attracts correspondence and high postage repels it, received notice of the intention to raise the rates without even an attempt to avert the mischief.

By the middle of December, or little more than six weeks from the time of the Post Office receiving notice to prepare for fresh legislation, the bill was in Lowndes's hands. Containing as it did some fifty clauses, and dealing with a matter of no little complexity, such despatch might do no discredit even to our own days of high pressure. At the beginning of the eighteenth century it was out of the common. But the explanation is simple. Swift, the solicitor to the Post Office, who was profoundly dissatisfied with the law as it stood, had for years past employed his leisure moments in framing clauses founded upon his conception of what the law ought to be, less probably in the hope of seeing them passed than with the view of giving relief to his feelings. These clauses he now collected, arranged, and added to, producing what he conceived to be a model measure. But while the bill had taken only six weeks to prepare, nearly double that period was occupied in revising it. Whatever may be thought of Lowndes's understanding, there can be no question about his industry. Day after day during the next three months he devoted to the task he had undertaken every moment he could snatch from his numerous other engagements. In conjunction with Swift, who now passed most of his time at Whitehall, he went through the bill clause by clause, discussing and arguing every point, and not seldom making alterations. Swift, as the representative of the Post Office, knew well what the Post Office wanted; but Lowndes knew, or thought that he knew, better, and in this as in other instances superior authority passed current for superior knowledge. It was not, however, to what for distinction's sake may be called the Post Office clauses of the bill that the chief interest attached. To these Lowndes added others, of which one, while dealing with a matter of the most delicate character, revealed an intention of which the Post Office had had no previous notice. The preparation of this clause severely taxed the abilities of its framers.

As the Post Office revenue was at this time vested in the Crown, the Crown would, of course, in the absence of express provision to the contrary, reap the benefit of any increase which additions to the rates of postage might produce. To divert the increase, or part of the increase, from the Crown to the public was the object of the clause on which Lowndes and Swift were now engaged. This clause having at length been settled to their satisfaction, the bill came before Parliament, and was with some modifications passed. The new rates as compared with the old were as follows:—

From London.	1660.			1711.		
	Single.	Double.	Ounce.	Single.	Double.	Ounce.
80 miles and under	2d.	4d.	8d.	3d.	6d.	12d.
Above 80 miles	3d.	6d.	12d.	4d.	8d.	16d.
To Edinburgh	5d.	10d.	20d.	6d.	12d.	24d.
To Dublin	6d.	12d.	24d.	6d.	12d.	24d.

FROM EDINBURGH, within Scotland.	1711.		
	Single.	Double.	Ounce.
50 miles and under	2d.	4d.	8d.
Above 50 and not exceeding 80 miles	3d.	6d.	12d.
Above 80 miles	4d.	8d.	16d.

From Dublin, within Ireland.			
40 miles and under	2d.	4d.	8d.
Above 40 miles	4d.	8d.	16d.

The old rates during the year ending the 29th of September 1710 had produced £111,461, and the new rates were estimated to produce £36,400 more. Of this increase the whole was to be paid into the Exchequer by weekly instalments of £700, so that a fund might be established for the purpose of carrying on the war; and of the surplus, if any, over and above £147,861, one-third was to be reserved to the disposal of Parliament for the use of the public. These provisions were to hold good for thirty-two years, after which the old rates were to be reverted to.

We have already seen how difficult the postmasters-general had found it, even with the lower rates of postage, to prevent the smuggling of letters; and of course, in exact proportion as the rates should be increased, the temptation to smuggle would become greater. This consequence had been foreseen and provided for. After declaring in the preamble that, as a condition of the new rates, provision must be made "for preventing the undue collecting and delivering of letters by private posts, carriers, higglers, watermen, drivers of stage-coaches, and other persons," the bill went on to give to the postmasters-general large powers of search. This clause was regarded as of the highest importance. Without it, indeed, even Lowndes would hardly have ventured to suggest that the rates should be increased. To his dismay, however, and, truth compels us to add, to the dismay also of the Post Office, the House of Commons, while passing the rates, rejected the searching clause. Only the declaration in the preamble remained, an enduring monument of a foolish intention.

Another clause must also be regarded as peculiarly Lowndes's own. This clause—which, unlike the foregoing, was not rejected—prohibited the postmasters-general and all persons serving under them from intermeddling in elections. They were forbidden under heavy penalties "to persuade any one to give or to dissuade any one from giving his vote for the choice" of a member of Parliament. Lowndes can hardly have believed it possible thus to padlock men's mouths. It is still more difficult to suppose that the clause can have been aimed at Frankland; and yet assuredly Frankland was the only person whom it affected. Postmasters and others, it may well be believed, continued to talk and to argue exactly as they had argued and talked before; but Frankland had to give up his seat. At the general election in October he had, there can be little doubt, received a hint of what was coming, for after sitting for his pocket borough of Thirsk for more than twelve years he retired from the representation.

So much of the new Act as originated with the Post Office was mainly directed to clearing up doubts, to supplying omissions, and to making that legal for which the law had not yet provided. Thus, legal sanction was given to the penny post, and competition with it was forbidden under severe penalties. Pence upon ship-letters were not only authorised but directed to be paid. The rates of postage to America and to the West Indies were confirmed; and power was given to impose rates upon letters to other places with which communication might be opened. The Act of 1660 had conferred upon the postmasters-general the exclusive right of "receiving, taking up, ordering, despatching, sending post or with speed, and delivering of all letters and packets whatsoever"; but it was silent on the subject of carrying. This omission the Act of 1711 supplied. The later Act also imposed restrictions on the common carrier. Hitherto it had been left in doubt what letters he might carry. These were now defined to be letters which concerned the goods in his waggon or cart; and they were to be delivered at the same time as the goods and without hire or reward.

It was not enough that the penny post should receive legal sanction. By this post, from its first establishment, a single penny had carried only within London proper. For delivery in the outskirts—as, for instance, at Islington, Lambeth, Newington, and Hackney, all of which were at this time separate towns—the Post Office received one penny more. So long, therefore, as the charge by the general post for a distance not exceeding eighty miles stood at 2d., it was a mere question of convenience whether towns in the neighbourhood of London should be served by that post or by the penny post. In either case the postage on a single letter was the same, namely 2d. But now that the initial charge by the general post was raised from 2d. to 3d., it became necessary to assign a limit beyond which the penny post should not extend; and this limit was fixed at ten miles, measured from the General Post Office in Lombard Street.

How little the Post Office had at this time entered into the inner life of the people may be judged by the fact that such restriction was possible. In 1711 there were towns distant nearly twenty miles from London—for instance, Walton-on-Thames, Cheshunt in Hertfordshire, and Tilbury in Essex—which had long been served by the penny post; and the penny post carried up to one pound of weight for the same charge for which the general post carried a single letter. Yet these towns were now deprived of the facilities which the penny post afforded without, so far as appears, exciting a murmur.[36]

Under the new Act the Post Office retained the monopoly of furnishing post-horses. It is to be observed, however, that the charge for each horse, although remaining the same as before—namely, 3d. a mile, with 4d. a stage for the guide—was now re-enacted apologetically, as though some compunction had begun to be felt at the interference with the freedom of contract. The explanation is perhaps to be found in the recent introduction of stage-coaches and the low prices at which these vehicles carried passengers. "There is of late," writes an author of the period, "an admirable commodiousness, both for men and women of better quality, to travel from London to almost any town of England and to almost all the villages near this great city, and that is by stage-coaches, wherein one may be transported to any place, sheltered from foul weather and foul ways; and this is not only at a low price, as about 1s. for every five miles, but with such speed, as that the posts in some foreign countries make not more miles in a day."[37] If a mode of travelling so luxurious as this appears to have been thought could be secured for less than 2-1/2d. a mile, a charge of 3d. a mile for a horse besides a guerdon to the guide may well have appeared to require justification.

It may here be noticed that, although the postmasters-general were under obligation to supply horses on demand, and, failing to do so, became liable to a penalty, the control which they exercised over the travelling post appears to have been of the slightest. It is true that they would now and again complain of a postmaster for keeping bad horses; but the badness would always be with reference to the horses' capacity to carry the mails. Whether they were fit or unfit for the use of travellers appears never to have troubled headquarters. Except, indeed, for some little exertion of authority on rare occasions and in circumstances out of the common,[38] it would almost seem that the postmasters-general had ceased to regard the travelling post as a matter in which they had any concern. It is not very clear why this should have been so. But perhaps the explanation is that in the case of the travelling post, unlike that of the letter post, a postmaster's interest and duty were identical; if horses were wanted, he was under the strongest inducement to supply them; and the danger to be apprehended was not that travellers would be neglected, but that they might be accommodated at the expense of the mails.

On one point, no doubt because it involved a question of prerogative rather than law, the new Act was silent; and yet it was a point of high importance and, as it afterwards became the subject of legal enactment, this may be a convenient time to mention it. We refer to the privilege conceded to certain persons to send and receive their letters free of postage, or, to use the term by which it was commonly known, the franking system. The persons who enjoyed this privilege were the Chief Officers of State and the members of the two Houses of Parliament. The Chief Officers of State, or ministers as they had now begun to be called, were entitled to send and receive their letters free at all times and without limit in point of weight. The members of the two Houses were so entitled only during the session of Parliament and for forty days before and after, and in their case the weight was limited to two ounces.

The privilege had already been greatly abused. Secretaries of State would not scruple to send under their frank the letters of their friends and their friends' friends as well as their own. In 1695 Blaithwaite, who was then Secretary of War, carried the practice to such an extent as to evoke from the postmasters-general a vigorous remonstrance. "We cannot deny," they said, "but this has been too much a practice in all tymes, and we are sure you will not blame us for wishing itt were amended, being soe very prejudicial to His Majestye's revenue under our management." The practice extended, and in 1705 a warrant under the sign-manual, after enumerating afresh the Officers of State who were entitled to frank, expressly charged them not "to cover any man's letters whatsoever other than their own," and, as regards any letters which might come addressed to their care for private persons, to send them to the Post Office to be taxed and delivered.

The abuses identified with the letters of members of Parliament were of wider scope. Lavishly as members might use their names as a means of franking, the use was not confined to themselves and their friends. On the part of the London booksellers and other persons who might hesitate to incur the risk of imitating another man's signature it had become a common practice to assume the name of some member of Parliament, and under that name to have their letters addressed to them at particular coffee-houses; and as their correspondents in the country adopted a similar device, the letters passing to and fro escaped postage. Cotton and Frankland had not been long at the Post Office before this practice arrested their attention, and in 1698 the warrant which granted to the members of the new Parliament the usual exemption from postage was expressly designed to check the abuse. "To prevent abuses," thus the warrant ran, "that were formerly practised[39] to the prejudice of our revenue by divers persons who, though they were not members, yet presumed to indorse the names of members of Parliament on their letters and direct their letters to members of Parliament which really did not belong to them," our will and pleasure is that members "will constantly with their owne hands indorse their names upon their owne letters, and not suffer any other letters to pass under their ffrank, cover, or direction but such as shall concerne themselves." Successive warrants issued between 1698 and 1711 were expressed in the same or nearly the same terms, what little variations there were only serving to shew that the practice against which the warrants were directed had become more general.

But now the postmasters-general could no longer conceal from themselves that, unwarrantable as might be the liberties taken with members' names, the members themselves were by no means blameless. That they were scattering their franks with boundless profusion was beyond doubt; and the question which the postmasters-general set themselves to solve was, How was this profusion to be checked? As the best expedient they could devise, they prepared for the Queen's signature a fresh warrant which, as a hint to members for the regulation of their own conduct, referred to Her Majesty's condescension in allocating a portion of the Post Office revenue towards defraying the expenses of the war. Of previous warrants copies had been posted up in the lobby of the House and in the Speaker's chamber. Of the present warrant copies were to be distributed with the votes so as to secure that every member should have a copy.

The immediate effect of the Act of 1711 was, as might have been foreseen, enormously to stimulate clandestine traffic. The Post Office could do little to check it. In London officers were appointed whose duty it was to frequent the roads leading into the capital and keep a watch on all higglers and drivers of coaches who were notoriously carrying letters in defiance of the law. In the country the postmasters-general could get nothing done. In vain they urged upon the Treasury the paramount importance of appointing officers who should travel about the country and be authorised to open the mail bags at odd times and unexpectedly. By no other means, they declared, was it possible to keep any check upon either the London or the country letters. The London letters might not be charged correctly by the clerks of the roads; and of the country letters, it was perfectly well known, only a very small proportion was charged at all. But all to no purpose. The officers whom the postmasters-general proposed to appoint were to receive for remuneration and travelling expenses together £1 a day, and the Treasury declined to sanction the expense.

This, even for the Treasury, has always appeared to us a masterpiece of perversity. That large sums were being diverted into the pockets of the postmasters had been admitted in the Act itself;[40] nor could it be denied that the tendency of the Act was to make these sums larger. And yet the abuse was to be allowed to go on unchecked because its correction would involve a small outlay. For four years this penny-wise and pound-foolish policy continued, and it was not until 1715, as the consequence of a strong representation from Frankland and Evelyn's successors, that the officers whose appointment these two postmasters-general had consistently advocated were added to the establishment under the title of surveyors. To surprise the mail bags in course of transit and to check their contents— such was the humble function originally assigned to officers who have since become as indispensable to the Post Office as the mainspring is to a watch or the driving wheel to a steam engine.

It may here be noticed that the decisions which the postmasters-general received were not all of them conceived in the same spirit. So different indeed was the treatment of questions relating to home communications and communications with foreign parts as almost to suggest that they had been referred to different tribunals. Was the packet service which had come to an end through Dummer's misfortunes to be re-established or not? The cost was far, very far, in excess of the receipts; and yet the direction to the Post Office was to consult the West India merchants, and to be guided by their wishes. The two packets between Falmouth and the Groyne, which had been left running at the close of the war, were after a time discontinued. They cost £1600 a year to maintain, and the annual receipts from the letters and passengers they carried were less than £450. Yet upon a representation from the merchants trading with Spain pointing out the inconvenience which the stoppage had caused them, the boats were restored at once. But all such questions were decided by the Lord Treasurer himself, and his decisions were communicated under his own signature, or else under the sign-manual.

Very different was it with questions affecting intercourse within the kingdom. These, urgently as the postmasters-general might press them, received little or no attention. They would seem indeed to have been relegated to subordinates, who having been instructed to keep down expense proceeded to obey their orders without discrimination. Whether the packet agent at Dover had in his cups refused to drink to the health of the ministers, or whether the postmaster of Chester had said that Queen Anne, had she pursued the same course as was pursued by Charles the First, would have met with the same fate—these were questions of vital importance which must be investigated with all convenient speed; but when the question was merely one of improving the internal posts of the country, it was treated at leisure, and no considerations of public convenience, or even of prospective gain, were allowed to weigh against the bugbear of present expense. In 1710, for instance, the Lord Provost and magistrates of Glasgow had petitioned that the foot-post to Edinburgh might be converted into a horse-post. The mail would thus arrive sooner and leave later, and, as the petitioners pointed out, letters would fall into it which had heretofore been sent by private hand. Between a horse-post and a foot-post the difference in point of cost was £20 a year; and for the sake of this small sum the Treasury had refused the request, just as they now refused to sanction the appointment of surveyors, although the postmasters-general clearly demonstrated that by no other means could the misappropriation of postage be checked, and that within a few months the cost would be covered many times over.

But the addition to the establishment of a few appointments more or less was not the most serious charge which the Act of 1711 entailed. The Post Offices over a great part of England were then in farm. How, within the area over which these Post Offices extended, was the State to derive any benefit from the higher postage? The postage, whatever it might be, was under their leases secured to the farmers; and the farmers were under no obligation to pay any higher rent than that for which they had stipulated. This difficulty, which had without doubt been overlooked, took a most unexpected turn. The farmers had had only a short experience of the new rates before they found that these rates, far from bringing them a golden harvest, were fast contributing to their ruin; that they were in effect prohibitive rates; that the letters passing to and fro were getting fewer and fewer; and that the increase of charge by no means made up for the decrease in number. In short, the Crown or those who represented the Crown had taken for granted that under the new rates the returns would be relatively higher than under the old, whereas the farmers found to their cost that the returns were actually lower. Never, perhaps, has there been a more striking demonstration of the unwisdom of high rates of postage. In this dilemma the postmasters-general had recourse to an expedient which appears to have been considered satisfactory on both sides. They cancelled all the leases, nine in number,[41] and under the title of managers, appointed the farmers to superintend the Post Offices embraced within the area over which their farms extended. The managers who had heretofore been at the cost of the postmasters' salaries were to be relieved from this and all other payments; and as remuneration for their services they were to receive one-tenth part of the net produce derived from the postage.

Two questions may here be asked, to neither of which is it easy to give even a plausible reply. Of these the first is, How did it happen that the postmasters-general, who without authority from Whitehall could not even convert a foot-post into a horse-post, were able on their own motion to sanction an arrangement, the practical effect of which was to add to the establishment not only a large number of small salaries, amounting in the aggregate to a formidable total, but also a dead-weight annuity of nearly £2000 a year? This is an obscurity which we confess ourselves unable to penetrate. We can only record the fact, a fact the more surprising because only recently Godolphin had laid it down under his own hand that in the Post Office "all extraordinary payments or allowances are to be vouched by warrant from Her Majesty or myself, or from the Lord High Treasurer or the Commissioners of the Treasury for the time being." The second question is hardly less perplexing. How, except in name, did managers differ from surveyors, whose appointment the postmasters-general were urging, and urging in vain? Or what could surveyors have done which it was not equally competent to managers to do? This question also we cannot answer. We only know that the very men who as farmers had rendered signal service to the Post Office, and earned the gratitude of the districts over which their farms extended, were found as managers to be of little use, even if they did not league themselves with the postmasters to intercept the postage.

Difficulties from an unexpected quarter added to the confusion into which, as the result of the Act of 1711, the Post Office was drifting. As soon as peace was declared, it became necessary to arrive at an agreement with France as to the conditions on which the British mails should pass through French territory. M. Pajot was still comptroller of the posts in Paris; and he proved to be hardly less untractable than before the war. Frankland

and Evelyn committed their case to the care of Matthew Prior, who was at that time minister plenipotentiary to the Court of France. Prior, who had hated his commissionership of customs because, as Swift tells us, he was ever dreaming of cockets and dockets and other jargon, could hardly be expected to give his mind to anything so prosaic as postage and letter bills. The matter, moreover, was one of a highly technical character, and, without fuller information than could be contained in the most precise instructions, a far abler negotiator than Prior could claim to be might easily have found himself overmatched. Pajot, presuming on his superior knowledge, put forward the most extravagant demands; and it was not until an expert had been sent from London, upon whom it would have been useless to attempt to impose, that he abated his pretensions. Extravagant demands were now followed by frivolous objections, and at the last moment, when the conditions were practically settled, he actually refused to proceed further unless "Her Britannic Majesty," an expression employed in the Post Office treaty, were altered to "The Queen of Great Britain."

Vexatious as these proceedings were, the result was more vexatious still. Before the war a lump sum of 36,000 livres a year had been paid for the transit of the British mails across French territory. Pajot now refused to accept any lump sum at all. He insisted that each letter passing through France should be charged for separately, according to the French postage; and high as the English postage was, the French postage was higher still. In vain the postmasters-general pointed out that by virtue of such an arrangement they would on many letters have to pay more than Act of Parliament permitted them to receive. Pajot replied in effect that this was their affair and not his; and no better terms could they get. The treaty was eventually signed, and its onerous provisions will best be shewn by an example. On a single letter from Italy the postage prescribed by the Act of 1711 was fifteenpence, and on a letter weighing one ounce sixty pence. This was all which the Act permitted the postmasters-general to collect; and yet, under the terms of the treaty, the postage for which they had to account to the French Post Office was in the one case twenty-one sous and in the other eighty-four.

To this treaty we are indeed indebted for one piece of information. It gives us—what is not to be found elsewhere—a definition of the terms single and double as applied to letters. It is strange that the Acts of 1660 and 1711, while imposing distinctive rates on single and double letters, nowhere define what single and double letters are. This omission the treaty of 1713 supplies. "That piece," the treaty provides, "is to be esteemed a single letter which hath no sealed letter inclosed, and that to be esteemed a double letter which hath inclosures and is under the weight of an ounce." It will be interesting to note how far the Post Office adhered to its own definition.

On the accession of George the First, when almost every place of honour and profit under the Crown changed hands, the Post Office did not escape; and Frankland and Evelyn were succeeded by Cornwallis and Craggs. The natural tendency of the provision which had made members of the House of Commons ineligible for the office of postmasters-general was to throw the office into the hands of peers; and although this tendency did not fully develop itself until later in the century, the appointment of Lord Cornwallis was a first move in that direction. Peers have in our own time been among the ablest of the many able administrators who have presided over the Post Office; but at the beginning of the eighteenth century the conditions attaching to the appointment were in some respects different from what they are to-day. The postmasters-general had to write their own letters; their attendance was both early and late and during fixed hours; and they were expected to reside at the Post Office. Whether from a disinclination to satisfy these conditions, or on the score of health, which he was constantly pleading, Cornwallis had not been long in Lombard Street before he retired into the country, and left the conduct of affairs pretty much to his colleague. Craggs—or Craggs senior as he was commonly called, to distinguish him from his son, the Secretary of State—was an industrious, plain-spoken man; and deeply as he afterwards became implicated in the South Sea Scheme, there is no reason to suppose that his proceedings as postmaster-general would not bear inspection.

Cornwallis and Craggs had been only a short time at the Post Office before they became profoundly impressed with what they found there. The managers withholding the postmasters' salaries, the postmasters recouping and a good deal more than recouping themselves out of the postage, the post-boys—for so they had begun to be called—clandestinely carrying letters for what they could get, the inordinate number of franked letters— these were among the abuses which arrested the new postmaster-generals' attention; but what excited their most lively surprise was that there should exist a branch of the King's revenue upon the subordinate agents of which there was absolutely no check. At length, on a representation from them as to the scandal of allowing such a state of things to continue, consent was obtained to the appointment of surveyors; and the dismissal of the managers speedily followed.

These remedial measures, though good as far as they went, affected only the internal administration of the Post Office. Of its troubles from without, and how they had been increased by recent legislation, Cornwallis and Craggs were no less sensible than their predecessors; but here they had no remedy to apply. "The additional penny," they wrote in March 1716, within eighteen months of their appointment, "has never answered in proportion, and we find by every day's experience that it occasions the people to endeavour to find out other conveyances for their letters." "The additional tax," they wrote again two years later, "has never answered in proportion to the produce of the revenue at the time it took place, the people having found private conveyances for their letters, which they are daily endeavouring to increase, notwithstanding all the endeavours that can be used to prevent them."

As with the clandestine traffic, so with the abuse of the franking privilege. In isolated cases, where the abuse was more than usually glaring, the postmasters-general would write to the erring member a letter of mild expostulation, affecting to believe him more sinned against than sinning;[42] but even if this had any effect in the particular instance, to stem the torrent was beyond their power. In Great Britain alone the postage represented by the franked letters, excluding those which were or which purported to be on His Majesty's service, amounted in 1716 to what was for that time, relatively to the total Post Office revenue, the enormous sum of £17,500 a year. In Ireland the members followed the example of their English colleagues, if indeed they did not improve upon it. In 1718 the Irish Parliament sat for three months, and in 1719 it sat for nine months; and it was only during the session, and for forty days before and after, that letters could be franked. Cornwallis and Craggs had now been some years at the Post Office; and yet, with all their experience of the extent to which the abuse of franking was carried, they were startled to see the effect which the duration of Parliament had upon the receipts. In 1718 the gross revenue of the Irish Post Office—and in the gross revenue was reckoned the postage on members' letters, the postage which these letters would have paid if they had not been franked—amounted to £14,592, and the net revenue to £3066. In 1719, although the gross revenue rose to £19,522, an amount higher by £4930 than in the preceding year, the net revenue fell from £3066 to £753. Such was the effect upon the revenue of a difference of six months in the duration of the two Parliaments.

To add to the postmaster-generals' troubles, the merchants of London, groaning under the onerous rates of postage, had recourse to an expedient in order to evade them. They associated themselves together, and all those who had occasion to write to a particular place, though to different persons, would write on the same piece of paper and under the same cover. The postmasters-general contended that these several writings should be charged as separate letters; the merchants contended that there was but one letter, and that it should pass for a single rate of postage.

Their next step was to dispute the postmaster-generals' reading of the statute. Under the law as passed in 1660, and re-enacted in 1711, merchants' accounts not exceeding one sheet of paper, and all bills of exchange, invoices, and bills of lading, were "to be allowed without rate in the price of letters"; in other words, the weight of these documents was not to be reckoned in the weight of a letter for the purpose of charging it with postage. This exemption, however, had hitherto been allowed only in the case of foreign letters; and the postmasters-general held that such was the intention of the statute. The merchants retorted that no such intention was expressed, and that to act as though it had been brought about this anomaly—that on a letter containing any one of the documents in question the charge from Constantinople was actually less than from Bristol. Was it possible that the Legislature could ever have enacted such an absurdity? It was an old contention, as old as the Post Office itself,[43] and the merchants took the present opportunity to revive it. On both questions Northey, the Attorney-General, advised that the Post Office should adhere to its ancient practice as the best expositor of the meaning of the new law; but excellent as this advice may have been, its adoption failed to satisfy the merchants and it was not until a declaratory Act had been passed that they ceased to contest the points.

Much the same sort of thing occurred a few years later in connection with the penny post. From the first establishment of this undertaking 1d. had carried only within the bills of mortality; for delivery beyond those limits had been charged 1d. more. Some persons now refused to pay the additional penny, on the ground that it was not prescribed by law. This was perfectly true. The penny post owed its legal sanction to the Act of 1711; and this Act merely provided that "for the post of all and every the letters and packets passing or repassing by the carriage called the penny post, established and settled within the cities of London and Westminster and borough of Southwark and parts adjacent, and to be received and delivered within ten English miles distant from the General Letter Office in London [shall be demanded and received the sum of] 1d." Again an Act of Parliament had to be passed in order to assimilate law and practice. This Act, which was not obtained until 1730, made legal the twopenny post, just as the penny post was made legal by the Act of 1711; although, as a matter of fact, both posts had been in existence since April 1680.

In 1721 Lowndes, who was still at the Treasury, called for a return of the Post Office income and expenditure. Ten years had now elapsed since the imposition of the new rates. Of these ten years eight, as compared with the eight which preceded them, had been years of prosperity and peace; the population had increased, and the reductions in the packet service had effected a saving of many thousand pounds a year. Certainly the circumstances had not on the whole been unfavourable for testing the results of the new policy. The return was rendered. During the year ending the 29th of September the gross Post Office revenue was, in 1721, £168,968, and in 1710, £111,461, being an increase of £57,507; in 1721 the cost of management was £69,184, as against £44,639 in 1710; and the net revenue, which in 1710 had been £66,822, was in 1721 £99,784, an increase of £32,962. But the case does not end here. Under the terms of the Act the sum of £700 a week, or £36,400 a year, was to be allocated to a specific object. This sum had been regularly paid into the Exchequer, and, after deducting it from the net revenue, there remained for the use of the Sovereign a balance of £63,384, or less than in 1710 by £3438.

While the contingency of a loss to the Civil List had not been either foreseen or provided against, elaborate precautions had been taken for the disposal of a surplus. If the gross Post Office revenue should exceed the sum of £147,861, the excess was to be divided between the Sovereign and the public in the proportion of one-third to the public and two-thirds to the Sovereign. As a matter of fact, the gross Post Office revenue in 1721 had exceeded, and exceeded by a considerable amount, the sum of £147,861; and yet there was no excess to divide. The plain truth is that, in preparing the Act of 1711, Lowndes had forgotten the cost of management. It must have sounded strange in the ears of an assistant Chancellor of the Exchequer to be told, as Cornwallis and Craggs did not scruple to tell him, that he had confounded gross and net revenue, and that by this blunder Parliament had been misled.

The Act of 1711, disastrous as it proved in its effects on the wellbeing and morality of the nation, is only one more instance of the mischief which may be done with the best intentions; and it was perhaps meet that its author should have remained long enough at his post to witness the results of his own handiwork.

CHAPTER X
RALPH ALLEN 1720-1764

There was one who realised not less fully than the postmasters-general themselves the difficulties by which they were beset. He knew well, even better than they, how letters were being kept out of the post and transmitted clandestinely, and how even on letters which fell into the post the postage was being intercepted. But while the postmasters-general regarded the evil as incurable, he thought that it might at all events be mitigated. This was Ralph Allen, the postmaster of Bath. Allen's experience in postal matters was probably unrivalled. He had, it might almost be said, been cradled and nursed in the Post Office. The son of an innkeeper at St. Blaise, he had, at eleven years of age, been placed under the care of his grandmother, who, on the post road being diverted from South to Mid-Cornwall, was appointed postmistress of St. Columb. Here the regularity and neatness with which the lad kept the accounts gained for him the approval of the district surveyor when on a tour of inspection; and shortly afterwards, probably through the surveyor's influence, he obtained a situation in the Post Office at Bath. It is said that while in this situation, intelligence having reached him that a waggon-load of arms was on its way from the West for the use of the disaffected, he placed himself in communication with General Wade, who was then quartered at Bath with his troops, and that it was by this service that he first brought himself into notice; but be that as it may, it is certain that when Quash the old postmaster died, Allen was appointed in Quash's room.

In 1719 Allen offered to take in farm the bye and cross-post letters, giving as rent half as much again as these letters had ever produced. It was a bold offer, and, coming as it did from a young man only twenty-six years of age, and presumably without capital, not one to be accepted precipitately. Allen proceeded to London and had frequent interviews with the postmasters-general. The earnestness of his convictions and the modest assurance with which he expressed them invited confidence, and on the 12th of April 1720 a contract was signed, the conditions of which were to come into operation on the Midsummer Day following.

Much as we desire to avoid the employment of technical terms, it is necessary here to explain that letters, exclusive of those passing through the penny post, were technically divided into four classes—London letters, country letters, bye or way letters, and cross-post letters. For purposes of illustration we will take Bath, the city in which Allen resided. A letter between Bath and London would be a London letter, and a letter from one part of the country to another which in course of transit passed through London would be a country letter. A bye or way letter would be a letter passing between any two towns on the Bath road and stopping short of London— as, for instance, between Bath and Hungerford, between Hungerford and Newbury, between Newbury and Reading, and so on; while a cross-post letter would be a letter crossing from the Bath road to some other—as, for instance, a letter between Bath and Oxford. It was only with the last two classes of letters that Allen had to do. The London and country letters were outside the sphere of his operations.

On the bye and cross-post letters the postage for the year 1719 had amounted to £4000. Allen was to give £6000 a year; and in consideration of this rent he was for a period of seven years to receive the whole of the revenue which these letters should produce. Some letters indeed were excepted, namely Scotch letters, Irish letters, packet letters, "all Parliament men's letters during the privilege of Parliament," and such letters as "usually goe free," that is, letters for the High Officers of State or, as we should now say, letters on His Majesty's service. No post under Allen's control, whether a new or an old one, was to go less than three times a week; and the mails were to be carried at a speed of not less than five miles an hour. He was also to keep in readiness "a sufficient number of good and able horses with convenient furniture," not only for the mails but for expresses and for the use of travellers. One condition of the contract may seem a little hard. Allen's own officers were to be appointed and their salaries to be fixed by the postmasters-general, and to these officers he was to give no instructions which had not first been submitted for the postmaster-generals' approval.

Allen by his sterling qualities had won the confidence of his fellow-townsmen at Bath, and there can be little doubt that they now gave him practical proof of the estimation in which he was held. It is difficult to understand how else he can have raised the funds necessary for the purposes of his undertaking. In the very first quarter, between the 24th of June and the 29th of September 1720, he expended in what may be called his plant as much as £1500, and made himself responsible for salaries to the amount of £3000 a year. But heavy as the expenses were, the receipts bore a most gratifying proportion. From the bye and cross-post letters the postmasters-general had received, at the highest, £4000 a year. Allen in his first quarter

received £2946. These first-fruits, while viewed by Allen with equanimity, threw the postmasters-general into transports of delight, such delight as men feel when they find themselves to have been true prophets. "See," they said in a letter to the Treasury dated the 10th of November, "how right we were. We told you that the greater part of the postage on these letters was going into the pockets of the postmasters, and that to accept Mr. Allen's proposal was the only way to check the malversation." But the promise of the first quarter was not fulfilled. The system of check and countercheck on which Allen relied for the success of his plan depended largely, as the postmasters were not slow to discover, on their own co-operation; and this they refused to give.

Nor can we feel surprise that it should have been so. Of the postmasters some received no salary at all, while others received the merest pittance. It could not in reason be expected that they would give their services gratuitously or, as the postmasters-general were pleased to think, in return for the copy of a newspaper once a week. Postmasters, like other men, must live, and they no doubt reasoned that, as the State did not pay them, they were forced to pay themselves. It must also be remembered that the offence of intercepting postage, heinous as it would now be considered, may in those days have been regarded in a somewhat different light. Some postmasters, as remuneration for their services, were authorised to withhold a certain proportion of the postage; and numerous were the complaints that in this particular the liberty accorded to some was not extended to others. It is probable, therefore, that many a postmaster, when accounting for less postage than he had actually received, excused himself on the plea that he was only doing without authority that for which authority had been given to others, and which should not in his judgment have been denied to himself.

But whatever apologies they may have found for their conduct, the fact remains that Allen's contract had been only a few months in operation before the postmasters resumed their old practices, and, seeing clearly enough that his plan when once fairly floated would deprive them of a profitable source of income, they not only withheld all co-operation but obstructed him by every means in their power. To such an extent indeed was this obstruction carried that at the end of three years Allen, far from realising the promise of the first quarter, found himself a loser to the amount of £270. Although things now began to improve, the improvement was slow, and in June 1727, when the contract expired, Allen had established his plan completely on only four out of the six main roads of the kingdom. On the Yarmouth road he had established it only partially, and on the Kent road not at all.

Circumstances so far favoured Allen that the demise of the Crown, which must in any case have terminated his contract, took place within

a fortnight of the date on which the contract would have expired in the ordinary course. The period of seven years for which it was made expired on the 24th of June 1727, and the King died on the 11th. A renewal of the contract could not in justice be refused. Not only had Allen been obstructed in the execution of his plan and put to heavy expenses which, except for such obstruction, would not have been necessary, but in fixing the amount of his rent a mistake had been made to his prejudice. He had agreed to pay half as much again as the bye and cross-road letters had ever produced, and it is true that the postage represented by these letters had amounted to £4000 a year; but it had been overlooked that the whole of this amount had not been collected, and that for the purpose of fixing the rent the sum of £300 should have been deducted on account of letters which could not be delivered, and on which, therefore, no postage had been received. Allen, while making no claim for the return of the amount overpaid, pleaded the fact of overpayment as an additional reason for enlarging his term. The postmasters-general were not less solicitous than Allen himself that his services should be continued. They had, during the last seven years, received on account of bye and cross-post letters £6000 a year, where before they had received only £4000, or, allowing for the sum not collected, £3700; and during the same period the country letters, far from falling off as had been predicted, had improved to the extent of £735 a year, a result which was attributed to the vigilance of Allen's surveyors. These reasons were regarded as conclusive, and, subject to the condition that he should appoint an additional surveyor and lose no time in completing his plan, Allen's contract was extended for a further period of seven years.

While Allen is perfecting his arrangements, it may not be amiss to glance at the condition of affairs as he found them. Houses were still unnumbered. On letters even to persons of position the addresses could be indicated only by their proximity to some shop or place of public resort. "For the Rt. Honable. the Lady Compton next door to Mr. Massy's Wachmaker in Charles Street near St. James's Square, London." "To the Right Honble. Lady Compton next door to the Dyall in Charles Street near St. James Squir—London." "Pray derickt for me att my Lady norrise near the Theater in Oxford."[44] To the Court and the Downs the post went every day; but to no town, however large, did it go more than thrice a week. Of cross-posts there were only two in the kingdom, the post from Exeter to Chester and the post from Bath to Oxford. Outside London, Chester was the only town in England which could boast of two Post Offices; and these two Post Offices were not for letters in the same direction. One was for general post letters, and the other for letters by the Exeter cross-road, an arrangement which presupposed a knowledge of topography not probably

possessed even in the present day. The cathedral town of Ripon had no Post Office at all. Not many years before, the inhabitants had asked for one and the request had been regarded as little less than audacious. "We could not think it reasonable," wrote the postmasters-general, "to put Her Majesty to the expense of a salary to a Deputy att Ripon." The utmost concession that could be obtained was that the letters for that town should be made up into a packet by themselves and put into the mouth of the Boroughbridge bag, and, on arrival at Boroughbridge, be despatched to Ripon at once by a messenger on horseback. This messenger was to deliver them with all expedition, and to remain at Ripon for replies, leaving only in time to catch the return-mail from the North. Charges on letters over and above the legal postage were general. Not a single letter passed between Yarmouth and the Great North Road without a charge of 3d. as the postmaster's perquisite. At Gosport a perquisite of similar amount was claimed on every bye-letter. In the neighbourhood of Chesterfield the inhabitants paid for every letter they received in no case less than 2d. in addition to the postage, and in some cases as much as 4d.; and so it was, with variations as to the amount, in every part of the kingdom. Only the wealthy could afford to use the post, and even they, on account of the want of facilities, used it sparingly. How far the post was at this time removed from being a matter of common concern might, if other evidence were wanting, be inferred from one solitary fact. In 1728 a book was published,[45] one chapter of which professed to give a detailed account of the posts of the period, and assuredly the account it gave was detailed enough; but of the posts as we understand them, that is to say, as a vehicle for the transmission of letters, there was from the beginning to the end of the chapter not a single word. By the term posts nothing more was meant than the post for travellers, and, for anything that appeared to the contrary, the letter post might have had no existence.

And perhaps this may be a convenient place to say a few words about those who had presided over the Post Office during the first five or six years of Allen's connection with it. Edward Carteret and Galfridus Walpole, who had succeeded Cornwallis and Craggs in 1721, possessed in a high degree the qualities which endear men to their subordinates,—a sense of justice, consideration for others, and a rooted dislike to high-handed proceedings. In these respects they bore a striking contrast to their immediate predecessors. We will give instances.

When Cornwallis and Craggs assumed the direction of the Post Office, their first step was to dismiss the secretary, Henry Weston. The circumstances were peculiarly hard. Weston's father had been receiver-general for the county of Surrey, and in this capacity he had contracted a heavy debt to the Crown. It was the son's ambition to pay off this debt and to provide a home

for his mother and sisters. By force of industry and self-denial he had just succeeded in securing both objects when a change of postmasters-general resulted in his summary dismissal. Weston naturally appealed against so arbitrary an act. Cornwallis and Craggs, to whom his antecedents were well known, while commending the young man as an object worthy of the royal benevolence, resented as unreasonable and little short of impertinent his reluctance to give up a situation which they desired for a nominee of their own.

Far different was the treatment accorded by Carteret and Walpole to those who were committed to their charge. Mary Lovell had for more than thirty years kept the receiving office in St. James's Street. On the 11th of March 1725 the Earl of Abercorn entered this office, holding in his hand a letter addressed to his son at Cambray, and inquired what postage had to be paid upon it. The woman replied that there was only 1d. to pay, this being the charge by the penny post, and that the remaining postage of 3s. would be payable on delivery. Abercorn questioned the accuracy of this information, and insisted on paying the entire sum at once. Lovell, feeling sure that a mistake had been committed, and anxious about the consequences, hurried to the Post Office, and having there ascertained that she should have received only 1d., called at Abercorn's residence, and with a humble apology refunded the difference.

Nothing more was heard of the matter until the following July, when a second very similar mistake appears to have revived the recollection of the first. Abercorn, who was then at Tunbridge Wells, took to the Post Office there a letter addressed to his son at Luneville and handed it to Comer, the postmaster, impressing upon him the importance of its prompt despatch, and desiring him to pay whatever postage might be required. It should be explained that at that time letters for Germany had to be prepaid, or else they were returned to the writers, whereas letters for France could not be paid except on delivery. Comer, jumping to the conclusion that Luneville was in France, paid no more than the inland postage of 6d., the consequence being that three or four days afterwards the letter, after being opened in London, was returned as insufficiently paid. Abercorn, naturally enough, was very angry, and, as is apt to be the case with angry persons, was not altogether reasonable. Luneville, without the addition of Lorraine or Germany, was an incomplete address. For this he would make no allowance; neither would he admit that it was necessary to open the letter in order to return it, and that the impression on the seal, a coronet and coat of arms, was not sufficient indication of the writer.

All this was natural enough; but it was strange that he should have reverted to the earlier of the two mistakes, and directed his resentment less against Comer than against Mary Lovell. He now charged her with insolence and an attempt at imposition, and declared that nothing would satisfy him except her dismissal. In pursuance of this object Abercorn proceeded to the Post Office, where he was received by Carteret and Walpole. Walpole said little, and what little he said was said courteously. Carteret spoke in both their names. He expressed surprise that the return of the amount overcharged on the letter to Cambray, accompanied as it had been by Lovell's humble apology, had not been considered satisfactory, and inquired what further satisfaction could be expected. Abercorn replied that he expected her to be turned out of her office as a person unfit to retain it. Carteret expostulated. Such a step, he said, would not be in accordance with Post Office usage; she was a poor and unprotected woman, no previous complaint had been made against her during the thirty years she had held the office; he had seen her himself, and felt sure that her professions of regret that she had given offence to his lordship were sincere. Impatient of what he afterwards described as an irksome expostulation, Abercorn rose to leave. Carteret and Walpole rose also, and accompanied him to the door. "I owe it to the North British peers," said Abercorn, turning on the threshold, "to acquaint some of their representatives with the treatment that I, their peer, have met with." "And I," haughtily retorted Carteret, "should care not if all the sixteen North British representing peers were present at this moment."

Allen's plan consisted in a system of vouchers and what he called post-bills, by means of which the postmasters might act as a check upon each other. The post-bill which accompanied the letters throughout their course was designed to distinguish the bye-letters from others, and to shew the total amount of postage to be collected; the voucher appears to have been nothing more than the acknowledgment which each postmaster gave of the amount to be collected by himself; and these two documents were sent periodically, once a month or once a quarter, to Allen's office in Bath, where they underwent a rigid scrutiny. Simple as this check was, it was only by ceaseless vigilance on Allen's part that he could get it carried out. To make in the post-bills entries which should have been made in the vouchers, to omit to send the vouchers to headquarters, to confound the bye-letters with the London and country letters—these were only some of the devices to which recourse was had in order to defeat the check.

Allen was better qualified probably than any other man living for the task he had set himself to perform. Of a temper which nothing could ruffle, with ample means at his command, and accountable to no one but himself for their disposal, and possessed of an amount of local knowledge which even at the present day is perhaps unrivalled, he enjoyed a combination of advantages which might have been sought elsewhere in vain. His patience indeed was inexhaustible. No subterfuge, not even a transparent attempt at imposition, would call forth more than a passing rebuke. "'Tis faulty," he would write, "'tis blameable"; and then, perhaps, from the following words would peep out, in spite of himself, a gleam of merriment at the clumsiness of the contrivance.

To a man of less easy temperament even the conditions under which he worked would have been intolerable. Under the terms of his contract Allen's surveyors were to be the officers of the postmasters-general, and to do as the postmasters-general bid them. This was no mere nominal condition. When Allen wanted something done, it may be in the extreme north or the extreme west of England, he might find that the surveyor whose business it would have been to do it had been summoned to London to wait upon the postmasters-general in Lombard Street. Hardly less provoking must have been the condition that the surveyors, though Allen's servants, were not to receive from him any instructions which the postmasters-general had not first approved. Ordinarily Allen was at Bath, and it was there that the instructions were prepared; yet they had to be sent to London for approval, and were seldom despatched thence to their destination until seven or eight days after the dates they bore.

But to any one of less modest and retiring disposition the severest trial would have been the manner in which the postmasters-general took credit to themselves for improvements which were exclusively his own. It was always "our" surveyors who had been instructed to do this, that, and the other, without the slightest acknowledgment that the instruction had come from Allen, and that it was he who supplied the money to pay and the wit to direct them. Only when the cost of some new arrangement had to be stated to the Treasury did his name appear, and then it was put prominently forward. "Your Lordships," the postmasters-general would write, with a confidence which must have possessed all the pleasure of a new sensation, "will of course approve our proposals. It is true that the cost they involve is considerable, but the whole of this will fall upon Mr. Allen, the farmer." But so placid was Allen's temper that these petty annoyances, irritating as they might have been to some men, passed unheeded.

As a qualification for the task he had undertaken, hardly less important than placidity of temper was the possession of ample means and his unaccountability to others for their disposal. With no one to please but himself, he enjoyed facilities in dealing with postmasters which the Post Office, under the most favourable circumstances, could never hope to possess. To one he would give what he called a complimentary salary; to another he would give, over and above his salary, a certain proportion of the postage; and a third would receive a substantial increase, not for what he had done or was doing, but for what he might do in the future. All, in short, who could control the actions of others Allen bound to himself by a community of interest.

But it was the extent of his local knowledge that constituted Allen's chief qualification for the task he had set himself to perform. This knowledge, acquired probably during the struggle to introduce his plan, may appear almost marvellous. There was hardly a town in England, and certainly no town of importance, with the trade and manufactures of which, and even with the character and disposition of its postmaster, he was not acquainted. At the present day it is the district surveyor who in Post Office matters affecting the provinces takes the initiative. In Allen's time the initiative came from Bath. In a single letter he would treat of some thirty or forty towns, and not only prescribe the order in which they were to be taken and the roads by which they were to be reached, but give the minutest instructions as to what was to be said and done on arrival there. In respect to only one town, a town without a Post Office, does Allen appear to have been uninformed, and that was Stowmarket. "When in that neighbourhood," he wrote to one of his surveyors, as though half ashamed of his own ignorance, "go over to Stowmarket and ascertain and let me know the distance of that town from Ipswich and from Eye, and also the nature and extent of its trade."

Lest we should be thought to exaggerate the difficulties with which Allen had to contend, Allen himself shall be our witness. The postmasters were strictly enjoined to stamp the bye and cross-post letters. This was their first duty, for without stamping no check was possible. "I need not tell you," Allen writes to one of his surveyors, "the mischief which has already attended the omission of this necessary part of their duty, nor the difficulty which I have hitherto met with to get this order observed; but when they find that their neglect will for the future hurt themselves, this evil will be stopped."

Hardly less difficult did he find it to make the postmasters send in their vouchers with even decent regularity. We will give a few instances out of many. Of Bodmin and St. Columb he writes, "Both these deputies are exceeding backward in transmitting their vouchers. Order them strictly to send them hither for the future within a week after every quarter." Richmond, Yorkshire, "instead of sending me his vouchers at the end of every month sends them considerably over the quarter and then in so great disorder as to be of little use to me in fixing my cheque account." Gosport, again, "persistently neglects to send his vouchers, without which, as you know, it is not in my power to state an exact account nor to fix the cheques which are necessary to prevent abuses." Grantham is little better, and as for Wolverhampton, Allen writing in April says, "He has sent me no vouchers since last Michaelmas, and by this obstinacy destroys my cheque and puts my affairs into great disorder."

The dead and missent letters were a source of continual trouble. How to dispose of dead letters and how to get back into their proper channel letters that had been missent were questions which not seldom perplexed even Allen himself. But it is not of this particular difficulty that we propose now to speak. Our present concern is with these two classes of letters only so far as they affected the relations between Allen and the postmasters. According to his instructions a postmaster who should find himself in possession of a dead or missent letter was to send it to Bath in order that allowance might be made for the postage with which, otherwise, he would stand charged. Hence arose various attempts at imposition, attempts to palm off, as though they were dead or missent, letters which were neither the one nor the other. But let Allen again speak for himself. "From Lancaster," he writes, "go through Kendal and Penrith to Carlisle, where I believe you will meet with a very great abuse. 'Tis thus: His dead letters for a good while since much exceed what can be rationally accounted for at that stage, and upon enquiry the greatest number of those letters appear to be sham letters all written by one hand and sent from different parts of the kingdom, which plainly shews it to be only a blameable contrivance by some people in that office to expect money from me for bits of paper never sent by the post but made by themselves. Some instances you will receive with these instructions. Be sure to suppress this dangerous abuse. Cause me a redress for the injury I have received and leave with Mr. Pattison a copy of my letter relating to stamps, which is the only method I can think of for an effectual cure of this evil."

The method to which Allen here refers afterwards became a rule of the office. It was to the effect that no allowance would be made in respect to any dead or missent letters which should not bear on their covers the name of the office whence the postmaster by whom the allowance was claimed had received them. If at that office they had been stamped, that was enough; but if they had been forwarded unstamped—and the stamping was as often omitted as not—the postmaster who received the letters was to write the name upon them. Allen's first experience of the working of this rule was a little singular. Mrs. Wainwright, the old postmistress of Ferrybridge, had sent up for allowance a number of unstamped letters without shewing whence she had received them. Allen returned the letters, explaining that as such information had not been given no allowance could be made. If Mrs. Wainwright felt any impatience at what she no doubt regarded as new-fangled ways, no evidence of it was allowed to appear. She simply sent the letters back with the name of the office whence they had reached her neatly written upon each. To Allen's dismay, the letters had all been opened and the information obtained from the inside.

The new rule, though good as far as it went, proved insufficient to check imposition; and Allen felt constrained to add an additional safeguard. For the future no postmaster was to have his claim allowed unless he should verify it on oath. This obligation brought its own troubles. By one the oath was omitted, by another it was objected to on conscientious grounds, a third would treat it as of small account, and all this meant additional work for Allen. "This officer," he writes of the postmaster of Salisbury, "constantly makes large deductions for missent letters" and on other grounds "without sending me the particulars of his demand or the office oath to the truth of his claim." The postmaster of Newark had conscientious scruples and objected to the oath in any form. "You have already," writes Allen, "been fully acquainted how tender I am in this respect; but if he still refuses to claim his demand for allowances by an oath framed in any shape, 'tis directly necessary to appoint an officer in that place who will obey their Honours' commands, for if his obstinacy should be suffered the rest of the kingdom who have readily complyed may raise new objections." No such scruples afflicted the postmaster of Stone in Staffordshire. Until lately "the errors made to my injury considerably exceeded those made to the hurt of that deputy"; but now "the articles to my hurt are dwindled to a trifle and the others much augmented, which causes Mr. Barbor to make constant and large claims on me for the difference. Only lately I received from him a statement of his demands on this head, with an oath at the bottom of it that the several articles to his prejudice were all true. But if it be the case, as I have always understood, that he never concerns himself with the bye-letters but leaves this business to his uncle, pray enquire of him how he came to send me such an oath."

The postmasters had been allowed to receive their correspondence free of postage; but Allen soon found that the privilege was being abused. The covers addressed to them would contain letters not for themselves alone but also for their neighbours in trade. Indeed the neighbours' letters would predominate, and, ordinarily, the address was a mere subterfuge. To check this abuse Allen established a rule that when addressed to postmasters none but single letters—letters without enclosures, were to pass free, and that all others were to be charged with full postage. The postage, however, was to be afterwards remitted in the case of any postmaster who should make oath that the letters in respect to which he claimed remission were on his private business. Here again Allen's belief in the efficacy of an oath was rudely shaken. The number and magnitude of the claims made upon him from Lancaster had arrested his attention, and he had laid them aside to be examined at leisure. Meanwhile the explanation came in a curious manner. He received a circular from a man of the name of Bracken asking him to subscribe towards the publication of a book relating to the treatment of horses.[46] This circular, as announced in the document itself, was being issued to all the postmasters in the kingdom; and it was in his capacity of postmaster of Bath that Allen received it. It further announced that answers should be sent under cover to the postmistress of Lancaster, the reason given being that they would thus escape postage.

Other malpractices were less easy of detection. All the claims, before they were passed, came under Allen's personal inspection; and to determine whether these were fraudulent or not needed no special aptitude. But whether at some distant part of the country two or more postmasters were in collusion, or whether without collusion they were bringing to account less postage than they collected, were questions the solution of which demanded qualifications of a different order. As the result of reflection or observation, or more probably of both combined, Allen laid down for his own guidance certain propositions as simple as they were no doubt sound. Of these one was that the correspondence passing between two given places, far from being liable to violent fluctuations, might be relied on to maintain a nearly uniform level. It is certain that in our own days, when locomotion is easy and the movements of large parts of the population are influenced by the weather and other considerations, the principle which this proposition embodies would not hold good; but in the earlier half of the eighteenth century Allen regarded it, and probably not without reason, as a safe guide. When, therefore, the correspondence passing between two places during a certain period had once been ascertained, he adopted this as a standard, and any variation of the amount immediately excited his suspicions. "At Christchurch and Ringwood," he writes, "fully inform yourself why the letters which formerly were sent between those places and Salisbury are now almost entirely sunk." At York, during the quarter ending Midsummer 1734, the postage on bye-letters amounted to £165, as against £176 during the corresponding quarter of the previous year. This he affirms must proceed, not from "deadness in trade," but from "some mismanagement in the office." Between Appleby and Brough the letters passing in December were fifteen, whereas in the two preceding months they had been only three. "Let me know at once," he writes, "the cause of the difference."

Another proposition which Allen established as a rule of conduct was that between two trading towns in the same neighbourhood there must almost of necessity be correspondence. He noticed with surprise that between Stone and Coventry, according to the vouchers sent him, not a single letter had passed during a whole quarter. "I will not say it is impossible," he writes to the surveyor, "that no letters should during this time pass between such trading places, but during your stay at Stone I must in a particular manner desire you will examine whether you receive none."

A third proposition was that there could not be what, if it be not a contradiction in terms, we will call a one-sided correspondence. He regarded it as an absolute certainty, amounting almost to an axiom, that whatever number of letters a town might receive, it would send the same or nearly the same number in reply. If, therefore, as between two towns, he found from his vouchers that one was sending to the other more letters than the other sent in return, he immediately concluded that something was wrong. It is interesting to note how his views on this point were confirmed by experience. During the year 1732 the postage on letters sent from Nottingham to Newark amounted to £25, whereas on those sent from Newark to Nottingham it amounted to only £13. Surely, writes Allen, the amounts should be nearly equal. Ascertain whether this comes "from faults, errors, or a real deadness in the correspondence," and to enable him to do this the surveyor was to take the Newark office under his care for a week or a fortnight. Here Allen speaks with confidence indeed, and yet as though some doubt might exist; but a few years later there is no doubt at all. "In the Chipping Norton vouchers," he writes, "another remarkable oddness is that the letters received by that deputy appear to be double the number sent from that office, which is not only different from any other well-managed office, but 'tis out of all rules of proportion with respect to correspondence." And again, "The receipt of Chipping Norton's letters are still double the number of what Mr. Mackerness in his vouchers enters as sent from his stage. I can't conceive how 'tis possible for this difference to arise where an office is justly managed. Fully examine into the cause of it."

But there were other irregularities which, as being further removed from observation, were still more difficult to check. Between Worcester and Bewdley there had been great delay. "The account sent me," writes Allen, "is that, tho' both these deputys are paid for riding their whole stages, by a private arrangement between themselves they exchange the mails at an alehouse on the road, and neither of them will ride beyond that place, tho' one of them should happen to arrive there several hours before the other can reach it." The postmaster of Lynn, in Norfolk, who was paid by Allen to keep a check upon other postmasters in the neighbourhood, calls his attention to their remissness in delivering letters. Sometimes, he states, they keep letters several days. On this account letters that would otherwise go by post are sent by friend or carrier. "I am perfectly ashamed," he adds, and when I remonstrate and "set forth the complaints of our gentlemen," the postmasters plead that they are not paid for delivery, "and therefore think themselves not obliged to send out their letters even to persons inhabiting within their own towns."

The post-boys were a constant source of trouble. "By the enclosed letter from Mr. Floyer of Worcester," Allen writes to his surveyor, "you will find that the post-boys on the cross-road convey letters between that city and Bristol by exchanging them from one hand to another without ever suffering them to be put into the mayl or baggs. Pray thank Mr. Floyer for his letter, diligently search the boys, and make whatever other inspection you find to be necessary. Mr. Lumley by the last post writ me that at Exeter he had made another new and great discovery of this kind, having found nineteen letters on the Oakhampton rider." "At Plymouth," he writes on another occasion, "formerly there was a particular house where the post-boys frequently met to exchange their letters, which they collected throughout the country from Exon to Truro. Inquire if this is still going on, and, if so, endeavour to detect them." On the cross-road between Bristol and Tiverton "several of the letters have been actually taken out of the baggs and delivered in some of the trading towns by the post-boys instead of the proper officers. This could not be if, according to instructions, these bags were always chained and sealed." At Wells, in Somersetshire, the postmaster has deprived the Bristol riding-boys of their perquisite of 1d. a letter "for dropping of letters" at the towns and villages through which they pass; and as to his own boys, he allows them no wages. This "must drive those unhappy boys to almost a necessity to rob the mails for their subsistence." "Then proceed to Rawcliff, in Yorkshire, where Mr. Carrack, the deputy of that place, will tell you that the riders of the branch between Doncaster and Hull embezzle great numbers of the bye-letters. Take his assistance to detect and then punish those fellows."

Heretofore we have spoken only of the difficulties with which Allen had to contend in dealing with persons more or less under his own control. But he had troubles from without as well as within. "Everywhere," he writes, "endeavour to inform yourself of and suppress all illegal conveyance of letters." "At Birmingham," he writes again, "endeavour to detect the carriers who, I am told, in the most open manner convey letters from that place to all the trading towns in that country." "Use your utmost vigilance to suppress the illegal collection of letters which, I am informed, is now carried on by one Twopotts and other persons, to the injury of the revenue, between Derby and Nottingham." Between Cowes and Southampton the illegal conveyance of letters "is now such a custom that we have seldom any go in the bag." "At every stage which you pass through cause to be fixed to the most public places some of the printed advertizements against the carriers and wherrymen, and take every other reasonable methode to surprize all private, illegal, conveyances of letters, and always have a particular regard of the followers employed in the dispersing of news from the country presses." This last injunction is best explained by another given a year or two later. A printer at Northampton was employing a large number of persons ostensibly to disperse newspapers, but really, as Allen affirmed, to collect letters. These persons, he wrote, no longer confine their operations to short distances, but "by meeting at the extremity of their divisions the servants of other printers exchange their letters." "Pray, therefore," he adds, "wherever country presses are erected, do your best to suppress this evil."

Allen when dealing with the posts displayed a degree of self-reliance which was hardly to be expected from one of his modest and retiring disposition. We will give an instance, and with the less hesitation because it will serve to shew his general way of transacting business. In 1736 the Duke of Devonshire, who had been spending the summer at Chatsworth, was much struck with the length of time which letters took to pass between Chesterfield and Manchester, and he begged the postmasters-general to apply a remedy. These two towns are about forty-six miles apart, and in 1736 there was no post between them. Not very long before, indeed, letters from one to the other would have had to pass through London, and even now they were taking a circuitous course by Ferribridge, Doncaster, and Rotherham. The Duke's application was referred to Allen; and Allen, without waiting to consult the local surveyor, proceeded at once to give his instructions. Between Manchester and Chesterfield there should certainly be a post; but this would not be enough. Derby must also share the benefit; and this could not be compassed without erecting a stage between that town and Nottingham, Nottingham being already in direct communication with Chesterfield. Lincolnshire must also be considered. True, there was a post from Nottingham to Newark; but between Newark and Lincoln, though only about seventeen miles apart, there was no communication except through Grantham, nor between Newark and Horncastle and Boston except through Stilton. The letters, moreover, on reaching the Great North Road had to await the arrival of the London mail. Not only did Allen determine that all this must be altered, but he sketched out the particular alterations that were to be made, and merely referred to the district surveyor with a view to ascertain what their effect upon the correspondence was likely to be.

The particulars which this officer furnished were curious. At Chesterfield, he reported, not a letter was delivered except on payment of a fee of 2d. or 3d., and sometimes even of 4d., over and above the postage. On each letter sent to the post it was the custom to pay 1d. The entire district, including not Chesterfield alone, but Sheffield, Nottingham, and Mansfield, was doing a very considerable trade in Manchester wares; but the letters which passed between these towns and Manchester were chiefly sent with the goods by carrier. Of post letters there were few, the postage for a whole year amounting to only £23. The correspondence might possibly increase by as much as one-third or £7:13:4 a year, if a post were put on between Manchester and Chesterfield; but this was doubtful, and the annual cost, owing partly to the badness of the road, would be £80. Between Derby and Nottingham a new stage could not be erected for less than £26. Nor could the Lincolnshire posts be improved as desired for less than £102, making altogether an increased annual charge of £208; and there was no probability of this increase of cost being covered, or nearly covered, by increase of correspondence. Allen was not to be deterred by any such consideration. The whole of the alterations were carried into effect; the postmasters-general received from the Duke a warm expression of thanks for their admirable arrangements; and Allen, who had devised them, and at whose expense they were made, did not so much as appear in the transaction.

In striking contrast with Allen's proceedings were those of the Post Office in the few instances in which it acted independently. Allen's energy, far from communicating itself to Lombard Street, appears to have extinguished what little energy had existed there before. Why should the postmasters-general exert themselves to do that which was done better and without expense to the Crown by another? And yet there were some, though rare, occasions on which independent action was called for. One such occasion presented itself in 1733, and it serves to shew how wanting the Post Office was in the local knowledge which Allen possessed in so remarkable a degree. Application had been made for a post to Aylsham in Norfolk. Among those who had lent their influence in support of the application was Lord Lovell, who had just been appointed postmaster-general in conjunction with Carteret, but who had not yet entered upon his duties; and Carteret, to oblige his new colleague, sent an officer specially from London with a view to facilitate arrangements. This officer, John Day by name, was furnished with written instructions. He was to proceed to Norwich, and there ascertain certain facts, any one of which could have been supplied by Allen at Bath without rising from his chair in Lilliput Alley. These were—how far Aylsham was from Norwich; whether the road between the two towns was a good or a bad one; whether under existing arrangements Aylsham ever received any letters, and, if so, how and whence; and particularly—an instruction which could hardly have been given except under the belief that Aylsham was south and not north of Norwich—whether the setting up of a post between the two towns would be a "hindrance to the grand mail betwixt Norwich and London." Day, having described the position of Aylsham, appears to have considered it unnecessary to give this last piece of information; but he told as news, which perhaps it was, that the London mail left Norwich on Mondays and Wednesdays at midnight, and on Saturdays at four in the afternoon.

Even where local knowledge was not wanting, the lack of funds which they could dispense at discretion placed the postmasters-general as compared with Allen at a serious disadvantage. We have seen how Allen dealt with the application from Chatsworth. Not many years later it devolved upon the postmasters-general to deal with a somewhat similar one from Kimbolton; and it is interesting to note the difference of procedure. From Kimbolton and St. Neots the course of post had been through Biggleswade and Hitchin, and in 1758 the inhabitants of the counties of Huntingdon and Cambridgeshire petitioned that it should be through Caxton. The effect of the alteration would be that letters for the two first-mentioned towns coming from the north or from Norfolk and Suffolk would, regularly three times a week, be brought to the towns themselves, and not, as had hitherto been the case, be left at Huntingdon, to be forwarded thence as opportunity offered by carriers and market people. St. Neots had a further interest in the matter. A considerable corn-market was held there on Thursdays; and the dealers complained that, leaving as the post did at twelve mid-day, they had no time to write their letters, whereas, by way of Caxton, it need not leave until five in the afternoon. On the score of convenience the change had everything to recommend it; but there was one drawback. To carry it into effect would involve a cost of £25; and this, the postmasters-general expressed their apprehension, the Treasury would not feel justified in incurring, as the increase of expense might be only partially covered by the increase of correspondence. Whether the Treasury consent was given or withheld we know not; but the mere fact that such an apprehension should have been expressed, and that the convenience of towns and extensive districts should have been made to depend upon the paltry consideration of a few pounds, goes far to shew that the Post Office, without the aid of private enterprise, would have made but little progress.

Allen's contract expired every seven years. In order to obtain a renewal of it he did not, according to a practice not uncommon with reformers, stoop to the pretence that he was on the point of introducing some important measure, which would be lost to the country unless his services were retained. On the contrary, he treated it as a pure business matter, and each time offered higher terms. Thus, in 1741, which was the first year of a new septennial period, he guaranteed the country letters to produce £17,500; in 1748 he guaranteed them to produce £18,000; and in 1755, £18,500. This being the class of letters of which it had been and continued to be predicted that with the extension of cross-posts the number must diminish, the postmasters-general regarded the advance as not unhandsome.

But, in consideration of his contract being renewed, there was another and far more important condition, which Allen undertook to perform. This was to convert tri-weekly posts into posts six days a week, and to take the whole expense upon himself. Accordingly, in 1741, the post began to run every day of the week except Sunday between London and Bristol, between London and Norwich, and between London and Yarmouth; and of course all the intervening towns participated in the benefit. In 1748 a further instalment followed. This time it was the Midlands and the west of England that were to be benefited; and on and after Monday the 26th of December the post went on the three days on which it had not gone hitherto to Birmingham, through Oxford, and to Exeter through Bristol. In 1755, the beginning of another septennial period, the six-day service was widely extended. Leicester, Derby, and Nottingham, Shrewsbury and Chester, Warrington, Liverpool, and Manchester were among the towns which were now to receive letters from London on every day of the week except Sunday. From Liverpool and Manchester the cross-post service to almost every part of the kingdom was at the same time improved. At the close of the nineteenth century, postridden as some of us think ourselves to be, we may find it sometimes difficult to believe that less than 150 years ago there was not a town in the kingdom which received a post from London on more than alternate days.

And yet Allen's activity, untiring as it was, went only a short way to regain for the Post Office the popularity it had lost. Various causes had contributed to this result. The chief of them, however, as it was the earliest in point of time, was of itself enough and more than enough to account for the distrust and hostility with which the Post Office appears to have been regarded towards the middle of the last century. As early as 1735 members of Parliament had begun to complain that their letters bore evident signs of having been opened at the Post Office, alleging that such opening had been frequent and was become matter of common notoriety; but it was not until six years later, in the course of inquiries which were being made into the conduct of Sir Robert Walpole during the last ten years of his administration, that the state of the case became fully known. It then transpired that in the Post Office there was a private office, an office independent of the postmasters-general and under the immediate direction of the Secretary of State, which was expressly maintained for the purpose of opening and inspecting letters. It was pretended, indeed, that these operations were confined to foreign letters, but, as a matter of fact, there was no such restriction. The office appears to have been established in 1718, and its cost, which was defrayed out of the secret service money, had since increased more than tenfold, and now reached the prodigious sum of £4700 a year. The establishment, exclusive of a door-keeper, consisted of nine persons, with salaries ranging from £200 to £1000; the head of the office or "Chief

Decypherer," as he was called, being Dr. Willes, Dean of Lincoln. It was in June 1742 that these shameful facts became known, through the report of a committee of the House of Commons; and, in the August following, Willes was gazetted Bishop of St. Davids.

To ourselves it may seem strange that the State monopoly of letters should have survived so terrible a revelation. It must be remembered, however, that in the middle of the last century the Post Office, owing mainly to the heavy charges it levied, had hardly become matter of general concern; that public opinion, as we now understand it, was only beginning to exist; and, above all, that the very conditions under which Post Office work was done precluded the idea of privacy. These conditions were absolutely inconsistent with the sanctity which now surrounds a letter. Letters were divided into two classes,—single and double; and to determine whether a letter was the one or the other demanded a close scrutiny, a scrutiny such as could not be exercised except by the strongest light that candles could give. In 1719 it had been laid down that a letter, however small, was to be charged as a double one if two or more persons joined in writing it. How could it be ascertained that the whole of a letter was in one and the same handwriting except by prying? Even the law itself, by the meagre protection it vouchsafed to letters, discouraged the idea of sanctity. For an offence of the pettiest kind, as for instance for stealing a pocket-handkerchief in a dwelling-house, the penalty was death. For opening or embezzling a letter the highest penalty which the law allowed was a fine of £20. It is significant of the change which has since taken place in the public sentiment that while in the case of almost every other description of offence the penalty has been enormously reduced, in the case of opening and embezzling letters it has been enormously increased.

Horace Walpole, writing more than twenty-five years later, never tired of mentioning the elaborate precautions he had taken to secure his correspondence against inspection. "I shall send this letter by the coach," he says, "as it is rather free-spoken and Sandwich[47] may be prying." "I always say less than I could, because I consider how many post-house ordeals a letter must pass"; and similar observations occur in a hundred different places. All this was sheer nonsense. It tickled the exquisite vanity of the man to affect to believe that his correspondence was of sufficient importance to attract the attention of the State. And yet truth compels us to admit that the infamous practice which the committee exposed did not cease with the exposure. The Treasury, while grudging every 6d. expended on the posts, continued regularly to remit more than £4000 a year for the maintenance of their inquisitors in Lombard Street; and it was not until George the Third had sat some years on the throne, probably under the Rockingham administration, that the corps was finally disbanded.

Apart from the grave cause of offence we have mentioned, it is a curious fact that during the last eighteen or twenty years of George the Second's reign hardly anything occurred in which the Post Office was concerned that did not in one way or another cause dissatisfaction to some section of the community. The Post Office, no doubt, was often to blame, sometimes deeply so; but even where this was not the case, where no blame attached either to itself or to any other office or person, it in no single instance, so far as we are aware, escaped a certain amount of obloquy.

This unfortunate result first shews itself in the case of the Falmouth and Lisbon packets. During the war with Spain it had only been necessary, as a defence against some Spanish privateers which infested the Channel, to provide the Dover and Harwich packets with arms and to make a small addition to their complement of men; but in 1744, when Spain was joined by France, a good deal more had to be done. The Dover and Calais packets, after the six months' grace allowed by the treaty of Utrecht, were taken off; the packets to the West Indies which had been discontinued since 1711 were revived; and the Falmouth and Lisbon packets were put on the same footing as during the last war. This the merchants trading with Portugal, an important body representing forty-eight firms, protested was not enough. The packets, they argued, afforded the only available means for remitting gold to Lisbon in exchange for commodities, and should, therefore, be of at least 300 tons and carry 100 men. It was true that this would be in excess by about seventy tons and forty men of what was provided during the last war; but the fact that during the last war some of the packets fell into the hands of privateers was of itself a proof that they were not of force and burthen sufficient. Besides, we had then an army in Spain, and the number of soldiers and passengers passing to and fro made fewer sailors necessary. Moved by these arguments, the Duke of Newcastle decided to comply with the merchants' request; but Pelham, on learning that the building and equipment alone would cost £34,800, revoked the Duke's decision. His Majesty's opinion he declared to be that the main object of a packet was to carry letters, and that for the carriage of letters light and swift vessels were the fittest. This, it will be remembered, was the opinion which had been expressed by William the Third more than fifty years before, and events had proved its soundness. Nevertheless, the merchants were highly displeased; and, of course, at that time they were no more able than they are now to distinguish between a refusal which originated with the Post Office and one that was imposed upon it by superior authority.

But the merchants—and here we speak not of those alone who traded with Portugal—had other and more serious cause of complaint. Their foreign letters were not delivered until twelve o'clock in the day, and, if a mail arrived by as much as a few minutes after twelve, it was not at the earliest delivered until the same hour on the following day. And if on this day a second mail chanced to arrive shortly before noon, the letters by the first mail were kept back so as to be delivered with those of the second in the evening. Thus, foreign letters received at the Post Office in Lombard Street a few minutes after mid-day on Saturday might not be delivered even in Lombard Street itself until the evening of Monday. To make matters worse, the foreign ministers residing in London had their letters delivered soon after the mail arrived, so that any persons whom these ministers might please to favour enjoyed an undue advantage.

The merchants now urged that this might be altered. Did not Sir Harry Furness, they asked, during the last war obtain permission to have his letters delivered immediately after the arrival of a mail? And was not this permission afterwards revoked on the ground that it had led to abuse? Matters were better managed abroad. At Amsterdam, for instance, if a mail arrived as late as nine o'clock in the evening, the letters were delivered to those who might call for them at any time before midnight, or else sent out for delivery early the next morning. At Rotterdam—this also was urged as an instance of better management—the English letters were never delivered till twelve hours after the mail had arrived, about which time those which had come by the same mail would be in course of delivery at Amsterdam. Equality of treatment was thus secured, and neither city had priority of intelligence. At Hamburg, again, as soon as a mail arrived—if in the day, a notice to that effect was fixed up at the Post Office and at the Exchange, the letters being delivered about three hours later; and if at night, the clerks were called out of bed, so that the letters might be sorted and ready for delivery the first thing in the morning. Sundays, moreover, were not excepted. As regards foreign gazettes, too, these all over Europe were delivered within a quarter of an hour after their arrival; yet in London the merchants had to wait for them many hours. And this was all the more hard to bear because the clerks in the Post Office, to whom gazettes were addressed, received them at once and communicated the contents to their friends. What could be more calculated to promote fraudulent insurance, one-sided bargains, and a system of overreaching generally? Such was the representation made by the merchants; and they concluded by asking that henceforth, except on Sundays, no longer interval should be allowed to elapse between the arrival and delivery of a foreign mail than was absolutely necessary for the purpose of sorting. The postmasters-general had no choice but to refuse the request. To have granted it would have defeated the object with which the Treasury were maintaining an office of their own within the Post Office building.

About this time, three or four years short of the middle of the century, the Post Office got into disgrace with travellers. Under the provisions of the numerous Turnpike Acts which had recently passed, the trustees of the roads were to measure distances and to erect milestones; and on these provisions being carried into effect the statute mile proved to be shorter, much shorter, than the reputed or Post Office mile.[48] So great indeed was the difference that the Post Office may be said to have been almost ridiculously out of its reckoning. Thus, from London to Berwick-upon-Tweed the distance, according to Post Office computation, was 262 miles; according to measurement, it proved to be 339 miles. To Holyhead the actual distance proved to be 269 miles; the Post Office had computed it at 208 miles. To Manchester the distance, according to the Post Office, was 137 miles; the actual distance was 165. Bristol, which proved to be 115 miles from London, had been reckoned as 94; Birmingham as 89 instead of 116; Warwick as 67 instead of 84; and so it had been throughout the kingdom. In every case the Post Office mile proved to be an unduly long one; and of course, as soon as milestones were erected authoritatively recording the statute miles, the postmasters charged accordingly. This change excited many murmurs. The traveller to Warwick who, at the rate of 3d. a mile, exclusive of a guide, had hitherto paid for the use of a horse 16s. 9d., had now to pay 21s. To Birmingham he had now to pay 29s. instead of 22s. 3d.; to Bristol, 28s. 9d. instead of 23s. 6d.; and so on.

The King's messengers fought hardest against the innovation, but without success. Finding the expense of their journeys to Berwick and Holyhead appreciably increased, they appealed to the Treasury for redress, and the Treasury invited the postmasters-general to explain under what authority they had raised their charges. The postmasters-general replied, as they had replied scores of times before on occasions of complaint from the public, that they had really nothing to do with the matter; that it was the postmasters who made the charges; and that in the opinion of the Attorney-General these officers were clearly entitled to be paid according to the new measurements. It had been expressly provided by Act of Parliament that all persons riding post should pay after the rate of 3d. for every British mile, and the British mile was a known statute measure common to all His Majesty's dominions. The Treasury were not satisfied, and insisted that the King's messengers should be charged according to the old scale. But this, as the postmasters-general pointed out, was not feasible, the Act of Parliament by which they were governed making no exception in favour of particular persons, but on the contrary enacting that all persons without distinction should pay at the rate of 3d. a mile.

At the headquarters in Lombard Street it was long feared that, on finding that the reputed mile exceeded the statute mile, those postmasters whose remuneration had been fixed according to the distance over which they carried the mails would claim an increased mileage allowance; but this, to their credit be it said, they never did. Such forbearance, however, had one ill effect. It tended to perpetuate error. For many years afterwards two sets of distances remained in vogue, the one right and the other wrong; the new set applicable to travellers, and the old set to mails and to expresses sent on the service of the State.[49]

The feeling against the Post Office, which had long been gathering force, now displayed itself in a remarkable manner. It had been the constant and uniform practice ever since the Post Office was established to charge letters containing patterns or samples with double postage. To this the merchants now demurred. They did not deny that such letters if weighing as much as an ounce should be charged as for an ounce weight; but they contended that if weighing less than an ounce they should be charged as single and not double letters. This contention was founded on the wording of the Act of Anne, which, after prescribing the postage which "every single letter or piece of paper" not being of the weight of one ounce was to pay, enacted that "a double letter" should pay twice that amount. Was a letter to be charged double because it had in it any enclosure—a sample of grain, for instance, or a pattern of cloth or of silk? or to constitute a double letter must not the enclosure be of paper?

This question the merchants now resolved to try; and accordingly at Bristol, at Manchester, and at Cirencester proceedings were commenced against the local postmasters for demanding and receiving more than the legal postage. It affords striking evidence of the widespread dissatisfaction then existing that in 1753 a practice as old as the Post Office itself should have been challenged for the first time, still more that it should have been challenged at three separate places, distant from one another, simultaneously. The action against the postmaster of Cirencester came on first. It was tried at the Gloucester Assizes before a special jury, when a special verdict was found upon the words of the statute, whether a letter containing a pattern or sample and not being of the weight of one ounce ought to pay double or single postage. The postmasters-general, anxious to avoid a multiplicity of suits, now opened communications with the merchants of Bristol and Manchester. Would it not be well that their suits should be abandoned? One special verdict would serve as well as a hundred such verdicts would do to settle the point of law between the Crown and the subject. Having succeeded in one county, what more could they expect in another? Or what advantage would follow that had not been already secured? These overtures came too late. The merchants were determined to fight to the bitter end. The suits came on both at Bristol and at Manchester; and at each of those places a special verdict was given in almost identical terms with that which had been returned at Gloucester.

Meanwhile the attorneys both in London and the country had passed resolutions to the effect that, if the point of law were decided in the merchants' favour, they would refuse to pay double postage on letters containing writs. The postmasters-general became alarmed. Single instead of double postage on letters containing writs as well as patterns and samples meant, according to the most moderate computation, a reduction of the Post Office revenue by £10,000 or £12,000 a year. This was a serious reduction, and how to prevent it was the question to which the postmasters-general now addressed themselves. It is characteristic of the time that the first expedient they devised with this object was simply to refuse to carry any more letters containing patterns and samples unless the senders of them should agree beforehand to pay double postage. They argued that, in view of the importance to the merchant to have his letters carried, any unwillingness on his part to enter into such an agreement would be easily overcome. A notice to give effect to their intention was already prepared; but before issuing it they took the precaution to consult the Attorney-General. His advice to them was that, admirable as the expedient might be, it was distinctly illegal. Should they, then, bring one of the special verdicts on to be argued in Westminster Hall and abide by the judicial decision? To this the Attorney-General could raise no objection, but he warned them that the decision was pretty sure to be against the Crown. Driven thus into a corner, the postmasters-general adopted a most questionable course. They advocated the passing of an Act which should declare a letter containing any enclosure, even though not of paper and not weighing as much as an ounce, to be a double letter; and this advice was followed. In a bill then before Parliament, having for its object to prevent the fraudulent removal of tobacco, a clause was inserted which effectually prevented the merchants from sending their patterns or samples and the lawyers their writs for single postage.[50]

It would be difficult to conceive a more irritating course. No doubt there was precedent for it. Early in the reign of George the First an Act had been passed enacting that bills of exchange written on the same piece of paper as a letter, and also letters written on the same piece of paper and addressed to different persons, should be charged as distinct letters: and, possibly enough, it might have been difficult to explain why a bill of exchange should pay double postage and not a pattern or a writ. It is also true that the fact of three several judges and three several juries in distant parts of the kingdom having been unable to agree as to the intent and meaning of a statute implied a real doubt. And yet it can hardly be denied that to solve that doubt by the brute force of an Act of Parliament, instead of bringing one of the special verdicts before the Courts to be argued, was a most provoking step. Nor would it have been calculated to appease the merchants if they had known, as the postmasters-general knew, that the entire rates of postage, as they then existed, rested on no legal sanction. The existing rates were imposed by the Act of Anne; and that Act imposed them for a period of thirty-two years, a period which had now expired, and after which it was expressly provided that the former and lower rates were to revive. It is true that early in the reign of George the First a further Act had passed, making perpetual the Post Office contribution of £700 a week to the Exchequer; but by a clumsiness of legislation, which is not unknown even in our own day, the latter Act, while making perpetual both the contribution and the power to levy it, had omitted to re-enact the rates out of which the contribution was to be paid. Virtually, therefore, these rates had lapsed through effluxion of time.

And what during the last forty or fifty years had the Post Office done— done, that is, independently of Allen—to promote the public convenience or to make amends for so much that had given offence? It had done four things, and, so far as we are aware, four things only. It had introduced the contrivance, with which we are all familiar, of external apertures in Post Offices, so that letters could be posted from the outside. It had brought the system of expresses up to a standard which, compared with what it was at the beginning of the century, might perhaps be considered high. It had, indirectly, been the means of eliciting from the Courts of Law an important decision. And it had accelerated the course of post between London and Edinburgh. In 1758 the time which the mail took to accomplish the distance was, at the instance of the royal boroughs, reduced between London and Edinburgh from 87 hours to 82, and between Edinburgh and London from 131 hours to 85.

The date at which apertures on the outside of Post Offices were first introduced is unknown to us even approximately. All we can do is to fix two distant dates at one of which the contrivance existed, and at the other it existed not. On the 3rd of November 1712 Oxford, the Lord Treasurer, received an anonymous letter, and, being anxious to discover the writer, he invoked the assistance of the postmasters-general with a view to ascertain where and by whom it had been posted. Any such inquiry at the present time would be absolutely futile. One hundred and eighty years ago the postmasters-general, after an interval of twenty-four hours, were able to reply not only that the letter had been posted "at the receiving office of Mrs.

Sandys, a threadshop two doors within Blackfryars Gateway," but that it had been posted "by a youth of about seventeen years old, in a whitish suit of cloathes, who was without a hat." It is difficult to believe that apertures can have existed then, and that the letter was not posted inside the office. That in 1757 the contrivance had come into existence, though possibly in a rude form, is beyond question. In that year an unfortunate woman was put on her trial for stealing a letter, and the sender was called upon to prove the posting. "On Tuesday the 7th of December 1756," he said, "I put this letter into the Post Office at the house of Mrs. Jeffreys at Bloomsbury, at about nine o'clock at night.... There is a window and a slip to put it into a little box from out of the street. I was not in the house. It is a very narrow box, and I was afraid my letter was gone down to the ground.[51] I asked Mrs. Jeffreys if my letter was safe after I had dropped it into the slip. She said your letter is safe and gone into the box." If the value of a contrivance depended upon the amount of ingenuity displayed in devising it, these apertures would be hardly deserving of mention; but in view of the convenience they afford, this short notice of them may not perhaps be considered out of place.

The Rebellion of 1745, while disarranging the posts, brought into vogue the system of expresses; and this system once established was not long in extending itself. An express cost 3d. a mile, and, no doubt, travelled faster than at the beginning of the century. The roads had since been improved; and it may well be believed that the postmasters, as their custom increased, kept better horses. It was probably the speed of the express as compared with the tardiness of the post which induced the wealthy, about the middle of the last century, largely to employ this mode of conveyance for their letters. It had indeed one drawback, a drawback such as in our own time has attended the use of telegrams. It was apt to excite alarm. "Let me," writes the good-natured Charles Townshend to his sister-in-law, Lady Ferrers, under date September 1759—"Let me now desire you to conclude whenever you receive an express that it brings you good news, for otherwise I shall be obliged to defer one day sending you any such account if it should not come to me on a post day, least the express should alarm you. I should not chuse to detain you one minute from the news I know your heart beats for, and yet I should not chuse to frighten you by the sudden manner of its arrival, for which reason I desire you will remember to receive whatsoever express I send with confidence and as a friend."

But the purpose for which an express might be employed was jealously restricted. A man might employ an express to carry a letter; but woe betide him if he employed the same agency for the purpose of disseminating news. The licensed carriers at Cambridge had recently been prosecuted and the postmasters on the Great West Road taken severely to task for doing this very thing. What are we to think of the intolerable state of bondage in which men were content to live when even the gentle Allen could give the following instruction? "At every stage," he writes to one of his surveyors, "you must forbid the deputies to send any express except to the General Post Office in London, unless it be for His Majesty's immediate service; and all other intelligence must be conveyed either by the common post or particular messenger."

In the middle of the last century, and for about thirty years before and after, the mails were being continually stopped and robbed by highwaymen. The reward which the Post Office offered on these occasions for the apprehension of the robber was invariably £200, this being in addition to the reward of £40 prescribed by Act of Parliament; and if the robbery took place within five miles of London, there was a third reward of £100 by proclamation. Numerous and diverse as the robberies[52] were, there is only one of which we propose to speak; and in this case an exception may well be made on account of the important decision which it was the means of evoking from the Courts. A highwayman had stopped the Worcester mail at Shepherd's Bush and rifled it of its contents. Finding himself in possession of a large number of Bank of England notes he adopted a novel expedient for disposing of them. He hired a chaise and four and proceeded along the Great North Road as far as Caxton, passing the notes as he went; and in order to give himself a wider field of operations he took the precaution of going one way and returning another. To Caxton he went through Barnet, Hatfield, Stevenage, and Bugden, and he returned by way of Royston, Ware, and Enfield. Except at Barnet, which was probably thought to be dangerously near to London, there was hardly a postmaster along the whole line of road who had not one or more of the notes passed upon him. The question now arose who was to bear the loss,—the person by whom the notes had been sent by post or the postmasters who had changed them into cash. At the present time the law on the subject is so well ascertained that no doubt could exist as to the answer; but such was not then the case. In order to try the point, it was arranged that the notes should be stopped, and that the sender of them should bring an action against the Bank of England to recover their value. The trial came on before the King's Bench in 1758, and, after learned pleadings on both sides, the Lord Chief Justice pronounced the decision of the Court. This was that any person paying a valuable consideration for a bank note to bearer in a fair course of business is unquestionably entitled to recover the money from the Bank.

An important legal decision, with which the Post Office had only the remotest concern, an improved system of expresses following as a natural consequence from circumstances over which the Post Office had no control, a simple contrivance to facilitate the posting of letters, and an acceleration of the mail between London and Edinburgh—this as the record of forty or fifty years' progress is assuredly meagre enough; and yet we are not aware of any omission. The plain truth is that during these years, except in the matter of bye and cross-post letters, the Post Office had retrograded rather than advanced. The rates of postage were higher now than at the beginning of the century. More, probably, than one-half of the public Acts of Parliament which passed during the reigns of the first two Georges were Acts for repairing and widening the roads. The roads had kept steadily improving; and the posts had failed to keep pace with them. While travellers travelled faster than in the reign of Queen Anne, letters were still being conveyed at a speed not exceeding five miles an hour. The friendly relations which had existed between the postmasters-general and the merchants existed no longer. These had been replaced by feelings of estrangement and animosity. Under Cotton and Frankland and under Frankland and Evelyn the Post Office enjoyed a reputation for personal integrity; but even this claim to distinction had now disappeared. Barbutt, the secretary, had recently retired under a cloud. Bell, the comptroller of the inland office, had been arrested on a charge of fraud.[53] Denzil Onslow, the receiver-general, had been declared a defaulter to the amount of £10,000; and Stone, Onslow's successor, after two or three years' tenure of the appointment, had died in debt to the Crown. The Post Office, when George the Third ascended the throne, was thoroughly discredited, and, despite Allen's exertions, men were beginning to ask themselves, Why cumbereth it the ground?

Allen died in 1764, leaving behind him a name which is still venerated, and justly venerated, in the city of Bath. For many years before his death he is reputed to have made out of his contract with the Post Office not less than £12,000 a year; and the greater part of this noble fortune he spent in acts of benevolence. As early as 1735 riches must have come pouring in upon him, for in that year he built for himself the stately house of Prior Park, not indeed for ostentation's sake, but in order to prove that the stone dug from his quarries on Combe Down was not the sorry stuff which interested persons in London had represented it to be. That house still stands; but, as was said at the time—and the statement holds good to this day—"his charity is seen further than his house, though it stands on a hill, aye, and brings him more honour too." In 1742 Allen served as Mayor of Bath; and in 1745, the year of the Rebellion, he raised a company of volunteers, which he clothed at his own cost. At Prior Park he dispensed a more than decent hospitality, numbering among his guests Pitt, Pope, and Fielding, Charles Yorke, and Warburton. Fielding has immortalised Allen's character but not his name in the person of Squire Allworthy; and Pope has immortalised both his name and his character in the lines—

> Let humble Allen, with an awkward shame,
> Do good by stealth and blush to find it fame.

Among Post Office reformers Allen stands absolutely alone in one particular. His connection with the Post Office, long as it endured, was not abruptly terminated. This we attribute partly to a natural sweetness of disposition, which provoked no enemies, and still more to that which on the part of reformers is the rarest of virtues, an entire abnegation of self. So long as a thing which he thought desirable was done, he cared not that others received the credit.[54]

CHAPTER XI
LEGISLATION AND LITIGATION 1764-1782

Brighter days were in store for the Post Office, but not yet. Meanwhile the clouds grew darker and darker. During the twenty years that followed Allen's death, partly as the result of ill-considered legislation and still more through the incompetence and helplessness of its rulers, the Post Office sank to a depth which, in England, probably no other public institution, or at all events none that still exists, has ever reached.

In 1764 and 1765 two Acts of Parliament were passed, one having for its object to prevent the abuses of franking, and the other to improve the posts. It would be hardly too much to say that both of these Acts had an exactly opposite effect to that which was intended. The first, far from preventing the abuses of franking, largely extended them; and the second imposed a deplorable restriction, a restriction for which any little advantages conferred at the same time afforded very inadequate compensation.

Under the Act of 1765, to take the later one first, the postage rates were reduced for short distances. Since 1711 the charge for carrying a single letter had been 3d. for eighty miles or under. Now it was to be 1d. for one stage and 2d. for two stages. For longer distances the charge was to remain unaltered. The speed of the post was raised from five to six miles an hour. Power was given to the postmasters-general to erect penny Post Offices in country towns; and—a provision which we have pronounced deplorable—the weight to be carried by the penny post was restricted to four ounces. Compensation for losses by the penny post had long ceased to be given. [55]

Such was the end of Dockwra's post as Dockwra had established it. With that eminent man it had been an object of the first importance that the penny post should carry up to one pound in weight; and now the weight was to be reduced to four ounces. And why? Because the penny post was little used for packets and parcels above four ounces? Exactly the contrary. It was because packets and parcels above four ounces were being largely sent by the penny post that the limit of weight was to be reduced.[56] These missives had been found a little inconvenient to manipulate and it was resolved, therefore, to exclude them. Such was the wretched policy of the time. Even in matters vitally affecting their own interests the public had as yet no voice and their wishes were not considered. On account of some trifling inconvenience, which a very little amount of ingenuity would have sufficed to overcome, the inhabitants of London and its suburbs were now deprived of accommodation which they had enjoyed uninterruptedly for eighty-five years.

In 1764 franking became for the first time the subject of Parliamentary enactment. To send and receive letters free of postage had been a privilege enjoyed by members of the two Houses of Parliament from the first establishment of the Post Office; but whereas it had hitherto been a concession granted by the Crown, it was now to be a right conferred by statute. The reason will be obvious. The revenue of the Post Office had recently been surrendered to the public during the life of the Sovereign, in exchange for a Civil List charged upon the Consolidated, or, as it was then called, the Aggregate Fund; and the Crown, having dispossessed itself of all property in the Post Office, was no longer competent to remit postage without the authority of Parliament. The Act which was now passed was designed to correct the abuses which experience had shewn to exist. The limits of weight and of time remained as before; that is to say, only letters not exceeding the weight of two ounces were to be franked, and these only during the session of Parliament and for forty days before and after. In other respects the conditions were slightly altered. Hitherto it had been enough, in the case of letters sent by a member, that he should sign his name on the outside; for the future not only was the outside to bear his signature, but the whole of the address was to be in his own handwriting. In the case of letters addressed to a member, none were to be exempt from postage unless directed to the place of his usual residence or to the place where he was actually residing, or, of course, to the House of Parliament. It had been hoped that these alterations of practice would check the abuses of franking. Vain expectation! No sooner had the concession been converted into a right than what little scruples existed before appear to have vanished, and franks were scattered broadcast over the country. Before eight years were over, the number of franks passing through the London office alone had nearly doubled, the postage from which they carried exemption being in 1765, the first year after the change, £34,734, and in 1772, £65,053; and this, be it observed, was no mere estimate, but the actual result as ascertained by the careful examination of each letter.

Another effect of the change of practice was to embroil the Post Office. The Post Office, in its efforts to protect itself against imposition, would charge letters when addressed to a member at a place where he was supposed not to be; and hence constant disputes and altercations.

Members, again, who were bankers or were engaged in trade insisted that letters addressed to them at their counting-houses, even though they did not reside there, should pass free. On these the Post Office claimed postage, and the members refused to pay it.

But it was in Ireland that the rage for franking broke out into the wildest excesses. In 1773 an inspector of franks was sent to several towns on the cross and bye roads, in order that he might ascertain and report to the postmasters-general the extent to which the abuse had grown. This officer visited nine towns altogether, and was absent from Dublin for sixty-three days, being at the rate of seven days at each town. At Waterford, during his stay there, 588 letters passed through the local Post Office purporting to be franked. The franks on only 354 of these were genuine; the rest were counterfeit. At Kilkenny there were 425 counterfeit franks to 510 that were genuine. At Clonmel, 526 counterfeit and 509 genuine. At Gowran, 212 counterfeit and 195 genuine; and so with the remaining towns. Altogether the number of letters with counterfeit franks was nearly as large as the number with genuine franks, and far exceeded all the other letters combined. However clear might be the evidence of fraud, and however conclusively it might be brought home to particular persons, it was of no use attempting to prosecute. Hear what Mr. Lees says on this point. Mr. Lees was Secretary to the Post Office in Ireland, and he had, under direction from Lord North, received instructions to take proceedings against a firm of solicitors in Londonderry who had been sending letters under forged franks. "A prosecution," wrote Mr. Lees, "will not be of the slightest avail. It has been tried over and over again, and, in the face of the clearest evidence, without success." "There is scarcely a magistrate to be found in Ireland who will take examinations on the Post Office laws; and certainly in no instance has this office prevailed in getting the bills of indictment found by a Grand Jury. This being so universally known, counterfeiting franks is drawn into such general practice that I believe there are very few merchants or attorneys' clerks throughout the kingdom who do not counterfeit in the name of one member or other. Nay, if I classed with them almost every little pretty Miss capable of joining her letters, I should not exaggerate the abuse." "As I have observed," he wrote further on in the same letter, "in every town of consequence throughout the kingdom the members resident, under their address, cover the correspondence of the principal merchants.... The postage arising on counterfeit covers alone amounts to more than a third of the revenue of this office."

Under the terms of the Franking Act newspapers were to go free which should bear a member's signature on the outside or which should be directed to a member at any place of which he had given notice in writing to the postmasters-general. This provision seriously affected the Post Office, though in a different way from the liberties which were being taken with letters. From the first establishment of the Post Office the six clerks of the roads had enjoyed the privilege of franking newspapers, and the emoluments derived from this source, originally insignificant, had been continually increasing. In 1764 they were certainly not less than £8000 a year, and may have been more. The Franking Act sapped this source of emolument. No sooner had that Act passed than the members served the Post Office with notice of the places to which they wished newspapers to be directed. These places did not in the first instance extend beyond the member's own residence and the residences of his constituents and friends; but after a while no such moderation was observed. The booksellers and printers, or news-agents as they would now be called, soon recognised the advantage it would be to them if they could get their customers' addresses put on the Post Office Register, and they experienced little difficulty in finding members who were ready to do them this service. There were four who were noted for their complaisance. These were Sir Robert Bernard, member for Westminster; Brass Crosby, member for Honiton and alderman for the City of London; Richard Whitworth, member for Stafford; and Richard Hiver.[57] These four members in little more than eighteen months served upon the Post Office no less than 744 separate notices. Altogether, at the close of the year 1772, there were 2024 such notices registered in Lombard Street, of which 765 were on behalf of constituents and friends, and 1259 on behalf of printers and booksellers.

As the natural result the clerks of the roads found their emoluments rapidly dwindling. Heretofore they had been, virtually, the great news-agents of the kingdom. Enjoying, in common with a few clerks at Whitehall, the exclusive privilege of sending newspapers through the post free, they had been exposed to little, if any, competition; but now that in the matter of postage the terms were equal, the advantage was all on the side of the private dealer. The private dealer procured his newspapers in the open market, whereas the clerks of the roads were required to procure them from a particular officer designated by the postmasters-general; and this officer was authorised not only to charge for the newspapers he supplied 1-1/2d. a dozen more than he gave for them, but to retain as his own perquisite one out of every twenty-five copies.

It may seem of little moment that, as the result of legislation, six persons more or less should find themselves in reduced circumstances. Such an event, unhappily, is not so rare as to call for special remark. But there was a good deal more than this in the present case. The profits which the clerks of the roads derived from the sale of newspapers had never been devoted to the exclusive use of the recipients. On the contrary, they were to a large extent common property. Out of these profits pensions were provided for Post Office servants who were past work; and from the same source inadequate salaries were raised to something like a decent maintenance. In additional salaries to brother officers and in pensions to officers who had retired, the clerks of the roads had in 1764 contributed as much as £6600; and even now, reduced as their profits were, they were contributing a little over £2000. They were, in effect, the mainstay of the establishment, and the falling off of their emoluments was being watched by the postmasters-general, hardly less than by those who were more immediately interested, with the gravest concern.

Nor was it calculated to reconcile the Post Office servants to the deprivations which they were already beginning to suffer that the members of other public offices, who had lost from the same cause as the clerks of the roads, but to a much less extent, had received compensation in full. The clerks in the offices of the Principal Secretaries of State, like the clerks of the roads, had been privileged to frank both letters and newspapers. By the Act of 1764 the privilege had, as regards letters, been taken away in both cases; and in both cases, as regards newspapers, it remained. Yet to the clerks in the offices of the Principal Secretaries of State was secured, by special Act of Parliament, compensation to the amount of £1500 a year, while the clerks of the roads received nothing; and, as though to add to the aggravation, this sum of £1500 a year was to be paid by the Post Office.

In Dublin the same difficulties were being experienced as in London and from the same cause. Emoluments were falling off and obligations could not be met. Among these obligations, however, there was one which was peculiar to Dublin. Before 1764 the clerks at the castle, like the clerks of the roads, had enjoyed the privilege of franking newspapers, and the exercise of this privilege by the two bodies simultaneously had been attended with so much friction that advantage had been taken of the passing of the Franking Act to effect a compromise. In consideration of the sum of £350 a year to be paid by the clerks of the roads the clerks at the castle undertook to abandon their privilege absolutely. A deed to this effect was prepared, and, in order that nothing might be wanting to give it formality, it was signed by the Earl of Northumberland, the Lord Lieutenant, on behalf of the castle, and by Lord Clermont, the Deputy Postmaster-General of Ireland, on behalf of the Post Office. Whence was the sum of £350 to come when the emoluments should be gone? Was a price to continue to be paid for the surrender of a privilege which had ceased to be of value? The Attorney-General for Ireland advised that the clerks of the roads were still liable to the last farthing of their salaries; and the clerks at the castle refused to abate one jot of their claim.

But we are anticipating. In 1767 the statute-book received an addition which, though differing widely both in intention and effect from the Franking Act and the Postage Act, cannot be allowed to pass unnoticed. This was an Act for the better paving, lighting, and regulating the streets of London, a first step in fact towards converting the London of Hogarth into the London of to-day. The mere preamble[58] of the Act brings home to us, hardly less vividly than Hogarth's pencil, the intolerable inconveniences under which our forefathers were content to live; but what concerns us at the present moment is that one section provided not only that the names of the streets should be put up but that the houses should be numbered. This numbering of houses quickly spread, and, although unnoticed by the Post Office at the time, was destined very materially to assist its future operations. As a consequence, too, and at no long interval, arose a new industry, namely the compilation of Directories—a thing that was impossible before—and hence the Post Office derived still further assistance.

About this time considerable improvements took place both in the Scotch and Irish posts. Between London and Edinburgh communication had been only thrice a week. In 1765 it was increased in frequency to five days a week, and posts on six days a week were at the same time established between Edinburgh and the chief towns of Scotland. The result was an immediate increase of revenue which much more than covered the increase of expense. Two or three years later the course of post between London and Dublin came under review. By virtue of an arrangement, which the fact of the communication being only thrice a week goes but a short way to explain, letters from England to Ireland were kept lying two whole days in the London Office and, similarly, letters from Ireland to England were kept lying two whole days in the Dublin Office. The packet which was due in Dublin on Saturday night rarely arrived before Sunday, and, unless it did so, the letters from England for the interior of Ireland did not leave Dublin until Wednesday morning. Nor was this all. The number of packets was extremely limited, and, owing to their constant employment by Government as express boats, it frequently happened that two and sometimes three and even four mails were sent by the same packet. In 1767 this was altered. Additional packet boats were placed on the station, and the post between London and Dublin and between Dublin and Belfast in one direction and Cork in another was increased in frequency from three to six days a week.

Between London and the chief provincial towns in England Allen had, as we have seen, established posts six days a week instead of three; but it was not until 1769, or nearly five years after Allen's death, that within the metropolis arrangements were made to correspond. Meanwhile the offices for the receipt of general post letters were kept open and the bellmen went about ringing their bells on only three nights of the week, namely Tuesdays, Thursdays, and Saturdays, and on the other three nights, except at the General Post Office, letters could not be posted gratuitously. On the nights of Monday, Wednesday, and Friday a receiver if called upon to take in letters was entitled to charge a fee of 1d. apiece, and this fee he retained as his own perquisite. Beginning with 1769 the receiving offices were kept open and the bellmen rang their bells on every night of the week, Sundays excepted.

An event or rather a series of events now took place, the result of which was largely to alter the character of the Post Office and to extend its usefulness. Recent legislation had done little for the public convenience. It had indeed provided that Penny Post Offices might be established out of London, and advantage had been taken of the provision in one single instance. In Dublin a Penny Post Office had been opened on the 10th of October 1773, or seventy years after the Countess of Thanet desired to open one and was refused permission at the last moment. But in other respects legislation had accomplished little beyond promoting the very abuses it was designed to prevent, and impairing the utility of Dockwra's post. Litigation was now to have its turn; and it is interesting to note the result.

The machinery for the dispersion of letters remained much as it had been since the first establishment of the Post Office. In London, in Edinburgh, and in Dublin there was, as there is now, a body of men whose duty it was to deliver from house to house; but with these three exceptions there was not, 120 years ago, a single town in the kingdom which could boast of its own letter-carrier. The postmaster was the sole Post Office agent in the place; it was he who delivered the letters if they were delivered at all; and for this service he was left to charge pretty much as he pleased. The public had grown tired of this state of things and strenuous efforts were now made to alter it.

The crusade began in the little town of Sandwich in Kent. It had been the practice of the postmaster there, at some former time, to deliver free the letters arriving by the bye and cross posts, and on the delivery of the London letters to charge a fee as his own perquisite. In 1772 a fee was being charged on the delivery of all letters. This charge the inhabitants now determined to contest. The case came on for trial in the Court of King's Bench and was decided against the postmaster, the Court being of opinion that wherever the usage had been to deliver free, there the usage should be adhered to. The postmasters-general were very uneasy. Out of the 440 post towns of the kingdom there were known to be not less than seventy-six which were in the same case as Sandwich and to which the decision of the Court must apply, towns where letters had at one time been delivered free and where they were so no longer; and not a day passed without bringing fresh and unexpected additions to the list. At Birmingham and at Ipswich, for instance, where a charge was now being made for delivery, old inhabitants could remember how forty or fifty years before letters had been delivered free. Was the Crown to be at the expense of letter-carriers at all of these towns, or were the postmasters, who were already complaining of the inadequacy of their remuneration, to forego their perquisites and make a house-to-house delivery as part of their duty?

The question was still under consideration when the town of Ipswich commenced an action. The point raised in this case was whether on the delivery of letters addressed to the inhabitants of the town the postmaster could legally demand any sum over and above the postage, and, if so, whether in the event of the demand being refused he could oblige the inhabitants to fetch their letters. Again the decision, this time by the Court of Common Pleas, was in favour of the public and against the Post Office. The postmasters-general were more than uneasy now. No sooner had the decision in the Ipswich case become known than town after town where letters had never yet been delivered free demanded a free delivery and threatened the postmasters-general with actions in the event of their demand being refused. Bath and Gloucester did more than threaten. They, like Ipswich, proceeded to trial; and again, for the third and fourth time, the decision was against the Post Office.

Thurlow was at this time Attorney-General. He held a strong opinion that in order to comply with the statute it was enough to deliver letters at the Post Office of the town to which they were addressed, and that there was no obligation to deliver them at the houses of the inhabitants. Still clinging to the belief that the decisions of the Courts must have proceeded more or less on the usage of delivery, he now determined to try the question in the case of a town where the usage had been for no delivery to be made without payment. The town of Hungerford in Berkshire was selected for the purpose. There, it could be proved, ever since the beginning of the century, letters had not been delivered except on payment of a fee of 1d. apiece.

The case came on before the Court of King's Bench in Michaelmas term 1774. Lord Mansfield, the Lord Chief Justice, was the first to deliver judgment. He was surprised, he said, the several Acts being so ambiguous and the usage so contradictory, that the Post Office had not applied to Parliament to explain the matter. That was the view of the Court when, in the other cases, it avoided the general question. He never liked to avoid general questions, for to decide them tended to prevent further litigation; but an important question of this kind, arising out of Acts that had "not yet spoke," and, whichever way it might be decided, involving more or less inconvenience, was essentially one for Parliament. And in the Bath case there were grounds on which the general question could, without impropriety, be avoided. There the postmaster when delivering a letter had demanded a certain sum as a duty. Now, a duty it certainly was not. If on the delivery of a letter Parliament had intended to impose a duty, it would have fixed the amount and made it part of the Post Office revenue; and not have left every postmaster free to fix what amount he pleased or might prevail upon people to give. And what a monstrous inconvenience it would be if every one had to go to the Post Office to fetch his own letters! How could the Court have laid down such a proposition as that? The thing was impossible. And it must be remembered that there could be no middlemen—men between the inhabitants and the postmaster—who for gain could set up an office to distribute the letters, because by law the postmaster could not deliver them except to the persons to whom they were addressed. These were the considerations which in the Bath ease induced him to avoid the general question, and he had been glad to feel able to do so, never doubting that the postmasters-general would apply to Parliament for a determination; but this, unfortunately, they had not done. Then there was the Gloucester case. He remembered it well. There the question was not whether there should be a free delivery, for at Gloucester letters had always been delivered free, but whether certain houses should fall within the limits of that delivery. All that the Court then decided was that in the case of these houses, forming as they unquestionably did a part of what was known as the town of Gloucester, the Post Office could not depart from its own practice. But the present case was different. Here the contention was that in the town of Hungerford there was not a single house at which the Post Office was required to deliver letters without being paid for it. Practically, no doubt, it was the Bath case over again; but the Court could not well avoid the general question a second time. The Post Office, in effect, sought to impose a duty; and this, he said it emphatically, the Post Office had not the power to do without the authority of Parliament, which authority had not been given. His mind was perfectly clear that within the limits of a post-town the Post Office was bound to deliver free; but how far these limits should extend was a question upon which he did not feel called upon to express an opinion.

The other judges were equally emphatic. The Post Office had urged in support of its contention that it sometimes happened—as, for instance, at Hartford Bridge—-that the stage or post-house was a single house with no other houses near. There, at all events, as soon as it had deposited the letters at the post house, the Post Office had discharged its duty. And if there, it was asked, why not elsewhere? If, said Mr. Justice Aston, the post house was a single house with no other houses near, the question did not arise; but, in the case, of towns, surely it would not be contended that each individual inhabitant was to resort to the post house every day in order to inquire whether there was a letter for him or not. To demand this penny within the limits of a post town, said Mr. Justice Willes, was contrary to the whole tenor and spirit of the Acts of Parliament; and where the post town was a small one like Hungerford, the demand was far more unreasonable than it would be in the case of London and Westminster. Yet in London and Westminster letters were delivered free. He should pay more regard to the usage of the city of London than to that of fifty such towns as Hungerford. Mr. Justice Ashurst was of opinion that even to usage too much importance might be attached. If it were really the case that at Hungerford, ever since the passing of the Act of Anne, a man living next door to the Post Office had had to pay over and above the postage 1d. for every letter he received, this in his opinion was a bad usage, an usage for which the Act afforded no justification, and the sooner it was laid aside the better.

The decision of the Court burst upon the postmasters-general like a thunderbolt. They had been assured that it would certainly be in the opposite direction; and now, to their dismay, they found themselves face to face with the prospect of, what they called, an universal delivery. What was to be done? The Post Office would be ruined. Of course the Attorney-General would advise an appeal to the House of Lords. As a matter of fact the Attorney-General advised nothing of the sort. Thurlow's private opinion continued to be what it had always been, that the Post Office was not bound to deliver letters beyond the stage or post house. He even went so far as to admit that, if once the Act were construed to require more than that, he knew of no manner of construction that would entitle the postmasters-general to refuse to carry letters into every hole and corner of the kingdom. Still, as two Courts had decided against the Post Office, he regarded it as useless to appeal to the House of Lords, where, no doubt, the opinion of the same judges would be taken and acted on. Then, inquired the postmasters-general, might not a writ of error be brought with a view to hang up the judgment of the Court of King's Bench until the matter should be settled by Parliament. "No," replied Thurlow, "I do not approve a writ of error being brought by an office of revenue avowedly to suspend a question."

Thus ended a controversy which in one form or another had extended over a period of more than two years. The postmasters-general urged indeed that Parliament should be asked to avert what they regarded as little short of a catastrophe; but the recommendation was not adopted, and the decision of the Court was left to take effect.

We have dwelt upon this matter at some length, because it was, in effect, a turning-point in the history of the Post Office. The enterprising spirit of the small towns, the independence of the judges, and the conspicuous fairness of the Attorney-General, make up no doubt a combination which it is pleasing to contemplate; and yet, if this were all, a shorter notice would have sufficed. It is because the Post Office was now to assume a new character, the character in which it is known to us at the present time, that we have thought it best not to omit any important particular. And how great the change was to be a moment's consideration will shew. Cotton and Frankland had, early in the century, done what little they could to make the Post Office popular. They had lost no opportunity of advocating cheap postage; they had lived among the merchants, and, as far as duty would allow, had consulted their wishes; and within the limits assigned to them had spared no efforts to promote the public convenience. But since then a different spirit had prevailed. By Cotton and Frankland's successors much had been done in restraint of correspondence and nothing, or next to nothing, in promotion of it. The Post Office had become, insensibly perhaps, but none the less surely, a mere tax-gatherer, and, like other tax-gatherers, its policy had been to exact as much and to give as little as possible. All this was now to be altered. An appeal had been made to the Courts; and the Courts in the most deliberate and solemn manner had affirmed this principle—a principle now so universally recognised and acted on as to excite our wonder that it should ever have been otherwise—that the Post Office was to wait upon the people, and not the people upon the Post Office.

It might be supposed that the decision of the Courts would have been immediately followed by the appointment of letter-carriers throughout the country, or else by additions to the salaries of the postmasters in consideration of their undertaking to make a house-to-house delivery gratuitously. Such, however, was not the case. At the towns which had taken a foremost part in the fray—at Hungerford and Sandwich, at Bath, Ipswich, and Birmingham—as well indeed as at other towns which were spirited enough to assert their rights, letter-carriers were no doubt appointed; but there was no sudden and general alteration of practice. On the contrary, the obedience which the Post Office yielded to the law as laid down by the Courts was a tardy and grudging obedience. As much as ten or eleven years later we find the postmasters-general acknowledging indeed the obligation under which they lay to appoint letter-carriers at any towns that might demand it, and yet taking credit to themselves that, as a matter of fact, no such appointments had been made except where the inhabitants had refused to continue the accustomed recompense for delivery.

The Courts of Law were at this time the best friends of the people. No sooner had they decided that every town which possessed a Post Office of its own was entitled to a gratuitous delivery at the door than a somewhat similar question came before them in connection with the penny post. For every letter delivered by the penny post the inhabitants of Old Street, St. Luke's, of St. Leonard's, Shoreditch, of Bethnal Green, and Spitalfields were required to pay an additional penny, that is a penny over and above the one which had been paid on posting; and this they had long regarded as an imposition. According to Dockwra's plan the second or delivery penny was to be confined to Islington, Hackney, Newington Butts, and South Lambeth, which in his day formed separate towns; but in course of time, as buildings extended, the Post Office appears to have exacted the same charge at intermediate places. Jones, a wealthy distiller of Old Street, now determined to try the question. Again the decision of the Courts was against the Post Office, and not only in Old Street, but in Shoreditch, Bethnal Green, and Spitalfields the additional penny had to be abandoned.

While these proceedings were taking place before the Courts, the Post Office had forced upon it a step which, even in those days of indifference, cannot have been taken without a pang. This was the dismissal of its most distinguished servant or rather of its only servant with any claim to distinction, and that of the highest. We refer to Benjamin Franklin. This eminent man had been appointed postmaster of Philadelphia in 1737, and after being employed in several positions of trust, had been promoted to be one of the joint postmasters-general of America in 1753. He had recently been sent to England with the object of averting war between the mother country and her transatlantic colonies, and, his mission having failed, he was now dismissed. The letter in which the decision was announced was as follows:—

To DOCTOR FRANKLIN.

GENERAL POST OFFICE, *Jan. 31, 1774.*

Sir—I have received the commands of His Majesty's postmasters-general to signify to you that they find it necessary to dismiss you from being any longer their deputy for America. You will therefore cause your accounts to be made up as soon as you can conveniently.—I am, sir, your most humble servant,

ANTHONY TODD,

Secretary.

Curt as this communication was, it was perhaps the best of which the circumstances admitted. Indeed, we are by no means sure that the terms of it were not arranged with Franklin himself. He was in London at the time. His relations with the Post Office had always been of the most cordial character. He did not, after receiving the letter, cease to visit Lombard Street; and before his return to America he wrote to the Post Office intimating that he would cheerfully become security for his colleague, who, as a consequence of his own dismissal, had to enter into fresh bond. At all events, whether Franklin had any hand in the preparation of the letter or not, the less said the better would seem to have been the opinion of the writer; just as a desire to let bygones be bygones is plainly shewn in the first letter which passed after correspondence was resumed. This letter is a curiosity in its way. It is dated the 25th of June 1783, and, ignoring all that had happened during the preceding seven years, begins as follows:—

TO DOCTOR FRANKLIN at PARIS.

GENERAL POST OFFICE, *June 25, 1783.*

Dear Sir—I must confess I have taken a long time to acknowledge the last letter you were pleased to write me the 24th of March 1776 from New York. I am happy, however, to learn from my nephew, Mr. George Maddison, that you enjoy good health, and that as the French were about to establish five packet boats at L'Orient, Port Louis, for the purpose of a monthly correspondence between that port and New York, you were desirous of knowing the intentions of England on that subject....—I am, dear sir, with the greatest truth and respect, your most obedient and most humble servant,

ANTHONY TODD.

In 1780, as part of a Licensing Act, the monopoly of letting post-horses which the Post Office had enjoyed uninterruptedly since 1603 was taken away. It is curious to note that a measure which 177 years before had been deemed essential to the maintenance of the posts was now withdrawn without, so far as we are aware, exciting a murmur; and, by a strange coincidence, at the very time the measure was being withdrawn in the United Kingdom, the deputy postmaster-general of Canada, who had recently arrived in London, was urging upon the Government a similar expedient as an indispensable condition without which the "maîtres de poste" between Quebec and Montreal would be constrained to throw up their appointments. Such is the difference between a new institution and an institution that is well established.

It should here be remarked that with the extinction of this monopoly passed away one of the original functions of the postmasters-general. Hitherto, lightly as the responsibility had rested upon them for the last hundred years or more, they had been masters of the travelling-post as well as the letter-post. For the future they were to be masters of the letter-post alone.

Little remains to be told of the eighteen years of which this chapter treats. In 1782, in consequence of a hint dropped by the Lord Chief Justice in the course of a trial, the Post Office did an eminently useful thing. It issued an advertisement counselling the public when sending bank notes by post to cut them into two parts and to send one part by one post and another by another. The counsel was adopted, and in an incredibly short space of time the practice became general. In the same year the Post Office servants were disfranchised. By an Act passed in the reign of Queen Anne they were forbidden either to persuade or to dissuade others in the matter of voting; and now they were forbidden to vote themselves. The only point of interest connected with the two Acts is perhaps their termination. While the later Act was repealed in 1868, the earlier one was not repealed until 1874; and meanwhile the postmaster-general sat in the House of Commons and offered himself for election. Little, probably, did he think that for every vote he solicited he rendered himself not only liable to a penalty of £100 but "incapable of ever bearing or executing any office or place of trust whatsoever under Her Majesty, her heirs, or successors."

The internal condition of the Post Office during the last few years of Lord North's administration was simply deplorable. The profits from the sale of newspapers kept growing less and less. The clerks of the roads, after paying the salaries and pensions which formed the first charge on their receipts, had left for themselves the merest pittance. These men, to whom an appeal for help had never been made in vain, were now in sore need of help themselves. The prospect was alarming, for if the clerks of the roads should fail to meet their engagements they would drag down with them a not inconsiderable part of the establishment. It was in 1778, when apprehension was highest, that the Commissioners of Land Tax for the city of London made a new assessment, and suddenly, without a note of warning, every Post Office servant in the metropolis found himself assessed to the land tax to the amount of 4s. in the pound. Not even the letter-carriers or maid-servants were excepted. At this time and during the two or three following years a general bankruptcy was imminent. Eventually the abatements were remitted and the salaries and pensions which had been charged to the clerks of the roads were in part transferred to the State; but not before many of the Post Office servants had compounded with their creditors and all had endured the severest privations.

Meanwhile the postmasters from America, ejected from their offices, had been flocking to this country and pleading for pensions on the English establishment. The packets were meeting with a series of disasters so far beyond the experience of former wars as to excite the most hostile comment. During the seven years ending August 1782 no less than thirty-seven were captured by the enemy. Of these four belonged to the Post Office, and sums for that time prodigious were expended to replace them. The others were owned by the captains who commanded them, and the owners received as compensation for their loss the sum of £85,000. Even the fabric of the buildings partook of the general decay. In Edinburgh the Post Office had had to be abandoned at a moment's notice, the arch which supported the main part of the structure having given way. In Dublin the roof had fallen in. In both Dublin and Edinburgh new Post Offices were being erected at heavy expense; while in London search was being made for new premises on the plea that those in Lombard Street were insufficient for present requirements.

To crown all, ugly rumours were afloat, rumours imputing corruption in the highest quarters. The postmasters-general were indeed to be pitied. The Post Office in more senses than one was falling about their ears.

CHAPTER XII
JOHN PALMER 1782-1792

The apathy of the Post Office about this time is incomprehensible. More than twenty years before, the General Convention of the Royal Boroughs of Scotland had called the attention of the postmasters-general to the intolerable slowness of the post on the Great North Road. "Every common traveller," they wrote, "passes the King's mail on the first road in the kingdom." At the present time the clerks of the roads were giving as one of the reasons why they were undersold in the matter of newspapers that, whereas they sent their wares by post, the booksellers and printers availed themselves of the more expeditious conveyance by stage-coach. Yet it seems never to have occurred to the postmasters-general that what was being done by others they might do themselves. The lesson that was lost upon the postmasters-general was to be learnt and applied by John Palmer, proprietor of the theatre at Bath.

Palmer had, while yet at school, been distinguished for a love of enterprise, an indomitable perseverance, and an activity of body which knew no fatigue and set distance at defiance. He had, through sheer persistency, obtained a patent for his theatre at Bath, which thus became the first Theatre-Royal out of the metropolis. At a time when the mail leaving London on Monday night did not arrive at Bath until Wednesday afternoon, he had been in the habit of accomplishing the distance between the two cities in a single day. He had made journeys equally long and equally rapid in other directions; and, as the result of observation, he had come to the conclusion that of the horses kept at the post-houses it was always the worst that were set aside to carry the mail, and that the post was the slowest mode of conveyance in the kingdom. He had also observed that, where security or despatch was required, his neighbours at Bath who might desire to correspond with London would make a letter up into a parcel and send it by stage-coach,[59] although the cost by stage-coach was, porterage included, 2s. and by post 4d. Not seldom, indeed, the difference would be more than 1s. 8d., for to prevent delay on the part of the porters in London one of these clandestine letters would as often as not have written on the back, "An extra sum will be given the porter if he delivers this letter immediately."

Starting from these premises Palmer, with characteristic energy, set himself to devise a plan for the reform of the Post Office. This plan was simply that the mails—which, to use his own words, had heretofore been trusted to some idle boy without character, mounted on a worn-out hack, who, so far from being able to defend himself against a robber, was more likely to be in league with one—should for the future be carried by coach. The coach should be guarded, and should carry no outside passenger. For guard no one could be better than a soldier, who would be skilled in the use of firearms. He should carry two short guns or blunderbusses, and sit on the top of the coach with the mail behind him. From this position he could command the road and observe suspicious persons. The coachman also should carry arms; but in his case they should be pistols. A speed should be maintained of eight or nine miles an hour. Thus, the distance between London and Bath would, stoppages included, be accomplished in sixteen hours instead of thirty-eight; and these stoppages should, in point of time, be largely reduced. As the coach arrived at the end of each stage there would be little more for the postmaster to do than to put into the mail bag the outgoing letters and to take out of the bag the letters that were coming in. Surely a quarter of an hour would be ample for the purpose. He must indeed be an inexpert postmaster who could not change his letters as soon as the ostler changes his horses. Strict punctuality should be observed. Each postmaster should be on the spot and to the moment to receive the mail when it arrived; and if it did not arrive to time, a man on horseback should be despatched to ascertain the cause of delay. This, in the event of the coach having been stopped by highwaymen, would secure immediate pursuit.

And how little would be the cost of the proposed reform. It was doubtful indeed whether there would be any additional cost at all. The mails were now being conveyed at a charge for boy and horse of 3d. a mile. It was certain that men might be found who for this rate of payment would be glad to convey them by coach. Especially would this be the case if the coaches which carried the mails were exempt, as they ought to be, from toll. Between London and Bath, for instance, the toll was, for a carriage and pair, 9s., and for a carriage and four, 18s. Exemption from this impost would of itself be no inconsiderable boon to the contractors. Besides, the speed and security of a mail coach would attract passengers. At all events something, it was clear, must be done. As matters stood it was an intolerable hardship that persons sending letters by coach should be subject to penalties. A coach might go at a time when there was no post; and a letter might require immediate despatch. Yet, rather than make use of the coach and pay half a crown, one was obliged to hire an express, which was less expeditious, at a cost of two or three guineas. Surely, if no other change were made, this at least should be conceded—that any one taking a letter to the Post Office and paying the proper amount of postage upon it according to its address should, after the letter had been impressed with the postmark and signed by the postmaster, be at liberty to send it by what channel he pleased.

Such were the main features of Palmer's plan. As a subsidiary, though by no means a necessary, part of it he made two suggestions which it may be well to mention, if only because they were afterwards adopted. These were—1st, that the mails, which from the first establishment of the Post Office had not left London until between midnight and three o'clock in the morning, should start at eight in the evening; and 2nd, that they should not be kept waiting for the Government letters when these happened to be late. This keeping the mails waiting for the Government letters had, at the beginning of the century, been a constant source of complaint. "We take this occasion of representing to your Lordship," wrote the postmasters-general to Lord Dartmouth on the 16th of March 1710, "the great inconvenience which happened to the business of this office on Tuesday's night's post by the inland mails having all been detained here till the receipt of the Court letters, which were not brought by the messenger from Whitehall before half-past six on Wednesday morning." A similar letter of remonstrance was at the same time addressed to Mr. Secretary St. John. But, of late years, so profound had been the supineness which reigned at the Post Office that it may, probably enough, have been considered of little consequence whether the mails were delayed or not. Palmer was unable to take this view. To him it appeared in the highest degree improper that, for the sake of a few letters which after all might be of no great importance, the Post Office business of the whole country should be thrown out of gear. Far better, he urged, that the mail should leave at the proper hour, and that these letters, if behind time, should be sent after it by express. A third suggestion he made, a suggestion admirable in itself, and yet one that at that time was little likely to be adopted. This was that the Post Office should take the public into its confidence, and invite them to make known their wants and suggest how best these wants might be supplied.

In October 1782, through the intervention of his friend John Pratt, afterwards Lord Camden, Palmer's plan was brought under the notice of Pitt; and Pitt, who was then Chancellor of the Exchequer in the administration of Lord Shelburne, at once discerned its merits. Nothing, however, could be done until the Post Office had had an opportunity of offering its opinion on the matter, and when this opinion was given—which was not until July 1783—Pitt was out of office; and, although he returned to power as minister in the following December, the struggle in which he then became engaged with an unruly Parliament, and afterwards a general election, effectually precluded him from giving attention to the posts until the summer of 1784.

Meanwhile Palmer devoted himself to the perfection of his plan. He traversed the whole of the kingdom by stage-coaches, noting down the time they occupied in accomplishing their journeys, the time they unnecessarily lost, and how they might be better regulated and made serviceable for the transport of the mails. He took the same opportunity of acquainting himself with the course of the post and carefully observed its defects and delays. Nor did he trust to his own exertions alone. In order to test the extent of clandestine traffic, he employed persons to watch the Bath and Bristol coaches as they started for London, and to count the number of parcels which appeared to contain letters. These persons assured him that the number was never less than several hundreds in the week, and in some weeks was as high as 1000.

The office of postmaster-general was at this time held by Lords Carteret and Tankerville. Carteret had only recently been raised to the peerage. Appointed thirteen years before as Henry Frederick Thynne in conjunction with Lord le Despencer, he had, amid the conflict of parties and the fall of successive ministries, contrived to retain his post. Tankerville, on the contrary, had come in and gone out with a change of Government. Called upon to preside over the Post Office in 1782, he had left it in 1783 and had returned in January of the following year. The part which these two peers took in connection with Palmer's plan appears to have been not injudicious. Without expressing any opinion of their own as to its feasibility or otherwise, they contented themselves with collecting and forwarding to Pitt the opinions of such of their subordinates as were presumably qualified to judge. These were the district surveyors, and their verdict was unanimously against the plan. Of the reasons for this judgment a specimen or two will suffice. By one it was objected that there could be no need for the post to be the swiftest conveyance in the kingdom; by another, that to employ firearms for the protection of the mail would encourage their use on the other side, and thus murder might be added to robbery; by a third, that not only did the posts as they stood afford all reasonable accommodation, but it was beyond the power of human ingenuity to devise a better system.

Of these and other objections Pitt made short work. He summoned a conference at the Treasury, at which were present the postmasters-general, Palmer, and the objectors; and having patiently listened to all that could be urged against the plan, he desired that it should be tried on what was commonly called the Bath road, the road between Bristol and London. This conference was held on the 21st of June 1784. On Saturday the 31st of July an agreement was signed under which, in consideration of a payment of 3d. a mile, five innholders—one belonging to London, one to Thatcham, one to Marlborough, and two to Bath—undertook to provide the horses; and on Monday the 2nd of August the first mail-coach began to run.

It is unfortunate that of the early performances of this coach no record remains. We only know that on the first journey it started from Bristol and not from London, and that Palmer was present to see it off; that, ordinarily, the distance was accomplished in seventeen hours, being at the rate of about seven miles an hour; and that, as a result, the expresses to Bristol, which before 1784 had been as many as 200 in the year, ceased altogether. Ten or twelve years later, indeed, the expresses for the whole of the kingdom were not one-fifth of what, before 1784, was the number for the city of Bristol alone.

Palmer's plan, once introduced, made rapid progress. Mail-coaches began to run through Norfolk and Suffolk in March 1785; and on the cross-road between Bristol and Portsmouth in the following May. On the 25th of July the plan was extended to Leeds, Manchester, and Liverpool, and during the next two months to Gloucester and Swansea; to Hereford, Carmarthen, and Milford Haven; to Worcester and Ludlow; to Birmingham and Shrewsbury; to Chester and Holyhead; to Exeter; to Portsmouth; to Dover and other places. The Great North Road was reserved to the last, and here the plan was carried into effect in the summer of 1786.

It may be convenient here to say a few words on the subject of nomenclature. Post-coach, a term in vogue about this time,[60] might not unnaturally be supposed to denote a coach in use by the Post Office. Such, however, was not the case. The term post-coach, like the kindred term post-chaise, was introduced probably early in the last century, and, so far as we are aware, was never employed in the sense of mail-coach. It should further be noticed that the term mail-coach, although we have employed it to make our meaning clear, did not come into use until after 1784. In that year, and for some little time afterwards, coaches which carried the mails were called diligences or machines, and the coachmen were called machine-drivers.

The plan of carrying letters by mail-coach was, on its introduction, sadly marred by a simultaneous or almost simultaneous increase in the rates of postage. Pitt had brought forward his budget on the 30th of June; and among the measures he proposed with a view to replenish an exhausted Exchequer was a tax upon coals. The proposal was not well received by the House, and it was afterwards withdrawn in favour of an increase of postage. Palmer took credit to himself that he had proposed the substitution. If, as would appear to be the case, the claim is well founded, one can only regret that he should thus wantonly have handicapped his own proceedings. It is true, no doubt, that he was about to make the post both quicker and more secure; that he would have a better article to dispose of, an article that would fetch a higher price. It is also true that his plan, weighted as it was, proved an unqualified success. And yet it is impossible to deny that his reputation as a Post Office reformer, high as it stands, would have stood still higher if his counsel had been on the side of reduction.

The rates prescribed by the Act of 1784, as compared with those of 1765, were as follows:—

	1765				1784.			
Distance.	Single	Double	Treble	Ounce.	Single	Double	Treble	Ounce.
	d.	d.	d.	d.	d.	d.	d.	d.
Not exceeding one post stage	1	2	3	4	2	4	6	8
Exceeding one and not exceeding two post stages	2	4	6	8	3	6	9	12
Exceeding two post stages and not exceeding 80 miles	3	6	9	12	4	8	12	16
Exceeding 80 and not exceeding 150 miles	4	8	12	16	5	10	15	20
Exceeding 150 miles	4	8	12	16	6	12	18	24
To and from Edinburgh	6	12	18	24	7	14	21	28

To and from Dublin
{ The Irish Post Office had only
{ recently been placed under the
{ authority of the Irish Parliament;
{ and the rates of postage, not only
{within Ireland, but between Ireland

{ and Great Britain, were awaiting
{ revision.

Within Scotland.
(Measured from Edinburgh.)

Not exceeding one post stage	1	2	3	4	2	4	6	8
Exceeding one post stage and not exceeding 50 miles	2	4	6	8	3	6	9	12
Exceeding 50 miles and not exceeding 80 miles	3	6	9	12	4	8	12	16
Exceeding 80 and not exceeding 150 miles	4	8	12	16	5	10	15	20
Exceeding 150 miles	4	8	12	16	6	12	18	24

The same Act which increased the rates of postage imposed, or sought to impose, additional restrictions upon franking. Some concessions indeed were made. Letters from members of Parliament, in order to secure exemption, need no longer be limited, in point of weight, to two ounces and, in point of time, to the session of Parliament and forty days before and after. As part of the superscription, however, were now to be given the full date of the letter, the day, the month, and the year, all in the member's handwriting; and the letter was to be posted on the date which the superscription bore. These restrictions, it was confidently expected, would correct the worst abuses and render the concessions harmless. But, curiously enough, like the restrictions of 1764, they had an exactly contrary effect to that which was intended. The members sent to their constituents and friends, for use as occasion should serve, franks that were post-dated. These the Post Office charged, as coming from places where the members were known not to be. The members remonstrated, demanding to be informed in what respects the conditions of the Act had not been satisfied. The dispute waxing warm, the matter was referred to Pitt; and Pitt, after testing the opinion of the House, decided that pending fresh legislation the charges should be abandoned. Practically, therefore, the abuses which the Act was designed to prevent were not only not prevented but were given wider scope.

Palmer maintained to the end of his life that during the two years which followed the starting of the first mail-coach he was thwarted and opposed by the Post Office. This charge, so far as it refers to those by whom the

Post Office was managed and controlled, we believe to be groundless. That he had difficulties with contractors and postmasters is beyond question. Contractors were at all times troublesome persons to deal with, but they were not Post Office servants; and postmasters might well be excused if they looked askance at the new plan. Their salaries, low as they were, had long been shamefully reduced by exactions at headquarters under the name of fees; and what little they had been able to make out of their allowances for riding-work was now threatened by a system under which that work was to be done by contract. But the charge was not confined to contractors and postmasters. It extended to those who controlled and directed the Post Office, to Carteret and Tankerville and to their confidential adviser, the secretary; and, as we believe, with very insufficient reason. Carteret was indifferent. Tankerville was sincerely desirous of a reform of the posts, from whatever quarter it might come. Anthony Todd, the secretary, was eminently a man of peace. Appointed to the Post Office in 1738, he had arrived at a time of life when to most men ease and quiet are essential; and not only was he well advanced in years but it was not in his nature to thwart or oppose any one. All he wanted was to be left alone; and he was shrewd enough to know that the best way to secure this object was not to molest others.

Between Todd and Palmer, indeed, there was little in common. Palmer, in everything he undertook, was intensely in earnest. Todd, on the contrary, could with difficulty get up even an appearance of earnestness about anything which did not concern himself. Even of his duty Todd took a view which must have been absolutely repugnant to Palmer. Lloyds's coffee-house was supplied by the Post Office with the arrivals and sailings of British ships, and it paid for the information no less than £200 a year. One-half of this amount went into Todd's own pocket; and yet, according to him, the giving of the information was a concession, an indulgence. "The merchants," he would write, "are indulged with ship news." To the Mayor of Shrewsbury, who had asked on behalf of the inhabitants for an earlier post, he deliberately wrote, "The arrival of the mail a few hours sooner or later can be of no great consequence." Not many years before, a despatch sent by express from Lord North to the Duke of Newcastle had been lost. Even to the minister Todd was not ashamed to write, "I dare to say there is no roguery in the case, but [that the letter has been] lost and trampled under foot in the dirty roads." Between a man who could take this view of his duty and Palmer, who was burning to perfect his plan, there could be little sympathy; but there was certainly no active antagonism. That, as Palmer extended his plan, doubts as to its merits arose at headquarters is perfectly true; but they were honest doubts, doubts which might excusably be entertained and which, if entertained, the Post Office was bound to express. Palmer, who regarded every one who was not for him as being against him, construed the expression of a doubt into an act of hostility.

Let us see what some of these doubts were, and whence they originated. In London, before the introduction of Palmer's plan, it had been the practice to wait for the arrival of all the mails before any one of them was delivered, so that in the event of a single mail being behind time, no delivery at all might take place until three or four o'clock in the afternoon or even later. Palmer, of course, altered this. But now his interest in the Bristol coach led him to an opposite extreme. The Bristol mail was delivered the moment it arrived; and all other mails, by how little soever they might be later, were kept waiting. Again, before 1784 the post was frequently diverted from the high road in order that adjacent villages might be served. On the Bath road, for instance, although on this road there were fewer diversions than on any other in the kingdom, the post left the turnpike road between Hungerford and Marlborough in order to go through Ramsbury. Under the new arrangement it would have defeated Palmer's object to leave the direct track, if indeed the state of the roads would have admitted of it; and as the coaches could not go to the villages, the villages had to send to the coaches. Not in these cases alone was there, at first, a very general failure to effect a junction. Along every road on which a mail-coach was started the bye and cross posts were deranged and thrown into confusion; and, as a consequence, the Post Office was swamped with complaints from those whose letters had been delayed.

Had this been all, it would have been little more than might be expected in the course of transition from one system to another; but other causes of dissatisfaction arose. The Act of Parliament regulated the rates of postage according to stages—2d. in the case of a single letter, for one stage, 3d. for two stages, and beyond two stages and not exceeding eighty miles 4d.; but what was meant by the term stage the Act nowhere defined. Virtually it was in the power of one man, by the simple expedient of reducing the length of the stages and so increasing their number, to raise the rate of postage between any two towns in the kingdom that were not more than a certain number of miles apart. And this is exactly what Palmer did. From Rochester to Dartford, for instance, had been one stage. The single stage was replaced by two stages; and the postage, which had been 2d., became 3d. From Newbury to Devizes had been two stages. The two stages were increased to three; and the postage was raised from 3d. to 4d. And so it was throughout the kingdom. Well might the postmasters-general write, as they wrote under date the 7th of December 1785, "We are now at a loss in many instances how to rate letters and what to call by the name of a stage."

But not even the increase of postage which resulted from shortening the stages gave so much offence as the earlier closing of the Post Office in Lombard Street. The Post Office had from the earliest times been kept open to at least twelve o'clock at night, and probably a little later. It now closed at seven o'clock in the evening, so as to admit of the mails starting at eight o'clock. Palmer had foreseen that objections might be raised to the change; but he was little prepared for the storm of indignation that followed. The first merchants in London, some of them bearing names still honoured in the city,—Thellusson, Lubbock and Bosanquet, Herries, Quentin Dick and Hoare,—protested in writing and afterwards waited on the postmasters-general in a body to support their protest. The leather-dealers followed suit, a body representing more than sixty firms. Some held that the Post Office should be kept open till nine o'clock, and others till ten or even eleven o'clock; but all were of opinion that seven was too early an hour to close. At a meeting held at the London Tavern, and presided over by one of the sheriffs, resolutions were passed, copies of which were afterwards presented to Pitt in person, not only condemning the early hour of closing but calling for the adoption of measures with a view "to remove the inconveniences which had hitherto been experienced from the establishment of mail-coaches." No wonder if the postmasters-general doubted the merits of a plan which exposed them to these complaints.

Nor was it only from without that troubles came. The letter-carriers were grumbling and more than grumbling; and not without reason. For more than seventy years they had been ringing bells in the streets after the receiving houses were shut—until 1769 on the three nights of the week called grand post nights, and since that date on the bye-nights as well—receiving as their own perquisite 1d. on each letter they collected. Hence the men had made a comfortable addition to their wages of 12s. a week; and now, owing to the closing of the Post Office at seven, the emoluments derived from this source were rapidly dwindling and promised soon to disappear altogether.

Between Carteret and Tankerville differences now arose which, in view of subsequent events, it is impossible to pass unnoticed. On the break-up of the Shelburne administration in 1783, when Tankerville left the Post Office and Carteret remained, the two postmasters-general had parted with mutual expressions of regard and goodwill. A questionable transaction in which Carteret had been concerned, a transaction partaking of the nature of a corrupt bargain, had indeed come under Tankerville's notice; but he willingly attributed it to the malign influence exercised by his predecessor, Lord le Despencer. This favourable construction his later experience had induced him to modify. One case in particular which occurred soon after his return to the Post Office had aroused the most painful suspicions. On

Monday the 2nd of August 1784, the same day as that on which the first mail-coach started, the Post Office of Ireland was separated from the Post Office of England. Into the reasons of this separation, being as they were political, we do not propose to enter. Suffice it to say that the Government of Ireland took advantage of the occasion to displace Armit, the secretary to the Irish Post Office, and to reappoint John Lees, who had been secretary from 1774 to 1781, when he was promoted to the War Office. On his reappointment Lees wrote to the postmasters-general in London recapitulating the conditions on which he had been appointed ten years before, and stating that to those conditions, onerous as they were, he proposed in the main to adhere. He was indeed under no obligation in the matter, for he owed his reappointment to the Irish Government; but of this circumstance he had no desire to avail himself. Armit had taken over the conditions from Lees; and Lees would now resume them from Armit. Let us see what the conditions were. In 1774 Barham, the packet agent at Dover, being compelled by ill-health to retire, was succeeded by Walcot, the secretary to the Post Office in Ireland, and Walcot was succeeded by Lees, who was new to the service. Barham, though superannuated, was during his life to receive from Walcot the full salary and emoluments of the packet agency, and Walcot was during the same period to receive from Lees the full salary and emoluments of the secretaryship. Lees was meanwhile to receive from Walcot a small allowance for acting as secretary. Thus far there was nothing unusual in the arrangement. On the contrary, it was an arrangement which in those days was very commonly made. That which was unusual, and which nowhere appeared in the official records, was an undertaking into which Lees had entered to the effect that, after Barham's death, he would make to a fourth person during that person's life an annual payment of £350. This engagement Lees, when reappointed in 1784, expressed himself unwilling to renew. He was quite prepared to resume the payment to Walcot, reduced only to the same extent as by recent legislation the secretary's emoluments had been reduced; but the reversionary payment to the gentleman whom he would designate by the initials A. B. rested on different grounds. From this he must beg to be released.

Now, who was A. B.? This was the question which Tankerville asked; and asked in vain. He could obtain no information on the subject. Meanwhile Carteret, who was extremely displeased and disquieted at the disclosure, caused an expression of his severe displeasure to be conveyed to Lees that he should have presumed to make public a transaction which was obviously designed to be private. Lees replied that, as he would be unable to keep the engagement, he was bound in honour to state so; that he had made known nothing more than was absolutely necessary in order to obtain an acquittance, namely, that after Barham's death an annuity of £350 had been agreed to be paid to some one; but who this some one was had been, and would continue to be, a profound secret. In London it had been whispered, and more than whispered, that A. B. was Carteret himself. On this point Lees was emphatic. The transaction, he said, concerns no postmaster-general, either living or dead. "With Lord Carteret it has personally no more to do than with the King of France."

Tankerville, though profoundly dissatisfied, resolved to let the matter drop; and during the next eighteen months the feeling of distrust with which he regarded Carteret did not prevent the two postmasters-general from working together harmoniously. It was not until June 1786 that an open rupture occurred. Some furniture had been ordered for the housekeeper's apartments, and Tankerville, regarding it as of too luxurious a nature, refused to countersign the bill unless the secretary could produce a precedent for the expense. This Todd might have had some difficulty in doing, as no housekeeper had resided on the Post Office premises since the year 1740; but instead of offering an explanation to that effect he waited for the next Board meeting, and, having already procured Carteret's signature to the bill, put it before Tankerville without remark. Tankerville, who never signed a document without examining its contents, inquired whether this was not the housekeeper's bill to which he had taken exception, and, on being answered in the affirmative, told Todd that he had been guilty of a gross impropriety. Carteret, who had made no secret of his opinion that it was no part of a postmaster-general's duty to check tradesmen's accounts, took Todd's part; whereupon Tankerville, whose temper was always running away with him, observed that he would do no jobs, and that if a good understanding between himself and Carteret were only to be procured by such means he would rather that they should continue on their present terms.

The next business set down for discussion had a termination still more unfortunate. The office of comptroller of the bye and cross roads had become vacant, and Carteret, whose turn it was to appoint, had appointed Staunton, the postmaster of Isleworth. In addition to a salary of £500 a year, the appointment carried a residence in the Post Office building; and as the residence occupied by the late comptroller had by Pitt's desire been given to Palmer, Carteret proposed that Staunton should be recommended to the Treasury for an allowance of £100 a year as compensation. Tankerville, who had been in personal communication with Pitt and ascertained that he would object to an allowance for such a purpose, declined to join in the recommendation, explaining the reason. Carteret's remarks implied, or seemed to imply, a doubt whether Pitt had really been seen on the subject, as alleged. Tankerville again lost his temper. High words ensued, and the Board broke up, Carteret declaring that it was impossible they should continue to act as joint postmasters-general, and that he should at once wait upon Pitt and inform him to that effect.

Carteret was as good as his word. In three days from the date of the Board meeting at which the altercation had taken place he waited upon Pitt; and Pitt, after labouring in vain to effect a reconciliation, at length dismissed Tankerville. Tankerville, who had been in constant communication with the minister on the subject of the abuses at the Post Office, and had sedulously applied himself to their correction, was hardly less surprised than he was indignant; and restating the origin of the disagreement between himself and his colleague, he demanded to be informed in what respects he had been to blame. Pitt replied that he could not enter into the merits of the question; that all it concerned him to know was that Carteret was necessary to him in the House of Lords; and that, as Carteret had expressed himself unable to act any longer with Tankerville, it had become essential to make another arrangement.

This decision as between two colleagues, of whom one was as clearly actuated by honesty of purpose as the other was not, a decision given too by a minister who had already established a character for purity of administration, seems so extraordinary that we must look for some further explanation. The truth we believe to be that owing to an ungovernable temper Tankerville was simply intractable, and had shewn himself to Pitt to be so. Even Todd, who with all his faults was essentially a man of peace, was unable to get on with him. "I am sorry to say," he wrote on one occasion, "your Lordship is the only postmaster-general I have not had the happiness to serve under with his perfect approbation." On another occasion he wrote to Carteret: "I have had a very unpleasant day of it. His Lordship is so completely jealous and wrong-headed, so that without entering into unpleasing particulars I had better leave him to his own thoughts." Tankerville's own letters afford evidence to the same effect. "I shall not be disposed to talk coolly on the subject of Mr. Dashwood, or hear anything you may have to say, unless you can prove him guilty of fraud, which I do not admit, but now tell you distinctly that I believe Lord Carteret has been indebted to you for that forced construction." Again, "I do not find that I cool very fast," Tankerville wrote from Brighton a week or so after the incident which had excited his ire. Ever his own worst enemy, he now spoiled a good ease, so far as it was possible to spoil it, by intemperate writing. Instead of keeping to the main question, he rambled off into side-issues which were all but irrelevant. Carteret had spoken of one interview with Pitt. Pitt had expressed himself as though there had been more than one. The point was absolutely unimportant. Yet

Tankerville fastened upon it, and, declaring that one or the other must have been guilty of untruth, called upon them as men of honour to reconcile the discrepancy.

Intemperate as Tankerville's language had been, it was impossible that things should remain as they were. Nothing but a public inquiry would satisfy the justice of the case; and on this he was resolved. It was a matter of regret to him to impeach Carteret's conduct; but there was no other method of vindicating his own. "The causes of my removal," he wrote, "shall be made as public as the injury; and, however gratified your Lordship and those in concert with you may at present feel by the success of your measures, I will take upon me to foretell that the triumph will soon be at an end. I have been removed; others will be disgraced." "When your Lordship," replied Carteret, "shall think proper to bring this matter before the public, I flatter myself my conduct will be unimpeached."

A Parliamentary Committee of Inquiry was granted, and met for the first time on the 16th of May 1787. The session terminated on the 30th of the same month. Short as the interval was, evidence enough was taken to substantiate all and more than all that Tankerville had alleged. The Committee reported that a payment of £350 a year had been exacted from Lees as a condition of his appointment as secretary to the Post Office in Ireland; that a payment of £200 a year had been similarly exacted from Dashwood, the postmaster-general of Jamaica; that, while Lees had engaged to pay only in a future event, the payment in Dashwood's case had begun from the date of his appointment; that both payments were in favour of the person who had been designated by the initials A. B.; that the transactions, though protested against at the time, had been insisted upon by Lords Carteret and Le Despencer; and that not only had no record of them been made in the official books, but they had been kept carefully concealed. The Committee further reported that scandalous abuses had been found to exist at the Post Office, abuses which should be examined into and corrected forthwith; and that of many of these the First Lord of the Treasury had been specifically informed by Lord Tankerville before the latter was dismissed.

The chief interest of the inquiry, however, centred in the question— who was A. B.? A. B. proved to be one Peregrine Treves, a so-called friend of Carteret's, who had never performed any public service either in the Post Office or elsewhere. "Are you not a Jew and a foreigner?" asked the inexorable Committee. "Yes," was the reply. "In consideration of what services," the Committee continued, "did you receive these grants?" "From friendship entirely," answered Treves.

Tankerville's prediction had been amply fulfilled. It was not he that was disgraced. Yet, curiously enough, Carteret made no sign. And even Pitt did nothing more than expedite the proceedings of a Royal Commission which was already sitting. This Commission had been appointed at his instigation some years before to inquire into the duties and the pay of certain public departments, of which the Post Office was one. It was now arranged that the Post Office was to be the next to come under review.

During these dissensions at headquarters Palmer's plan had made steady progress. Many of the irregularities inseparable from the introduction of a new system had been corrected. The cross-posts had been fitted to the mail-coaches, so that failures of connection were daily becoming fewer; and when the merchants found that answers to their letters were being received in less than half the usual time, and with a degree of punctuality never experienced before, their complaints respecting the early closing of the Post Office appear to have died away. The Post Office revenue bore evidence to the improved state of things, the net receipt during the quarter ending the 5th of January 1787 being £73,000, as against £51,000 during the corresponding quarter of 1784. According to all experience, the increase in the rates of postage should have had the effect of reducing the number of letters; but so far was this from being the case that the number of letters had increased in spite of the increase of rates. The truth is that clandestine correspondence had to a large extent ceased. There was no longer any temptation to send by irregular means, at a cost of two or three shillings, and at the risk of detection, a letter which would be conveyed at least as expeditiously and for one-third of that amount by mail-coach.

Palmer, who had to this time been assisted by persons selected by himself and not belonging to the Post Office, now bestirred himself to procure for them an established position. Public and private interests were for once identical. Hitherto there had been only three surveyors for the whole of England; and of these one had resided in London. At Palmer's instigation, England was now divided into six postal districts, and a surveyor allotted to each. A seventh or spare surveyor was held in readiness to be detached to any part of the kingdom where his services might be required. Each surveyor was to reside in the centre of his district, and his functions, shortly stated, were to keep an accurate record of the posts and of the persons under his charge, to see that these persons did their duty, to facilitate correspondence and to remedy complaints. The resident surveyorship, an appointment which had been created in 1742, was abolished as no longer necessary, Palmer himself being at hand to give what advice the postmasters-general might require. The mode of remuneration was also altered. Hitherto the surveyors had received a salary of £300 a year without any allowance for travelling, the consequence being of course that they had travelled as little as possible. For the future the salary was to be only £100; but as an inducement to them to move about within their own districts, they were to have one guinea a day when absent from their headquarters. The whole of the additional appointments were conferred upon Palmer's nominees, and for the seventh or spare surveyorship he selected Francis Freeling, a young man of promise, who during the last two years had been actively engaged in regulating the mail-coaches throughout the country.

It was about this time or a little earlier that the conditions of Palmer's own employment were, at length, definitely settled, but not by any means to his own satisfaction. His first stipulation was that, besides being absolutely free from the control of the postmasters-general, he should have a commission of 2-1/2 per cent upon all increase in the net Post Office revenue, which should follow as the result of his own plan. Thus, the net Post Office revenue before August 1784 being estimated at £150,000, he stipulated for one-fortieth part of the excess over that amount. To this Pitt agreed; but freedom from the control of the postmasters-general was a point which it was out of his power to concede. The Act of Parliament constituting the Post Office would not admit of it. Even nominal subjection to the postmasters-general was so irksome to Palmer that he was constantly pressing that a special Act might be passed to give him perfect freedom. Nor was this all. The increase in the rates of postage which came into operation one month after the starting of the first mail-coach was estimated to produce £90,000 a year, and Pitt deemed it only reasonable that this amount should be added to the previous revenue of £150,000, making £240,000 altogether, before Palmer could be allowed to draw his percentage. Of this variation of the original understanding Palmer bitterly complained, not seeing apparently that, as the increase of rates had been recommended by himself, the complaint reflected on his own singleness of purpose in making the recommendation.

Eventually it was decided that, in addition to a commission of 2-1/2 per cent upon the net revenue in excess of £240,000, Palmer should receive a salary of £1500; but even this settlement was not arrived at without grumbling on Palmer's part, and without serious misgiving on the part of the Post Office. Pitt highly approved the percentage, holding that it would serve as a constant incentive to exertion. Tankerville, while not denying the expediency of such a mode of remuneration, questioned its legality. Under the Act of Anne, which a subsequent Act had made perpetual, the Post Office revenue was appropriated to certain specific purposes; and he doubted the propriety of diverting any part of it as a reward for services, however meritorious. Clarendon, Tankerville's successor, entertained the same scruples; and except by the postmasters-general no appointment within the Post Office could be made. Palmer's objection, on the contrary, was to the amount of salary, on the ground that £1500 did not represent the fortieth part of £90,000. Pitt declined, however, to give way; and on the 11th of October 1786 Palmer was appointed comptroller-general of the Post Office on the terms prescribed by the minister.

There can be no question that Palmer bargaining for terms is Palmer seen in his least pleasing aspect. The best that can be said is that he was candid enough not to disguise his object, which was to amass a fortune. At Bath he had in his boyhood seen Ralph Allen living in a large house and dispensing hospitality on an extensive scale, and he could not bring himself to understand why the difference between his own and Allen's remuneration should be in the inverse ratio to the value of their improvements. And not only did Palmer exhibit an unworthy jealousy of Allen, but he did that good man, as we think, an injustice. When urging his own claims on the minister, he constantly insisted that Allen, on the introduction of his plan, had no difficulties to contend with, and that he kept that plan a secret. Never was there a more untenable position. That Allen had difficulties to contend with and how he overcame them we have seen in a preceding chapter; and the charge of keeping his plan a secret is refuted by the conditions of his contract, which prevented him from giving an instruction even to his own servants until it had been submitted to headquarters. No doubt it was not known until after his death that Allen had derived from the Post Office an income of £12,000 a year. His wealth had been supposed to come from the stone-quarries he possessed on Combe Down. But this was not the contention. What Palmer insisted upon was that, while he had disclosed his plan, Allen had kept his plan secret, and that, if only on that ground, the balance of merit was on his own side.

In December 1787 the Commission of Inquiry commenced its labours. Exactly a century had elapsed since the Post Office had undergone a similar ordeal, a period too long for any public department to be left to itself; and meanwhile abuses had taken root and flourished. One hundred years before there had been no sinecures. Now the principal officers attended, some of them only occasionally and others not at all; and attendance, when attendance was given, often extended no later than to one or two o'clock in the afternoon. The receiver-general, for instance, attended on three days a week; and the accountant-general attended once or twice in three months, when the quarterly balance had to be made up. Court-post employed a deputy, to whom, out of a salary of £730, he made an annual allowance of £58. The solicitor, like court-post, was an absentee, but, unlike him, was careful not to part with even a fraction of his salary. In this case the deputy received as remuneration one-third part of the law charges incurred—a form of payment calculated more perhaps than any other to promote litigation. In the Penny Post Office were three principal officers—a comptroller, an accountant, and a collector. Of these the first two gave no attendance, and the third attended only occasionally, their duties being imposed upon the chief sorter, who, in all but salary, was practically the head of the department.

Meagre salaries were bolstered up by fees and perquisites, many of them of an outrageous character. While the senior letter-carrier was rigidly restricted to 312 candles in the year, a number not perhaps in excess of his actual requirements, there was hardly an officer reputed to be of any position in the Post Office, whether an absentee or otherwise, who was not provided with coals and candles for his private use. Although to some the supply of these articles was greater than to others, the usual annual allowance was, in the case of a subordinate, four, and, in the case of the head of a department, ten chaldron of coals, and in both cases thirty-two dozen pounds of candles. As the holder of two appointments, although he discharged the duties of only one of them, the comptroller of the bye and cross roads received a double allowance. Many commuted with the tradesmen whose duty it was to supply the articles for a money payment. Altogether the allowance to Post Office servants for their private use in town and country, and irrespective of what was consumed in the official apartments, exceeded in a single year 300 chaldron of coals and 20,000 pounds of candles.

The postmasters-general had long ceased to reside in the Post Office building; and yet to them was supplied, besides coals and candles, what was euphoniously termed tinware, by which is to be understood kitchen utensils. The expenditure on their account under the three heads during two years and a half was, for coals £2230, for candles £700, and for pots and pans £150.

Of stationery there was also a gratuitous supply for private as well as official use. One fee was a peculiarly cruel one, exacted as it was from a class of public servants who were unable to protect themselves. All postmasters whose salaries amounted to as much as £20 were forced to renew their deputations every three years, with no other object than to enrich the harpies at headquarters. On each renewal the same fee had to be paid as on appointment, namely £4:11s.; and of this amount 30s. went to each of the postmasters-general, 10s. to the secretary, 10s. to the solicitor, and 1s. to the door-keeper. The remainder was for stamp duty. Postmasters were also required to pay a fee of half a guinea before receiving a warrant to exempt them from serving in public offices. Christmas-boxes given by the merchants, and designed for the letter-carriers and other subordinates, were to a large extent appropriated by their superiors. From this source the comptroller of the foreign office, with an official income of £1300, was not ashamed to derive £34 a year. Others from the same source derived smaller amounts. Newspapers for reading were supplied in profligate profusion. One head of department was allowed for his own use two morning and five evening papers; another was paid £42:16s. a year to supply himself with what papers he pleased. All, whether absentees or not, received an annual payment under the title of drink and feast money, the lowest amount being £1:17s. and the highest £3:17s., and this was in addition to three or four so-called feasts given annually at the cost of the department. These with percentages on tradesmen's bills were some of the fees and perquisites which were now dragged to the light.

Out of the whole number there was only one which, besides being moderate and unobjectionable, possessed a certain interest as denoting the connection which had at one time subsisted between the Post Office and the Crown. This was a fee of 1s. received by the chief sorter at the General Post Office on the occasion of a birthday in the Royal Family; and as the Royal Family now consisted of twenty-one members, his emoluments from this source amounted to one guinea in the year.

There were two points on which the Royal Commissioners appear to have received less than full information. These were expresses and registered letters. Expresses, according to the old custom of the post, were still going at the rate of only six miles an hour, while the mail-coaches were going at the rate of eight. To this difference the Commissioners called attention; but they were silent as to the fees which some expresses paid, being apparently under the impression that all were treated alike. As a matter of fact, however, expresses had by this time been divided into two kinds—the public express and the private express. The public express, that is the express on public affairs, was allowed to pass without a fee, no doubt because the Post Office dared not impose one; but on every private express, in addition to the authorised mileage, was charged, if from London, a fee of 12s. 6d., and if from the country, a fee of 2s. 6d.; and of course in this, as in every other case, the fees were for the benefit of individuals.

On the subject of registered letters addressed to places abroad the Commissioners merely expressed the opinion that the registration fee, instead of being any longer treated as a perquisite, should be applied to the use of the public; but they nowhere stated, and perhaps had not been informed, what this fee was. It may be interesting if we supply the omission. The fee for registering a packet of value was, outwards[61] 21s., and inwards 5s. It seems incredible, and yet such is the unquestionable fact. For every letter registered for abroad the comptroller of the foreign office received 10s. 6d., the deputy-comptroller 4s. 6d., and six clerks 1s. apiece. One guinea for registration! And it was all the more monstrous because there can be little doubt that at one time letters had been practically registered without any fee at all. An Order in Council dated as far back as July 1556 had ordained "that the poste between this and the Northe should eche of them keepe a booke and make entrye of every letter that he shall receive, the tyme of the deliverie thereof unto his hands with the parties names that shall bring it unto him, whose handes he shall also take to his booke, witnessing the same note to be trewe." In 1603 another Order in Council passed, requiring that "every post shall keepe a large and faire leger paper booke, to enter our packets in as they shalbe brought unto him, with the day of the moneth, houre of the day or night, that they came first to his handes, together with the name of him or them, by whom or unto whom they were subscribed and directed." In 1680 Dockwra, when establishing his penny post, was careful to provide that letters on reaching any one of his seven sorting offices should be "entered"; and in a mere detail of treatment, it may well be believed, he followed the practice of the general post. In 1707 letters from abroad arriving at Harwich were not to be forwarded to the Court at Newmarket until the addresses had been copied. And more than this. In 1709 two letters between London and Ostend had been delayed, and it became important to discover where the delay had occurred. "We find them," wrote the postmasters-general, "both duly entered in Mr. Frowde's books, and are satisfy'd they were regularly dispatched from this office." Now Mr. Frowde was comptroller of the foreign office. It may be added that, small as was the force employed at the end of the seventeenth and beginning of the eighteenth centuries, it is difficult to account for the length of time which was then occupied in dealing with a mere handful of letters except on the hypothesis that there was a good deal more to be done than to sort and to tax them. And now the Post Office, upon no better authority than its own will, was exacting a fee of 21s. and 5s., according as the letter was outwards or inwards, for doing what some eighty years before had been done for nothing. The sums extorted from the public under this head were in 1783 £121, and in the following year £240.

As regards the working arrangements, Palmer, in virtue of the power he possessed as comptroller-general, had already corrected those that were most faulty. Until lately, the letter-carriers' walks had been so extensive that many of the deliveries could not be accomplished within five or six hours. Palmer had arranged that no delivery should occupy more than two hours or two hours and a half at the utmost, counting from the time of despatch from the General Post Office. It had been the practice for the junior clerks, the clerks with the least experience, to sort the letters for delivery, the consequence being that they reached the letter-carriers' hands in so confused a state that they had to be sorted again. Hence it had been by no means unusual for an interval of four or five hours to elapse between the arrival of the last mail and the going out of the letter-carriers. By appointing some of the most intelligent letter-carriers to sort the letters in the first instance, Palmer had reduced the interval to one hour on ordinary, and to one hour and a half on extraordinary occasions. As many as 400 postmasters had returned their letter-bills in one week, and on the plea of having been overcharged had claimed and been allowed deductions. Palmer had checked this abuse by arranging that in the case of those postmasters who were in the habit of returning their letter-bills the charges should be twice told. He had also reduced the amount expended on extra duty by £2000 a year. Heretofore, if a man had chosen to absent himself, the Post Office had provided a substitute. For the future the substitute was to be provided at the absentee's own expense.

But although Palmer had already corrected the most faulty of the arrangements, some still existed which could not be pronounced good. The accountant-general was intended to be a check upon the receiver-general; yet, instead of keeping an independent record of the sums received, he merely transcribed or caused to be transcribed the entries from the receiver-general's books. The accountant-general, again, was required to certify every bill before the postmasters-general passed it for payment; but as he was not empowered to call for vouchers or for the authority under which the expenditure had been incurred, his certificate conveyed nothing more than that the bill had been rightly cast. The accounts themselves appear to have been rendered in the strangest manner. The article "Dead Letters," for instance, was made to serve a variety of purposes. Under this article postmasters were accustomed to claim chaise-hire, law charges, and even pensions to private persons.

The packet service was a part of the Post Office which the Commissioners would fain have avoided if they could; but the public voice was too strong for them. The enormous expenditure which this service involved had long excited murmurs, and the opportunity which now offered of investigating the causes of it was one which could not with any regard to propriety be missed. Accordingly the inquiry was entered upon; but with a desire to restrict it as far as possible the Commissioners did not extend their investigations beyond the packet station at Falmouth, where more than three-fourths of the expenditure was incurred. To ourselves, who are under no obligation to observe a similar limit, perhaps a little more latitude may be allowed.

The continental mails by way of Dover and Harwich went at this time only twice a week; and by a curious arrangement these mails started from the General Post Office at midnight, although the inland mails for the same towns and going by the same route started at eight o'clock in the evening. At Harwich the packet station had abandoned itself to smuggling. In 1774 two packets, the *Bessborough* and the *Prince of Wales*, were seized for having contraband goods on board. Not a single voyage had these packets made during the last two years without committing a similar infringement of the law. The Commissioners of Customs, whose patience was exhausted, now commenced proceedings in the Court of Exchequer, and were prevailed upon to abandon them only upon the captains, who were also owners of the vessels, paying by way of fine two-third parts of their appraised value—amounting to £306 in one case and to £272 in the other—of which sums one-half was to go to the Crown and one-half to the officer by whom the goods had been discovered. This high reward was not long in reproducing the occasion on account of which it had been given. In November 1777 another seizure took place, this time of three packets simultaneously, two of them being the same as had been seized in 1774. The third was the *Dolphin*. On this occasion the Commissioners of Customs determined that the vessels should be prosecuted to condemnation. In vain the postmasters-general urged that the law was a hard one which made the captains responsible for offences which, it was alleged, they had done their best to check. The customs authorities were inexorable. It was not long, however, before the Post Office became possessed of certain facts which, when investigated, proved beyond a doubt that there had for years past been collusion of the grossest character. On every voyage contraband goods—chiefly tea, coffee, and gin—had, with the connivance of the local officers of customs, been imported in large quantities; and of these only a part, a comparatively small part, had been seized. Thus, the Post Office servants received from the goods that were left to them ample, and more than ample, compensation for those that were taken away; and the servants of the customs received from their Board in London both credit and reward for their vigilance. Nor was it by any means certain that the seizure of the packets in 1774 and again in 1777 was not another phase of the same collusive arrangement.

At Falmouth the case was somewhat different. Smuggling, indeed, was going on there just as it was at Harwich. As far back as 1744 the customs had issued process against the captains of two of the Falmouth packets for having contraband goods on board. The case is only worthy of mention as shewing the loose notions which at that time prevailed even in high quarters on the subject of clandestine traffic. The postmasters-general of the day, Lord Lovell and Sir John Eyles, told the Board of Customs in so many words that their conduct was unhandsome. It was vain, they urged, to endeavour to prevent "these little clandestine importations and exportations" on board the packets; and if violent measures were to be resorted to, as in the present instance, no captain "of real worth and character" would be found to command, and "no fit and able" seamen to serve. Again, in 1776 the *Greyhound* packet was seized at the port of Kingston in Jamaica for attempting to smuggle spirits. Early in 1788 the *Queen Charlotte* packet was condemned and sold at the same port and for the same cause. In 1786 a special agent sent down to Falmouth by Tankerville reported that, according to common repute, no packet either proceeded on a voyage or returned from one without hovering about the coast for the purpose of shipping or unshipping goods.

But, rife as smuggling was, it was something more than an infringement of the customs laws that now brought the packet station at Falmouth into notoriety. During the seventeen years ending the 5th of April 1787, the cost of the packets had exceeded £1,038,000; and of this amount about £800,000 had been expended at Falmouth. At the present day, when a single mail steamer costs perhaps as much as £300,000, the sum of £1,000,000 sterling would not go far to create and maintain a fleet; but a century ago it was considered, even when spread over a period of seventeen years, an enormous expenditure, an expenditure such as, in the language of the Royal Commissioners, almost to surpass credibility. And certainly there seems to have been good ground for this opinion. The packets altogether were only thirty-six in number, of which twenty-one were stationed at Falmouth. These were of no more than 200 tons burthen, and were navigated with thirty men, five of them being the property of the Post Office and fifteen being hired. For each of the hired boats was paid the annual sum of £2129, and for each of the others the annual sum of £1529, these sums including the charge of manning and victualling. The sixteen packets stationed elsewhere than at Falmouth were hired at ridiculously low prices, at Dover for £412 a year each, at Harwich for £469, and at Holyhead for £350. To expend upon the packets under such conditions as these more than £1,000,000 sterling in the course of seventeen years required no small amount of ingenuity. How was it managed? This was the question which the Royal Commissioners now set themselves to solve.

The grossest abuses were found to exist. The hire of the packets had been paid when they were under seizure for smuggling, and under repair, and even when they were building. In the case of packets that were building and under repair the victualling allowance paid when there were no men to victual had amounted in twelve years and a half to £56,000. When packets had been taken by the enemy the hire of them had been paid for months beyond the date of their capture; and this was in addition to compensation to the owners, which, however old and rotten the packet might be, was fixed at her original value when taken into the service. Compensation to the captains had also been given for the loss of their private property and of provisions. For provisions the compensation had always been as for six months' supply, although the supply that was actually on board might not be enough for one month; and for their private property the captains had been compensated at their own valuation. Whatever they had asked they had received without examination and without question. This astounding prodigality indulged in at the expense of the State is easily explained. The Post Office servants in London, down even to the chamber-keeper, had shares in the packets; and of these servants the one who possessed by far the largest number of shares was Anthony Todd, the secretary. Todd also received a commission of 2-1/2 per cent upon the entire sum expended on the packet establishment of the kingdom. Thus, the very man whose duty it was to check the expenditure had a direct personal interest in making the expenditure as high as possible.

The salary of the Secretary to the Post Office remained, as it was fixed in 1703, at £200 a year; and whatever Todd received over and above that amount, he received without authority. Let us see what his actual receipts were. In addition to his proper salary of £200, he had what was called a bye salary of £75. Bye had at one time meant out of course or clandestine; and this meaning would perhaps not be inappropriate here. He had for coach hire £100 a year. He had another £100 a year from Lloyds's coffee-house. He had from fees on commissions and deputations £154 a year. He had every year twenty chaldron of coal and twelve dozen of wax and sixty-four dozen of tallow candles, valued by himself at £103. He had an unfurnished residence with stables in the Post Office building; and he received annually from the East India Company eight pounds of tea and two dozen of arrack. But this was by no means all. As former clerk in the foreign branch, an appointment which he still retained, he had a salary of £50 and an allowance of £100 a year for so-called disbursements, which he never made. He had also, in his capacity of clerk, £15 a year for coach-hire and ten chaldron of coal and thirty-two dozen of candles, valued at £40. Besides all this, he had his commission of 2-1/2 per cent upon the entire packet expenditure of the country, from which source he derived in the year 1782 no less than £2136. Altogether, Todd's modest salary of £200 a year had, by his own unaided exertions, been converted into an annual income of more than £3000.

The extent of Todd's emoluments, his commission on the packet expenditure, the outrageous character of some of the fees and perquisites which he and others were receiving, the absenteeism, the abuses generally— all this had long been known to Pitt. Much he had heard from Tankerville, and still more, probably, from Palmer. But before either Palmer or Tankerville became connected with the Post Office, Pitt had been aware of many, if not most, of the abuses which prevailed there. As early as 1782 one of his first acts after becoming Chancellor of the Exchequer in the Shelburne administration was to give peremptory orders that no more packets were to be either built or purchased without Treasury authority. For such authority it had hitherto been the practice to ask before setting up new packets, but not before replacing old ones—packets that were worn out or alleged to be worn out, or that had been lost or captured. This was a distinction which had existed since packets were first established, and to which, nearly a hundred years before, Cotton and Frankland had attached great importance. It was now to exist no longer. In 1783 Pitt called for a return of the fees and perquisites received at the Post Office, and it was not until after this return had been furnished and possibly in consequence of it that the Commission of Inquiry was appointed. "Did you ever communicate this transaction to Mr. Pitt," inquired the Parliamentary Committee in 1787. "I did," replied Tankerville, "but found him not ill-informed on the subject in general."

It may seem strange that with the knowledge which he unquestionably possessed respecting the prevalent abuses Pitt should have allowed them to go on so long uncorrected. The explanation we believe to be twofold. In the first place he was unwilling to do or suffer to be done anything which might interfere with the introduction of Palmer's improvements. This was a point on which Pitt never ceased to betray the utmost anxiety. To embark on any general system of reform might conflict with the new plan. Let the plan be established first and the abuses could be corrected afterwards. Hence it was, no doubt, that of all the public offices to be inquired into, the Post Office, in spite of the notoriety which its abuses had acquired, was taken last. But this, although the primary explanation, was not, we suspect, the only one. Incorrupt himself, Pitt was extraordinarily tolerant of corruption in others. Witness his defence of Melville. Even of Carteret's transaction with Peregrine Treves he could never be brought to admit more than that it was not a proper one. This tolerance in others of what he would have scorned to do himself we attribute to a conviction on his part that abuses were less to be charged against individuals than as the result of a bad system which made the abuses possible; and what, if we mistake not, Pitt had proposed to himself was to bring to bear upon this system the force of public opinion. A ruthless exposure, we have little doubt, had been in contemplation; and yet when the time for exposure came, Pitt held back. Whether it was that the abuses proved too flagrant to be published with safety or that their correction would involve more time or more money than could then be spared, the fact remains that, after receiving the report of the Commission, Pitt locked it up in his despatch box and kept it there for the space of four years; and not even the postmasters-general could procure a copy.

But secret as the report of the Commission was kept, the procedure at the Post Office was about to undergo a radical change. A change indeed had already begun. Tankerville, on his dismissal in August 1786, had been succeeded by Lord Clarendon; and Clarendon died in the following December. Then followed an interval of eight months, during which Carteret alone administered the Post Office and, as was usual on such occasions, drew the double salary. At length, as Carteret's colleague, Pitt appointed Lord Walsingham; and from that moment irregularity and disorder were at an end. Nothing escaped Walsingham's vigilant eye. To neglect or evasion of work he shewed no mercy. The man honestly striving to do his duty had no better friend. His industry and power of work were simply amazing. All instructions were prepared by him. Not a single letter of any importance was received at the Post Office without the answer to it being drafted in his own hand. Generous to a fault with his own money, he regarded the money of the public as a sacred trust, a trust which could not be discharged too scrupulously. Carteret's opinion was well known, that it was no part of a postmaster-general's duty to check accounts. Walsingham, on the contrary, would allow no account to be passed until he had checked it; and his checking went a good deal beyond the casting. Unless the articles were necessary and the charges reasonable, and unless they were proved to be so to his satisfaction, the account had a sorry chance of being passed. The official hours of attendance had hitherto been pretty much what each man chose to make them. To Walsingham all hours were alike; and at all hours he exacted attendance from others. "It is utterly impossible," wrote the head of one department, "for the accounts to be ready for your inspection to-morrow evening." "I will not fail," wrote the head of another, "to do myself the honour of waiting upon your Lordship to-morrow morning at eight precisely."

Walsingham, on entering upon his duties at the Post Office, was concerned to find that to documents requiring to be signed by the two postmasters-general Carteret attached his signature first. Carteret's peerage dated from 1784, and Walsingham's from 1780. Surely the peer of older creation should sign first; and such, Walsingham found on inquiry, had been the practice hitherto. Pitt, though overwhelmed with business, was called upon to decide the momentous question. He was sorry, he said, that in the preparation of the patent the practice of the Post Office had been overlooked. It was a strange practice, a practice different from that of all other public offices. There the senior, the one who was first to enter the office, took precedence of the junior whatever his rank; and Carteret having been mentioned first in the patent must unquestionably sign first. But this, he added, need not be drawn into a precedent, and, on a new patent passing, the old practice of the office might be reverted to. We may here mention that a few years later the Earl of Chesterfield became Walsingham's colleague; but on that occasion Walsingham does not appear to have raised the question again or to have been unwilling to conform to the new practice. And, indeed, whether Walsingham signed before or after Carteret must to every one except himself have appeared of the least possible importance. Sign in what order he might, Walsingham's influence soon became paramount. Carteret might give what instruction he pleased, but unless endorsed by Walsingham a Post Office servant obeyed it at his peril. Walsingham, on the contrary, gave instructions without reference to his colleague, and exacted prompt and implicit obedience.

With many of the qualities of a great man, Walsingham was strangely wanting in one particular. He had no sense of proportion. A trivial point hardly deserving of a moment's consideration he would elaborate as carefully as a measure involving large and important issues; and a clerical error or a slight indiscretion he would visit as severely as misconduct of the gravest character. Nor must we omit to mention a habit in which he indulged to an extent that has probably never been surpassed. This was a habit of annotating. Nothing came officially before him, whether a letter or a report or a book, without being covered in the margin and every available space with notes and queries; and, to add to the distraction which this mode of criticism seldom fails to cause, they were in so small and crabbed a hand as to be always difficult, and sometimes even with the aid of a magnifying-glass impossible, to decipher.

There was only one person that had the slightest influence with Walsingham. This was Daniel Braithwaite, who, holding nominally the situation of clerk to the postmasters-general, was really their private secretary. Braithwaite was a Fellow of the Royal Society. Of consummate tact and judgment, and endowed with a peculiar sweetness of disposition, he contrived during difficult times to tone down asperities and to accommodate many a dissension which promised to become acute. Passing through his hands a harsh admonition was turned into a gentle reproof, and an imperious command into a courteous message. But under this softness of manner and a deference of language so profound that even Walsingham quizzed him on the number of "Lordships" he would introduce into a single letter, there lay concealed a solidity of character which few would have suspected. Honest Braithwaite he was called, and well he deserved the epithet. By a simple inquiry, a request for information or the expression of a doubt, he would nip some wild project in the bud, and, where occasion required, he would not hesitate to speak his mind freely. A young man, Stokes by name, who had been appointed to assist Braithwaite, had miscopied a date in one of Walsingham's numerous drafts, or rather, feeling sure that the date as it stood was wrong, had altered it to what he believed to be the right one. Walsingham, who was absent from London at the time, wrote back that Stokes was to be suspended. Braithwaite's sense of justice was shocked, and he refused to carry the order into effect. "If a mistake in copying," he wrote, "deserves so severe a punishment as suspension, what am I not to fear for disobedience, and yet I really cannot execute the task your Lordship has imposed upon me. For God's sake, my dear lord," he proceeded, "let me most earnestly entreat you to mitigate the severity of this sentence, and, if a reprimand at the Board is not sufficient, give poor Stokes a holiday and impose the fine for a substitute upon me. At any rate," he added, "pray leave the case to be decided at a Board or refer it to Mr. Todd." Walsingham did refer the case to Todd, but not before he had sternly demanded of his refractory henchman whether he had never read Beccaria on Crimes and Punishments. "No," replied Braithwaite, "I have not read Beccaria on Crimes and Punishments; but Beccaria, say what he may, will never convince me that it can be right to punish a mistake as though it were a crime." Honest Braithwaite! He prevailed in the end, and stood in Walsingham's confidence even higher than before.

At a Board meeting on the 20th of July 1787, less than a fortnight after taking up his appointment, Walsingham in the presence of the captains who were ashore, and who had been summoned to London for the occasion, gave notice of his intention to reduce the packet establishment at Falmouth. That establishment consisted of twenty-one boats of 200 tons each, and manned by thirty men. It was proposed that for the future there should be twenty boats of 150 tons each, and with a complement of eighteen men. These boats would cost about £3000 apiece to build, and would not be the property of the Government. The Government would simply hire them, giving as the price of hire £1350 a year, which was to cover everything, wages and victualling included. The owners would also have the passage money, estimated at £150, for each boat. Large as this reduction was, the Treasury desired that it should be carried further, that only the boats to America should be of as much as 150 tons, and that those for the West Indies and for Lisbon should be of 100. The captains, who had not relished the proposed reduction even to 150 tons, were half-amused and half-indignant. Why, they asked, should the boats for America be the largest? Were hurricanes unknown in the West Indies? And could not the Bay of Biscay boast of tremendous seas? Boats of 100 tons would be positively dangerous. No passenger would go by them; nor would any merchant trust them with bullion, from the freight of which the Post Office derived a considerable income.

The postmasters-general had also on their side the result of experience. In 1745, when the packet service to the West Indies, which had ceased in 1711, was re-established, boats of 100 tons had been tried and had proved to be altogether insufficient. Moreover, it was in the highest degree important, as a means of checking smuggling, that the boats should not be restricted to one route. The intention was that they should be interchangeable, so that their port of destination should be uncertain; and to this end the tonnage of one should be the tonnage of all. The Treasury appear to have remained unmoved by these representations. At all events no decision was received; and Walsingham, after waiting for what he no doubt considered an unreasonable time, took silence for assent and proceeded to carry his recommendations into effect.

The economical results which had been looked for were not immediately realised. The boats hitherto in use may not perhaps have been built with the view of facilitating smuggling; and yet, crowded as they were between decks with cupboards, they could hardly have been better adapted to the purpose. In the new boats no receptacles were to be allowed in which clandestine goods could be concealed; the holds were to be only large enough to contain the stores and provisions for the voyage; the seamen were no longer to remain unrestricted as to the size and number of their boxes; and in other respects stringent regulations were laid down to prevent illicit traffic. Finding what they called their ventures stopped, the crews of the packets refused to go to sea without an increase of pay all round. These ventures, they contended, had been recognised from time immemorial and went in place of so much wages. How else would it have been possible for them, many of them men with wives and families, to subsist on a pittance of 23s. a month? The Post Office was forced to yield to the demand; and as the immediate result of his first essay in the cause of economy, Walsingham had the mortification of seeing the cost of the packet establishment increased by more than £2300 a year.

From Falmouth Walsingham turned his attention to other ports where packets were stationed. At Dover and at Harwich the establishments were too small to admit of any reduction. At the latter port, indeed, what little change took place was on the side of increase, the victualling allowance being raised from 7-1/2d. a day for each man to 9d., so as to be uniform with that given at Falmouth; and for the same reason the seamen's wages were raised from 23s. a month to 28s.

With Holyhead the case was different. Here Walsingham had resolved upon making a reduction, and it was only on an earnest remonstrance from the Marquis of Buckingham, the Lord-Lieutenant of Ireland, that he abandoned his intention. The Holyhead packets were at this time five in number, and they were of seventy tons each and carried twelve hands. Walsingham held that this tonnage and complement of men were more than enough; and Buckingham maintained a directly contrary opinion. Between England and Ireland, he urged, the number of passengers was increasing every year, and surely this was not a time to lessen the confidence of the public in the security of the packets. The danger of navigation in those seas could not, he felt sure, be appreciated. He had himself crossed the Channel in all weathers. Once he had been nearly lost, and not on that occasion alone he had seen the crews, though at their full complement, absolutely prostrate with their exertions. Could it be known that, for purposes of passenger traffic, the captains of the Holyhead packets had recently built and fitted out at their own expense a sloop named the *Duchess of Rutland*; and that for this sloop, which, although vastly superior in point of accommodation to any one of the packets, was of no higher tonnage, the complement had been fixed at twelve hands? This would shew what was the opinion on the point of those who were most competent to judge. The fact, moreover, that Ireland had undertaken to pay to Great Britain the sum of 2d. on every letter passing to and fro placed the English Post Office under a sort of moral obligation not to reduce the amount of accommodation and security existing at the time the undertaking was given. Such were the arguments by which Buckingham prevailed upon Walsingham to abandon his intention. He at the same time hinted that there were other objects to which Walsingham's energies might more properly be directed. "Does your Lordship know," he asked, "that an immense communication of letters is kept up by the Liverpool packets[62] which sail weekly to Dublin?"

One line of packets remains, the line between Milford Haven and Waterford. Here five boats were employed, of which three were of eighty tons and the others somewhat less; and the service was six days a week. This, though the youngest of the packet stations, was by no means the least interesting. It had been opened in April 1787; and in the first year the proceeds from passengers alone amounted to more than £1200. No doubt had been entertained that in the matter of letters there would be an equally satisfactory account to render; but it soon became evident that all hopes on this score must be given up. The Irish Post Office was no longer subject to the Post Office of England; and in the supposed interests of Dublin, which regarded with jealousy the postal facilities enjoyed by the southern towns, advantage was taken of this freedom from control to checkmate the new service. From Waterford the post for Cork had been used to start at two o'clock in the afternoon, an hour most convenient for the packets. Under orders from Dublin it was now to start at twelve; and, as shewing the vexatiousness of the proceeding, an express leaving Waterford as late as four o'clock would overtake the mail at Carrick, a distance of no more than fifteen miles. Under the same orders Limerick was forbidden to send letters by way of Waterford; and the post between this town and Clonmel was reduced from six days a week to three. This was a state of things which, under the system of Home Rule then existing, Walsingham was powerless to remedy. He could only lift his hands in amazement that such perversity should be possible.

But it was not exclusively or even mainly to the packet establishment that Walsingham's attention was directed. There was no part of the Post Office with which he did not make himself thoroughly acquainted; and in the course of his investigations nothing struck him more than the pitiable condition of the clerks of the roads. The case of these men had been gradually getting worse and worse. It is true that ten years before a part of the salaries and pensions for which they were responsible had been transferred to the State; but the relief thus afforded had been neutralised and more than neutralised by the decrease which had since taken place in their emoluments from the franking of newspapers. Of these emoluments, indeed, little now remained. In the seventeen years from 1772 to 1789 the notices served upon the Post Office by members of Parliament to send newspapers into the country free had risen from a little more than 2000 to 7000, and the number of newspapers which these 7000 notices covered amounted to no less than 65,760 a week. In the face of such competition the special privilege enjoyed by the clerks of the roads was practically valueless, and Walsingham and Carteret clearly discerned that to compensate them for the loss of their emoluments by an increase of salary was an act dictated no less by justice than policy.

The case indeed was urgent if a catastrophe were to be averted; and Carteret, whose experience led him to believe that the salaries would not be increased with the consent of the Treasury, proposed to increase them without. Walsingham was shocked at the audacity of the proposal, and read his colleague a homily on the constitutional proprieties. "I know," replied Carteret, "we shall have the power of increasing salaries with the consent of the Treasury, but many may starve before that consent comes." Even Walsingham admitted the gravity of the occasion; and with the full knowledge that at this time no representation from the Post Office reached the Treasury which did not come under Pitt's own observation, the two peers, after recommending a substantial measure of relief, concluded their letter thus: "We shall find ourselves compelled, if the present weight of Parliamentary and official duties shall make it impossible for your Lordships to give us the authority we request in the course of a week, to take it upon ourselves to issue the money at our own risk, or the persons who are the object of this relief will be unable to attend their duty, and the business of the office will be literally at a stand." Whatever Pitt may have thought of the somewhat unusual terms of this address, he allowed no sign of dissatisfaction to escape him, and the authority sought was given.

As long as Walsingham confined his attention to the packets and the clerks of the roads, there was no danger of a collision with Palmer. Palmer, on the contrary, offered his congratulations to Walsingham on the improvement which he had been instrumental in making in these officers' condition. It was when Walsingham gave an instruction which even indirectly affected the inland posts that Palmer's jealousy was aroused. This he regarded as his own peculiar domain, a domain upon which even the postmasters-general themselves were trespassers; and a trespass or what he considered as such he never lost an opportunity of resenting. The earliest and not the least curious illustration of these pretensions appears in the case of the King's coach. In the summer of 1788 the King repaired to Cheltenham for the purpose of drinking the waters, and Walsingham, who was above all things a courtier, had arranged that during the royal visit a mail-coach should be stationed at that town for the exclusive use of His Majesty. The coach was to be a new one, sent down from London for the occasion, and the leading contractor on the Cheltenham road, one Wilson by name, was to provide the horses. The royal visit at an end, the contractor's bill was sent in, and Palmer, in forwarding it to Walsingham, professed to be extremely dissatisfied with the magnitude of the charge. On the sale of the horses and harness alone, after only a month's use, there had been a loss of £550. "Nothing," he said, "could have been more absurdly or extravagantly conducted." But the thing was done. It would be useless to dispute the payment. Besides, it would "soil the compliment" designed to His Majesty. "We must," he added, "take more care next time, for, had it been properly settled, the loss at most could not have exceeded £300."

The actual arrangement for the coach had been made not through Palmer but through Bonnor, Palmer's lieutenant; and to him Walsingham now applied for further information. Bonnor's reply was a strange compound of candour and insolence. It was indeed not to be wondered at, he said, that his Lordship's indignation should be roused by the magnitude of the bill. Had the matter been left as originally settled under Mr. Palmer's orders, Wilson could never have made so monstrous a claim. By those orders he had been given to understand that, the coach being designed as a mere compliment to the King, not more than 1d. a mile would be allowed at the outside. And "so the undertaking stood 'till your Lordship ordered the circular letter to the horse-keepers respecting Sir George Baker's[63] being accommodated with the mail horses if he had occasion. Your Lordship will recollect that I remonstrated against it, and urged the impossibility of Wilson ever allowing his mail horses to be taken out of his stables for posting, and the regularity of the work destroyed, and the cattle drove along by people he knew nothing of; to which your Lordship was pleased to say that Wilson had no business to trouble his head about that; that, whatever his expenses were, he should be paid; and that no feelings of his about his horses or anything else should prevent the thing being done in the best possible style."... "Thinking as little in the delivery of the message as your Lordship did in sending it that such an advantage would be taken, I of course obeyed the directions, and it seems that this is the ground upon which the charge is made out as it is."

Walsingham was not satisfied, and resolved to contest the bill. Palmer now took alarm, and urged every consideration he could think of to dissuade Walsingham from his purpose. To have recourse to a Court of Law might seriously damage his infant undertaking. A legal dispute had been avoided hitherto, and, with a cunning and refractory set of persons such as the contractors were, might have the effect of raising the present terms of conveyance. These terms were low, lower than the Post Office was likely to obtain again; and the mail-coaches were running smoothly. It would be a thousand pities to introduce an element of disturbance. Besides, how unpleasant it would be to his Lordship to be subpœnaed as a witness; and, in the hands of an expert counsel, how supremely ridiculous the whole business might be made to appear! The King's jaunt with a mail-coach in attendance! For his own part, when he had been unfortunate enough to be imposed upon, he generally found it best to put up with the imposition and to take more care another time. Nor should it be forgotten that the matter might have been much worse. When first he had heard of the arrangement, he had rebuked Bonnor for his extravagance; and Bonnor had produced two letters from his Lordship in justification. These letters shewed not only that no expense was to be spared, but that it had originally been in contemplation to have two coaches, and that it was only owing to Bonnor's earnest expostulation that the idea of a second coach had been given up. Surely it was cause for congratulation that the bill was no higher. Had two coaches been established instead of one, Wilson might have clapped on another £1000. As the bill stood, it was a gross imposition, an imposition which must condemn him in the eyes of all honest men; and yet it would be pure madness to go to law. These arguments prevailed, and Walsingham abandoned his intention of contesting the bill. He did not at this time see, what he saw clearly enough some years later, that in retaliation upon himself for presuming to interfere Wilson had been cajoled or coerced into making an exorbitant demand, and that of the several persons who were concerned in the transaction Wilson himself was the least to blame.

This may be a convenient place to notice a point in which the practice of 1788 differed from that of the present time. It was only a few months after his return from Cheltenham that the King was taken with the serious illness which so nearly proved fatal. On the 9th of November the accounts from Windsor were such as to leave little room for hope. On the 10th intelligence reached the Post Office at three o'clock in the afternoon that, contrary to all expectation, the King was still living; and on the 14th a form of prayer was issued, to be used in all churches, for His Majesty's recovery. At the present time a circular of this kind would reach the Post Office already addressed to the persons for whom it was intended, and the Post Office would do nothing more than carry and deliver it like an ordinary letter. But such was not the case in 1788. The form of prayer, as it was issued by the printer, was sent to the Post Office in bulk, and the Post Office despatched fifty copies to the postmaster of each town with instructions to distribute them "with all possible expedition to the rectors, vicars, or resident ministers of your town and all places in your delivery." The point is hardly deserving of mention, for, of course, it would make little difference to the postmaster whether the copies were sent in bulk or as single letters. He would be bound to deliver them in either case. It is more worthy of note that, as the number of Post Offices in England was at this time only 608, and the area subordinate to each of correspondingly wide extent, to go over the whole of his delivery at one time as these instructions obliged the postmaster to do was no slight undertaking, and one which, owing to the paucity of letters, he had probably not been required to perform on any previous occasion. In this instance, however, we may feel sure that a sense of loyalty alone precluded all disposition to murmur. With far other feelings, it may well be believed, was an order regarded which had been issued rather more than thirty years before. The year 1756 was a year of scarcity; and, under direction from Whitehall, postmasters were to frequent the local markets and to ascertain and report the price of corn. This is the first instance on record of postmasters having been employed outside their own proper duties as such. It may be added that two years later the Duke of Newcastle sent down in hot haste to Lombard Street to inquire the latest prices, when it was explained to His Grace that, despite the course which had been adopted in 1756, the Post Office was not an office for the collection of agricultural returns.

It is a common practice to laugh at public offices for their rigid adherence to routine. This, we think, is not quite reasonable. No doubt it is calculated to excite ridicule, and indeed to irritate beyond all endurance when a course obviously proper in itself is condemned because, forsooth, there is no precedent for it; and we are by no means sure that some public servants would not be all the better for taking to heart the maxim—Wise men make precedents, only fools require them. But, without the order and regularity which a strict adherence to routine can alone produce, the business of a Government department must inevitably drift into a state of hopeless confusion. This is a truth which persons outside the public service have always found it hard to accept; as well indeed as persons inside who have entered late in life or after their habits are formed. Palmer was of the latter class; and a striking instance now occurred of his inability to adapt himself to the requirements of his new situation. Walsingham had asked whether the surveyors were keeping their journals regularly. These officers, besides a small salary, were now receiving an allowance of one guinea a day when travelling; and not only was a journal indispensable in order to shew whether they had been travelling or not, but the keeping of one had been made an express condition of the allowance being given. No subordinate cared to pass on the inquiry to Palmer, implying, as this might seem to do, a doubt. Walsingham had no such scruple and wrote to Palmer asking that the journals might be sent to him for examination. Palmer's reply will explain how it is that the records which now exist respecting himself and his achievements are so surprisingly few. There were no journals, he said. The surveyors' own letters, with their bills of expenses attached, were sufficient evidence of the journeys they had made. And these bills and letters, he added, as soon as the charges which they represent have been paid, "are and must be useless paper, for if I did not constantly clear my office both of their as well as my own and the other officers' rubbish, I should be buried under it." The auditors of the imprests had recently made good progress, but, fortunately for the Post Office, they were still many years in arrear.[64]

Among Walsingham's correspondents was George Chalmers, a merchant of Edinburgh. Chalmers was no mere maker of crude and impracticable suggestions. He had thirty years before been instrumental in shortening the course of post between Edinburgh and London. Before 1758 the Great North Mail, as it was called, went three days a week and occupied eighty-seven hours in going from London to Edinburgh, and 131 hours in going from Edinburgh to London. Thus, a mail leaving Edinburgh at twelve at night on Saturday did not reach London until eleven o'clock on Friday morning. Chalmers, in a paper of singular ability, dwelt upon the absurdity of the various detentions, ranging from three hours at Berwick to twenty-four hours at Newcastle, which made the course of post longer by nearly two days in one direction than in the other, and shewed how, by avoiding these unnecessary delays and getting rid of a diversion of twelve miles to York, the distance might be accomplished between London and Edinburgh in eighty-two hours, and between Edinburgh and London in eighty-five.

The plan was adopted, and some years later, in recognition of its merits, Chalmers received from the Government a gratuity of £600. More recently he had prevailed upon the Post Office to increase from three to six days a week the service between London and Edinburgh, and from Edinburgh to the principal towns in Scotland; and in London, at his suggestion, the letter-carriers who collected letters by the sound of bell, or bellmen as they had begun to be called, were being employed after nine o'clock at night.

It was not, therefore, as a novice in Post Office matters that Chalmers now entered into correspondence with Walsingham. His present representation was in the nature partly of a suggestion and partly of a complaint. He had been staying some time in London, and was surprised to find that at the capital of the first commercial nation in the world the Post Office closed as early as seven o'clock in the evening. He contended that it ought not to close before ten. But it was in respect to his own native city of Edinburgh that he felt and expressed himself most warmly. Edinburgh was without a penny post. He was himself an old man or he would undertake to farm one, although, in his judgment, the farming of such an institution, until at least it was well established, was not for the public interests. But surely, whether farmed or not, a penny post should be opened without delay, and on his return to Edinburgh he would let Walsingham know how this could best be done. Nor was the want of such a convenience by any means the chief thing of which the inhabitants of Edinburgh had to complain. Since 1758 their post had not gone out until eight o'clock at night. Now, to suit Palmer's arrangements, it went out at half-past three in the afternoon; and, more than this, the diversion to York, which it had cost such pains to get rid of some thirty years before, had been revived. Thus, between Edinburgh and London the course of post was actually longer now than before the introduction of mail-coaches by as much as five hours. Were a little more consideration to be given to the correspondence of the country and a little less to the convenience of passengers, more than these five hours might be saved. At all events the mails might start from Edinburgh at eight o'clock as before, and from London at ten, and yet arrive at their destination no later than now. For himself, he thought it hardly decent that passengers should be allowed to travel by the same coaches as the mails, and predicted that a time would come when the mails would have coaches to themselves. Much of this, Chalmers added, he had pointed out to Palmer some time before, and the only result was an angry letter which had terminated a friendship of years. Even as he now wrote, another letter had come to hand in which Palmer told him, almost in so many words, to mind his own business.

Walsingham was at this time at Old Windsor. Hither it was his habit to repair whenever he had anything of more than ordinary interest to engage his attention; and such was the case at the present moment. He had recently had lent to him, under a pledge of the strictest secrecy, a copy of the Report of the Royal Commission which had sat upon the Post Office in the preceding year; and this Report he was now having copied under his own eye with a view to the preparation of an elaborate criticism upon it. But though absent from London he relaxed not his hold upon the Post Office for a single moment. Each morning's post brought to Lombard Street its own budget of drafts, to be written out fair, of questions to be answered, of scoldings to be given, and of instructions to heads of departments in the minutest details of their duty. Walsingham absent was a far more important personage than Carteret present; and a mandate from Old Windsor superseded any that might be given on the spot. It was while Walsingham was thus engaged that he received one morning from Palmer a few hurried lines, of which the last were as follows: "You ought not, meaning as well as you do, to be unpopular anywhere. Nor must you. You fret me now and then, tho' you don't intend it, and I am angry with myself for it." A visit from Palmer on the following morning, especially as that morning was Sunday, was little calculated to lessen the surprise with which Walsingham must have read this letter. The truth is that Palmer had repaired to Windsor with the intention of resigning his appointment; but the courteous reception he met with from Walsingham disconcerted his plan, and he returned to London as he had come, with the letter of resignation in his pocket.

The reasons which Palmer afterwards gave for his conduct on this occasion throw a flood of light upon his character. These reasons were: 1st, That Walsingham was ready to listen to proposals for improving the Post Office, come from what quarter they might, thus leaving it to be inferred, as Palmer put it, either that he was himself incompetent to effect improvements or else that there was a sinister design to detract from his reputation. 2nd, That from himself, though vitally interested in its contents, a report was being kept which clerks from his own office had been sent down to Windsor to copy. 3rd, That the same feeling of distrust was evidenced in the constant pressure which was being put upon him to require the surveyors to keep journals. How hollow these reasons were, a very little consideration will shew. In the course of the correspondence with Chalmers, on which the first of Palmer's reasons was obviously founded, Walsingham had been careful to state that, while ready to consider proposals for establishing a penny post in Edinburgh, he must decline to interfere with any of Palmer's arrangements. The second reason, though more plausible, was the merest pretext. Not a month before, with the full knowledge of what was going on at Windsor, Palmer had offered to send down, if required, the whole of his office to assist. And more than this. Although Walsingham could not in honour disclose a document which had been lent to him under a pledge of secrecy, Palmer must have been perfectly well acquainted with so much of the Report of the Royal Commission as dealt with his own undertaking, for it is beyond all question that this part of the Report had been written by himself. There was no other man living who was capable of writing it; and even if there had been, the opinions, the recommendations, the mode of expression, the disparagement of Ralph Allen, all of which are common to the Report and Palmer's private writings, unmistakably betray the author. The third reason requires little remark. Walsingham would have neglected his obvious duty if he had not taken steps to establish some check upon the travelling expenses claimed by the surveyors; and the experience of the hundred years which have since elapsed has failed to devise any better check than the journal. The keeping of the journal, moreover, had been an express condition imposed by the Treasury when the allowance of a guinea a day was authorised.

Walsingham treated Palmer on this occasion with great kindness. Rightly judging that jealousy was at the root of the whole matter, he followed up the conversation which had taken place at Windsor by a letter, in which he exhorted Palmer to speak out, to declare his sentiments freely, and to dismiss idle apprehensions. Then came a full statement from Palmer, written, as he expressly declared, "not as a justification but as an apology for my suspicions," and explaining the object and the motives of his visit on the preceding Sunday. "Your habits are not my habits," he concluded; "I would give a great deal for but a part of your correctness and inveterate attention to business and accounts." Walsingham's reply, which came by return of post, was an invitation to dinner. Palmer accepted it, and the courteous and hearty welcome he received called forth his warmest acknowledgments.

The duty of the mail guards, as their title implies, was to guard and protect the mails. This body of men, as it existed during the first forty or fifty years of the present century, was one of which the Post Office might well be proud. The very nature of their employment engendered in them a habit of self-reliance and an independence of character which invested them with a peculiar interest. But it was not always so. When mail-coaches were first established, Palmer had it in contemplation to employ retired soldiers as mail guards, on the ground that soldiers would be accustomed to firearms; but constitutional objections prevailed and the contractors who furnished the mail-coaches with horses were required also to furnish firearms arms and the men to use them. The result was not satisfactory. For economy's sake men were employed of little or no character, and the weapons with which they were supplied were of the most worthless description. More than worthless, they were dangerous. "Cheap things;" they were declared to be, "that burst and often did mischief." Accordingly, at Palmer's suggestion, the Post Office undertook to appoint its own mail guards. Honest and faithful as these men always were, it was only by degrees that they grew into the fine body they afterwards became. At first the novelty of their position led them into little excesses such as were never heard of in later years. Thus, a statute passed in 1790 imposed a penalty of 20s. on any mail guard who should fire off the arms with which he was entrusted for any other cause than the protection of the mail; and even this enactment appears to have been insufficient to correct the abuse against which it was directed. "These guards," writes Pennant two years later, "shoot at dogs, hogs, sheep, and poultry as they pass the road; and even in towns, to the great terror and danger of the inhabitants."[65]

It must not be supposed, because Palmer's name is associated with the establishment of mail-coaches, that to these his attention was exclusively confined. In virtue of his appointment as comptroller-general he exercised control, subject of course to the postmasters-general, over the whole of the Post Office, the offices of account excepted; and he now took advantage of this position to create a newspaper office. Newspapers had long been a source of trouble. By the clerks of the roads they were not only posted in good time but were tied up in bundles, covered with strong brown paper, and addressed to the postmasters of the respective towns, who took out the contents and had them delivered. So long as the newspapers were thus dealt with, no inconvenience resulted from their being mixed up with letters; but from the moment that the distribution passed into the hands of the printers and dealers the case was different. The newspapers were now posted at the last moment, and, being clumsily folded and still wet from the printing press, they damaged and defaced the addresses of the letters with which they came in contact in the mail bags. The inconvenience had been tolerated for years. As early as 1782 the postmasters-general had contemplated the creation of a newspaper office, an office in which newspapers might be dealt with separately from letters, but nothing had been done. Palmer now took the matter in hand and carried it through with his usual vigour. Having satisfied himself that a separate office was necessary, he forthwith established one, appointed to it eighteen sub-sorters and fixed their wages; and not even the postmasters-general were aware of what he was doing until it was done.[66]

Such an instance of energy, worthy as we may think it of imitation, would be impossible on the part of any one who had been brought up in the public service, because he would have learnt that no wages can be fixed or new offices created without the consent of the Treasury. In the Post Office, too, the postmasters-general alone were legally competent to make appointments. But to Palmer these were the merest trifles, if indeed he gave them a thought. To create a newspaper office was a right thing to do, and he had done it; and to haggle about the circumstances of the doing appeared to him sheer pedantry. Not so thought Walsingham. It ill accorded with his sense of propriety that a number of new places should have been created without the requisite authority which the Treasury alone could give; but that to these places, whether authorised or not, a subordinate should have presumed to make appointments—a power which by the postmaster-generals' patent was vested in themselves alone—struck him as little short of an outrage.

Unfortunately for Palmer, another irregularity on his part came to light at the same time. The mail guards' wages had been fixed at 13s. a week; but of this sum Palmer paid only 10s., retaining the balance for the purpose of providing uniforms, pensions, and an allowance during sickness. Again, the plan was excellent; but it was unauthorised, and had the effect of leaving in Palmer's hands, without any means of checking it, a sum of liberated money amounting to about £900 a year.

Walsingham now called upon Palmer to give the details of his plan, with a view to its being properly authorised, and to submit the names of those whom he had appointed to the newspaper office, so that their appointments might be confirmed. Palmer would do neither the one nor the other. Walsingham persisted in his demand, and Palmer persisted in his refusal. No course remained but to submit the matter for Pitt's decision; and Pitt decided in Walsingham's favour. Palmer, said the minister, had the power of suspending Post Office servants but not of appointing them, although the postmasters-general, it might well be believed, would consent as a matter of favour to accept his nominations. Pitt also agreed that the mode of dealing with the mail guards' wages was highly irregular. The decision of the minister was communicated to Palmer, but it had not the slightest effect upon his conduct. The mail guards' wages continued to be dealt with as before; and the appointments to the newspaper office remained unconfirmed.

Pitt's decision was not given until the autumn of 1789; and meanwhile other matters had occurred to strain the relations between Walsingham and Palmer. Chief among these was Walsingham's inveterate habit of scribbling. Both men were endowed with an amount of energy which nothing could repress; but while Palmer expended himself by rushing from one part of the country to another as fast as horses could carry him, Walsingham's sphere of activity was restricted to writing. And well he exemplified the law that force asserts itself in proportion to the limits within which it is confined. His notes and questions were literally endless. At one time all the ingenuity of

Lombard Street, with the assistance of erasers and acids, is being exercised to remove remarks he has written upon a document which, not being the property of the Post Office, had to be returned. At another, he has sent for a blank form of contract, of which only a single copy remains in the Office. "I implore your Lordship," writes the sender, "to let me have it back, and that the margin may not be written on." Palmer, to whom pens, ink, and paper were an abomination, would think nothing of posting a hundred miles and more to avoid the necessity of writing a letter; and by Bonnor, Palmer's lieutenant, who always aped his master as far as he dared, answers to the questions put to him would be withheld altogether or reserved for the next Board meeting. "I can perceive," wrote Todd to Walsingham about this time, "you are hurt that neither Mr. Palmer nor Mr. Bonnor pay a proper regard to your many observations."

Another matter occurred at this time which, while only indirectly affecting Palmer, was not calculated to promote harmonious relations. Bonnor, who had sent some accounts to Windsor for Walsingham's signature, wrote two or three days later, urging that they might be signed and returned at once, and giving as a reason the importunity of the letter-carriers. "What these poor oppressed creatures will do," he said, "I know not. They all came in a body this morning and gave a most affecting description of the distresses with which their wives and families laboured, their credit exhausted, not a shilling to buy bread, and each having between £30 and £40 of hard-earned wages due to them from a public office whose revenues are every day increasing." This struck Walsingham as very strange. The letter-carriers were paid by weekly wages; and what, over and above their wages, they had earned for extra duty should also have been paid weekly. Besides, the accounts had been in his hands for only two or three days, whereas for the last twelve months and more he had been pressing for their production, and had only now succeeded in getting them.

There was a mystery somewhere, and, as the best means of solving it, Walsingham called for the vouchers. Bonnor now lost himself in excuses. The vouchers were essential to his reputation. He could not part with them. If once they left his hands, they might be lost. It could not but be known to his Lordship how often this had happened with official papers passing to and fro. Besides, to inspect the vouchers would be to pry into his private concerns. This was enough for Walsingham, and he directed the accountant-general to look into the matter forthwith. The examination revealed a curious state of things. The amounts which the letter-carriers had earned for extra duty had not been paid for a whole year, and a part of the money which had been issued for that purpose had been applied to the payment of the persons irregularly appointed to the newspaper office.

More than this. The accounts shewed, or professed to shew, that during the last eighteen months the mail-coach contractors had received in payment of their services the sum of £20,000; but the receipts for more than £16,000 of this amount bore no dates, and others were signed by Bonnor himself. "Signed," to use his own words, "by myself for money paid by myself to myself." In short, the so-called vouchers were no vouchers at all. Bonnor now made an apology, which, in point of abjectness, has probably seldom been equalled; and Walsingham, unwilling to force matters to extremities, let him off with a sound dressing. This disclosure did not tend to restore either harmony or confidence. Palmer, it is true, gave no heed to accounts; but Bonnor was under his protection, and Palmer resented a censure upon his lieutenant and friend even more than a censure upon himself.

We doubt whether in England a public department has often been in so singular a position as that which the Post Office occupied during the six months beginning with September 1789. Carteret had been dismissed;[67] and Westmorland, Carteret's successor, whose patent had been delayed owing to the absence of the law officers from London, had not even entered upon his duties as postmaster-general before he wrote to announce his appointment as Lord-Lieutenant of Ireland. Meanwhile Palmer resolutely withheld obedience from the orders of his chiefs, backed though those orders were by the minister; and Walsingham was powerless to act. Minutes indeed he prepared by the score, proposing the most drastic measures; but Carteret refused to sign because he was on the point of going out, and Westmorland refused to sign because he had only just come in, and had no intention of remaining. Walsingham's signature alone carried no legal force. It was not until the following March, the March of 1790, that the office of postmaster-general was again properly filled by the appointment of Lord Chesterfield as Walsingham's colleague.

At the risk of interrupting the course of our narrative we cannot refrain from mentioning here in its chronological order memorial which was at this time received from certain merchants of the city of London trading with foreign parts. This memorial, or rather the counter-memorial to which it gave rise, is interesting if only as serving to shew that the conservative instinct— an indisposition to change, is not confined to public offices. The delivery of inland letters had been recently expedited; but foreign letters continued to be delivered as of old. Lest the practice in the case of these letters should seem to be overstated, we give it in the memorialists' own words. "It is the practice of the Post Office," they write under date the 20th of January 1790, "if a mail does not arrive before one o'clock to withhold the delivery of the letters till the next day, and even to protract the delivery till after the same hour the succeeding day, provided any other mail be expected or due.

This happening on a Saturday (a case by no means uncommon), the letters are kept back till the Monday, when three other mails being due, and they not arriving perhaps till the stipulated hour of one, the delivery of the mail which arrived on Saturday is not made till between three and four o'clock on the Monday and sometimes later. Thus the advice of property shipt to a great amount on which insurances should immediately have been made, the receipt of remittances on which the credit of many persons may depend, and the general information so essential in commercial affairs are cruelly withheld for upwards of fifty hours without the least apparent necessity." The remedy which the memorialists proposed was moderate enough. They asked nothing more than that, in the case of mails arriving before four o'clock in the afternoon, letters might be given out to persons who should call at the Post Office for them in two or three hours after the mail had come in, such as were not called for being, at the expiration of that interval, sent out by letter-carrier; and that, in the case of mails arriving after four o'clock, the letters might be delivered at ten o'clock on the following morning.

The unfortunate merchants who signed this memorial little bethought themselves of the storm they were raising. Other merchants, also trading with foreign parts and more numerous than those who advocated an earlier delivery, put forward a counter-memorial strongly protesting against any change. The custom of postponing until the following day the delivery of all foreign letters arriving at the Post Office after one o'clock was, they said, a wise custom, a "custom recommended by our ancestors," and one that could not be altered save to their own great prejudice. The original memorial had been studiously kept from themselves, and "this most extraordinary proceeding" they could only ascribe to a well-founded apprehension on the part of the promoters that otherwise the impropriety of the "novelty" which they sought to introduce would be exposed. The remonstrants added that many and cogent reasons might be given in support of the existing usage; but, unhappily, they omitted to state what these reasons were. Doubtless, however, jealousy lest others should obtain priority of information was at the bottom of the protest; although it is not very clear how, under a regulation that was to be common to all, any one in particular would enjoy an undue advantage.

The Post Office, unassisted in this instance by Palmer, declared the change to be, if only on account of want of space, impossible. The average number of letters arriving by each foreign mail were at this time—from France 2500, from Holland 2000, and from Flanders 1500, or 6000 altogether. At the present day, when as many as 500 sacks full of letters come by a single mail, and several mails may arrive simultaneously, 6000 letters more or less make little appreciable difference. One hour at most is enough for three men to sort them. But in 1790 the office in which the foreign letters were sorted possessed but a single table and a single alphabet or sorting rack.

Although want of space was the ostensible reason for refusing an earlier delivery, there was another, not avowed indeed, and yet which, there can be no doubt, materially influenced the decision. This will be best explained in the words of the comptroller of the foreign letter department. "The delivery of foreign letters," writes this officer to Walsingham, "is so complicated with *the secret office*[68] that any alteration will deserve the most serious consideration when you come to the Board."

It would hardly excite surprise if Chesterfield, on entering upon his duties in Lombard Street, had fallen under the influence of a colleague who, besides being possessed of a strong will, had had some years' experience in Post Office administration; but, as a matter of fact, he does not appear to have surrendered his private judgment. On one point, indeed, he took a view somewhat different from Walsingham. Walsingham regarded Palmer, in so far as he withheld obedience from the postmaster-generals' orders, as simply an insubordinate servant. To Chesterfield, on the contrary, Palmer was an object of no common interest. That two peers of large social influence, deriving their authority direct from the Crown, and to some extent supported by the minister, should be held in check by one man, and that man a subordinate, was an incongruity which struck Chesterfield's imagination. It amused him. It interested him. He could not withhold his meed of admiration from the masterful spirit which fought single-handed against long odds, and not always without success. The very terms Chesterfield employed, while implying a consciousness of defeat, implied also a certain amount of homage to the victor. It was always as "our Master," "our Dictator," "our Tyrant" that he referred to Palmer; and it is difficult to believe that a man who could thus playfully express himself would have proved implacable.

For ourselves, we have little doubt that, if at this time Palmer had demeaned himself with only moderate reserve, all might yet have been well; but it must be admitted that, from now till the end of his official career, his conduct was strangely aggressive. We have already seen how he made appointments to the newspaper office without reference to the postmasters-general, and how, in their despite, he retained in his own hands a considerable balance arising out of deductions from the mail guards' wages. He now went further. He declined to attend the Board meetings: he not only omitted but refused to answer inquiries which the postmasters-general addressed to him; he persistently withheld the surveyors' journals, if, indeed, he had required journals to be kept; he claimed to make contracts and to introduce what measures he pleased without the postmasters-general being so much as consulted; and because Walsingham and Chesterfield would not admit the claim, he suffered the contracts to expire, and the mail-coaches were run on mere verbal agreements. "Except the warrants we have signed," wrote the postmasters-general in October 1790, "there is no record whatever in our possession of any of Mr. Palmer's proceedings since his appointment."

From disobedience Palmer proceeded to defiance. We will give instances. The proprietors of the mail-coach between Carlisle and Portpatrick had demanded payment at the rate of 2d. a mile, and Palmer had agreed to the demand. This was just double the usual rate, and the postmasters-general, fearing that if given on one road it could not be refused on another, determined, before signing the warrant presented for payment, to obtain Treasury authority. Palmer, knowing that delay would thus be caused, protested that no such authority was necessary, and, in order to enforce his protest, stopped four mail-coaches, for which was being paid more than the usual allowance of 1d. a mile, namely, the coach to Falmouth, the coach to Bristol, the coach to Plymouth, and the coach to Portsmouth—coolly informing the postmasters-general that he had done so "under the idea that appears to influence their Lordships, that paying a higher rate to the proprietors on one road might induce others to make a similar demand." He next inquired whether the postmasters-general were to be understood as preferring a cart to the mail-coach, even though a cart should be the more expensive of the two. As nothing had been said about a cart, the postmasters-general remarked that this could only be meant for insult. Insult! rejoined Palmer, he was as little capable of offering an insult as he was of putting up with one; and then he proceeded to charge the postmasters-general with the grossest partiality. The postmasters-general had increased the salary of the postmaster of Tewkesbury beyond what Palmer conceived to be necessary. He denounced the transaction as extraordinary and ill advised, and, while himself professing to believe that it proceeded only from motives of benevolence, expressed his conviction that others would regard it as "a job." Smuggled goods had been found in the mail-box of the Dover coach; and coach, horses, and harness had, in consequence, been seized by the Commissioners of Customs. The same man who, in order to force a decision, had stopped four mail-coaches in a single morning, now rated the postmasters-general soundly because they did not at once and without inquiry take steps to get the Commissioners' proceedings reversed. "The comptroller-general," wrote Palmer on another occasion, "has informed their Lordships of his motives for not answering several of the postmaster-generals' minutes, which he trusts cannot but be satisfactory to them. The same reasons will prevent him from answering any others their Lordships may send but such as appear to him absolutely necessary."

But the particular case which brought matters to a climax was connected with Scotland. Palmer had sent two officers to Edinburgh, not to promote the conveyance of mails by coach, but to reform the internal management of the Scotch Post Office; and these officers had given orders for various changes to be made. Robert Oliphant was at this time deputy postmaster-general for Scotland, and from him alone, according to the terms of his commission, were Post Office servants in Scotland to receive instructions. It was by mere accident that the postmasters-general heard of the proceedings of Palmer's agents in Edinburgh, and, as soon as they did so, they wrote to Oliphant desiring that the proposed changes might be suspended until he had reported his opinion upon them and received authority from London for carrying them into effect. They at the same time wrote to Palmer, sending him a copy of their letter to Oliphant, and giving him to understand that he had exceeded his powers.

Palmer now threw off all restraint. He charged the postmasters-general with superseding his commission; he cautioned them against further interference with his regulations, and he appealed to the minister, to whom alone he declared himself to be responsible. It was true, he said, that he was nominally responsible to the postmasters-general, but, except for a legal difficulty connected with the constitution of the Post Office, he would have received an independent appointment. His commission had been made out as it stood merely as a matter of present necessity; and that in such circumstances they should venture to supersede it appeared to him a hasty and ill-advised measure—a measure not consistent with the judgment and temper which usually guided their proceedings. He had a profound veneration for the nobility of the country, and he could give no stronger proof of it than by stating that he still retained his respect and esteem for them in spite of their unhandsome conduct. The more he reflected on this conduct, the more he was struck at the haste and violence of it. Was it reasonable to suppose that he would consent to carry out his plan in trammels and fetters, and, liable as the postmasters-general were to change, to submit his regulations to them to be checked and controlled? The considerations for which he had received his appointment were twofold—for the good he had done in the past, and for the good he might do in the future. "When, therefore," he continued, "your Lordships from mistake or ill-advice shall send me any commands that I think may go to mischief instead of good, I shall most certainly not observe them; and if I apprehend ill consequences from any you may think proper to send to any of the officers under me, I shall take the liberty, for your Lordships' sake as well as my own and the public's, to contradict them."

It was impossible that this state of things should continue. Palmer had appealed to Cæsar; and to Cæsar he should go. Such at least was the postmaster-generals' intention, and they so far carried it into effect as to state their case in writing; but an interview with the minister, though solicited over and over again, the minister always found some excuse for declining. "We shall wait with the utmost impatience to hear from you that you have found a leisure moment when we may wait upon you to explain the nature of the question between Mr. Palmer and us." "The postmasters-general," they wrote again after a long interval, "present their compliments to Mr. Pitt. He will see by the enclosed copy of a minute from Mr. Palmer how totally the business of this Office must stand still, as far as respects the comptroller-general's department, till they can have the honour of seeing Mr. Pitt." And again, a fortnight later, "the postmasters-general present their compliments to Mr. Pitt, and take the liberty to remind him of the comptroller-general's two last minutes, and desire to have the honour of waiting upon him on Wednesday next at any hour he may be pleased to appoint previous to their holding their usual Board."

But all to no purpose. The truth is that Pitt was heartily tired of these unhappy dissensions. Palmer was doing, and doing admirably, the task which he had set himself to do. He might not indeed be all that could be desired. His conduct might be masterful and his pretensions absurd. Yet much allowance was to be made for a man who had undertaken a difficult business, and whose efforts had been crowned with success. And lamentable as the dissensions might be, there was no certainty that interference would effect a reconciliation. On the contrary, it might serve only to widen the breach, and, to judge from the past, this was the more likely result. And should the breach prove irreparable and a decision have to be given against the reformer who had done so much for his country, and from whom yet more was expected, it would be little short of a disaster. Better that matters should remain as they were than incur such a risk. We can well believe that some such considerations as these influenced Pitt in avoiding an interview; and doubtless he was confirmed in his decision by what he learned from another quarter. Palmer was a friend of Camden's, and Camden was a friend of Pitt's. To this common friend Palmer gave his own version of the differences between himself and his chiefs; and this version, which was altogether different from the one which the postmasters-general gave, was studiously impressed upon Pitt to their prejudice.

Thus matters stood when, early in 1792, in consequence of some discrepancies in the accounts, the postmasters-general determined that letters for the city by the first or morning delivery should be checked. Care had been taken that the check should not be of a nature to retard the delivery;

and yet, strangely enough, the delivery became later and later every day. At length a public advertisement appeared inviting the merchants and traders to meet at the London Tavern on Wednesday the 15th February in order to consider the subject. The meeting was held under the presidency of Alderman Curtis, one of the members of Parliament for the city; and strong resolutions were passed directing the postmaster-generals' attention to the delay, and calling upon them to explain and remove the cause.

Charles Bonnor, the deputy comptroller-general, owed all he possessed to Palmer. It was by Palmer that he had been brought into the Post Office in July 1784, and the same influence procured for him shortly afterwards a salary of £500 and an allowance of £150 a year for a house. Warm in his attachments as he was fierce in his animosities, the great reformer extended to Bonnor a confidence which probably no other man possessed, and during his frequent absences from London kept up with him a correspondence in which he poured out his inmost thoughts. This person, stung with jealousy at some fancied coolness on Palmer's part, now published a pamphlet in which he charged his friend and benefactor with wilfully delaying the delivery of the morning letters, and then promoting the meeting at the London Tavern in order to protest against a mischief of his own making. According to Bonnor, Palmer had spared no effort to induce persons to attend the meeting, and had furnished Alderman Curtis, the chairman, with materials for denouncing the Post Office. All this, it was alleged, had been done in order to bring the postmasters-general into discredit, and to create a demand that Palmer might have larger powers given him and be left to deal with Post Office matters according to his unfettered judgment.

The postmasters-general were overwhelmed with astonishment. At first they could not bring themselves to believe that the pamphlet was authentic, and it was not until they had been reassured on this point that they began to make inquiries. Palmer, of course, denied the charge, and Bonnor reaffirmed it. Meanwhile the resolutions passed at the London Tavern had been sent to the Post Office; and the postmasters-general, not knowing what to believe, simply referred them to Palmer, with a request that he would explain the cause of the late delivery. Palmer's reply shews the frame of mind he was in. "The cause of the late delivery," he answered, "as well as every other existing abuse in the Post Office, arises from the comptroller-general not having sufficient authority to correct it." The postmasters-general naturally inquired in what respects his authority was insufficient to prevent the late delivery, and to what other abuses he referred. Palmer, without specifying what these abuses were, replied that among the causes which had produced them were "an unfortunate difference in opinion, and an equally unfortunate interference in his office"; and then he proceeded to ask for larger powers, which the postmasters-general, consistently with the terms of their patent, were unable to give.

A few days later Palmer did that which should perhaps have been done before. He suspended Bonnor. The postmasters-general also took action, but at the very moment when it might have been better if they had remained passive. They inquired the reason of Bonnor's suspension, and Palmer returned no reply. After waiting a week, the postmasters-general decided that, as no reason had been given, the suspension must be taken off; and Bonnor was directed to resume duty. On presenting himself for this purpose, however, Palmer refused to give up the key of his room, and sent him word that, if he dared to come to the Office again, the constables would have orders to turn him off the premises. The postmasters-general had put themselves in a false position. If their intention was to try conclusions with Palmer, they had selected the worst possible ground. Their only choice now was between submitting to defiance of their authority and supporting a worthless subordinate against his illustrious chief. They elected the latter alternative; and the suspension which had been imposed upon Bonnor was transferred to Palmer.

An interview with the minister had now become indispensable; and at length, but not without a great deal of pressure, Pitt fixed the 2nd of May for the purpose. Chesterfield was at Bath, slowly recovering from an attack of the gout. He was reluctant to leave his colleague unsupported on the occasion; and yet for a man who was still far from well it was a long and tedious journey to London. Should he go or should he not? A decision could not be longer delayed, as the 1st of May had already arrived. He ordered horses to be put to his carriage, then he countermanded them, then he changed his mind again, and finally, in response to a sudden twinge of the gout, he finally abandoned his journey, and determined to write to Walsingham a letter such as he might shew.

Chesterfield, unlike Walsingham, wrote a beautiful hand, a hand that was clear and easy to read; but on this particular occasion, in order that Pitt might have no excuse for not reading the letter, he wrote more clearly and legibly than usual. He had—thus the letter ran—been in fifty minds whether he should not repair to London and take part in the interview with Pitt; but he was still so lame that he durst not venture on so long a journey. His desire to be present had not indeed been prompted by the slightest doubt as to what Walsingham would do or say. On the contrary, he had the fullest confidence that his colleague would strictly adhere to the resolution which they had adopted, that on no consideration could Palmer remain with them at the Post Office. This resolution the experience which they had gained since his suspension had served to strengthen, for how much better and with how much greater regularity had they gone on since they had in fact as well as in name been postmasters-general. All this would doubtless be pressed upon Pitt, and, should he waver in the least, he must be informed of their ultimatum, which nothing could make them change. If, contrary to expectation, they should be driven to that option, they must be satisfied to retire from an office where they had done their duty and could do it no longer. To the full extent of the resolution they went hand in hand to Pitt, and this point could not be pressed upon him too strongly. Should he begin to propose any middle measures, Walsingham should stop him at once. It would be disgraceful to listen to them. "Our resolution once taken, no power, no persuasion, no influence ought to shake it, and I am confident nothing will."

Walsingham waited upon the minister at the appointed time. Pitt received him courteously indeed, but coldly. Walsingham stated his case. Pitt said little, but that little clearly shewed that his leanings were in Palmer's favour. Palmer had done good service to the public. Was it impossible that he should be restored to duty? Or, much having been alleged and nothing proved, might not a court of inquiry be held by which the questions at issue between him and his chiefs should undergo a thorough and impartial investigation? After these and other questions had been put and answered, Walsingham produced Chesterfield's letter. Pitt read it from beginning to end, folded it up, and returned it. Formal civilities followed, and the interview was at an end. That night a letter from Walsingham informed Chesterfield that assuredly two persons would be dismissed from the Post Office, and that of these two persons Palmer would not be one.

The postmasters-general were in a state of sore perplexity. Of Pitt's intentions they entertained not the slightest doubt. "The Post Office chair," wrote Chesterfield, "totters under us"; and again, "I see that can the ingenuity of man detect a flaw in our proceedings, we are to be the victims." The doubt which the postmasters-general felt concerned their own conduct. Rightly or wrongly, they believed that they were powerful enough to depose the minister, and the question which now agitated their minds was whether they should have recourse to so violent a measure, or whether they should simply resign. Bonnor saved them from the necessity of coming to a conclusion on the point. This person had hoarded up the private correspondence which, during years of close intimacy and friendship, had passed between himself and Palmer; and among the correspondence were many compromising letters. Such of these as he could readily lay his hands upon Bonnor, with incredible baseness, now carried to Walsingham, and Walsingham in an evil moment accepted them.

The temptation was no doubt strong. Even in the eyes of the postmasters-general themselves it was a comparatively small matter that they were on the point of losing their places. But it was by no means immaterial to them that they should appear to Pitt, as they were conscious of appearing at the present time, in the light of false accusers, persons who had brought false charges, or at all events charges which they could not substantiate; and these letters would prove all, and more than all, that had been alleged or even suspected. They laid bare the story of the King's coach. They shewed how on that occasion the contractor had been cajoled into making an exorbitant charge in order that Walsingham might be deterred from again interfering in what Palmer regarded as his own peculiar province. They shewed also how, from that time to the present, a deliberate plot had existed at headquarters to hinder and thwart Walsingham in everything he undertook.

And yet they were private letters, letters which had passed under the seal of confidence. It is by no means the least strange part of a strange and painful business that it appears never to have crossed the mind of either Walsingham or Chesterfield that this was a class of evidence which could not with propriety be used. Bonnor, not content with the letters he had already produced, searched his correspondence through from the time that he and Palmer became connected with the Post Office, and hailed any additional testimony he was able to collect against his former friend and benefactor with fiendish delight. He literally revelled in the shameless task he had set himself to perform. Evidence-hunting he called it. "We shall not only prove all that has been asserted," he wrote, "but a great deal more; and on the grand point of his premeditating a thorough and complete confusion in the business of the inland office, for the declared purpose of thereby disgracing the postmasters-general, I have proof that for strength and conviction no holy writ can exceed. But," he added, "I have a great deal to work up yet."

As soon as the unholy brief was completed, a second interview took place with the minister. Pitt appears again to have said little, even less than on the previous occasion. He had been deceived. The postmasters-general must take their own course. The rest is soon told. Two official minutes were prepared, the one in Lombard Street and the other at Whitehall. By the postmaster-generals' minute Palmer, the insubordinate Post Office servant, was dismissed.[69] By the minister's minute Palmer, the distinguished Post Office reformer, was granted a pension equal to double the amount of his salary. His salary was £1500, and he derived another £1500 a year from his percentage. The pension which Pitt conferred upon him was £3000. To this was added later on, after an interval of many years, a Parliamentary grant of £50,000.

Bonnor—we blush to record it—received as the reward of his infamy the place of comptroller of the inland department. His promotion brought him little pleasure. The Post Office servants, with all their faults, were loyal to the backbone, and they could ill understand being presided over by one who was branded with the foulest of all private vices, with treachery to a friend and ingratitude to a benefactor. His subordinates would hold no communication with him beyond what their strict duty required. His equals shunned him. Outside the Post Office, go where he would, he received the cold shoulder. Never was man left more severely alone. At the end of two years fresh postmasters-general came who, under the plea of abolishing his appointment, dismissed him with a small pension. Then he became insolvent, and was thrown into prison. Released from confinement at the end of the century, he published pamphlet after pamphlet, having for their object to vindicate what he was pleased to call his good name; but these vindications, though replete with professions of honour, proved nothing more than that the writer was a poltroon as well as a traitor.

CHAPTER XIII
THE NINETIES: OR, ONE HUNDRED YEARS AGO

The spirit of activity which Palmer had infused into the Post Office did not cease with the cessation of his official career. Those who served under him had been selected by himself; and they had been selected on account of qualities which the withdrawal of his dominating influence was calculated rather to stimulate than to check. These men now came to the fore, and not only ably sustained their late master's work but inaugurated important measures of their own.

But before proceeding to chronicle the acts of Palmer's successors, we propose to give a few particulars which will serve better perhaps than a mere record of leading events to shew the state of the Post Office at the time that Palmer left it; and in this relation the project with which his name is mainly identified shall have precedence.

In 1792 sixteen mail-coaches left London every day, and as many returned. These were in addition to the cross country mail-coaches, of which there were fifteen—as, for instance, the coach between Bristol and Oxford or, as it was commonly called, Mr. Pickwick's coach.[70] Those leaving London started from the General Post Office in Lombard Street at eight o'clock in the evening, and they travelled every day, Sundays included.

There is still extant at the Post Office in St. Martin's-le-Grand the model of an old mail-coach, as fresh and as perfect as the day it was painted. This model bears upon its panels four devices—one a cross with the motto, *Honi soit qui mal y pense*; another a thistle with the motto, *Nemo me impune lacessit*; a third a shamrock under a star, with the motto, *Quis separabit?* (ah! who indeed?); and a fourth, three crowns with the motto, *Tria juncta in uno*. It is commonly reputed to be the model of the first mail-coach, and as such we have seen it represented in foreign publications. We feel constrained in the interests of truth to expose this fiction. The first mail-coach ran between Bristol and London. The model bears upon it the words, "Royal Mail from London to Liverpool." The first mail-coach carried no outside passengers. The model has places for several passengers outside. The first mail-coach began to run on Monday the 2nd of August 1784. On the model, below one of the devices, appears in small yet legible figures the date 1783. But although certainly not the model of the first mail-coach, we are by no means sure that it is not still more interesting. We have little doubt that it is a model which, before mail-coaches began to run, was prepared for Pitt's inspection.

In 1787, owing to the faulty construction of the original mail-coach and the wretched materials of which it was made, hardly a day passed without one or more accidents. Occasionally, indeed, the Post Office would receive notice of as many as three and even four upsets or breakdowns in a single morning. Palmer at once discerned the origin of the disease and the remedy; and the latter he proceeded to apply with his usual resolution. Having satisfied himself that a patent coach which was being constructed at this time fulfilled the necessary conditions more completely than any other, he agreed with the patentee, one Besant by name, to supply whatever number of coaches might be required. It was a mere verbal agreement, an agreement confirmed by no writing of any kind; yet no sooner was it made than Palmer addressed a circular to all the contractors of the kingdom, reproaching them with the shameful condition of their coaches. This, he told them, was due to the miserable sums they gave to the coach-maker, sums so low as to oblige him to use the most worthless materials; and as to repairs, even if they made him an allowance for these, it was so inadequate to the continual mending which vehicles constructed of such materials required that he merely put in a clip or a bolt where the fracture might happen to be, and then returned them in as dangerous a condition as before. Such a state of things, Palmer continued, would no longer be tolerated, and, as fast as Besant could turn them out, the new patent coaches would be sent down to replace those that were now in use. For providing them and keeping them in thorough repair, for which of course the contractors had to pay, the patentee's terms would be five farthings a mile or 2-1/2d. a mile out and in. After this summary fashion did Palmer clear the country of the mail-coaches of original construction.

In 1792 the only mail-coaches on the road were those supplied by Besant. They were constructed to carry five passengers, four inside and one out. The coachman was not a Post Office servant; yet he, like the mail guard, was provided with uniform. The mail guard carried firearms. He carried also a timepiece; and this timepiece was regulated to gain about fifteen minutes in twenty-four hours, so that, when travelling eastwards, it might accord with real time. Of course, in the opposite direction, a corresponding allowance was made. The mail guard's position was one of no little responsibility. Not only were the mails under his personal charge, but he had to see that the coach kept time, that there was no undue delay for the purpose of obtaining refreshments, that the harness was in serviceable condition, and, generally, that matters along the road were conducted with order and propriety. If in any one or more of these respects there were any defect, it was the mail guard's duty to report the circumstance. Should the harness be reported as in bad condition, and the contractors fail to replace it on demand, a new set was sent down from London at their expense; and should a coach persistently keep bad time, a superintendent from headquarters was deputed to travel by it until proper time was kept. This was equivalent to a heavy fine, as the superintendent travelled free, and for the seat he occupied a passenger would have been charged at the rate of 4d. a mile. The fees which at this time it was usual to pay to the mail guard and coachman were moderate enough, only 1s. apiece at the end of the "ground"; and if the "ground" was less than thirty miles, only 6d. Even at this rate the gentlemen of Devonshire bitterly complained that between Exeter and Taunton they had to pay two coachmen.

The chief superintendent of mail-coaches at this time was Thomas Hasker, a man whose heart and soul were in his duties. Hasker has left behind him copies of letters written by himself or by his instructions; and these letters, though expressed in homely language, throw such a flood of light upon the ways of the road a century ago that we make no apology for quoting from them. "The Bristol coach," he writes to the postmaster of Marlborough, "is the fastest in the kingdom, and you must not detain it for the coach from Bath." Again, to the postmaster of Ipswich he writes, "Tell Mr. Foster to get fresh horses immediately, and that I must see him in town next Monday. Shameful work—three hours and twenty-two minutes coming over his eighteen miles." The Dover coach had long been keeping bad time. "I must beg you to attend to this directly," writes Hasker to the contractors, "or we shall be obliged to put three fresh guards on the coach, and keep a superintendent constantly up and down till time is kept." The contractors for another coach had failed to replace their harness when desired, and a set had been sent down from London. "The harness," writes the indefatigable superintendent, "cost fourteen guineas, but as it had been used a few times with the King's royal Weymouth [coach], you will be charged only twelve, which sum please to remit to me." Thanks to the widening of the roads, it is only in thoroughfares more or less crowded that the device can now be practised to which the following refers: "Your coachman, Pickard, lost thirty-seven minutes last night coming up, and by so doing he always hinders the Manchester coach; he leaving Leicester first keeps on before, and prevents the other coach from passing. This is the case every night that Pickard comes up."

But it is the instructions to the mail guards which bring home to us most vividly the ways of the road a hundred years ago. Thus, to the mail guards on the Exeter coach: "You are not to stop at any place whatever to leave any letters at, but to blow your horn to give the people notice that you have got letters for them; therefore, if they do not choose to come out to receive them, don't you get down from your dicky, but take them on to Exeter and bring them back with you on your next journey." And again to the mail guards on another coach: "If the coachman go into a public-house to drink, don't you go with him and make the stop longer, but hurry him out." This hurrying out had sometimes to be applied to passengers, and not always with success. "Sir," writes Hasker to a mail guard who had complained of the futility of his efforts in this direction, "stick to your bill, and never mind what passengers say respecting waiting overtime. Is it not the fault of the landlord to keep them so long? Some day when you have waited a considerable time (suppose five or eight minutes longer than is allowed by the bill), drive away and leave them behind. Only take care that you have witness that you called them out two or three times. Then let them get forward how they can. Let the innkeeper [of the house] where they dine know that you have received this letter."

While thus urged to correct others, the mail guards had sometimes to be corrected themselves. Fines ranging from 2s. 6d. to 5s. were imposed for omitting to date the timetable or for dating it wrongly; and on one occasion an unfortunate guard was fined as much as one guinea because some bags for which he should have called at the Stafford Post Office were left behind. Also to delegate one's duties was strictly prohibited. "It has been reported to Mr. Hasker," writes Hasker's lieutenant, "that you send your mail to the Post Office by the person called Boots, and do not go with it yourself. You have been wrote to two or three times before on this subject. Therefore, if the irregularity be repeated, you will certainly be discharged." Occasionally advantage would be taken of a complaint to read a lesson to the complainant. A mail guard had been reported for impertinence by certain contractors who were notorious for the indifferent lights with which they supplied their coach. After replying that he had been severely rebuked for his conduct, Hasker slily adds, "but perhaps something may be said for the feelings of a guard that hears the continual complaints of passengers against bad lights and the disagreeable smell of stinking oil, especially when through such things the passengers withhold the gratuity which the guards expect."

On the part of the mail guards, however, the commonest irregularity, and the irregularity most difficult to check, was the carrying of parcels and of passengers in excess of the prescribed number. "In consequence"—so runs a general order which was issued about this time—"of several of the mail guards having been detected in carrying meat and vegetables in their mail-box to the amount of 150 pounds weight at a time, the superintendents are desired to take opportunities to meet the coaches in their district at places where they are least expected, and to search the boxes to remedy this evil, which is carried to too great a length. The superintendents," the order proceeds, "will please to observe that Mr. Hasker does not wish to be too hard on the guards. Such a thing as a joint of meat or a couple of fowls or any other article for their own family in moderation he does not wish to debar them from the privilege of carrying." Truth compels us to add that at the time to which we refer it was not only meat and vegetables that the mail guards carried. They carried also game. In later years the country gentleman was probably the mail guards' best friend, but at the end of the last century he did not hesitate to charge them with being in league with poachers, and not infrequently threatened prosecution. The mail-box indeed was admirably adapted to purposes of secretion. Occupying a part of the space which even in these early days was known as the boot, it opened not, as the boot opened, from behind but from the top, immediately under the mail guard's feet; and no one but himself had access to it. Constant were the injunctions to the superintendents to meet the coaches at unexpected places for the purpose of search. "Search," writes Hasker, "as many mail-boxes as you can, and take away all game not directed and anything else beyond a joint for the guard's family, and send it to the chief magistrate to be disposed of for the benefit of the poor of the parish." The temptation to carry an extra passenger or two was even greater than to carry parcels. What degree of indulgence was shewn to this form of irregularity appears to have depended upon the part of the coach in which the extra seat was provided. To be detected in carrying a passenger on the mail-box was certain dismissal.

Although it is not our intention to treat of mail-coaches otherwise than as vehicles for the transmission of letters, it may perhaps be permitted to us to pause here a moment and inquire where, at the end of the last century, the passengers' luggage can have been stowed. Of the boot a part, as we have seen, was given up to the mail-box; and the roof, upon which, within our own recollection, the luggage would be piled to nearly half the height of the coach itself, was forbidden, or almost forbidden, ground. "To load the roof of the coach," writes Hasker, "with large heavy baskets would not only be setting a bad example to other coaches, but in a very short time no passenger would travel with it." "Such a thing," he adds, "as a turtle tied on the roof directed to any gentleman once or twice a year might pass unnoticed, but for a constancy cannot be suffered." This objection to a load on the roof appears to have been common to the Sovereign and the subject. In 1796 the Court proceeded to Weymouth; and, as usual, a royal mail was in attendance. The King, who took the liveliest interest in the performances of this coach, and examined the way-bill daily, discountenanced roof-loads. The royal injunctions on this head Hasker, who was a plain-spoken man and no courtier, conveyed to, his subordinates thus: "Take care not to load the royal mail too high, and when any of His Majesty's servants travel by it do not load the roof upward, as you know he ordered that no luggage should be put on the top when his servants rode, and, indeed, at all times. Now upwards [*i.e.* on return from Weymouth to Windsor] there can be no occasion, for there are waggons and other conveyances to bring the luggage up." The possible use of waggons and other conveyances notwithstanding, we cannot help thinking that the traveller by coach of a hundred years ago must have been content with a far smaller quantity of luggage than would satisfy the traveller of to-day.

That the roof of the coach, whether loaded or not, had its drawbacks for travellers is sufficiently evident from Hasker's correspondence. "The York coachman and guard," he writes after a spell of bad weather which had rotted the roads, "were both chucked from their seats going down to Huntingdon last journey, and coming up the guard is lost this morning, supposed from the same cause, as the passengers say he was blowing his horn just before they missed him."

The King's interest in his mail-coach was not confined to the inspection of the way-bill. It was usual, before the Court repaired to Weymouth, for the coach to make a certain number of trial trips, and the King would go to the castle gates to see it pass. "His Majesty," writes Hasker, under date the 12th of August 1794, "came down to the park gate to see the mail-coach the first and second day, and told me he was much pleased to see it so well done and regular, and that he was glad Mr. White did not work it." Mr. White had worked it on a previous occasion, and had not given satisfaction. At the end of each season the King gave still more practical proof of the interest he took in his coach by sending thirty guineas for distribution among the mail guards and coachmen.

But, gratified as Hasker must have been by these marks of royal condescension, there was one thing which, with his concurrence, even the King should not do, and that was, detain the mail. Owing to the letters from the Court being late, the coach, on several successive days, had not started from Weymouth until after the appointed hour. Chesterfield was the minister in attendance, and Hasker addressed to him a letter of respectful remonstrance. Of course he did not know, he said, whether the mail had been detained by His Majesty or by His Majesty's postmaster-general; but in either case he prayed it might be considered how bad an example it was, and what disorder was being introduced into the service. According to present arrangements, the coach should leave Weymouth at four in the afternoon. It might be appointed to leave at five or even six if desired, and yet reach

London on the following day in time for the last delivery; but whatever hour might be fixed, he adjured his Lordship that it might be observed.

How completely the mail-coach had by this time extinguished the express may be judged from the following instruction to the packet agent at Yarmouth:[71] "You will observe the reason why you keep the mail to send by the mail-coach is that, tho' you detain it four or five hours, it arrives as soon at the General Post Office as if sent by express, for the coach travels in sixteen or seventeen hours, and the express in not less than twenty or twenty-one, sometimes more." Nor is it less interesting to note the change of sentiment which had recently taken place as to the importance of despatch. Only a few years before, as we have seen, the inhabitants of Shrewsbury had been informed that it could be of no consequence whether their letters arrived four or five hours sooner or later. Now, in order to accelerate the letters contained in a single bag, no expense is to be spared. "If," the same instruction continues, "any mail arrives within an hour after the mail-coach is gone, perhaps a post-chaise and four might catch it at Ipswich."

But, to quit details, the broad results were these. Palmer, when introducing his plan, had promised security and despatch; but not economy. On the contrary, he had made no secret of his opinion that the use of mail-coaches would involve a considerable increase of expense. The result was a surprise even to himself. Before 1784 the annual allowance for carrying the mails ranged from £4 to £8 a mile, £8 being paid where the mails were heavy—as, for instance, on the Great North Road from London as far as Tuxford. In 1792 the terms on which the mails were carried were exemption from tolls and 1d. a mile each way, or an annual allowance of a little more than £3 a mile. Palmer had estimated the total cost of his plan at £30,000 a year. The actual cost only slightly exceeded £12,000.

Hardly less reason had he to congratulate himself on the score of security and despatch. Before 1784 scarcely a week passed without the mails on one road or another being robbed. So great had the scandal become that the Post Office built a model cart—a cart wholly constructed of iron and reputed to be robber-proof. This cart had not long begun to run before it was stopped by highwaymen and rifled of its contents. In 1792 eight years had passed since the introduction of Palmer's plan; and during this period not a single mail-coach had been either stopped or robbed. This immunity from robbery was in more ways than one equivalent to a further saving. Before 1784 heavy expenses were incurred annually for prosecutions. One trial alone, a trial which made no little noise at the time, namely that of the brothers Weston, cost no less than £4000. This source of expense had now, of course, disappeared. As regards despatch, before 1784 the post travelled between five and six miles an hour. In 1792 the mail-coaches were travelling about seven miles an hour. Telford had not yet levelled the hills nor Macadam paved the roads; and rollers were unknown. A speed of seven miles an hour at the end of the last century was probably far more trying to horses than a speed of ten miles an hour later on.

It would be beyond our province to inquire—interesting as the inquiry would be—to what extent the exchange of commodities between town and town dates from the introduction of mail-coaches; and whether it was not at this period that, with some noted exceptions, the local repute which certain towns enjoyed for the manufacture of particular articles began to spread. Ours is a humbler purpose; or we might be tempted even to contend that Palmer's plan, by the facilities it afforded for intercourse, exercised an influence—slow it may be, but none the less sure—upon the habits and condition of the people.

We will illustrate our meaning. Before the introduction of mail-coaches in 1784 the town of Penzance in Cornwall was not indeed without a post; but the post it possessed was hardly worthy of the name. In 1790 letters were conveyed there by cart from Falmouth regularly six days a week. Now, of the condition of Penzance not many years before the earlier of these two dates we are informed on unimpeachable authority. "I have heard my mother relate," writes Sir Humphry Davy's brother and biographer, "that when she was a girl[72] there was only one cart in the town of Penzance, and that if a carriage occasionally appeared in the streets it attracted universal attention. Pack-horses were then in general use for conveying merchandise, and the prevailing manner of travelling was on horseback. At that period the luxuries of furniture and living enjoyed by people of the middle class at the present time were confined almost entirely to the great and wealthy; in the same town, where the population was about 2000 persons, there was only one carpet, the floors of rooms were sprinkled with sea-sand, and there was not a single silver fork. The only newspaper which then circulated in the west of England was the *Sherborne Mercury*, and it was carried through the country not by the post but by a man on horseback specially employed in distributing it." Penzance can never be otherwise than a most interesting town; but one finds it difficult to believe that, after being brought into communication with the outside world on six days of the week, it can long have retained its pristine charm and simplicity.

Let us now see what, at the time of Palmer's retirement, was the condition of the country Post Offices. Bristol, after long ranking next to London in wealth and population, had yielded place to other towns. Foremost among these stood Manchester. Manchester, following suit to the capital, had recently numbered its streets; it was publishing local directories; and it enjoyed the reputation of being, the capital itself not excepted, the dearest town in the kingdom. At the present time the Post Office at Manchester gives employment to about 1400 persons. In 1792, with the exception of a single letter-carrier, the whole of the Post Office business there was conducted by an aged widow assisted by her daughter. Dame Willatt had recently achieved some little local notoriety. She had, as an inducement to persons to post early, imposed a late-letter fee. For this proceeding, not at that time uncommon and not disapproved at headquarters, she had been summoned to the Court of the Lord of the Manor, and had been cast in damages.

Bath enjoyed a double distinction, a distinction due less probably to its population as compared with that of other towns than to the fact that, being Palmer's native place, it was constantly under his eye as it had been under the eye of Ralph Allen before. This highly-favoured town was, outside London, the only one in the kingdom which could boast of what, with any regard to the meaning of words, could be dignified by the name of a Post Office Establishment; and the postmaster's salary was in excess of that which any other postmaster received. This salary was £150 a year, and the establishment, over which Ralph Allen's successor presided, consisted of one clerk and three letter-carriers.

No other town had more than one letter-carrier; and many towns had not even this. Whether the accommodation was provided or not appears to have depended less upon the necessities of the place than upon the disposition of the inhabitants. Thus, the little towns of Sandwich in Kent and Hungerford in Berkshire, in recognition of the gallant conflict they had waged with the authorities, had each a letter-carrier of its own, while Norwich, York, Derby, Newcastle, and Plymouth had none. Besides Bath only four towns received an allowance for a clerk or assistant, namely Manchester, Norwich, York, and Leeds. Elsewhere the postmaster and a letter-carrier, if letter-carrier there was, were the sole Post Office representatives.

At Bristol the postmaster's salary was £140,—the next highest after that given at Bath. At Liverpool, Manchester, Birmingham, and Chester the salary was £100; at Exeter, York, Newcastle, Leeds, and Plymouth £80; at Sheffield £60, to which amount it had been recently raised from £50; at Derby, Carlisle, and Gloucester £40; at Brighton and Nottingham £30; at Leicester £25; and at Southampton £20. At Tunbridge the postmaster, in addition to a salary of £20, received an allowance of equal amount for keeping an office at Tunbridge Wells. Ripon, despite the rebuke it had received in 1713 for its audacity in asking for a Post Office, had now been accommodated with one. At Chepstow pence were still being paid on the delivery of letters, not because the inhabitants had not discovered their rights but out of consideration to the aged postmistress, whose emoluments they were unwilling to diminish. Birkenhead, Torquay, and Bournemouth,[73] of course, did not exist. Eastbourne existed indeed, but not as we know it now. Hither the letters were carried three times a week from Lewes. At Ramsgate, then a village served from the neighbouring post-town of Sandwich, an office for the receipt of letters was kept at a cost of £6 a year. The whole of the Isle of Wight had but one postmaster and one letter-carrier. To the Channel Islands there was no post.

On Palmer's retirement the office of chief adviser to the postmasters-general devolved almost naturally upon Francis Freeling, the surveyor located at headquarters. Todd still held the appointment of secretary, but after a service of more than fifty years he was unequal to the exertion which the exigencies of the time required. Between Todd and Walsingham, moreover, there was little in common. Their relations, indeed, had always been most friendly; but the views they entertained on Post Office questions were more often than not at variance. "It is a matter of great entertainment to me," wrote Walsingham, as early as October 1788, "to see how totally we differ in all our official opinions." From this time Todd took less and less part in the duties of his office, and confined himself almost exclusively to its social amenities. This was a sphere in which he excelled. At his table in Lombard Street the postmasters-general themselves and such as they might choose to meet them were frequent guests, and "his old hock in his old parlour" passed into a by-word.

Freeling, on the contrary, possessed advantages which not only pointed him out as Todd's successor when Todd should be pleased to retire, but peculiarly fitted him to deal with the circumstances of the moment. In the prime of life, of good address and prepossessing appearance, and with a knowledge of every detail of Post Office organisation such as only constant visits to different parts of the kingdom could give, he soon contrived to make himself not only useful but indispensable; and before any long period had expired the postmasters-general appointed him joint secretary with Todd, an arrangement by virtue of which one was to be the acting and the other the sleeping partner; one was to do the work and the other to draw the pay. It was new to the postmasters-general to have about them some one who was not only able but willing and anxious to impart information on every official question as it arose, and they could ill conceal their glee at the altered state of affairs. "One of the complaints made by us of Mr. Palmer," they wrote about this time, "was that he did what he thought fit without making the least communication to the Board, or without there being a single record of anything which he did or objected to either before or after it was done"; ... but "Mr. Freeling reports distinctly to us upon every application that we refer to him, or that is made to the Board, amounting to above two hundred reports every quarter for the current business." Freeling was now exposed to a serious danger, a danger to which many a reputation has succumbed, namely, that of being transformed from a man of action into a mere scribe; but this was a temptation which he stoutly resisted. Without relaxing his efforts to maintain and improve upon Palmer's plan, he was careful not only to keep the postmasters-general informed of what he was doing, but to do nothing which had not first been duly authorised.

The period immediately following Palmer's retirement was one rather of honest endeavour than of solid achievement. The first and most pressing question to arise was that of insufficiency of accommodation at headquarters. The inland office, this being the office in which the mails were made up for despatch, was not only close and ill-ventilated, but altogether too small for its purpose. More post-towns were required in various parts of the kingdom; but it was impossible to add to the number of towns for which bags would have to be made up until more space should be provided. Some persons thought it would be best at once to take a step which in any case would probably have to be taken in the not remote future, and to build a new Post Office on other and more extensive premises. Such, however, was not the opinion of the postmasters-general. They were naturally unwilling to advocate the heavy expenditure which such a measure would involve except upon proof of its absolute necessity. Mainly on this ground, but also partly because premises in so central and convenient a position as those which the present Post Office occupied were not to be had, authority was sought and obtained for nothing more than the erection of a new inland office.

But, as the postmasters-general found to their cost, it is one thing to obtain an authority and another thing to carry it into effect. On part of the ground on which the office was to be erected stood two houses, the lease of which had not long to run; and the Drapers' Company, to whom the property belonged, declined to extend the term. This difficulty was at length overcome, and the houses were in course of demolition, when projecting into the very centre of the space designed for the new office was found the wall of an old house belonging to Sir Charles Watson, and this house he refused to let the Post Office have unless it would also take seven other houses which he possessed in the immediate neighbourhood. At the present time houses in and about Abchurch Lane would probably fetch twenty-five years' purchase. Fifteen years' purchase was the sum then demanded, and it was considered a hard bargain. Eventually Watson consented to grant a ninety-nine years' lease; but it was a lease not only of the single house that the Post Office wanted, but of all eight houses, seven of which it did not want. What they called their mortifications and disappointments at an end, the postmasters-general proceeded to build.

Still more unsatisfactory was the result of an attempt that was made or intended to be made about this time to improve the post with the Continent. Communication with France was only twice a week, and Walsingham desired to treble it. In France, as in England, the post went to the water's edge on six days of the week, and he could see no reason why, except on two days, it should stop there. He entertained a strong opinion that between the two countries communication should be daily.

There was also another matter to be settled with our neighbours. During a period of sixty-six years, namely, from 1713 to 1779, the postage on a single letter between London and Paris had been 10d.; and, to avoid the keeping of accounts, this sum had been collected and retained by the Post Office of the country in which the letter was delivered. In 1779, when owing to the war communication between Dover and Calais was stopped, letters from Paris reached England through Flanders, and on these letters when put into the post in Paris a charge of 4d. was made in addition to the 10d. to be paid on delivery in London. It had been thought that in 1783, on the termination of the war, this charge would be abandoned, and that the old postage of 10d. would be resumed. Such, however, was not the case. The Post Office authorities in France adhered to the 4d. charge and defended it. The old postage of 10d., they argued, was all very well when they had no packets of their own and England performed the sea service. But now France had her own packets, and the distance between Paris and Calais being far greater than between London and Dover, it could not in reason be expected that on a letter between the two capitals she would be content with no higher postage than that which England received. The charge of 4d. upon letters for London when put into the post in Paris must be maintained, even though they no longer went through Flanders. It was a matter of internal regulation with which England had no concern. Without contesting this view of the case, the home authorities regarded the 4d. charge as a most vexatious impost. Not only had it the effect of diminishing the correspondence, but many of the letters which still passed were carried by private hand from Paris to Dover and there posted, so that the British Post Office received upon them only 4d. apiece, this being the postage from Dover to London, instead of 10d., the postage from Paris. In 1787 Palmer had, by Pitt's direction, gone over to France in order to adjust the matter and to promote a six days' post between the two countries; but he returned without effecting either object.

Circumstances now appearing more favourable, Walsingham determined to make fresh overtures. An emissary had already been selected for the purpose, and was on the eve of departure when a new and unexpected difficulty arose; the merchants of London, to whom the intention to increase the frequency of communication with France had become known, met to protest against the project. A hundred years before they would have gone to the Post Office, talked the matter over with the postmasters-general, and, after an exchange of opinions, an agreement would have been come to as to what was best to be done. Now they assembled in their numbers at the London Tavern and resolved "that any addition to the present number of post days to France or to any other part of the Continent is unnecessary, and would be highly inconvenient and injurious to the merchants of London." The resolution was unanimous, and copies were sent to the postmasters-general and the minister. For the merchants of London Walsingham entertained a sincere respect; but in this particular matter, convinced that they did not know what was for their own good, he determined to proceed in their despite. Unhappily, however, at this conjuncture the resumption of hostilities with France extinguished for the time all hopes of improved communication with the Continent.

Another project, in which the Post Office and the merchants possessed a common interest and a common desire, was also doomed to failure. The practice of cutting bank notes into two parts and sending one part by one post and another by another had now become general. The expedient, though efficacious, was a costly one. A letter with an enclosure, however light, paid double postage; and double postage between two places no farther apart than London and Birmingham was 10d. To send two halves of a bank note each in a separate letter would, of course, cost twice that amount. This was a heavy insurance to pay. The Post Office, in its desire not to discourage a practice which diminished temptation to dishonesty, was hardly less anxious than the merchants themselves that the amount should be reduced. Accordingly Walsingham proposed that in all cases where a bank note was sent by two separate posts the second letter, that is to say, the letter containing the second half, should, on proof being given of its contents, be charged with only single postage. A notice to the public announcing the change had already been prepared when he learnt to his chagrin that the proposed regulation would be illegal. In the case of a letter with an enclosure the law prescribed double postage, and it was no more in the power of the Post Office to reduce the amount than to forego it altogether.

But these were failures which it is only interesting to record as evidence that at the Post Office, after Palmer had left it, there was no want of directing energy or of a desire to study the interests of the public. It is pleasant to turn to matters in respect to which good intentions were not unattended with results. But before leaving 1792, the year in which these disappointments occurred, we must not omit to notice that it was at the end of this year that the letter-carriers were for the first time put into uniform. Palmer, who was now playing the part of the outside critic, condemned the innovation as a piece of unnecessary extravagance. But Palmer did not know the reasons for it. The letter-carriers when in private clothes were exposed to temptation from which the wearing of uniform would protect them; and more than one recent case had brought the fact into painful prominence. Nor can it be denied that, so long as there was no distinctive dress, letter-carriers in want of a holiday were a little apt to take one without permission, supplying their place by persons of whose character they knew little or nothing. It was in order to check irregularity of this kind and as a means of protection to themselves and the public that uniform was now introduced. The uniform consisted of a scarlet cloth coat with blue lapels and blue linings of padua; a blue cloth waistcoat, and a hat with gold band.

It should also be noticed that about this time the Post Office servants in London were in some measure relieved from the pecuniary cares by which they had long been oppressed. The Commissioners of Inquiry in their Report of 1788 had recommended for the Post Office a new establishment; and now, after an interval of nearly five years, this establishment was approved by the King in Council. The new salaries were not high. At the present time they would be considered low; but such as they were, they were higher than the salaries they replaced. Jamineau's recent death, moreover, by relieving the clerks of the roads from payment of the commission[74] which this officer received on all newspapers with which they dealt, enabled them to reduce their price for franking, the result being an immediate extension of sale. On the whole, the Post Office servants in London were, at this time, in comparatively comfortable circumstances, or at all events above the reach of actual want. The starvation and bankruptcy with which they had at one time been threatened had been staved off by a grant, which Pitt renewed year after year while the Commissioners' Report was under consideration. This grant amounted to £3000, of which £2000 were for distribution in the sorting office, and £1000 in the other offices.

The year 1793 was signalised by a remarkable development of the penny post. This institution, which had as yet been established nowhere but in London and in Dublin, was now to be extended to Edinburgh, to Manchester, to Bristol, and to Birmingham. In Edinburgh the ground had been to some extent preoccupied. The keeper of a coffee-house in the hall of the Parliament House had sixteen years before set up an office from which letters were delivered throughout the city at 1d. apiece; and this office still remained open and prospered. To compare Williamson's undertaking with Dockwra's would be to compare a mouse with an elephant; and yet it may not be uninteresting to note the different treatment which the two men received. Dockwra was prosecuted, fined, and his undertaking confiscated.

Williamson was granted a pension. "We have also," write the postmasters-general under date the 19th of July 1793, "to beg your Lordship's permission to authorise us to allow to Mr. Williamson of Edinburgh £25 per annum, he having long had the profits of 1d. a letter on certain letters forwarded through his receiving house at Edinburgh, which he will lose by our having established a penny post there. We have made it a rule," they add, "always to propose that those who suffer in their incomes from regulations which are certainly beneficial to the public should receive compensation for the loss they sustain."

At Manchester the establishment of the penny post followed upon other and important alterations. The inhabitants of that town had long complained of the inadequacy of their postal arrangements; and measures had recently been taken, the very extent of which serves to shew how serious must have been the defects which they were designed to supply. The aged postmistress was granted a pension of £120, with the reversion of one-third of that amount to her daughter; and in her room an active postmaster was appointed at a salary of £300. Four clerks were at the same time appointed, at salaries ranging from £50 to £100, and five additional letter-carriers, making six altogether, at wages of 12s. a week. Thus, Manchester suddenly found itself in possession of a Post Office establishment with which, outside London, that of no other town in the kingdom could compare. As a sequel to this important extension of force a penny post was opened in July 1793; and no sooner had the boon been conferred upon Manchester than it was extended to Bristol and to Birmingham.

It is interesting to note what at these three towns was the financial effect of giving postal facilities. During the year 1794-95 the penny post brought a clear gain to the revenue—in Manchester, of £586; in Bristol, of £469; and in Birmingham, of £240. It is a curious fact that, with this experience to guide them and with an anxious desire to extend the system, the Post Office authorities, after sparing no pains to inform themselves on the subject, came to the conclusion that neither at Liverpool nor at Leeds nor at any other town in England would a penny post defray its own expenses.

But it was in London that the penny post attained its highest development. This branch of Post Office business had long been shamefully neglected. Of the officers concerned in it those above the rank of sorter were only three in number—a comptroller, an accountant, and a collector. Of these the collector attended only occasionally, and the accountant and comptroller not at all. This neglect had its natural effect upon the receipts. During the last twenty years and more, notwithstanding the increase which had during this period taken place in the population and trade of the metropolis, the revenue of the penny post had remained almost stationary. Up to 1789 the highest sum it had ever produced in one year was £5157 net. This was in 1784, and for the five following years the receipts went on decreasing until, attention having been called to the decline, there was a sudden rebound. In 1792 the revenue was—gross £10,825, and net £5561.

Palmer, who was well aware of the discreditable condition into which the Penny Post Office had fallen, proposed to take it in farm, and offered as a consideration to forego his salary and percentage; but this was a proposal the acceptance of which was strongly deprecated by the Commissioners of Inquiry who sat in 1788 no less than by the postmasters-general. It was their unanimous opinion that the penny post should be retained in the hands of the State. Palmer, still clinging to the hope that other counsels might prevail, put off effecting improvements which would afford the strongest arguments against the adoption of his own proposal; and in 1793, in spite of the changes which had been going on all around, the Penny Post Office remained much as it had been during the last twenty years.

The man who now took the reform of the penny post in hand was Edward Johnson. Johnson was a letter-carrier. He had been appointed by Palmer or on Palmer's recommendation; and he soon gave proof of more than ordinary ability. Palmer not infrequently exposed him to a severe ordeal. When unable or unwilling to attend the postmasters-general himself, he would send Johnson in his stead, a substitution which they resented as unseemly; and thus some little prejudice had been excited against him. This prejudice, however, had disappeared with the cause of it, and Johnson now stood high, deservedly high, in the postmaster-generals' favour.

In 1793, in addition to the numerous receiving houses where letters for the penny post might be taken in, there were in London five principal offices—one known as the chief Penny Post Office, and situated in Throgmorton Street, opposite Bartholomew Lane; another called the Westminster Penny Post Office, and situated in Coventry Street, Haymarket; a third, the Hermitage Office in Queen Street, Little Tower Hill; a fourth, the Southwark Office in St. Saviour's Churchyard, Borough; and a fifth, the St. Clement's Office, in Blackmore Street. Between these five offices there was little or no connection; at no two of them were the number of collections or deliveries the same or the hours at which they were made; the letter-carriers were altogether too few for the ground which they had to cover, so that punctuality and despatch were impossible; and even those whose walks lay near the ten-mile limit, before proceeding to deliver their letters, had to come to London to fetch them.

Johnson proposed to change all this. He proposed to reduce the number of principal offices from five to two, retaining only the chief office and the office in Coventry Street; to increase the number of collections and deliveries; to give the same number to all parts served by the penny post, namely, six in the town and three in the suburbs, or, as the suburbs were then called, "the country," and everywhere, as far as possible, to observe the same hours; to post these hours up in every receiving house, so that the public might be made acquainted with them and act as a check upon their being observed; and, instead of requiring the letter-carriers in the remoter parts to come to London for their letters, to send their letters to them by mounted messengers.

Johnson's last proposal, though following almost naturally from what had gone before, well-nigh staggered the postmasters-general. It was that, in order to carry his plan into effect, the number of penny post letter-carriers should be more than doubled. The existing number was eighty-two, and the number which Johnson proposed was 181. This, even at the present time — large as are the numbers with which the Post Office has been accustomed to deal — would be considered a heavy, an exceptionally heavy, increase. In 1793 it was regarded as portentous, and the postmasters-general anxiously sought means to reduce it; but Johnson, besides being perfect master of his subject, possessed two faculties which by no means always go together. He possessed the faculty of devising a good scheme and the faculty of explaining it; and the lucid explanation he now gave convinced the postmasters-general that they could not do better than adopt his plan in its entirety. Contrasting the time which a letter took to pass between various parts of London with the time which it would take if his suggestions were adopted, Johnson had no difficulty in shewing that from his plan the public would derive facilities for intercourse to which they had hitherto been strangers.

There were, perhaps, no two places between which the course of post was more difficult to manage than Marylebone and Limehouse. Under the existing plan a letter from one of these two places, however early it might be posted, might not reach the other on the same day, and, even if it did so, an answer could not be received before the afternoon of the following day. Under Johnson's plan a letter might be received, an answer returned, and the answer answered, all on the same day. Places less inconveniently situated in relation to each other were to receive a still larger measure of benefit. Between persons residing in Lombard Street and the Haymarket, for instance, five letters might pass to and fro between the hours of eight in the morning and seven in the evening. This was within the town limits. Within the country limits the general effect of Johnson's plan may be stated thus: that to letters from London answers might be returned sooner by two posts if the letters were for places not more than five miles distant, and, if for places distant between five and ten miles, sooner by a period ranging from one to three days. The last-mentioned places, moreover, were to have three posts a day instead of one post.

Pitt was no less favourably impressed with Johnson's plan than the postmasters-general were; but before sanctioning it he resolved to await the passing of an Act for the redress of certain anomalies, or what were considered to be anomalies, in the practice of the penny post. This Act was passed in 1794; and immediate steps were taken for carrying the plan into effect. A proud day for Johnson must have been the 8th of September. On that day a public notice appeared announcing the changes that were about to take place; and this notice bore his signature. Only the other day he had been a letter-carrier, and now, by reason of a promotion which did hardly more honour to himself than to the postmasters-general who made it, he signed as deputy-comptroller of the Penny Post Office.

The financial results of Johnson's plan exceeded all expectation. For the last year of the old system the gross revenue of the penny post was £11,000. For the first year of the new system it was £28,560; and for the second year £29,623. Johnson had proceeded on the principle—a principle which from the first establishment of the Post Office has never yet been known to fail—increase facilities for correspondence and correspondence itself increases.

Johnson had made one mistake, a mistake which he frankly acknowledged and did his best to repair. He had fixed the wages of the letter-carriers too low. It was not that he had been indifferent to the interests of the class from which he had recently emerged, but that he had feared to overweight a measure which, even as it stood, he had almost despaired of carrying. The wages, as fixed on his recommendation, ranged from 9s. to 16s. a week. Then came that terrible winter—the winter of 1794-95. We have ourselves been witness to an excessive absence from duty on the part of Post Office servants during the epidemic of influenza in 1890. But the number that were absent then, relatively to the whole force, were not to be compared to the number that were absent in the spring of 1795; neither was their absence due to so grievous a cause.

In the spring of 1795 the penny post letter-carriers, unlike the letter-carriers of the general post, had not yet been supplied with uniform, and, through sheer inability to supply themselves with such articles of clothing and of food as the severity of the weather required, nearly one-half of the whole number were unable to follow their employment. Johnson took great blame to himself for what he had done; nor did he rest until he had procured for the letter-carriers a substantial increase all round. This increase ranged from about 2s. to 6s. a week for each man, and involved a total cost of £1600 a year. Also in matters of detail Johnson effected several improvements, of which we will mention only one. The receptacle for letters at the receiving houses in London had hitherto been an open and movable box. The box was now, on his recommendation, to be fixed and provided with a key. The key was to be kept by the receiver, and he alone was to have access to the letters.

The Act of 1794 contained provisions which it is impossible to pass unnoticed. The penny post from its first establishment in 1681 had differed from the general post in this—that letters sent by it had to be prepaid. By the general post prepayment had not indeed been prohibited, but it had been discouraged; by the penny post it had been compulsory. This was now altered, and it was left to the option of persons using the penny post whether they would prepay their letters or not. It is difficult to repress a pang at the disappearance of a provision to which Dockwra, the founder of the penny post, attached the highest importance; and yet it must be admitted that the change was not made without a reason. Messengers and servants entrusted with letters to post would destroy the letters for the sake of the pence which had been given them to pay the postage; and to such an extent had the abuse been carried that some persons made it a rule not to use the penny post at all unless they could post their own letters.

Another provision of the Act of 1794 was to relax a restriction imposed by the Act of Anne. Before 1711 the penny post had been so extended as to include many places distant from London as much as eighteen and twenty miles. Then came the Act of Anne, restricting the penny post to a circuit of ten miles. And now the ten-mile limit was abolished, and the postmasters-general were empowered, not in London alone but also in country towns wherever the penny post might be established, to extend it at their discretion.

A third provision of the Act of 1794 was designed to correct what was considered a flaw in a previous Act. It is interesting to note what this flaw was. When Dockwra established his post, he insisted that on letters going by it the postage should be 1d. and no more. This penny, however, in the case of letters for places situated beyond the bills of mortality, was to carry only to the receiving house; for delivery at a private house was to be paid a second penny, commonly called the delivery-penny. The Act of Anne merely provided that letters by the penny post should be charged 1d., and was silent on the subject of the second or delivery-penny; and a subsequent Act, passed in 1731, made the delivery-penny legal.

Now what was the consequence of all this? The consequence was that as between two letters, the one passing from London to a place outside the bills of mortality and the other passing from a place outside the bills of mortality to London, there was a difference of postage. In the one direction the postage was 2d. and in the other 1d. The Act of 1794 imposed a postage of 2d. in both directions; and here we see not indeed the origin of the twopenny post but the twopenny post fully established.

The reform of the penny post was soon followed by that of the dead letter office. This office was established in 1784. How, before that year, dead letters were treated is perhaps one of the obscurest points of Post Office practice. We know that letters which could not be delivered and letters which had been missent were always treated together. We know that in 1716 these letters had become so numerous that an officer was specially appointed to check them. We know that to Ralph Allen, fertile as he was in resources, how to deal with this class of letters was a constant source of perplexity. We know that Todd, writing to Foxcroft, the deputy postmaster-general of America, in February 1775, says: "Amongst other regulations made here of late the dead, refused, and unknown letters returned to this office have been opened by the proper officers, and returned to the writers"; but without adding who "the proper officers" were. And we know that as late as 1783 there was in London a letter-carrier whose special duty it was to "take care of the unknown and uncertain letters."

But when we have stated this, we have stated all. Whether there was any recognised mode of dealing with dead letters, or whether any one into whose hands these letters came dealt with them as he judged best, according to circumstances, are questions upon which we have absolutely no information. In 1784 only a part of the dead letters and letters that had been missent went to the newly-created dead letter office. Another and larger part, consisting of bye-letters or letters that in the ordinary course would not reach London, were dealt with in the bye-letter office. No letter was returned to the writer until after the expiration of six months, and on its return no postage was charged. In 1790 Palmer reduced from six months to two the period before which letters were returned, and on his own motion, without reference to the postmasters general, charged them with postage. Grave doubts were entertained as to the legality of this charge, and Pitt, as soon as he heard of it, ordered it to be discontinued.

In 1793 Barlow, a clerk in the secretary's office, who had charge of the dead letter office, introduced two changes of practice which, obvious as they may now appear, were then regarded as evidence of no little merit. He arranged that missent letters, instead of being sent to London to be dealt with in the dead letter office, should be forwarded to their destination from the place where the missending was discovered; and also—a change which gave great satisfaction in naval and military circles—that letters for the army and navy should be sent where the army and navy were known to be, and not to stations and quarters which they were known to have left simply because the letters were addressed there.

About the same time the dead letter office received most valuable help in the discharge of its duties from the publication of what was, virtually, the first County Directory. For some years past three Post Office servants had been engaged in compiling a list of all the names and addresses they could collect throughout the different counties of England. This list, though still far from complete, now filled six large folio volumes. The venture which had been undertaken with a view to profit was financially a failure; but as a means of helping to forward letters with imperfect addresses it proved an unqualified success.

Thus matters stood in 1795, when Barlow proposed a further reform. The inspector of the "bye, dead, and missent letters," as they were called, had neglected his duties. These letters were not sent to London until they had lain for three months in the country offices, and after their arrival he had suffered a still longer period to elapse before proceeding to dispose of them. Barlow now proposed that these letters also should be placed under his control, and the proposal being approved, the dead letter office began to assume the shape in which, though under another name, we know it to-day. To the general practice one exception was made. On the first opening of penny post offices in country towns many letters could not be delivered on account of their imperfect addresses. The novelty and cheapness of the post, it may well be believed, induced persons to use it who possessed little skill in writing, and no knowledge of the mode in which superscriptions should be prepared. It was a duty imposed on the surveyor who was engaged in establishing the post to open these letters and return them to the writers on the spot.

Another office was established about this time, an office for dealing with the American and West Indian letters. The merchants had recently complained that these letters were continually missent, letters for one of the West India Islands being sent to another, and letters for places served from Halifax being sent to Quebec and *vice versâ*. The truth is that until lately some profit had been derived from the sorting of these letters; and the most experienced officers, who knew the circulation abroad almost as well as they knew the circulation at home, had been glad to sort them. The comptroller of the inland department—for, curiously enough, it was there and not in the foreign department that the letters were dealt with—had received one guinea a night and the clerks 5s. a night for dealing with them; but these unauthorised additions to salaries had now been stopped, and the West Indian and American mails were left to be sorted, just as any other mails were sorted, by seniors and juniors in common.

It was impossible that mistakes should not occur. To assist in the disposal of inland mails there were what were called circulation lists, lists shewing to what towns letters for particular places were to be sent; but in the case of the American and West Indian mails there were no such aids to inexperience, and the letters were to a large extent sent haphazard. Freeling now altered this. He procured from abroad circulation lists corrected to the latest date. Four experienced officers were selected, who were made specially responsible for the West Indian and American correspondence; they were to devote to it two hours a night over and above their ordinary hours; and for this extra attendance they were each to receive a special allowance of £30 a year.

Freeling's last safeguard is interesting as shewing what may be done with a limited correspondence. Two books were to be kept, of which one was to be reserved for Government letters. In this book were to be entered the date on which each individual letter was posted, the date on which it was forwarded to Falmouth, and the name of the packet by which it was despatched. The second book was, in Freeling's own words, "to contain observations of different kinds to enable the clerks the better to satisfy the merchants applying for information" respecting the letters they had posted. It would perhaps be hardly an exaggeration to say that between England on the one hand and America and the West Indies on the other there are at the present time more sackfuls of letters passing than there were single letters one hundred years ago.

About the same time, but a little later, an important change took place in the treatment of letters arriving from the East Indies in the ships of the East India Company. These letters came to the India House in boxes addressed to the directors, and so escaped all but the inland postage. Some of them indeed did not pay even that, for if addressed to persons in or near London they were delivered by the Company's servants, who charged and retained as their own perquisite a fee varying from 2s. 6d. to 10s. 6d. on each letter. The practice was of old date, as old probably as the East India Company itself, and was held to be not illegal. It is true that a vessel was forbidden under a penalty of £20 to break bulk or to make entry into port until all letters brought by the master or his company should be delivered to some agent of the postmasters-general; but both the captain and the directors were held to be exempt from liability under this provision, the captain because he was presumably ignorant of what the boxes contained, and the directors because the penalty attached to the captain and not to them.

The legality of the practice not being contested, nothing remained but to make overtures to the directors; and, on this being done, they readily consented that for the future all letters arriving by their ships, except such as were for themselves and their friends, should be forthwith sent to the Post Office to be dealt with as ship letters. The public derived no little advantage from the change. The postage from India was actually less than what the company's servants had been accustomed to exact as fees; and the letters were now delivered at once, whereas the company's servants would seldom deliver them under three or four days after their arrival at the India House, and sometimes not for a whole month.

Contemporaneously with the Act of Parliament regulating the penny post was passed another establishing a post to the Channel Islands. This was essentially a war post, a post which, except for the war between England and France, might have been postponed far into the present century. Hitherto letters for the Channel Islands had been charged with postage only as far as Southampton, and from Southampton they had been carried to their destination by private boat. Again and again had the Post Office been urged by those who wanted employment for their vessels to establish a line of packets to the islands; but to all such overtures the postmasters-general turned a deaf ear. Boats were passing to and fro regularly four or five times a week, and the owners of these boats were ready and glad to carry the letters for the ship-letter postage of 1d. a letter. Why then, it was asked, should the Post Office be at the expense of maintaining a line of packets which, unless it were put on a footing out of all proportion to the importance of the service, would give absolutely less accommodation than that which existed already?

Thus matters stood when war broke out and all communication with the islands was stopped. Even now the postmasters-general had grave doubts as to the propriety of establishing a line of packets. It was true that the correspondence with the Channel Islands was considerable. During the year 1792 the number of letters on which ship-letter postage had been paid was 21,570, namely, 20,070 at Southampton and 1500 at Dartmouth and other ports on the south coast—making, on the assumption that the letters were as many in the opposite direction, a total correspondence for the year of about 43,000 letters.

And yet there were serious considerations on the other side. Unless an Act of Parliament were passed providing a packet rate of postage between the mainland and the islands, the Post Office would have no exclusive right of carrying the letters, and the moment the war ceased the packets might be deserted in favour of the private boats. If, on the other hand, such an Act were passed, popular as the measure might be while the war lasted, it could not fail to be unpopular as soon as the war ceased. Private boats would then be an illegal means of conveyance, and correspondence would be restricted to the packets, however few these might be in number, and however wide the intervals between the despatches.

Another expedient remained, but this was one which had been tried during the last war, and the postmasters-general were not prepared to repeat it. The *Express* packet, Captain Sampson, belonging to the Dover station, had been temporarily detached to Southampton to keep communication with the Channel Islands open. As some set-off against the cost, the Post Office had counted upon saving the ship-letter pence; but here again the want of an authorised packet postage made itself felt. Sampson, though in receipt of a salary and at no expense for the boat he commanded, claimed and received the ship-letter pence, the postmasters-general regarding themselves apparently as legally incompetent to resist the demand. Without denying that a line of packets might be necessary for purposes of State, the postmasters-general now declined to promote one on Post Office grounds. Of the necessities of the State they were not the judges, and, if the State required the adoption of such a measure, it was for others to take the initiative.

The decision at which the Government arrived appears in the Act of 1794, which established a line of packets between England and the Channel Islands. The packet station was to be at Weymouth, the passage from Weymouth being shorter than from Southampton, and Southampton Water being difficult to leave when the wind was contrary. For a single letter the postage, over and above all other rates, was fixed at 2d., and for a double and treble letter in proportion. Thus the cost of a single letter from London to the Channel Islands would remain the same as before. Hitherto there had been paid 4d. for postage from London to Southampton, 1d. to a factor at Southampton, 1d. for conveyance across, and 1d. to the island post office — for the islands had a post office, although it was a private one, and not under the control of the postmasters-general — making 7d. altogether. Now the charge would be the same, namely, postage to Weymouth 5d., and 2d. for the packet postage. By the same Act of Parliament rates of postage were imposed within the islands similar to those which existed in England.

The abuses of franking now came under notice again. Ten years had elapsed since the passing of the Act which provided that a letter, to be exempt from postage, must bear on the outside, as part of its superscription, its full date written in the member's own handwriting, and be posted on the date which the superscription bore. Of course, the object of the provision was to confine the privilege to members themselves, and to prevent them from obliging their friends at a distance with franks; but this object was almost universally defeated by the simple expedient of sending to their friends franks that were post-dated. It was a common occurrence for franks dated on the same day and by the same member to be sent from places three or four hundred miles apart.

The bankers who sat in Parliament were the chief offenders. Little did they think that an exact account was being kept of every frank that passed through the London Post Office, or assuredly they would hardly have ventured to keep their friends and customers supplied, as it was their practice to do, with the means of evading postage. How many bankers sat in Parliament in 1794 we are not informed; but whatever the number was, we know that during the three months ending the 10th of October in that year there passed through the London Post Office no less than 103,805 letters franked by them, a number larger by one-fifth than the letters of the Court and all the public offices of the State combined.[75] During the same period those members of Parliament who were merchants and not bankers contented themselves with the comparatively modest number of 27,111. Two or three years before it had leaked out that the Government were considering whether a strenuous effort should not be made to abolish the franking privilege altogether, and it was no secret to the Post Office that in anticipation of such an event the banking houses which had a partner in Parliament had concerted arrangements for sending their letters by the coaches in boxes.

The Government were now resolved that, if the abuses of franking could not be stopped, they should at all events be restricted, and with this object a bill was brought in which passed into law in 1795. Under this statute the weight which a member could frank was reduced from two ounces to one ounce; no letter was to be considered as franked unless the member whose name and superscription it bore was within twenty miles of the town at which it was posted either on the day of posting or on the day before; and in the course of one day no member was to send free more than ten letters or to receive free more than fifteen.

The same statute which restrained the abuses of franking made a not unimportant concession. In an Act passed in 1753 a clause had been inserted providing that a letter containing patterns or samples, if it did not weigh as much as one ounce, was to be charged as a double letter and no more. This was now improved upon. Under the Act of 1795 a packet of patterns or samples might, on certain conditions, pass as a single letter. These conditions were that it did not exceed one ounce in weight, that it was open at the sides, and that it contained no writing other than the name and address of the sender and the prices of the articles of which he sent specimens.

A few months later another advance was made. At Lombard Street great inconvenience had been caused by the late arrival of the letters from the West End. The sorting began at five o'clock in the evening, and the mails were despatched at eight; but it was not until nearly seven that the bulk of the letters from the West End were brought in by the runners. Thus, while the first two hours of the evening were hours of comparative idleness, the last hour was one of extreme pressure. Occasionally, we are told, there would at a quarter before seven o'clock be lying on the sorting table as many as 14,000 letters, all of which had to be disposed of by eight. At the present day 14,000 letters would be regarded as a mere handful. In 1796 it was a number which it taxed the utmost resources of the Post Office to dispose of within the allotted time.

How to relieve the pressure between the hours of seven and eight was now the question to be solved; and the presidents who had succeeded to Bonnor's place when this person was got rid of suggested that the object might be attained if, instead of the letters from the West End being brought to the General Post Office by runners, light carts were employed to bring them. Two carts would be enough for the purpose. One might start from Charing Cross and the other from Duke Street, Oxford Street, picking up bags at the different offices on their way. Thus the letters would reach Lombard Street earlier by some thirty minutes than heretofore, and there would be more time to sort and charge them. The drivers should, of course, be armed. The plan was adopted, and answered well; and this was the origin of what is called the London Mail-Cart and Van Service, a service in which are now employed daily as many as 550 vehicles.

Since the introduction of mail-coaches the robbery of mails on the main roads of the kingdom had entirely ceased. Now and then, but very rarely, there had been pilfering from a mail-coach as, through the default of those in charge, it stood at an inn door unguarded; and there had, no doubt, been one serious case of theft. On the 24th of October 1794 a man, giving the name of Thomas Thomas, went down by the mail-coach from London to Bristol, and returned on the following day. This journey he repeated on the 2nd, 3rd, and 4th of November, and on the last-mentioned date, when the guard's back was turned, he took advantage of the mail box being left unlocked to steal the mails. But this was a case of theft, and not of robbery.

During the twelve years which had elapsed since Palmer's plan was established there had not been one single instance in which a mail-coach had been molested by highwaymen. Far otherwise was it with the horse and cross-post mails. In 1796 the distance over which these mails travelled was, in England, about 3800 miles, and hardly a week passed without intelligence reaching headquarters that in some part or other of their course they had been stopped and robbed. Some roads enjoyed an unenviable notoriety in this respect, as, for instance, the road between Barton Mills and Lynn in Norfolk, the road between Bristol and Portsmouth, and, above all, the road between Chester and Warrington. Between these two places, indeed, the mail had only recently been robbed on four different occasions.

Manchester and other towns now took the matter up, and urged that mail-coaches might be established on the roads where the robberies took place, not because coaches were necessary to carry the letters, but on account of the security which they afforded. Freeling proposed as an alternative that the horse and cross-post mails should be guarded. To supply the existing post-boys, or riders, as they were then termed, with firearms would have been worse than useless. They were mere boys—many of them not yet fourteen years of age—and with firearms in their possession they would have been more likely to shoot themselves than their assailants. Accordingly, Freeling proposed that no riders should be employed who, besides being of approved character, were not between the ages of eighteen and forty-five; that they should each be furnished with a brace of pistols, a cutlass, and a strong cap for the defence of the head; and that, in consideration of an increased allowance to be made by the Post Office, the postmasters whose servants the riders were should be required to provide them with better horses than those hitherto in use.

Of all the plans which, through a long course of years, were submitted to Pitt for the improvement of the posts this was the only one to which he demurred. He did not, indeed, deny its efficacy; but it would involve a cost of at least £6000 a year, and, pressed as he was for money, he declined to say more than that the plan might be carried out if the persons interested were willing to bear the additional expense, but not otherwise. For us with our present knowledge it is easy enough to see that the surest and most popular way of transferring the expense to the public would have been to cheapen the postage. In 1796 no other way appeared feasible than to make the postage dearer. To this object the postmasters-general now devoted themselves, and before many months were over they had prepared a bill which, with some modifications, was adopted by the Government and passed into law.

In the new Act, which came into operation on the 5th of January 1797, the ambiguous term "stage" was dropped, and the whole of the rates were fixed according to distance, thus—

On and After the 5th of January 1797.

	Single Letter.	Double Letter.	Treble Letter.	Ounce.
	d.	d.	d.	d.
Not exceeding 15 miles	3	6	9	12
Exceeding 15 and not exceeding				

30 miles	4	8	12	16
Exceeding 30 and not exceeding 60 miles	5	10	15	20
Exceeding 60 and not exceeding 100 miles	6	12	18	24
Exceeding 100 and not exceeding 150 miles	7	14	21	28
Exceeding 150 miles	8	16	24	32
To and from Edinburgh	8	16	24	32

Within Scotland the rates were raised by 1d. for a single letter, by 2d. for a double letter, and so on. Another important change was made. Hitherto, in the case of letters from Portugal and America, the packet postage had carried them to their destination. For the future these letters were to be subject to the inland rates as well as the packet rates. Thus the packet rate from Lisbon had been, on a single letter, 1s. 6d. It was now to be 1s.; but if for London the letter would be charged with the inland rate of 8d.—this being the postage from Falmouth—and if for Edinburgh with 8d. more, or 2s. 4d. altogether. As the packet postage from America remained unchanged, namely, 1s. for a single letter, the inland rate was in this case a pure addition.

The postmasters-general were now doomed to a serious disappointment. Their proposal to raise the rates of postage was, there can be no doubt, dictated, at all events in part, by a desire to carry out the project of guarding the horse and cross-post mails. Pitt had stated that he would approve this project if the persons interested would bear the expense of it; and unquestionably the expense, and much more than the expense, was thrown upon the persons interested by the higher sums which they had now to pay for their letters. The postmaster-generals' object, however, had not been avowed, and no understanding had been arrived at. Their proposal to raise the rates of postage had met with ready acceptance. Their proposal to guard the horse and cross-post mails, though repeated again and again, continued to be rejected.

Although much had been done during the last few years to introduce order and regularity among the packets, some little mystery still surrounded their proceedings. In March 1798, out of twenty packets on the Falmouth station there was not one in port to carry the mails to Jamaica and the Leeward Islands; and this was the second time within twelve months that the same thing had occurred. The West India merchants waited on the postmasters-general to complain. On this occasion an armed cutter was borrowed from the Admiralty to take out the mails; but the fact remained that between the 5th of April 1793 and January 1798 no less than nineteen packets, all of them belonging to the Falmouth station, had been captured by the enemy, and that the Post Office had had to replace them at a cost of close upon £50,000.

The merchants demanded, as they had done a year before, that the packets should be armed. Armed indeed in some sort they were already, but only with six four-pounders apiece, and with small arms so as to be able to resist row-boats and small privateers. The merchants urged that this was not enough. The postmasters-general replied that they could do no more, that the true policy was not to arm the packets with a view to their engaging the enemy, but so to construct them that they might outsail him. The merchants met to consider the reply which had been given, and, as the result of their deliberations, they prepared a memorial, copies of which were sent to the postmasters-general and the minister. In this memorial misgivings were expressed which, even at this distance of time, it is impossible not to share. During the last three years the average duration of voyage had been, from Falmouth to Jamaica, forty-five days, and from Jamaica to Falmouth, fifty-two days. These, as the memorialists pointed out, were not quick voyages; still less were they quick voyages for vessels which had been specially constructed with a view to expedition. It was extraordinary, too, built and equipped as the packets were, that out of nine that had been recently captured eight should have fallen a prey to private ships of war, which presumably enjoyed far less advantages in point of sailing. The conclusion at which the merchants felt constrained to arrive was that "in the mode of loading or navigating the packets some abuses exist sufficient to counteract the advantages of their construction."

And yet, mysterious as their proceedings were, ample evidence is at hand that the packets were both willing and able to fight as occasion required. Indeed, to this period belong some of their smartest engagements. We will give one or two instances. On the evening of the 17th of October 1797 the *Portland* packet, Captain Taylor, was lying becalmed off the island of Guadeloupe when a French privateer, the *Temeraire*, bore down upon her. The privateer carried sixty-eight men and the packet thirty-two. A light breeze springing up, the *Portland's* head got off shore, and for the time she contrived to elude her antagonist, who followed her all night under easy sail. At daybreak the same distance separated the two ships as on the preceding evening; but as the *Temeraire* began to overtake the *Portland*, Taylor fired the first shot. The shot was returned, and the privateer hoisting the bloody flag grappled the *Portland* and boarded her on the lee quarter. Laying hold of the jib-stay Taylor ordered it to be lashed to the packet, and called upon the passengers and crew to open their musketry.

A fierce engagement ensued, which ended in favour of the *Portland*. Out of sixty-eight men on board the privateer no less than forty-one were either killed or wounded. A treacherous shot fired after she had struck her colours carried off the captain of the packet in the moment of victory, and as he was endeavouring to allay the carnage.

Among the passengers on board the *Portland* were four military officers, captains in the English army. That these officers in no small measure contributed to the result may be taken for granted; but silent as to their own deeds they extolled in the highest terms the prowess of the captain and crew, and it was from the independent testimony which they and the other passengers bore that the gallant action became known to the postmasters-general.

Another and still more brilliant engagement had taken place a few years before. On the 27th of November 1793 the *Antelope* packet, Captain Curtis, sailed from Port Royal in Jamaica with twenty-nine men. She, like the *Portland*, had on board a few passengers, among whom were Colonel Loppinott, an independent witness to the events that followed, and a young man of the name of Nodin. Nodin had been a midshipman in the Royal Navy, and, having resigned his commission, was on his way home to England to seek for other employment.

On the morning of the 1st of December, when the *Antelope* was about five leagues off Cumberland harbour in the island of Cuba, the *Atalanta*, a French privateer, hove in sight and immediately gave chase. The privateer carried eight carriage-guns and sixty-five men. The packet carried the usual six four-pounders, and out of her crew of twenty-nine men four had died of fever and two others were prostrate from the same cause, so that her complement was practically reduced to twenty-three. The pursuit continued until the morning of the 3rd, when, the *Atalanta* coming within gunshot and hoisting French colours and the bloody flag, broadsides were exchanged. The two ships now grappled, and on the part of the privateer an attempt was made to board both fore and aft. Fore, the assailing party, fifteen in number, were swept away by the guns; aft, where there were no guns, the assault was also repulsed but at a cost of life which made the disproportion between the numbers on the two sides even greater than before. Among those that were killed in this sally was the captain of the packet; and the mate having been severely wounded, the command devolved upon John Pascoe, the boatswain. Another attempt was now made to board, and, like the first, was successfully resisted.

This result was largely due to Nodin's intrepidity. Standing by the helm and armed with a pike and a musket he alternately used these weapons with deadly effect. As the men climbed the sides, he sprang forward and cut them down with his pike; then he returned to the helm and righted the ship; then seizing his musket he loaded it and flew to quarters; and as he was cool and collected and a sure marksman every shot told. On the repulse of the second attempt to board, the privateer's grappling-rope was cut and she tried to sheer off; but this Pascoe prevented by lashing her square sail-yard to the fore-shrouds of the packet. The privateer's fire now began to slacken, which was only a signal to the others to renew their energies. The *Antelope* poured in volley after volley of small-arms; and at length the marauders cried out for mercy and, expecting none, some of them jumped into the sea and were drowned. Altogether, when the bloody flag was torn down from the mast-head of the *Atalanta*, only thirty men remained out of the sixty-five with which she had begun the combat; and of these thirty one-half were wounded. The troubles of the packet were not yet at an end. As the smoke cleared away she was found to be on fire; and it was not until the mainsail, quarter cloths, and hammocks had been cut away that she was able to carry her prize into Anotta Bay.

The officers and crew of the *Antelope* did not go unrewarded. For distribution among the survivors and the families of those who had been killed the House of Assembly in Jamaica voted the sum of 500 guineas; 375 guineas were afterwards presented for the same purpose by the Society for Encouraging the Capture of French Privateers; the postmasters-general showered small pensions and gratuities; and—what was the highest compliment of all—the *Atalanta*, though a droit of admiralty, was given up to the captors.

It was always when passengers were on board that the Post Office heard of these brilliant achievements on the part of the packets. We are not sure that this fact may not help us to unravel the mystery which perplexed the merchants. May it not be that, when the check exercised by the presence of passengers was removed, the packets at the end of the last century, like those of a hundred years before, went in quest of adventure and matched themselves against superior force or otherwise engaged in illicit operations? The series of captures which the merchants could not understand, and, where there were no captures, the dilatoriness of the voyages, would thus be explained.

The usage of the Post Office one hundred years ago differed in not a few particulars from the usage of to-day. At the present time no postmaster-general would think of calling for a daily return of the number of letters passing through the London office with the amount of postage paid or to be paid upon them. Yet such a return was, a century ago, sent to the postmasters-general regularly every morning, and it was esteemed the most important paper of the day. At the present time any instruction which may have to be given to the sorting office is entered in what is called the Order Book; and this book is signed by all whom it concerns. One hundred years ago, all instructions were made known by the presidents reading them aloud in the sorting office on Mondays and Saturdays, when the men were assembled for the purpose. It was thus that appointments, promotions, and punishments were also announced. One hundred years ago, when a letter-carrier's walk became vacant, a bell was rung, and, the letter-carriers being collected together, the vacancy was offered to the senior, and if the senior declined it, to the next in rotation, and so on. When a Post Office servant died, his salary was paid not only to the date of death but to the end of the current quarter.

Another practice then existed, a practice dictated, as some may think, by convenience and common sense. It was that counsel engaged in Post Office cases gave receipts for their fees. In connection with this practice a curious incident occurred. Walsingham had ordered an independent inquiry to be made into the solicitor's accounts, and, in the course of the investigation, the inspector came across a heap of receipts signed, or purporting to be signed, by some of the most eminent lawyers of the day. Walsingham had suspected imposition before, and now he was sure of it. The solicitor, had he been asked, would no doubt have explained, as indeed was the case, that the practice dated from 1703, and originated with Godolphin, who, failing to see why counsel engaged by public offices should be exempt from doing what all other persons were required to do, issued peremptory injunctions that in legal cases no more fees should be paid by the Post Office for which receipts were not given.[76] Instead, however, of addressing himself to the solicitor, Walsingham referred to Kenyon, the Lord Chief Justice; and Kenyon's reply, as Walsingham himself admitted, filled him with astonishment. It was simply that when attorney-general he had always given receipts for fees from public offices, understanding when he was appointed that such was the practice, and that it had long been so.

One more custom we may mention as existing a century ago, a custom which was then abandoned, but not without manifest reluctance on the part of those whose interest it was to keep it alive. At the present time our friends at the Treasury are credited with taking advantage of the accident of their position to get themselves appointed to the best situations in all the public offices of the State. One hundred years ago the blackmail which these gentlemen levied upon the public offices took another form, a form a little coarser perhaps but less provoking. At the beginning of each year they exacted tribute which, disguised under the name of New Year's gifts, were really New Year's extortions. The correspondence which passed between the Treasury and the Post Office, when these extortions ceased, unlike official correspondence generally, is so short and to the point that we cannot do better than give it in full:—

The TREASURY to the POST OFFICE.

TREASURY CHAMBERS, Oct. 10, 1797.

My Lords—The Lords Commissioners of His Majesty's Treasury having had under their consideration a Report of the Select Committee of the House of Commons on Finance in the last session of Parliament respecting this office, I am commanded by their Lordships to acquaint you that they have determined that the practice of receiving New Year's gifts by any person in this department shall be discontinued, and that your Lordships may not send them as heretofore.—I am, my Lords, etc.,

GEORGE ROSE.

The POST OFFICE to the TREASURY.

GENERAL POST OFFICE, Jan. 13, 1798.

My Lords—We beg leave to acknowledge the receipt of Mr. Rose's letter of the 10th of October acquainting us of your Lordships' determination that the practice of receiving New Year's gifts by any person in your department must be discontinued, to which we shall pay proper attention.

It is necessary to state to your Lordships that Mr. Rose's letter, although dated the 10th of October 1797, was not brought to this office until the 1st of January 1798; but it was received in due time to enable us to attend to the purport of it.—We are, my Lords, etc.,

Chesterfield.
Leicester.

It is needless to add that hitherto these New Year's gifts had been despatched from the Post Office on the evening of the 31st of December.

Nine years had now passed since the Royal Commissioners had reported upon the condition of the public offices; and four years had passed since the Report had seen the light. Pitt had been deliberate enough in approving the recommendations; but having done so, he had no intention that they should remain inoperative. And yet he had little confidence that such would not be the case unless some external influence were brought to bear. Accordingly recourse was had to an expedient which might perhaps with advantage be sometimes adopted at the present day. At Pitt's instigation a Special Committee of the House of Commons was appointed to ascertain and report how far the recommendations of the Royal Commissioners had been carried into effect.

The Post Office, on the whole, came well out of the ordeal. Abuses had been corrected; useless offices had been abolished; and men were no longer drawing salaries for duties which they did not perform. There was, however, one notable exception. Todd, the secretary, had during many years ceased to do any work; yet he had not ceased to draw his full salary; neither had he ceased to retain his shares in at least one of the Post Office packets. The Committee denounced his conduct in terms which far exceeded the ordinary bounds of parliamentary usage. Their language indeed, as applied to a man of more than eighty years of age, might even be pronounced to be cruel. And yet scathing as the censure was, it fell upon callous ears. With a tenacity worthy of a better cause the old man still clung to his place and his shares. The postmasters-general now brought pressure to bear. As regards the shares, which Todd had held unknown to his masters, they insisted upon his selling them; but his place of secretary they were either unwilling or unable to wrest from his grasp.

Death at length put an end to the scandal. In June 1798 Todd yielded up at once his life and his office; and Francis Freeling, according to a long-standing promise, became Secretary to the Post Office in his stead.

CHAPTER XIV
FRANCIS FREELING 1798-1817

The name of Francis Freeling has been placed at the head of this chapter, not because, in devising new means of correspondence or extending means that already existed, he is to be classed with the distinguished men who preceded him—with Palmer and Allen, with Dockwra and Witherings—but because for more than a generation he exercised a paramount influence in Post Office matters, and during this long period whatever was done affecting the communications of the country was done upon his advice.

The first act of importance in which Freeling was concerned after his appointment as secretary was the establishment of the ship letter office, an office which owed its origin to the suggestion of Frederick Bourne, a clerk in the foreign department. Hitherto the packet boats, where packet boats existed, had been the only means by which correspondence could be legally sent out of the kingdom; and yet in the neighbourhood of the Exchange there was hardly a place of public resort at which letters for America and the West Indies, as well as other places abroad, were not collected for despatch by private ship. There was no concealment about the matter. At Lloyds, and the Jamaica, the Maryland, the Virginia and other coffee-houses, bags were openly hung up, and all letters dropped into these bags, including those for places to which there was communication by packet, were taken on board ship, and, without the intervention of the Post Office, despatched to their destination, the captains receiving for their transport a gratuity of 2d. apiece.

Illegal as the practice was, Pitt was unwilling to suppress it. The Act which made it illegal to send by private ship letters which might be sent by packet had been passed in the time of Queen Anne, and he could not reconcile it to himself to enforce a law some ninety years old which had never yet been set in motion. Bourne's idea was to sweep all ship-letters into the post, and to charge them inwards with a fixed sum of 4d. and outwards with half the packet rate of postage. If with the place to which a letter was addressed there was no communication by packet, the rate was to be fixed at what presumably it would be if such communication existed. Pitt favoured the idea and adopted it—subject, however, to one important qualification. Instead of being compulsory the Act, should an Act be passed, was to be permissive. On this point Pitt was determined. It was only in return for some service that the Post Office was entitled to make a charge. And what was the service here? To seal the bags? This he could not regard as a substantial service—a service for which a charge should be made. The ship was a private ship, her commander was not a servant of the Post Office, and the bag of letters he carried might be, and not infrequently was, for countries in which neither the Post Office nor any other branch of the British Government had an accredited agent.

Surely in such circumstances anything in the shape of compulsion was out of the question, and all that should be done was to invite the merchants to bring their letters to the Post Office, when the Post Office would undertake to find a private ship that would carry them. A bill on these lines was brought in and passed; and on the 10th of September 1799 the ship letter office was opened, Bourne being appointed to superintend it under the title of inspector. The new measure failed of its object. On letters entering the kingdom fourpences were no doubt collected, because, until these letters had been deposited at the local Post Office, no vessel was allowed to make entry or to break bulk. But letters leaving the kingdom left it just as they had been used to leave it before the ship letter office was established. It was in vain that the Post Office tempted the keepers of coffee-houses by the offer of high salaries to become its own agents. All overtures to this end were resolutely declined; and during many years the letters by private ship that were sent through the post stood to those that were received through the same agency in no higher proportion than one to eighteen.

In 1801 the Post Office was called upon to make to the Exchequer a further contribution to the amount of £150,000. What would have struck consternation to the hearts of most men was to Freeling a source of unmixed pleasure. Not only had he a perfect craze for high rates of postage, but it had long been with him a subject of lament that under the law as it stood no higher charge was made for a distance of 500 miles than for a distance of 150. This in his view was a glaring defect, and he now set himself to remedy it. The new rates—which, as he lost no opportunity of making known, were exclusively of his own devising—were adopted by the Government, and having passed the Houses of Parliament came into operation on the 5th of April. As compared with the old rates, they were as follows:—

Before the 5th of April 1801.

	Single.	Double.	Treble.	Ounce.
	d.	d.	d.	d.
Not exceeding 15 miles	3	6	9	12
Above 15 and not exceeding 30 miles	4	8	12	16
" 30 " 60 "	5	10	15	20
" 60 " 100 "	6	12	18	24
" 100 " 150 "	7	14	21	28
Exceeding 150 miles	8	16	24	32

On and After the 5th of April 1801.

	Single.	Double.	Treble.	Ounce.
	d.	d.	d.	d.
Not exceeding 15 miles	3	6	9	12
Above 15 and not exceeding 30 miles	4	8	12	16
" 30 " 50 "	5	10	15	20
" 50 " 80 "	6	12	18	24
" 80 " 120 "	7	14	21	28
" 120 " 170 "	8	16	24	32
" 170 " 230 "	9	18	27	36
" 230 " 300 "	10	20	30	40
" 300 " 400 "	11	22	33	44
" 400 " 500 "	12	24	36	48
" 500 " 600 "	13	26	39	52
" 600 " 700 "	14	28	42	56
Exceeding 700 miles	15	30	45	60

Thus the postage on a single letter was—from London to Brighton, 6d.; from London to Liverpool, 9d.; and from London to Edinburgh, 1s. A letter weighing one ounce is now carried from London to Thurso for 1d. In 1801 the charge was 5s.

On letters to or from places abroad, "not being within His Majesty's dominions," the postage was at the same time raised by 4d., 8d., 1s., and 1s. 4d., according as the letter was single, double, treble, or of the weight of one ounce.

But there was worse to come. By the Act of 1801 the London penny post—that post which had been established 120 years before, and which, its founder had predicted, would endure to all posterity—was swept out of existence. For us who are now living it is difficult to conceive that such an enormity should have been possible. Yet there is the fact. After the passing of the Act of 1801 the London penny post had ceased to be. Where 1d. had been charged before, the sum of 2d. was to be charged now.

The same Act contained another provision, which it is impossible to regard otherwise than as a wanton interference with trade. The Legislature, from the earliest days of the Post Office, had shewn indulgence to merchants' accounts not exceeding one sheet of paper, to bills of exchange, invoices, and bills of lading. All these, in the language of the Act establishing the Post Office—the Act of 1660—were to be "without rate in the price of the letters"; and a similar provision was contained in the Act of Anne. Owing, however, to a faulty construction of the clause it was doubtful whether the exemption was confined to foreign letters or whether it applied to inland letters as well. The merchants contended that inland letters were included; otherwise, as they pointed out, a letter might "go cheaper to Constantinople than to Bristol." The postmasters-general, on the other hand, insisted that the exemption applied only to foreign letters, and, in order to set doubts at rest, they early in the reign of George the Second procured an Act to be passed declaring their interpretation to be the right one. As regards foreign letters, therefore, there had never been the slightest doubt as to either the intention or the practice. When enclosed in letters going or coming from abroad, merchants' accounts not exceeding one sheet of paper, bills of exchange, invoices, and bills of lading had from the first establishment of the Post Office been exempt from postage; and now after an interval of more than 140 years this exemption, like the penny post, was swept away. Henceforth these documents were to be charged as so many several letters.

Yet one more provision in the Act of 1801 it is necessary to notice as introducing a novel principle. This Act gave power to the postmasters-general to grant postal facilities to towns and villages where no Post Offices existed, provided the inhabitants were prepared to pay such sums as might be mutually agreed upon. As the postmasters-general were already authorised to establish Penny Post Offices wherever they might see fit out of London, the object of this fresh power may not be very clear. It was not that the Post Office might be able to charge for the local service more than 1d. a letter, for in no single instance, so far as we are aware, was more than 1d. charged, but that in arranging the local service the Post Office might have a freedom of action which it did not possess under the statute empowering it to establish penny posts. In short, the object of the power was to enable the Post Office, in concert with the inhabitants of the towns and villages concerned, to try experiments.

As a natural consequence of the high rates of postage, the illegal conveyance of letters now became general. This was an offence to which Freeling gave no quarter. Wherever information could be obtained that letters were being conveyed otherwise than by post, there a prosecution was instituted. The extent to which the policy of repression was carried less than a century ago may seem incredible. In Scotland, for instance, every carrier and every master of a stage-coach as well as many others were served with notice of prosecution. In that part of the kingdom alone no less than 1200 prosecutions were instituted simultaneously. Even Parkin, the solicitor to the Post Office in England, was absolutely aghast at the zeal of his colleague over the Border, and counselled moderation. Freeling, on the other hand, expressed entire approval, declaring that the Scotch solicitor was to be encouraged and not restrained. Nor were the prosecutions merely nominal. An unfortunate Post Office servant, or rider as he was called, had been detected in carrying forty unposted letters. This man, whose wages did not exceed a few shillings a week, was sued upon each letter, and adjudged to pay forty separate penalties of 10s. apiece.

Lord Auckland and Lord Charles Spencer were at this time postmasters-general. Spencer had been only recently appointed. Auckland had held his appointment for a couple of years, and by virtue of his seniority took the lead. Seldom, perhaps, has there been a more kindly postmaster-general, or one who to an equal extent enlivened by sprightly sallies the dull monotony of official work. The postmaster of Tring had opened a letter from Freeling to Sir John Sebright. The postmaster pleaded that the opening was accidental; Freeling maintained that it was wilful, and recommended the man's dismissal. Auckland ordered him to be reprimanded for culpable negligence. It may, no doubt, he said, have been a wilful act; but it may also have been an act of inadvertence. And then, in order to remove any feeling of soreness which Freeling may have entertained at his recommendation being set aside, he good-naturedly added, "*Multi alii hoc fecerunt etiam et boni.*" "I have," he continued, "a fellow-feeling on the occasion. My appetite for reading is as much sickened as that of any man-cook for the tasting of high sauces; and yet so lately as last night I tore the envelope of a letter which a little attention would have shewn was not for me."

On another occasion two postmistresses—the postmistress of Faversham and the postmistress of Croydon—simultaneously announced their intention of marrying, each for the third time, and asked that their offices, which as married women they would be incompetent to continue to hold, might be transferred to their future husbands. Auckland gave the permission sought, adding, in the case of the postmistress of Faversham, "I meet the repeated applications of this active deputy with great complacency, and in the words of Lady Castlemaine's answer to our mutton-eating monarch—

> 'Again and again, my liege, said she,
> And as oft as shall please your Majesty.'"

Bennett, the man to whom the postmistress of Croydon was engaged, had been known to her for some time, and she bore testimony to his qualifications for the post to which he aspired. "The Croydon lady, who is also laudably prone to a reiteration of nuptials," wrote Auckland, "rests her case on grounds less solid. I have no doubt of her judgment and testimony respecting the ability of Mr. Robert Thomas Bennett; but for the sake of the precedent the sufficiency should be certified either by the surveyor of the district, or by the vicar or some principal inhabitant."

With such pleasantries as these Auckland beguiled the tediousness of official work; but in serious matters, matters affecting the interests of the public, he appears to have exerted little will of his own. Once, indeed, he expressed some misgiving as to the propriety of the course pursued. It was in the case of the Scotch prosecutions. "I own," he said, "that I was a little surprised to find that so large a measure as that of commencing 1200 prosecutions has been undertaken without our special cognisance; but this circumstance," he added, "is in some degree explained." The reproof, if reproof it can be called, could hardly have been milder; and yet as coming from Auckland it was a severe one. It had not the effect, however—nor probably was it designed to have the effect—of checking the general policy on which Freeling had embarked. That policy was one of repression, and in England hardly less than in Scotland prosecutions went merrily on.

Indeed, the repressive powers of the Post Office, large as they were already, were yet not large enough to satisfy headquarters. Freeling discerned clearly enough that, if only a sufficiently high consideration were offered, persons would always be found to carry letters clandestinely. Might it not be possible to strike at the source of the mischief, and make it penal for persons clandestinely to send them? The tempters would thus be reached as well as the tempted. At all events the experiment should be tried.

With this object Freeling now devoted himself to the preparation of a bill, one clause of which rendered liable to penalties persons sending letters otherwise than by the post. The bill, which was throughout of a highly penal character, eventually passed into law,[77] but not without grave misgivings on the part of Eldon, the Lord Chancellor, and Ellenborough, the Chief Justice. It was only in deference to the urgent representations of the Post Office that these two eminent men consented to the introduction of the measure, and, while waiving their objections to it, they strongly recommended that "great lenity should be used in its execution." It will be interesting to note how far this recommendation was acted on.

Having settled the postage rates to his satisfaction, Freeling obtained permission to carry out his favourite project of guarding the horse-mails. The arguments in favour of this measure were overwhelming. During the five years which had elapsed since the Treasury had refused their assent, these mails had been stopped and rifled of their contents on fifteen different occasions; and on the last of these—when the Lewes mail was robbed in the neighbourhood of East Grinstead—bills had been stolen to the amount of nearly £14,000. During the same period seven persons had been executed for participation in these felonies; three were awaiting trial; and the cost of prosecutions amounted to £2000 or £3000 a year. The annual cost of Freeling's plan, as he now proposed to modify it, would not exceed £1500. Moved by these considerations, the Treasury gave at length the necessary authority, and the horse-posts throughout the country, except on the less important roads, were provided with a strong cap for the protection of the head, a jacket, a brace of pistols, and a hanger.

We have said that during the last five years—the five years ending in August 1801—the horse-mails had been robbed on fifteen different occasions. One of these robberies occurred between the towns of Selby and York. It was a commonplace robbery enough, with little or nothing to distinguish it from any other; and yet for a reason which will presently appear we give a copy of the letter in which the particulars were reported to headquarters:—

To Francis Freeling, Esq.

Post Office, York, *Feb. 22, 1798.*

Sir—I am sorry to acquaint you the post-boy coming from Selby to this city was robbed of his mail between six and seven o'clock this evening. About three miles on this side of Selby he was accosted by a man on foot with a gun in his hand, who asked him if he was the post-boy, and at the same time seized hold of the bridle. Without waiting for any answer he told the boy he must immediately unstrap the mail and give it him, pointing the muzzle of the gun at him whilst he did it. When he had given up the mail, the boy begged he would not hurt him, to which the man replied he need not be afraid, and at the same time pulled the bridle from the horse's head. The horse immediately galloped off with the boy, who had never dismounted.

He was a stout man dressed in a drab jacket, and had the appearance of being a hicklar. The boy was too much frightened to make any other remark on his person, and says he was totally unknown to him.

The mail contained the bags for Howden and London, Howden and York, and Selby and York. I have informed the surveyor of the robbery, and have forwarded hand-bills this night to be distributed in the country, and will take care to insert it in the first papers published here.—Waiting your further instructions, I remain with respect, sir, your obliged and obedient humble servant,

Thomas Oldfield.

Let us now go forward to the year 1876. In that year this identical bag, for which a reward had been offered at the time without result, was placed in our hands, having been found concealed in the roof of an old wayside public-house situated not far from the scene of the robbery, and then in course of demolition. The original documents were called for and produced; and thus, after an interval of nearly eighty years, the bag and the official papers in which its loss was reported have come together and found one common resting-place. Of the identity of the bag there is no question. Not only do the form and texture proclaim it to be of the last century, but it bears upon it the word "Selby," and a medallion with the letters "G. R."[78]

The troubles which had long been brewing with the mail-coach contractors now came to a climax. In 1797 an Act of Parliament had been passed imposing a duty of 1d. a mile upon all public carriages. The mail-coach contractors bitterly complained of this impost, and not without reason. A penny a mile was all they received for carrying the mails, and the new statute virtually took this 1d. away, leaving them without any payment at all for their services. It had been overlooked that the mail-coach was not as other coaches were. The ordinary stage-coach was at liberty to carry as many passengers as its proprietor pleased, and it was no unusual thing for eight or nine and even ten to be carried inside, the number outside being limited only by considerations of safety. The mail-coach, on the contrary, was rigidly restricted to five passengers—four inside and one out—and the Post Office rejected all proposals for so altering the construction of the coach as to admit of its carrying more.

Then came the year 1799, a year of scarcity, during which all kinds of horse provender reached unprecedented prices. The Government refused to bring in a bill exempting the mail-coaches from the new duty; and it only remained for the Post Office to raise the allowance which the contractors received from 1d. to 2d. a mile, a measure involving an additional payment of £12,000 a year. The second penny, however, was granted only as a temporary allowance, terminable at the end of one year and three-quarters, and, unlike most allowances given under a similar condition, it actually ceased at the appointed time.

The clamour of two years before now broke out afresh and with redoubled force. The tax on public carriages remained; and horse provender had become no cheaper. Did not justice demand that the additional penny should continue to be paid? The Post Office was disinclined to contest the claim; but acting under orders from above—orders which assuredly would not have been given had Pitt remained minister—it proceeded to bargain, and at length, after much haggling, the contractors were prevailed upon to accept one-half of the temporary allowance or an additional 1/2d. a mile for a further period of eighteen months, viz. from the 10th of October 1802 to the 5th of April 1804, when the question was to be again considered. A temporary expedient of this nature seldom answers; and the present was no exception to the rule. Eventually the Post Office had to give rather more than need have been given in the first instance, and after 1804 the mails were carried at an average rate of 2-1/8d. the single or 4-1/4d. the double mile.

Other alterations followed. To the postmasters' salaries an increase was made all round, an increase small indeed individually but large in the aggregate. What had been done for Manchester eight years before was now done for Liverpool. The Post Office there was remodelled and a penny post established. An end was, about the same time, put to a most objectionable arrangement. As a reward for their services in promoting Palmer's plan, three of the surveyors had been appointed to postmasterships, and these appointments they held in addition to their own proper appointments as surveyor. Thus, one of their number was postmaster of Gloucester, another postmaster of Honiton, and a third postmaster of Portsmouth.

These appointments were now taken away, but under circumstances calculated to leave the least possible soreness among those from whom they were taken. Not only were the salaries of all three raised from £100 to £150 a year, but the son of the surveyor who was postmaster of Gloucester was appointed to Gloucester, and the daughter of the one who was postmaster of Honiton was appointed to Honiton. The postmaster of Portsmouth, who had neither son nor daughter to succeed him, was, in accordance with a practice then very common, assigned the sum of £80 a year out of his successor's salary. This sum he received in addition to his own salary of £150 as surveyor.

In 1805, for the third time within eight years, the Post Office was called upon to make a further contribution to the Exchequer; and again Freeling devoted himself to the congenial task of revising and increasing the postage rates. Unwilling to destroy the symmetry of his own handiwork, he simply suggested that to the rates as prescribed by the Act of 1801 should be added—1d. for a single letter, 2d. for a double letter, 3d. for a treble letter, and 4d. for a letter weighing as much as one ounce. The suggestion was adopted, and after the 12th of March, the date on which the new Act was passed, the postage on a single letter was—from London to Brighton, 7d. instead of 6d.; from London to Liverpool, 10d. instead of 9d.; and from London to Edinburgh, 1s. 1d. instead of 1s.

But this was by no means all. In London, as we have seen, the penny post had, four years before, been converted into a twopenny post; and now the twopenny post, in respect to letters for places beyond the general post limits, was converted into a threepenny one. Thus, Abingdon Street, Westminster, was within the limits of the general post delivery, but Millbank was beyond them. Accordingly, a letter for Millbank, even though posted no farther off than Charing Cross, was to be charged 3d., while the charge on a letter to Abingdon Street remained at 2d. as before.

The Act of 1805 introduced a still further complication. Letters from the country addressed to any part of London that was outside the limits of the general post were to be consigned to the twopenny post, and, in addition to all other postage, to be charged with the sum of 2d. Thus, of two letters of the same weight delivered at the same time and by the same person, one, originating in the country, would have to pay 2d., and the other, originating in London, would have to pay 3d.

To record, therefore, that in 1805 the postage on a single letter—as, for instance, between London and Plymouth—was 10d., although in one sense correct, would give an imperfect idea of the real state of the case. Plymouth was one of the towns which possessed village or convention posts. Suppose a letter from one of the villages to which these posts extended to have been addressed to Knightsbridge or any other part of London situated outside the general post boundary. The postage would have been not 10d. but 10d. + 2d. + whatever might have been agreed upon for the village accommodation.

But more than this. There were certain towns through which, though lying off the direct road, the mail-coaches passed for a consideration. Such towns were Hinckley in Leicestershire, Atherstone in Warwickshire, and Tamworth in Staffordshire. Here, in consideration of the accommodation afforded by the mail-coach passing through, the inhabitants undertook to pay in addition to all other postage 1d. on each letter. A day came when they sought to be relieved from this impost. Vain aspiration! Had they not agreed for a penny a letter? And, for any relief that the Post Office would give, a penny a letter they should pay to the end of time.

It may safely be affirmed that at the present day no increase of postage would produce a corresponding increase of revenue. Such, unhappily, was not the case at the beginning of the century. People did not then write unless they had something to say which could not be left unsaid without loss or inconvenience. Trade, moreover, was rapidly expanding, and, as a consequence of the war, the ports were closed. Thus, correspondence was driven inland; and upon inland correspondence, unlike correspondence with foreign parts, the Government received the whole of the postage. But be the cause what it might, it must be owned that, in respect to the returns which they brought to the Exchequer, the three increases of postage made in 1797, 1801, and 1805 answered expectation. This, though not a justification, is perhaps their best excuse. In 1796, the year before the first of the three increases was made, the net Post Office revenue was £479,000; in 1806, the year after the last of them, it was £1,066,000. The same result is apparent in the case of what, for distinction's sake, we will still call the London penny post, although the London penny post had become a twopenny and threepenny one. In 1796 the net revenue derived from this source was £8000; in 1806 it was £41,000.

Among those who about this time criticised the doings of the Post Office was William Cobbett. Cobbett was regarded by Freeling as a base calumniator with whom no terms were to be kept; and yet on a dispassionate retrospect it is impossible to deny that on the whole his criticisms were just, and that such of them as appeared in print[79] were expressed in not intemperate language. At the present time far stronger language is used every day under far less provocation. Of Cobbett's numerous subjects of complaint we will mention only two—the so-called "early delivery" of letters and the treatment of foreign newspapers; and these have been selected because they serve to illustrate, better perhaps than any others, the practice of the Post Office eighty or ninety years ago. The latter of the two subjects serves also to explain much that would otherwise be inexplicable.

The "early delivery"—a species of accommodation confined to London—was not what its name would seem to imply, because no letters were even begun to be delivered before nine o'clock in the morning. It was really a preferential delivery, a delivery restricted to those who chose to pay for it. For a fee or, as the Post Office preferred to call it, a subscription of 5s. a quarter or £1 a year, any one residing within certain limits, including the whole of the city and extending westward as far as Hamilton Place, could get his letters in advance of the general delivery. It was managed thus. At nine o'clock or a little after the letter-carriers started from Lombard Street; and those for the remoter districts, in addition to their own letters, took letters for the districts through which they passed in proceeding to their own and, without waiting for the postage, dropped them at the houses of subscribers. The postage was collected in the course of the week by the regular letter-carrier of the district.

Against this preferential delivery, a delivery purchased by individuals at the expense of the general public, Cobbett very justly inveighed. Freeling, on the other hand, defended it as a priceless boon to merchants and traders who desired to receive their letters before the appointed hour. He omitted to explain, however, why a boon which could be bought by some could not be given gratuitously to all. It is a curious fact that this early delivery, essentially unfair as it was, continued to exist for more than thirty years after the period of which we are now writing. As late as 1835 and 1836 it was still in vogue, and not only the merchants and traders of London but the denizens of the squares were largely availing themselves of it. But it was chiefly in the city that the practice flourished. Thus, on the morning of the 9th of May 1828, out of a total of 637 letters for the Lombard Street district no less than 570 were "delivered early."

The second of Cobbett's complaints, or rather the second which we propose to notice, had reference to the treatment of foreign newspapers. What this treatment was at the beginning of the present century may appear hardly credible to us who live at the end of it. Except at the letter rate of postage, no newspapers could either enter or leave the kingdom unless they were franked;[80] and the power of franking them was restricted to Post Office servants. This power was as old as the Post Office itself; and so was the practice of exercising it for a consideration. What was new was an arrangement or understanding between Freeling and Arthur Stanhope, the head of the foreign department, by virtue of which Stanhope in conjunction with his subordinates franked newspapers for the Continent, and Freeling franked those for America and the British possessions abroad.

Here was a mine of wealth. Newspapers were rapidly increasing in number and postage was rapidly rising. Of course, so long as the price charged for franking was kept well below the cost of postage, the demand for franks would be brisk. Before the century was sixteen years old Freeling and Stanhope were drawing from this source more than £3000 a year each. Cobbett had had personal experience of the system. He had paid a visit to America, and having while there been supplied with a newspaper from England, he had on his return been presented with a bill for nine guineas as the price of franking. Not only did he refuse to pay the bill, and persist in his refusal in spite of repeated applications, but he inveighed in his paper against the practice which made such a charge possible. This was in 1802. He now, in December 1805, renewed his attack upon the Post Office; but this time it was in respect to the manner in which newspapers were treated on their arrival in England, a treatment still more extraordinary than that which they received on despatch.

The matter is somewhat complicated, and in order to explain it we must go back a few years. Till the breaking out of the French Revolution and the Continental wars which succeeded it, foreign intelligence had long been uninteresting and was little sought after. The few newspapers that were published in London had confined themselves almost exclusively to domestic matters. Then came a sudden change. Domestic matters fell into the background. The whole country was eager to learn what was taking place on the other side of the Channel. Newspapers multiplied apace. Where there was one before, there were now half a dozen, all hungering for foreign intelligence. Here was an opportunity for the clerks in the foreign department of the Post Office. These clerks, in conjunction with their comptroller, had the exclusive right of franking newspapers for the Continent, just as newspapers circulating within Great Britain were franked by the clerks of the roads. They had also, by virtue of their position, unequalled facilities for getting newspapers from abroad, and of these facilities they now availed themselves to the utmost.

It would not be correct to state that at this time they established a foreign news-agency, for this they had done long ago; but what had hitherto been an insignificant business now became a large and important one. It may be interesting to trace its progress. At the time of which we are writing—from 1789 onwards—the foreign correspondence was seldom in course of distribution in London till the afternoon, owing to the then established custom of waiting till two o'clock for any mail that might be due. Thus, a foreign mail arriving at three o'clock in the afternoon of one day might not be delivered until the same hour in the afternoon of the following day.

Another curious custom prevailed at this time. It was considered right, as a matter of international courtesy, that no foreign newspapers should be delivered until the foreign ministers had received their correspondence; and this correspondence, though delivered separately from the general correspondence, was seldom delivered earlier. Meanwhile the newspapers were held in reserve by the clerks, ready to be delivered to their customers as soon as delivery was permissible by the rule of the office. This was a state of things which readily lent itself to malpractices. The person whom the comptroller appointed to distribute the foreign newspapers was an old woman of the name of Cooper, and in her custody they remained during the close time, the time during which the foreign ministers' correspondence was preparing for delivery. This woman had a son who assisted her in the distribution, a young man of some ability and of no principle. He was not slow to take advantage of his position. From the foreign newspapers, while in his mother's custody, he jotted down the points of interest and sold his jottings to the London newspapers. The profits he derived from this source assumed such proportions that in the course of a few years he was reputed to have amassed a not inconsiderable fortune. From one newspaper alone, the *Courier*, he received no less than £200 in a single year.

Thus matters went on, save only that owing to the establishment of a second delivery of foreign correspondence the interval during which newspapers lay at the Post Office was shortened, until the year 1796, when Stanhope's appointment as comptroller put an end to one scandal merely to establish another. No sooner had Stanhope taken up his appointment than the clerks, who had long protested in vain against Cooper's conduct, broke out into fresh complaints; and the arrangement was then made which called forth Cobbett's invective. Why, argued Stanhope, should not that which Cooper has been doing clandestinely be done openly and under official sanction? It is true a rule exists that foreign newspapers must not be delivered in advance of the foreign ministers' correspondence; but a carefully-compiled summary of the contents of a newspaper is a very different thing from the newspaper itself. This, surely, might be delivered to the London editors without a breach either of the rule itself or of the considerations on which it was founded.

Such were Stanhope's arguments, and he proceeded to put them into practice. With few if any exceptions, the editors of the London newspapers, both morning and evening, fell into the plan. French and Dutch translators were engaged, and into their hands the foreign newspapers were placed as soon as they arrived at the Post Office. For each summary the charge was one guinea, and as there were generally two summaries a week, the sum which each editor paid was a little over £100 a year. The entire proceeds, after payment of expenses, were divided in certain proportions between Stanhope and his subordinates.

In 1801 and again in 1802 Cobbett had inveighed against a practice which thus amerced the editors of the London newspapers; but he might as well have preached to the winds. The practice was far too remunerative to be abandoned without a struggle. It is true that no one need take a summary unless he liked; but if he omitted to take one, it was at the cost of having only stale news to publish.

At the close of 1805 circumstances were somewhat altered, and Cobbett renewed his attack. Communication by Dover was closed, and correspondence from the Continent could reach England only by Holland and Gravesend. The best arrangements of which the circumstances admitted were made for keeping up the supply of foreign newspapers and summaries; but after a while they broke down, and the Post Office was forced to seek the assistance of the Alien Office. This office had agents at Gravesend, and undertook during the emergency to do what had hitherto been done by the Post Office. Cobbett saw his opportunity, and was not slow to take advantage of it. It had been dinned into his ears that it was through the Post Office alone that foreign newspapers could be legally obtained, and that the department could make what arrangements it pleased for their distribution. But arrangements which in the hands of the Post Office were tolerated only because they had, or were supposed to have, legal sanction had now been transferred to the Alien Office. What, then, asked Cobbett, had become of the law? To this inquiry the Post Office did not find it convenient to vouchsafe a reply.

But a still more formidable antagonist than Cobbett was about to deliver an assault. This was the *Times* newspaper. The *Times*, although among what Cobbett called "the guinea-giving papers," seldom made use of the summaries which the guineas purchased, regarding them as meagre and unsatisfactory. Drawing from other and more fertile sources, it contrived in the matter of priority of intelligence to distance all competitors. On one occasion, indeed—a remarkable feat for those days—it even forestalled the "Court," or, as they were now called, the "State" letters, which, unlike the ordinary letters, were delivered the moment the mail arrived. It was in 1807, when George Canning was Foreign Secretary. Canning had not yet opened his despatches, and was amazed to find in his morning's paper information of which he had received no previous notice, and which, as he afterwards found, the despatches contained. Indignant that his intelligence should have been thus anticipated, he instantly wrote to the Post Office demanding an explanation. Angry as Canning was, the reply he received can hardly have failed to evoke a smile. This reply was that the Continental newspapers from which the *Times* had derived its information had been obtained not from the Post Office but from the Foreign Office, and that they had reached this office in Canning's own bag under a cover addressed to himself.

The *Times* had long protested against the intolerable delay which foreign newspapers sustained at the Post Office. Especially had it protested against the absurdity of a system which, while withholding the newspapers themselves, yet permitted a summary of their contents to be published. But it had still more personal grounds of complaint. Letters for the *Times*, sealed letters addressed by permission to the Under-Secretaries of State, were excluded from the Foreign Office bag and kept back for the general delivery because, forsooth, the clerks at the Post Office were pleased to feel sure that these letters contained foreign newspapers, and feared that by forwarding them they would damage their own interests.

Such were the amazing liberties taken with correspondence in those days. No wonder that the *Times* proceeded to resent the outrage. In its issue of the 9th of May 1807 appeared an article which, after charging the Post Office with extortions and with sacrificing public convenience to the avarice of individuals, proceeded to declare that its administration was a disgrace to the Government. Freeling's indignation knew no bounds. That the charge was just never seems to have occurred to him. In his view it was nothing less than a libel—a libel of the most malignant character. Never had man been more cruelly wronged than himself. The postmasters-general, Lords Sandwich and Chichester, had been only four days in office, and their chief-officer was as yet unknown to them. Obviously the intention was to damage this officer's reputation in the eyes of his new masters. But this intention should be frustrated. A criminal information should be filed. No; not a criminal information, for thus the aggressor's mouth would be closed. It should be a civil suit or action at law; and then the aggressor would be at liberty to tell his own tale, and all the world should see how little justification there was for his aspersions.

At this time it was not known to Freeling that letters for the *Times* sent under cover to the Under-Secretaries of State were being diverted from the ordinary course; and when, a little later on, the fact of diversion became known to him, the terms in which he expressed his sense of the impropriety were such as even the aggrieved newspaper would probably have held to leave nothing to be desired. But to apologise and arrest proceedings—these were things which would appear not to have come within the sphere of contemplation. An action had been begun, and it must proceed to the bitter end. A righteous cause is not necessarily one that can be defended at law. Such would seem to have been the case in the present instance, for when the action came on for trial, the *Times* failed to appear, and judgment went by default.

Freeling was jubilant over the result. Here was a triumphant vindication of his own and Stanhope's proceedings. A charge had been brought—a charge as serious as any that could be levelled against a public department, and not even an attempt had been made to substantiate it. This was a happy termination of an unhappy business. So, at least, thought Freeling; but, as a matter of fact, the business was far from being terminated yet.

On the 27th of July, within three weeks of his reporting to the postmasters-general the result of the action at law, appeared a second article headed "Post Office," in which the iniquities of the system were ruthlessly exposed. Strong language, indeed—language such as two months before had brought the *Times* within the meshes of the law—was carefully avoided, and the article confined itself to a bare narrative of facts. But the case against the Post Office lost nothing on this account. The facts spoke for themselves, and these, stated in their naked simplicity, constituted an indictment, to the weight of which no words could add. We can well believe that from this period the *Times* received its foreign newspapers in due course; but in other respects the only effect which the appearance of the second article had upon the Post Office was to spoil the triumph which it was celebrating over the result of the first. As to changing their practice and setting their house in order, this appears not to have occurred to either Freeling or Stanhope. On the contrary, they regarded themselves as deeply-injured persons, and, by dint of sheer importunity, induced the postmasters-general to consent to a second prosecution. Wiser counsels, however, prevailed. The attorney-general, to whom the official papers were sent, took care not to return them, and to the present day the Post Office is without these interesting records.

It is time we inquired what measure of success had attended the experimental posts—the posts by which, under mutual agreement between the Post Office and the inhabitants, small towns and villages were to be connected with post towns. Village posts, they were sometimes called; but more commonly fifth-clause posts, from the clause of the Act under which they were established. At first they answered well, but in 1807 an authoritative decision to the effect that franked letters and newspapers conveyed by a fifth-clause post were exempt from charge tended materially to disconcert arrangements. Franked letters, though exempt from charge by the general post, were not exempt either by the penny posts in the country or by the twopenny post in London; and it had been taken for granted that they, as well as newspapers, would not be exempt by the fifth-clause posts.

But it had now been decided otherwise, and this made all the difference. In arranging these posts nothing more had been aimed at than to make them self-supporting, and in adjusting the receipts and expenditure franks and newspapers had been counted as so many letters; but if these were to be eliminated, the balance would be on the wrong side. A service that was not self-supporting was, at the beginning of the century, regarded by the Post Office authorities as an abomination; and saddled as they were with a number of fifth-clause posts which had ceased to pay their own expenses, it became a serious question what was best to be done.

A decision was precipitated by the action of the little town of Olney in Buckinghamshire. Olney had at one time received from headquarters in Lombard Street what was called "an allowance in aid of its post"; but when fifth-clause posts were introduced this allowance ceased, and the inhabitants, in consideration of their being supplied with an official messenger from Newport Pagnel, agreed to pay over and above all other postage the sum of 1d. on each letter delivered. This agreement had now existed for several years, and the inhabitants had grown a little tired of it, being of opinion that a private messenger of their own could be procured on easier terms. Accordingly they petitioned headquarters to reduce the rate they were paying from 1d. to 1/2d. a letter, and, the request being refused, they proceeded to consider whether their agreement should not be terminated.

This having come to Freeling's ears, he stopped the post at once, and the inhabitants were left to get their letters as best they could. Not even notice of his intention had been given. Nor was this all. These capricious and discontented people, he said, should have imposed upon them a penny post. Under a penny post they would still have their pence to pay; and the pence would be payable, not, as under the fifth-clause post, only on the letters delivered, but on those collected as well. This, while operating as a punitive measure, would have the incidental advantage of adding to the revenue. Freeling was a bold man, and yet, bold as he was, his courage deserted him in this instance. At the last moment, after arrangements had been made for converting the fifth-clause post into a penny post, the order for conversion was revoked. To impose a penny post, he argued, would be no injustice; it would not even be a hardship, and yet these unreasonable people would be sure to represent it as such. They would urge that at one time their town had received an allowance in aid of its post; that then a foot-messenger had been established, and they paid 1d. on each letter delivered; and that now because they proposed to replace this messenger, as the Act of Parliament gave them power to do, by a messenger of their own, who would perform the service at a cheaper rate, an older Act was brought to bear upon them which, while obliging them to pay 1d. on each letter collected as well as delivered, made the employment of their own messenger illegal.

Such were the arguments by which Freeling excused himself to the postmasters-general, as though an excuse were necessary, for not going on with the high-handed proceeding he had originally contemplated. In the result, Olney was given a Post Office of its own, being made in technical language a sub-office under Newport Pagnel, the post town. A rule was at the same time laid down to the effect that fifth-clause posts should no longer be maintained except in the case of small towns. To connect these with post towns fifth-clause posts might still be continued; but, in the case of villages and hamlets, they were to be replaced by penny posts. From this rule the fifth-clause posts received their death-blow. Such of them as were village posts were promptly converted into penny posts; and such as were town posts, as the small towns acquired Post Offices of their own, became gradually merged in the general posts of the kingdom.

The Post Office, which during the last ten or fifteen years had done much to impair its own utility, was now to receive a check from without; and this in respect to a branch of its service which was perhaps least open to criticism. The mail-coach system had continued to prosper. In 1811 the number of mail-coaches constantly running in Great Britain was about 220, and the extent of road over which they travelled was between 11,000 and 12,000 miles a day. The country gentry and the commercial classes vied with each other in demanding an extension of the system. Towns lying off the main road were glad to pay 1d. a letter in addition to the postage on condition of the mail-coach passing through them on its way. The mail-coach, moreover, apart from the facilities it afforded for communication, brought traffic in its train. It gave, in the language of the time, publicity to the roads. Palmer had, more than twenty years before, noticed this result and commented upon it. He found as a matter of experience that wherever a mail-coach was set up other traffic followed, and the post-chaises along the road were furbished up and better conducted.

But popular as the new system was on the whole, there was one class of persons with whom it was distinctly the reverse. These were the trustees of the roads. With them the exemption from toll which the mail-coaches enjoyed was a constant source of complaint. Nor was it calculated to abate their discontent that the Post Office, in whose favour the exemption was granted, possessed the power, a power which it constantly exercised, of indicting the roads if they were not kept in proper repair. The state of the trusts was at this time far from flourishing. In the neighbourhood of London and other large towns where traffic was considerable the tolls were low and the receipts high; but in the remoter and less populous parts of the kingdom the exact converse held good. There the tolls were high and the receipts low.

To take the kingdom as a whole, the case stood thus: In very few instances indeed had any part of the debt on the turnpike trusts been discharged, and in fewer instances still had a sinking fund been established with a view to extinction of debt by process of time. With these rare exceptions, nothing more had been done than to keep up payment of the interest agreed upon, while in many instances no interest at all was being paid or interest at a reduced rate. In some instances indeed, the receipts from the tolls were not enough to defray even the cost of maintenance and repairs.

It is not to be wondered at if in these circumstances the trustees of the roads looked with longing eyes to the £50,000 a year which was the estimated value of the tolls that, except for their exemption, the mail-coaches would have had to pay. Of course the postmasters-general were strongly opposed to the surrender of this large amount; and yet there was one consideration which told heavily against them. It was this, that in Ireland the mails were not exempt from toll. Under an Act passed by the Irish Legislature in 1798, an Act which still remained in force, an account was kept of all tolls leviable at the turnpike gates through which the mail passed, and this account was paid quarterly by the Post Office authorities in Dublin. Why, it was asked, could not a similar system be adopted in Great Britain? It was also urged, and not without force, that in the matter of weight the mail bore to the coach which carried it a very small proportion. The coach with its loading complete weighed from thirty-three to forty cwts., while the mail seldom weighed more than one cwt. For the sake of so small a proportion was it equitable that exemption should extend to the whole?

A strenuous and united effort was now made to force the mail-coaches to pay toll. The question came before Parliament, and a Committee was appointed to inquire and report. The result could hardly have been in doubt. It was by the landed proprietors, the men who had seats in Parliament, that the turnpike roads had been made, and they were generally the creditors on the turnpike funds. The Committee was unanimous in recommending that the exemption from toll which the mail-coaches enjoyed should absolutely cease and determine.

On the Committee's report no action was taken in the session of 1811; but if the Post Office supposed that the matter would be allowed to drop, it was doomed to disappointment. Early in the following year Spencer Perceval forwarded to Lombard Street for any observations the postmasters-general might have to offer upon it a bill having for its object to repeal the exemption. The postmasters-general suggested certain alterations, but upon the subject-matter of the bill, coming as it did from the Prime Minister, and their views being already well known, they confined themselves to once more expressing a doubt whether such a measure could be necessary. In May Perceval was assassinated; and now the postmasters-general fondly hoped that the matter was at an end. What then was their dismay at learning a month or two later that the Government was resolved to proceed with the bill. The same letter that conveyed this intelligence contained a suggestion as strange as it was original. This was that, in order to meet complaints, the mail-coaches on certain roads should be withdrawn. The postmasters-general, little supposing that such a suggestion could take practical shape, simply replied that not a whisper had yet reached them to the effect that mail-coaches were considered in excess; that, on the contrary, they were being constantly urged to increase the number.

The bill was finally withdrawn; but heavy was the price which had to be paid. With those who were advocating the measure Vansittart, the new Chancellor of the Exchequer, effected a compromise behind the back of the Post Office. There was indeed ample room for a satisfactory adjustment. For the conveyance of the mails the mail-coach proprietors received from the Post Office £30,000 a year; they paid to the Government for stamp duty £40,000 a year; and the exemption which they enjoyed from toll was estimated to represent £50,000 a year. These figures seem almost to suggest a feasible arrangement; yet the compromise actually effected took another form. It was that, in accordance with the suggestion of a few months before, mail-coaches should be withdrawn.

Nor was this mere empty talk; Vansittart had pledged himself to specific performance. And now began a general dis-coaching of the roads. The mail-coaches running between Warwick and Coventry, between Shrewsbury and Aberystwith, between Aberystwith and Ludlow, between Edinburgh and Dalkeith, between Edinburgh and Musselburgh, between Chichester and Godalming, between Dorchester and Stroudwater—all were discontinued at once. Notice to quit was served upon the mail-coaches between Worcester and Hereford, between Hereford and Gloucester, between Hereford and Brecon, between Alton and Gosport, and between Plymouth and Tavistock. And, what was hardly less important, numerous applications for mail-coaches which, except for Treasury interference, would have been granted, were refused. By Pitt the mail-coach had been regarded as a pioneer of civilisation; in the eyes of Pitt's successors it was a mischievous encumbrance.

Vansittart, having dealt one deadly blow at the Post Office, now proceeded to deal another. The war with France had exhausted the Exchequer, and, as part of the ways and means, he called upon the Post Office for a further contribution of £200,000 a year. Once more the screw was turned; and, oppressive as the postage rates were already, they were as from the 9th of July 1812 increased as follows:—

						Single.	Double.	Treble.	Ounce.
						d.	d.	d.	d.
Not		exceeding	15	miles		4	8	12	16
Above	15	and not exceeding	20	miles		5	10	15	20
"	20	"	30	"		6	12	18	24
"	30	"	50	"		7	14	21	28

"	50	"	80	"	8	16	24	32
"	80	"	120	"	9	18	27	36
"	120	"	170	"	10	20	30	40
"	170	"	230	"	11	22	33	44
"	230	"	300	"	12	24	36	48
"	300	"	400	"	13	26	39	52
"	400	"	500	"	14	28	42	56
"	500	"	600	"	15	30	45	60
"	600	"	700	"	16	32	48	64
Above	700	miles			17	34	51	68

This is the highest point to which the rates of postage have ever attained in this country. Freeling would have resented so much as a suggestion that the institution which had now for some years been under his exclusive management was not in the most perfect order to which human foresight and ingenuity could raise it; and yet to the dispassionate observer it may be permitted to doubt whether eighty years ago the Post Office was not in some important particulars more open to criticism than at any time since its first establishment.

Let us compare for a moment the beginning of the nineteenth with the end of the seventeenth century. In 1695 the postage from London to Liverpool or to York or to Plymouth was, for a single letter, 3d.; in 1813 it was 11d. In 1695, wherever letters were being carried clandestinely, the policy was to supplant; in 1813 the policy was to repress. In 1695 the King would not consent to a single prosecution even for the sake of example; in 1813, when the Post Office revenue had passed from the King to the people, prosecutions were being conducted wholesale. In 1695 a circuitous post would be converted into a direct one, even though the shorter distance carried less postage; in 1813 a direct post in place of a circuitous one was being constantly refused on the plea that a loss of postage would result. In 1695 London enjoyed the advantage of a penny post, and this post carried up to one pound in weight; in 1813 the penny post had been replaced by a twopenny and threepenny one, and, except in the case of a packet passing through the general post, the weight was limited to four ounces. In 1813, moreover, the complications were bewildering. In some places there were fifth-clause posts, and in others penny posts; and the charge by these posts was in addition to the charge by the general post. Some towns, over and above all other charges, paid an additional 1d. on each letter for the privilege of the mail-coach passing through them. Of two adjoining houses one might receive its letters free of any charge for delivery and not the other. This difference was to be found in towns where building was going on—as, for instance, at Brighton—old houses being considered within, and new houses without, what was called the usage of delivery.

In London itself the complications, if possible, were more bewildering still. The threepenny post began where the twopenny post ended. Thus far the practice was simple enough. But the general post limits did not coincide with the limits of the twopenny post: and the limits of both the twopenny post and the general post differed from those of the foreign post. Indeed, it is probably not too much to say that in 1813 there was not a single town in the kingdom at the Post Office of which absolutely certain information could have been obtained as to the charge to which a letter addressed to any other town would be subject. More than ten years later Post Office experts examined before a Committee of the House of Commons were unable to state what, even on letters delivered in London, would in certain cases be the proper postage.

It may here be asked how it was that with rates so oppressive and so vexatiously levied the public were induced to tolerate them. The mail-coaches were popular except with the road trustees; and there is reason to think that even these, or at all events the principal persons among them, only professed a dislike which they did not really feel. The Post Office packets were also popular, and well they deserved to be, distinguishing themselves as they were about this time by deeds of even more than usual daring.

But these considerations, added to the personal popularity which Freeling himself enjoyed, are altogether insufficient to account for the extraordinary patience of the public under the treatment which eighty or ninety years ago they endured at the hands of the Post Office. The explanation we believe to be that the heavy rates of postage, and not a few of the vexations incidental to the levying of them, were tacitly accepted as a part, a necessary part, of the load of taxation which the people were called upon to bear as a consequence of the war in which England was engaged. We further believe that, in respect to its acts of aggression, the Post Office escaped criticism mainly because its proceedings, irritating as they were to individuals, were not generally known. This want of publicity is specially noticeable in the matter of prosecutions. At the present day a single prosecution undertaken by the Post Office would be the subject of comment in every newspaper in the kingdom. Eighty or ninety years ago, numerous as the Post Office prosecutions were, there was not a newspaper in the kingdom that gratuitously published particulars or even announced the fact. Often did the postmasters-general lament this reticence, believing as they did that to make known their repressive measures, and the amount of penalties inflicted, must have a deterrent effect upon the illicit traffic;

and at length, for want of any better means of securing publicity, they gave directions that, wherever a prosecution took place, hand-bills giving full particulars were to be struck off and affixed to the doors of the local inns.

The question which two years before had agitated the minds of the road trustees was now revived in Scotland. Among those who pressed for the establishment of mail-coaches none were more persistent than the large landed proprietors north of the Tweed; and as soon as their demands were acceded to, none were louder in their denunciations of the injustice which exempted mail-coaches from toll. The Government yielded at length to the pressure that was brought to bear, and in 1813 an Act was passed repealing, so far as Scotland was concerned, exemption from toll in the case of mail-carriages with more than two wheels. The same Act, in order to indemnify the Post Office for the loss it would thus sustain, imposed an additional postage of 1/2d. upon every letter conveyed by mail-coach in Scotland.

The Post Office was not quite fairly treated in this matter. No sooner had the Act passed than the trustees of the roads raised the tolls. At the old rates the mail-coaches, had they not been exempt, would have had to pay £6865 a year; at the new rates, now that they were exempt no longer, they had to pay £11,759 a year, or more by nearly £6000 than the additional 1/2d. of postage had been estimated to yield. Nor was this all. Some of the Road Acts contained a clause empowering the trustees to demand the sum of 1d. for every outside passenger. This power had never yet been exercised; but now the demand was rigorously enforced in the case of passengers by the mail-coaches, and by these coaches only.

Thus unhandsomely dealt with, the Post Office proceeded to do in Scotland what under other circumstances it had done two years before in England. It reduced the number of its coaches. This excited many murmurs. From Glasgow, for instance, a mail-coach had been running through Paisley to Greenock. This was now replaced by a horse post, and the district was not only relieved from the payment of the additional postage of 1/2d. a letter, but—a boon which had long been earnestly sought—was given three posts a day instead of two. Yet all three towns refused to be comforted, and bitterly reproached the postmasters-general for depriving them of their mail-coach. The convenience of travellers, however, was not a matter of which the Post Office took any account. The Post Office was concerned with the transmission of letters; and wherever these could be transmitted with the same or nearly the same expedition and at less expense by other means, the mail-coaches were discarded.

About this time two measures were introduced which shew a strange forgetfulness of what had gone before. Of these one was a reorganisation of the returned letter office, and the other the passing of a fresh Ship Letter Act. Hitherto, of the letters which could not be delivered only those had been returned to the writers which contained property or enclosures of apparent importance. The others had been torn up and sold as waste paper. Now all were to be presumed to be of importance to the writers and to be returned accordingly. The propriety and even the legality of charging such letters had been questioned in Palmer's time, and Pitt had decided that they were not to be charged. This was now forgotten, and the Post Office proceeded not only to return every letter that could not be delivered, but to charge it with postage. To Freeling, who regarded the Post Office as a mere engine of taxation, the temptation was no doubt a strong one. The measure, before being definitively adopted, had been tried experimentally for one year; and it was found that out of 189,000 letters returned to the writers more than 135,000 were accepted, producing a clear revenue of £4421.

By the new Ship Letter Act the charge on a single letter arriving by private ship was raised from 4d. to 6d., and, what was far more important, no letters were to be sent by private ship except such as had been brought to the Post Office to be charged. The directors of the East India Company, who would seem to have strangely overlooked the bill during its passage through the House, implored Government to get the Act repealed. It was true, they urged, that their official correspondence was exempted from the operation of the Act; but dependent on them in the East was a small army of servants whose private letters had hitherto gone free, and, under the provisions of the Act, would go free no longer. With the East Indies there was no communication by packet, and surely it was introducing a new principle for the Post Office to make a charge where it did not perform a service. Did not the charge in such a case become a mere tax upon letter-writing?

Freeling, on the other hand, maintained that no new principle was involved, inasmuch as the previous Act, the Act of 1799, recognised the sending of letters by ships other than packet boats and charging them with postage. This was perfectly true; but he forgot to add that, whereas the Act of 1799 was permissive, the Act of 1814 was compulsory, that under the one Act it was optional with the senders of letters whether they would take them to the Post Office or not; and under the other, if they did not take them to the Post Office, they rendered themselves liable to severe penalties. He might indeed have gone further, and said that in 1799 Pitt and the whole of the administration of which Pitt was the head scouted the very idea of anything in the shape of compulsion being employed in the matter.

The Ship Letter Act of 1814 proved a complete failure. It contained no provision obliging private ships to carry letters, and the private ships between England and India were almost entirely in the hands of the East India Company. No wonder, therefore, that the Company, when asked whether it might be announced to the public that bags would be made up at the Post Office to be conveyed by their ships, replied in the negative. The Court of Directors, their letter said, are not without hopes that Parliament will consent to revise the Act, and meanwhile they "do not see fit to authorise the commanders or owners of any of their ships to take charge of any bag of letters from the Post Office subjected to a rate of postage for sea conveyance." Freeling was filled with dismay. "A vital impediment," he exclaimed, "to the execution of the Act."

The expectations of the India House were not disappointed. In the next session of Parliament the Act of 1814 was replaced by another which granted larger exemptions to the Company and disarmed its opposition. The later Act gave power to the Post Office to establish a line of packets to India and the Cape of Good Hope, and, until a line should be established, to employ as packets any ships it pleased, including ships of war. The mails were to go once a month. By packet—in which term is included the ship which the Post Office might be pleased to designate as packet for the occasion—the postage on a single letter was fixed at 3s. 6d.; by private ship it varied according to direction, outwards 1s. 2d. and inwards 8d.

Such were the main provisions of the Act of 1815; but there were others which introduced new principles. As a result of the action of the East India Company in the preceding year, it was now for the first time made compulsory upon private ships to carry letters when required to do so by the Post Office,[81] and the Post Office was empowered to pay for their carriage a reasonable sum. This sum was to go by way of remuneration to the owners of the vessels, and to be in addition to a gratuity of 2d. a letter which the commander was to receive as his own perquisite. A still more important provision, a provision which assuredly could not have emanated from the Post Office, was one in favour of newspapers. By packet the postage on a letter to India or the Cape weighing as much as one ounce was to be 14s.; on a newspaper of no greater weight, if stamped and in a cover open at the side or end, it was to be 3d. This was the first enactment that provided for newspapers going outside the limits of the United Kingdom for less than the letter rate of postage.

What was virtually a most interesting experiment was now about to be tried. To India and the Cape the Post Office had no packets of its own; and before private ships could be employed as packets, the consent of the owners had to be obtained and the amount of payment to be agreed upon. Practically, the Post Office was at the mercy of others. Mails had to be sent once every month; ships of war could not always be employed; and should the shipping interest combine, the postmasters-general would have to pay pretty much what owners chose to demand. To the credit of that interest nothing in the shape of combination took place. During the first sixteen months the mails were despatched five times by His Majesty's ships, four times by ships of the East India Company, and seven times by ships belonging to private owners. His Majesty's ships carried the mails, of course, without charge. The East India Company, with admirable generosity, placed their ships at the disposal of the Post Office and refused to receive any payment. And the ships belonging to private owners were engaged, the first of them for £500 and the other six for sums ranging from £50 to £150. Altogether, the sum expended during more than a year and a quarter in transporting the mails to India and the Cape of Good Hope did not exceed £1250; and the postage during the same period amounted to £11,658. In the following year, the year 1817, even better terms were obtained, the owners of private ships engaged as packets receiving in no case more than £125, and in one case as little as £25.

The East India Company's generosity was not reciprocated by the Post Office. His Majesty's ship *Iphigenia*, which was lying at Portsmouth, had been appointed to carry out the mails, and the India House had sent down its despatches to be put on board. In strictness these despatches should have been sent through the Post Office, inasmuch as the *Iphigenia* had been appointed a packet for the occasion; but as the India House paid no postage on its correspondence, whether sent by packet or by ships of its own, it was a mere technical irregularity.

Freeling maintained, however, that there was an important distinction which ought to be observed. It was true that no question of postage was involved. It was also true that the India House would have been at liberty to put its despatches on board the *Iphigenia* had she been sailing for India without being appointed a packet boat; but as she had been so appointed, the intervention of the Post Office was necessary, and without that intervention the commander ought not to have received them. Accordingly, Freeling urged upon the Government, though happily without success, that orders should be sent to Portsmouth to have the despatches removed from the ship to the local Post Office, to be there kept until instructions should be received from Lombard Street that they might be again taken on board.

On the close of hostilities in 1815 domestic matters began once more to occupy a place in men's thoughts; and it was next to impossible that the Post Office should escape attention. Its heavy and capricious charges, its high-handed proceedings, its disregard of the public requirements, its prosecutions, its constant indictment of roads which it largely used and yet contributed nothing to maintain, and, above all, the fact that its administration was virtually in the hands of one man, and that man not the nominal head, who could be reached by constitutional means—signs were not wanting that these and other matters had created an amount of dissatisfaction which must sooner or later find expression. Yet Freeling either could not or would not see. Were not his immediate superiors, the postmasters-general, satisfied with his management, so satisfied indeed that they seldom, if ever, found it necessary to pay a visit to Lombard Street? And had not the contributions which, under his guidance, the Post Office kept pouring into the Exchequer raised him high in the Chancellor's favour? If so, what more could a loyal and industrious public servant desire?

That Freeling was elated with what he considered his unbounded success is clear from a letter which about this time was written to the Treasury, enclosing a return of the Post Office revenue, and shewing how it had responded to the successive increases of rate which had been imposed during his tenure of the office of secretary. This letter, drafted by himself, as all the official letters were, though signed by the postmasters-general, concluded thus: "We flatter ourselves that we shall not be considered as exceeding the limits of our duty in drawing your Lordships' attention to a circumstance which has made a strong impression on ourselves in the course of our inquiry, namely, that the office of secretary during the whole of this flourishing period has been executed by the same faithful and meritorious servant of the Crown." The return, with a copy of this letter appended, was afterwards presented to Parliament.

There is no more tolerant assembly in the world than the House of Commons; and yet even the House of Commons is intolerant of egotism. It may have been, and probably was, a mere coincidence, but the fact remains that from the date of the presentation of this return Freeling's influence began to wane.

CHAPTER XV
IRELAND 1801-1828

At the Union with Ireland the Irish Post Office was not merged into the Post Office of England as the Scotch Post Office was merged at the Union with Scotland. The existence of two separate establishments, presided over by different heads, who had not always the same objects in view, and were influenced by different considerations, was not unattended with inconvenience.

Between the Post Offices of the two parts of the kingdom, moreover, there were differences not only of practice but of law, the statutes passed during the seventeen years that the Post Offices were separate not having been repealed at the time of the Union. Thus, the law which regulated franking was stricter in Ireland than in England, although, it must be confessed, the practice was looser. The law prohibiting the illicit conveyance of letters was also stricter. In England the Post Office was not empowered to search for letters; in Ireland the Post Office might search both vehicles and houses from sunrise to sunset. In England the mail-coaches were exempt from toll; in Ireland no such exemption was allowed. In Ireland, again, the Post Office was legally bound not, as in England, to deliver letters but only to carry them; and except in Dublin there was not a single letter-carrier in the kingdom. Even the constitution of the two Post Offices, though apparently similar, was really different. In Ireland, as in England, there were two heads commonly called joint postmasters-general; but whereas in England the assent of both was necessary to make a decision operative, in Ireland the assent of one was sufficient. This, while probably designed to facilitate the despatch of public business, was, as will be seen later on, attended with a curious result, a result which the framers of the statute can have little contemplated.

Of such differences of practice as were not rendered necessary by any difference of law it may be sufficient to mention a few. In England the mail-coach contractors supplied horses only; in Ireland they supplied coaches as well. In England the contract was for short periods and for short distances, seldom for more than one or two stages; in Ireland, where there was little or no competition, the contract was for the whole of the road over which the coach travelled, and for as much as twenty and even thirty years. Meanwhile no alteration was possible except with the contractors' assent. In England the horse-posts were provided upon the most advantageous terms of which each particular case would admit; in Ireland the obligation to provide them was imposed upon the local postmasters, who received for the service, cost what it might, one uniform rate of 5d. a mile. In London there was no despatch on Sundays; in Dublin the mails were despatched on Sundays as on other days. In Dublin, again, the men who collected letters by the sound of bell, bellmen as they were now called, received not as in London 1d. a letter but 1d. a house, a difference of which the inhabitants were wont to shew their appreciation by sending to a single house for delivery to the letter-carrier the letters of an entire street.

In Dublin there was one institution to which there was no counterpart in London. This was the British Mail Office, an office set apart for the management of the mails passing between England and Ireland. Other mails were dealt with in the Inland Office; but those to and from England were considered of such paramount importance as to deserve exceptional treatment. At the present day the term "office" as applied to the public service conveys the notion possibly of a palace and certainly of a building or part of a building consisting of several rooms. The British Mail Office, though destined to play a not unimportant part in the history of the Irish Post Office at the beginning of the present century, consisted of one room only, and this room was exactly six feet square.

The establishment of this office was one of many measures which owed their origin to Lord Clancarty, who was joint postmaster-general with Lord O'Neill from 1807 to 1809. Clancarty enjoyed an honourable distinction. Other postmasters-general were habitual absentees, their visits to the Post Office, if visits they made, being confined to the rare occasions on which they passed through Dublin on their way to London and back. Clancarty, on the contrary, devoted to his official duties all the powers of a keen intellect and a singularly energetic nature. Shortly after his appointment he proceeded to London, and having made himself master of the system pursued in the Inland Office in Lombard Street, returned to Dublin, resolved that, as far as circumstances would permit, a similar system should be established there.

A formidable difficulty, however, presented itself in the different hours of attendance in the London and Dublin offices. In London the attendance was daily, on every night and every morning; in Dublin it was only on alternate days, on every other night and every other morning. How to get rid of this difference was the question which Clancarty now set himself to solve. There was at this time in the Inland Office a clerk of the name of Donlevy, whose parts pointed him out as qualified to take the lead among his fellows. Clancarty sent for this young man, and told him that under the plan which was about to be introduced he would have to attend daily. Donlevy objected that a plan which would involve such attendance was an unreasonable, an oppressive plan, and that no man's constitution, strong as he might be, would stand it. "But," said Clancarty, "I will make you vice-president." "My Lord," replied Donlevy, "I am very much obliged to you; but under the conditions proposed I would not accept even the office of president." "Very well," rejoined Clancarty, laying his watch on the table, "I will give you three hours to consider of it." Long before the three hours had expired, Donlevy, who knew the character of the man with whom he had to do, and what would be the penalty of refusal, had accepted the vice-presidentship, and opposition to the introduction of daily attendance was at an end.[82]

But Clancarty was an exception to the general rule. Lord Rosse, who succeeded him and remained postmaster-general in conjunction with O'Neill for more than twenty years, was, like his colleague, an habitual absentee; and the consequence was to place large power in the hands of the chief permanent officer on the spot. This was Edward Smith Lees, who had been appointed joint secretary with his father in 1801, and who on his father's death some years afterwards became sole secretary. The power which Lees must in any case have possessed as chief resident officer was enormously increased by the fact to which we have already referred, that the signature of either of the two postmasters-general was sufficient. Of this fact Lees took advantage to an extent which may seem incredible. If the particular postmaster-general to whom the case was referred agreed to the course recommended, no reference to the other appears to have been considered necessary; but if he did not agree, a reference to the other took place without the fact of disagreement being made known, or even an intimation that his colleague had been consulted. By thus playing off one postmaster-general against the other, Lees generally contrived to secure approval of his own recommendations; but when, as occasionally happened, such approval could not be obtained from either, he claimed and exercised the right, as chief officer on the spot, to take his own course.

Thus Lees, like Freeling, was an autocrat within his own domain; but the means by which the two men attained this result were essentially different. Freeling kept the postmasters-general informed of every incident, however trivial. Lees gave no information which could with decency be withheld. Freeling supported his views by a perfect wealth of explanation. Lees explained no more than enough to carry his point. Freeling's candour, like his loyalty, knew no bounds. It is to his candour, indeed, that we owe our materials for criticising his own proceedings. Lees's candour and loyalty, on the contrary, so far as these can be said to have had any existence, were held in rigid subjection to considerations of expediency and personal advantage.

The circumstances attending the appointment of Lees's brother, a searcher in the Customs at Wexford, to a position in the secretary's office only inferior in point of rank and emolument to his own, well exemplify the mode in which the business of the Irish Post Office was conducted during the first two or three decades of the present century. The minute appointing him was signed, not by O'Neill and Rosse, nor by either of them, but by one of Lees's own subordinates, and purported to embody a decision come to at a Board at which the two postmasters-general were present. "At the Board"—so ran the minute—"present the Earls." The whole thing was a fiction from beginning to end. The Earls had not been present, and there had been no Board. Indeed, as Lees was afterwards forced to admit before a Committee of the House of Commons, during a period of twenty years that O'Neill and Rosse had been joint postmasters-general and he their secretary, he had seen them only once together in the same room, and that was in the drawing-room at Parsonstown.

The example set in high quarters was not without its effect below. Every one seems to have been left to do pretty much as he liked. The force was maintained at a level very far in excess of the actual requirements, and it was no uncommon thing for one-half of the entire number to absent themselves without notice in a single morning. Some of the clerks never attended at all, while others gave to their Post Office duties only such fragments of their time as they could snatch from other and more lucrative employments. Thus, one was a clerk in a private bank, another a clerk in a merchant's office, a third was a surgeon, several held appointments under the Customs or the Imprest Office, and many were practising attorneys. To most of these the object of holding an appointment in the Post Office appears to have been not so much the salary attaching to it as the privilege which they enjoyed, or rather which they assumed to themselves, of sending and receiving their letters free. The attorneys, indeed, were credited with a still less respectable motive. All, as soon as a mail arrived, helped themselves to their own letters and the letters of the firms in which they were interested. The president of the Inland Office held a valuable appointment in the Bank of Ireland, and was not in a position to check on the part of his subordinates a license which he allowed to himself. The receiver-general, the highest financial officer on the establishment, was a private banker and money-lender, and, beyond signing the balance-sheet at stated periods, the only Post Office function he performed was to frank his own correspondence.

That in Ireland the Post Office arrangements were made subservient to private interests does not admit of a doubt. A suspicion will indeed now and again cross the mind that even in England the readiness to raise the rates of postage, and the hostility shewn to newspapers except when supplied by the clerks of the roads, were not unconnected with personal considerations; but what in the case of England is at best only a matter of suspicion becomes in the case of Ireland an absolute certainty. In Ireland, as in England, the clerks of the roads had from the first establishment of the Post Office enjoyed the privilege of franking newspapers; but soon after the British Mail Office had been established by Clancarty, two other clerks, styling themselves express clerks, undertook to supply newspapers express. Their plan was very simple. In London the newspapers were made up in a parcel addressed to the express clerks; and these clerks had in readiness messengers of their own, who proceeded to deliver the newspapers as soon as they arrived in Dublin and without waiting, as others had to do, for the sorting of the mail. This alone would have given to the express clerks a considerable advantage over the ordinary news-vendor. But, more than this, the British mail was irregular in its arrival, and the latest hour in the evening at which a delivery by letter-carrier took place in Dublin was seven o'clock. The express clerks delivered the English newspapers by their own messengers as late as eleven o'clock.

In the case of the country the advantage which the express clerks enjoyed was still greater. The mails for the interior of Ireland left the Inland Office in Dublin at seven o'clock in the evening; but under a rule, on the observance of which the authorities rigidly insisted, no mails from the British Mail Office were to be received in the Inland Office for despatch the same evening unless they were brought there ready sorted full twenty minutes before that hour. Practically, therefore, as the sorting occupied about twenty-five minutes, mails from England arriving later than a quarter past six were detained until the following evening. No such detention, however, was sustained by the express newspapers, which, addressed as they were to the express clerks, could be forwarded up to the last moment. It may readily be supposed that, with such advantages in their favour, the express clerks and the clerks of the roads, for the two bodies had amalgamated and formed one common purse, found many customers. That they realised and fully appreciated their position will be seen from the following advertisement which was issued no longer ago than April 1822:—

British Newspaper Office, General Post Office.

The clerks of roads and clerks of express newspapers having, under the authority of the postmasters-general, reformed their establishment in this department for the transmission of British and foreign newspapers, lottery, commercial, army and navy lists, periodical and other publications, the nobility and gentry of Dublin are respectfully informed that they can be supplied with those articles either by an express delivery (which is made by special messengers immediately on the arrival of the packets) or by the regular course of post.

Country correspondents will have a peculiar advantage, as upon all occasions when a packet arrives before the despatch of the inland mails but too late for general transmission, their newspapers will be forwarded at the last possible moment.

Newspapers exchanged at pleasure any time during the period of subscription.

Subscriptions to be paid in advance.

Further particulars known by application to Messrs. Leet and De Joncourt, General Post Office, who will receive subscriptions.

Daily attendance from twelve till four o'clock.

London daily newspapers to Dublin by general delivery, £10:17:6 per annum.

Leet and De Joncourt were the two express clerks; but among the clerks of the roads, on whose behalf they wrote as well as their own, was Lees, the secretary, who participated in the profits derived from the sale of newspapers, and received the lion's share.

The news-vendors bitterly complained. That the newspapers supplied by the express clerks and clerks of the roads should be exempt from postage[83] was bad enough; but that they should also enjoy priority of transmission and delivery was past all endurance. How was it possible to compete under such conditions as these? The booksellers also complained, for the express service, though originally confined to newspapers, had now extended to periodicals as well. On a *Quarterly* or *Edinburgh Review*, for instance, when sent by coach from Dublin into the country, the bookseller's customers had to pay for carriage from 1s. 8d. to 2s. 6d., whereas the express clerks and clerks of the roads sent it, through the medium of the post, carriage free. A heavier indictment remains. The law permitted the examination of newspapers passing through the post with a view to ascertain whether they contained unauthorised enclosures; and it was confidently alleged that of this power the Post Office servants took advantage in order to retard the transmission and delivery of newspapers that were not supplied by themselves. A ring, the news-vendors maintained, had been formed at the Post Office, and they were the victims.

The management of what was technically termed the alphabet appears to have been influenced by similar considerations. This was nothing more than a rack with divisions corresponding to the letters of the alphabet, into which might be sorted ready for delivery all correspondence addressed to the Post Office to be called for. Such was its primary object; but in course of time the bankers and merchants, finding that through the alphabet they could get their letters sooner than if delivered by letter-carrier—as soon indeed as the mail arrived—made use of this expedient for their ordinary correspondence, readily paying for the accommodation a fee ranging from three to five guineas a year. This had gone on for a considerable period, when Lees appears to have been suddenly seized with compunction at the unfairness of a practice which, in the matter of delivery, gave to one man an advantage over another; and he issued instructions that henceforth, after the arrival of each mail, there should be a certain interval during which letters should not be delivered from the alphabet. The pretence imposed upon no one. Men readily discerned that in proportion as the advantages of the alphabet were restricted the express service was rendered more valuable.

It would be unjust to the memory of the Irish Post Office of seventy years ago not to mention here one good practice and, as far as we know, the only good one that then existed. By virtue of an arrangement with, the War Office, soldiers' wives, on presentation of a formal document with which the military authorities provided them, could draw from any Post Office in the kingdom a certain sum of small amount until the entire sum mentioned in the document was exhausted. Thus, a soldier's wife desirous of joining her husband could pass from one end of the country to another, and, without carrying anything in her pocket, could be supplied with money on her way. Of this practice, curiously enough, not a vestige now remains.

It is also pleasant, amid so much indifference as was at that time exhibited to the convenience of the public, to be able to record one instance to the contrary. Thomas Whinnery, the postmaster of Belfast, had read an account of the alphabet at Liverpool—how the letters were sorted into a rack according to the initials of the merchants to whom they were addressed, so as to be ready to be delivered when they should be called for—and he resolved to introduce something of the same kind into his own office. Instead, however, of adopting the alphabetical order he assigned to each merchant a particular number, letting him know what his number was, and instead of a fixed rack as at Liverpool he contrived a revolving one; and this, with the numbers conspicuously exhibited over each division, he placed in full view of a window opening to the street. Thus, any one looking through the window could see for himself whether there were any letters for him, and was saved the trouble of inquiring.

Equality of treatment as between man and man had not yet become one of the canons of the Post Office, and even Whinnery, well-meaning as he was, made a distinction as remarkable as it was invidious. Belfast not being supplied with an official letter-carrier, he employed a man of his own to deliver the letters, and charged on their delivery 1d. apiece. The letters, however, instead of all being delivered at one time, were arbitrarily divided into two classes, termed particular letters and ordinary letters; and the delivery of the ordinary letters was not begun until that of the particular letters was finished, a difference in point of time of two and a half hours. In order to maintain the distinction, the man had actually to go over the same ground twice. Particular letters were defined to be letters for merchants and other busy men, letters to which it was presumably of importance that replies should be given promptly.

We have said that in Ireland the mail-coach contracts were not, as in England, for short distances but for the whole of the road over which the coach travelled. The explanation is that, while in England the local inn-keepers were eager to horse the mail for one or two stages, in Ireland, where the coach had to be provided as well as the horses, the venture was too serious to be undertaken lightly, and the contracts fell into the hands of a few persons of means who dictated pretty much their own terms. Thus, in Ireland the cost of conveying the mails by coach was considerably higher than in England, though forage and labour were cheaper.[84]

All this was soon to be changed. In one of the early years of the century a young lad had arrived in Dublin, a lad without means and without friends, a foreigner who was unable to speak one word of English, and yet who, despite these drawbacks, did for the country of his adoption more probably than was accomplished by all the legislation that took place during the fourscore years and more over which his life extended. This was Charles Bianconi, a man to whom the Post Office owes a debt of gratitude which, as it seems to us, has never been sufficiently recognised. After serving an eighteen months' apprenticeship to a foreign print-seller in a small way of business, Bianconi passed the next two or three years of his life in hawking prints about the country on his own account, and in 1806, at the age of twenty, he turned carver and gilder and opened a shop at Carrick-on-Suir. From Carrick he removed shortly afterwards to Waterford, and finally settled down at Clonmel.

The experience of these few years determined Bianconi's future career. While roaming over the country with his prints for sale, he had had forcibly impressed upon him the difference between a pedlar like himself who was doomed to tramp on foot and his more fortunate fellow who could post or ride on horseback. At Carrick the want of facilities for travelling had been brought home to him in a hardly less cogent manner. Gold-leaf for the supply of his shop he had to fetch from Waterford, and Waterford is distant from Carrick twelve or thirteen miles. Between the two towns, however, the only means of communication was by water, and by water, owing to the windings of the river, the distance is twenty-four miles. A single boat, moreover, was then the only public conveyance, and, besides being obliged to wait for the tide, it took from four to five hours to accomplish the journey. From this time Bianconi appears to have become possessed with the idea that his mission in life was to devise some cheap and easy means of communication between town and town. Imbued with this notion, he gave up his shop in the summer of 1815, and started a single-horse car for the conveyance of passengers from Clonmel to Cahir, a distance of about eight miles. At the end of the same year he started similar cars from Clonmel to Cashel and Thurles, and from Clonmel to Carrick and Waterford. From such humble beginnings sprang that splendid service of cars which, extending from Sligo and Enniskillen in the north to Bandon and Skibbereen in the south, and from Waterford and Wexford in the east to Galway and Belmullet in the west, carried passengers daily over more than 4000 miles of road at an average cost to each passenger of 1-1/4d. a mile.

But we are anticipating. The Post Office, largely as it availed itself in later years of the means of communication which Bianconi placed at its disposal, was slow to perceive the advantage which his enterprise offered. The country postmasters were wiser in their generation. Located on the spot, and with their perception quickened by the motive of self-interest, they made use of the cars as fast as these were put on the roads. No sooner had a car been started from Clonmel than the postmaster sent by it the mails which he had been used to send by horse-post. For this service he received an allowance of 5d. a mile. Bianconi performed the service for him for an allowance of 2-1/2d. a mile. The same thing took place elsewhere. It was not until the year 1831, when the Post Office of Ireland was amalgamated with that of England, that Bianconi was brought into direct relations with headquarters. Meanwhile, through a strange lack of vigilance on the part of the Irish authorities, his very existence was ignored, and the postmasters continued to receive 5d. a mile for a service which, wherever Bianconi's cars extended, they were getting done for one-half of that amount.

But it is not only with the Irish Post Office in relation to its internal affairs that this chapter proposes to deal. The communication between England and Ireland or rather between the capitals of the two countries had, since the Act of Union, been under constant review, and it becomes important to see how, during the first two or three decades of the present century, this communication stood both by sea and by land.

By the Act of 1784, which made the Irish Post Office independent of that of Great Britain—an Act not repealed by the Union—Great Britain and Ireland were to receive, in respect to letters passing between the two countries, each its own proportion of the postage. The Channel service remained; and with this Ireland was to have nothing to do, at all events in the first instance. Great Britain was to provide the packets and to receive the packet postage. Ireland, on the other hand, until she should have established packets of her own, was to receive from Great Britain the sum of £4000 a year "in lieu as well of the profits of the said packets as in compensation for other purposes." This arrangement appears to have worked smoothly enough until after 1801, when, owing to the increase of correspondence as a consequence of the Union, the Irish Post Office began to complain that the conditions were hard, and that Great Britain had the best of the bargain. Surely, under the very terms of the statute, Ireland was entitled to have packets of her own; and if this were denied her, did not justice demand that the conditions should be reconsidered? The question had come before successive Governments and always with the same result—that the existing arrangement was not to be disturbed. What Pitt and Portland and Perceval had decided was not to be done Lees now proceeded to do on his own account.

We doubt whether travellers of the present day who cross from Holyhead to Dublin in the magnificent boats which modern science has provided have any idea of the misery to which our grandfathers were exposed in making the passage. His Majesty's packets afforded the best, if not the only means of transit; and these were six in number, and ranged from 80 to 100 tons in burthen. Customs duties were at this time levied on goods passing between the two countries, and passengers' luggage was subjected to strict examination. Thus, to the discomforts of a sea-passage made in vessels of light tonnage were added the vexations incidental to a rigorous search of personal baggage; and these vexations were rendered all the greater by faulty arrangements. Passengers were unnecessarily detained, and often, even after detention, had to proceed on their journey leaving their luggage behind. In course of time, indeed, an exception was made in the case of peers and members of Parliament. After December 1819, as the result of incessant complaints, the luggage of these privileged persons was allowed to pass unexamined on their giving a certificate on honour that it contained no articles liable to duty; but at the time of which we are writing, the year 1813, all travellers, whether of high or low degree, were treated alike.

Despite conditions which at the present day would be considered intolerable, the number of passengers carried to and fro by the Holyhead packets was between 14,000 and 15,000 a year;[85] and there can be no doubt that the advantage which the British Post Office derived from this traffic was considerable. It is true that the fares went to the captains; but of course, except for the fares, the Post Office would have had to pay more for its packets. These were supplied at an annual cost of £365 apiece, or £2190 altogether; and such being the terms on which boats could be hired, Lees was confirmed in his opinion that Ireland would do better if, instead of receiving from Great Britain a compensation allowance of £4000 a year, she were to provide her own packets and share the packet postage.

Freeling took a different view. The better the bargain was for the British Post Office, the more determined he was that with his consent the terms should not be altered. And, more than this, he little relished the prospect of competition between English and Irish packets. Indeed, so long had he been accustomed to deal with a monopoly that the very name of competition was hateful to him. At this very time he tried, and tried in vain, to repress a boat which had been set up between Weymouth and the Channel Islands in opposition to the packets. Another similar attempt which he made a little later was hardly more successful. The War Office had chartered vessels to convey troops between Bristol and Waterford, and these vessels had assumed the title of "Government Packets," a title which, according to Freeling, induced persons to go by them who would otherwise have gone by the Post Office packets from Milford. Lord Palmerston was then Secretary at War, and we think we see the twinkle in his eye as he replied to Freeling's letter of remonstrance. Freeling's objection was of course to the Bristol boats being styled packets, but he had spoken of them by the title by which they were known of "Government Packets." The contractors, wrote Lord Palmerston, had been directed to drop the word Government forthwith, and the boats would henceforth be called War Office packets, to distinguish them from the packets employed by the Post Office.

Attached to the Irish Post Office, by virtue of a contract which had yet some years to run, were boats called wherries. Originally designed to carry between the two countries special messengers and despatches during the period immediately succeeding the Union, they had long lost their original character, and were now being employed in picking up what goods and passengers they could, and transporting them across the Channel in opposition to the packets. These boats were not ill adapted to the purpose which Lees had in hand. On the 19th of July 1813 he despatched a letter to Freeling, incidentally mentioning that "as the intended packet station at Howth had sufficient depth of water for the vessels belonging to the Irish Post Office, it was in contemplation, until such time as the regular packets should be stationed there, that the mails from Ireland should be despatched in its own vessels, and that, as soon as the arrangements now in progress should be completed, the measure would take effect." This letter was received in London on the 23rd of July, and on the next day intelligence reached Lombard Street that the mail from Ireland had been refused to the British packet and had been given to the Irish wherry.

And now might be witnessed a most unedifying spectacle—in Dublin Lees placarding the walls of the city with advertisements,[86] vaunting the merits of his own packets; at Holyhead the authorised packets arriving without the mails, and the mails being brought by boats which did not arrive until after the mail-coach for London had started; and in London Freeling wringing his hands and invoking the aid of the Government to check the vagaries of his brother-secretary on the other side of the Channel. "For the first time," he wrote, "the postmasters-general of Great Britain have not the means of redressing grievances connected with their own department, and the most serious remonstrances may be expected from the merchants and traders of London on this alarming and unnecessary evil."

The prediction was a safe one. Not only were the mails often one day behindhand in arriving in London, but the letters they brought were charged with an additional rate of postage in respect of the distance between Dublin and Howth. The merchants flocked to the Post Office to inquire the reason. No reason could be given them, and they were invited to let their applications for a return of the charge stand over until the postmasters-general should have informed themselves on the subject. Some assented; others accused the postmasters-general of trifling, and demanded instant redress. Matters had thus gone on for a fortnight when Lord Liverpool, to whom an appeal had been made, directed that the wherries should be withdrawn. One is left to suppose that this direction cannot have been communicated in the proper quarter, for as a matter of fact it had no result. In vain the captains of the packets applied at the Dublin Post Office for the British mails. All such applications met with a flat refusal, and the mails continued to be sent by the wherries as before. At length an end was put to the scandal, but not until it had lasted for more than six weeks.

The question now arose whether for the forty-four days during which the wherries had acted as packets the compensation of £4000 a year which Ireland received from Great Britain should not be withheld. Freeling had not only taken it for granted that such would be the case, but had been unable to conceal his regret that this was the only penalty of which the circumstances would admit. Liverpool, however, decided otherwise. Lees might have been wrong-headed and even perverse, but there could be no doubt that law was on his side. Accordingly, the compensation was paid for the period during which the packets had not carried the mails, and not long afterwards the Government brought in a bill raising the amount which Ireland was to receive from £4000 a year to £6000.

We now pass over six years. In July 1819 a curious invention, which had for some little time been in practical operation on the Thames between London and Margate, was brought into use between Holyhead and Dublin. This was no other than a vessel propelled by steam. Two vessels of this class were now set up by private individuals styling themselves the Dublin Steam Packet Company; and of this company, to the amazement of the authorities in Lombard Street, Lees had become a director. The quality which the new vessels possessed of being able to go against wind and tide, and the comparative speed with which they accomplished the passage, soon commended them to the favour of the public; and the consequence was a reduction to the extent of nearly one-half in the number of passengers by the Post Office packets.[87] The matter was serious, for it was in consequence of the fares which the captains received that they let their boats to the Post Office at little more than a nominal sum: and of course this sum would have to be increased according as the fares diminished.

We now see the Post Office at its best. Not possessing in the case of passengers a monopoly such as influenced and often perverted its action in the case of letters, the department proceeded to do much as private persons with sufficient capital at command would have done in similar circumstances, namely to build better boats than those already employed, and endeavour by the superior excellence of its service to recover the custom it had lost. Orders were given for two steam packets, the best that Boulton and Watt could build; and on the 31st of May 1821 the *Royal Sovereign*, of 206 tons burthen, with engines of 40 horse-power, and the *Meteor*, of somewhat smaller dimensions, began to ply. "Hitherto," wrote the postmasters-general eight days later, "they have answered the most sanguine expectations that had been formed of them; the letters have been delivered in Dublin earlier than was ever yet known, and Ireland has expressed herself grateful for the attention that has been shewn to her interests."

The Post Office behaved in this matter with a moderation which was altogether wanting where its monopoly was concerned. To be outdone by a private company, to employ inferior boats, boats of an obsolete type and of a low rate of speed—this would not be creditable to a public department, still less to a department whose special function it was to carry the correspondence of the country at the highest speed attainable; and properly enough the Post Office might take steps to establish its pre-eminence. But it would be quite another thing for a public department to undersell a private company, and, by charging lower fares, to run its boats off the line. This, it appeared to the authorities in Lombard Street, would exceed the bounds of fair competition. Accordingly the fares by the Post Office steam packets were fixed at the same amounts as those charged by the company; and these fares were somewhat higher than those which had been charged by the sailing packets. By sailing packet, for instance, the charge for a cabin passenger had been one guinea, by steam packet it was £1:5s.; for a horse the steam packet charge was £1:10s. as against one guinea by sailing packet, and for a coach £3:5s. as against three guineas.

These charges, which were fixed with the express object of not exposing the company to undue competition, had not been long in force before Parliament intervened. The Select Committee on Irish Communication protested in the interests of the public against the raising of the fares, and the Post Office was constrained to submit. The substitution of steam packets for sailing packets bore immediate fruit. The number of passengers carried by the Post Office between Holyhead and Dublin, which in 1820 had sunk to 7468, rose in 1821 to 13,737 and in 1822 to more than 16,000; and for some years the Holyhead packets were not only self-supporting but produced a clear gain to the revenue of more than £6000 a year.

The change which had been made at Holyhead was not long in extending itself to other packet stations from which there was communication with Ireland. Between Milford and Waterford sailing packets were replaced by steam packets in April 1824, and between Portpatrick and Donaghadee in May 1825. By sailing packet the average duration of voyage between the last-mentioned stations had been seven hours and forty-eight minutes. During the winter of 1825-26, a winter unexampled for the derangement of sea-communication, the average time which the little Post Office steamers *Arrow* and *Dasher* took to perform the voyage was less than three hours and a half.

And yet, despite these exertions to maintain its superiority, the Post Office was not to remain in undisputed possession of the Irish traffic. Private steamers had begun to ply between Liverpool and Dublin, and the fares by these steamers were lower than by the Post Office packets from Holyhead. As a natural consequence, the passenger traffic to which the Post Office looked to recoup itself for the heavy expense to which it had been put in replacing sailing packets by steam packets was diverted to Liverpool.

Nor was it only in the matter of passengers that the Post Office lost by the competition. Its reputation also suffered. The mails for Ireland left Liverpool at three o'clock in the afternoon, before the Exchange was closed, and reaching Holyhead by way of Chester and Llangollen at six o'clock on the following morning, did not arrive in Dublin until the afternoon. The private steamers, on the contrary, did not leave Liverpool until the business of the day was over, and arrived in Dublin on the following morning. Hence comparisons were drawn not favourable to the Post Office; and it by no means tended to allay dissatisfaction that the owners of the private steamers were refused permission to carry the mails. This they had offered to do, in one case for nothing more than exemption from harbour and light dues; but at that time, strange as it may appear to us with our present experience, it was a fixed principle with the Post Office that private firms even of the highest eminence were not to be entrusted with the carriage of the public correspondence. Accordingly it was decided that between Liverpool and Dublin the Post Office should run its own packets, and the new service began on the 29th of August 1826. The opening was marred by a lamentable disaster. Early in September the *Francis Freeling* packet, a recently-built cutter named after the secretary, and reputed to be the finest vessel of its kind afloat, foundered during a heavy gale and all the passengers and crew were lost.

The new service, while an unquestionable convenience to the public, did not altogether satisfy the Post Office. It is true that, as a consequence of the increased accommodation, the letters for Ireland passing through Liverpool nearly doubled in number; but this satisfactory result was not without alloy. During the past few years the art of building as applied to steamboats had made rapid progress; and not only were the packets on the Liverpool station larger than those stationed at Holyhead, the horse-power of the engines being 170 in the one case as against 40 in the other, but they were altogether better equipped. The fares by the Liverpool route as fixed by the Post Office were also relatively lower, and to any one proceeding from London or the large manufacturing towns of the North the distance to be travelled by road was shorter. As a consequence, the diversion of traffic from Holyhead to Liverpool, notwithstanding the longer sea voyage, proceeded still more rapidly than when the steamers from the latter port were in private hands; and the Holyhead service, which had for some years produced a clear profit of many thousand pounds a year, was now carried on at a loss.

To the Post Office authorities, indeed, there was in connection with the four packet stations in communication with Ireland only one thing which gave them unqualified satisfaction. It was this—that to the Post Office belonged the credit of being first to demonstrate by practical experience that, to use Freeling's words, "steam vessels could force their way at all seasons of the year and in weather in which no sailing vessel, be her qualities what they might, would attempt to put to sea." Whether the claim is well founded or not we have no means of judging; we only know that it was made.

By land, at the beginning of the present century, communication with Ireland was in a more backward state than it was by water; and since the Union a very general opinion had prevailed that this communication should be improved. It would perhaps be too much to say that the British Post Office proved obstructive in the matter; but there can be no doubt that it did not lend the assistance it might have done, and the reasons are obvious. In the first place, a little soreness existed. No sooner had the Act of Union passed than the Government decided that between London and Dublin there must be an express in both directions daily. This, as the postmasters-general pointed out, would cost more than £4000 a year, and, as it was not required for Post Office purposes, the Post Office should not bear the cost. Accordingly the question as to the source from which the cost should be defrayed was reserved for future consideration; but after the express was well established, the Post Office received notice that it must defray the cost itself, and it continued to do so for twenty years and more. This was always a sore point with Freeling, and he constantly adduced it as an instance of unremunerative work.

Another reason which kept Lombard Street back from assisting to improve the communication with Ireland was that the British and Irish Post Offices approached the subject from different points of view. With the British Post Office the main object, an object which in its judgment was sufficiently well attained already, was the transmission of letters; with the Irish Post Office, as indeed with that section of the public which could best make its voice heard, the main object was the transport of passengers. Yet a third reason, we can well believe, was the conviction that for any improvement that might be made, though primarily for the sake of Ireland, the British and not the Irish Post Office would have to pay. These three reasons, we cannot doubt, were at the root of the manifest indisposition displayed by the British Post Office to meet what had gradually become a very general demand.

The first strenuous effort to induce the authorities in Lombard Street to improve the communication with Ireland was made in 1805, the prime mover in the matter being John Foster, the Chancellor of the Irish Exchequer. At this time the mail-coach between London and Holyhead went by a circuitous route through Chester. Foster maintained that it should go direct through Coventry and Shrewsbury. By Coventry the distance was 264 miles, and by Chester 278 miles—a difference, in point of time, of more than two hours.

It was alleged that by the shorter route other delays which now took place might be avoided; but how important was a saving of even two hours may be judged from the fact that the time of the mail-coach leaving Holyhead was fixed with reference, not to the arrival of the packet from Dublin, but to the arrival of the coach in London. All the mail-coaches were timed to reach London early in the morning, so that the letters they brought might go out by the morning delivery. To effect this object, the mail-coach by the Chester route had to leave Holyhead at seven o'clock in the morning, an hour by which it was barely possible for the packet from Dublin to have arrived. During the whole of the year 1804, for instance, the Dublin mails arrived at Holyhead in time to catch the coach to London on only twelve occasions; and, of course, when the mails did not catch the coach, they had to remain idle at Holyhead until the following morning.

If, argued Foster, the route be by Shrewsbury and Coventry, the coach can leave Holyhead so much later that the occasions on which the Dublin mail does not arrive in time to catch it will be not as now the rule but the exception. Freeling set the suggestion aside as impracticable. The coach, he maintained, must go through Chester. At Chester centred all the correspondence from the great manufacturing towns of the North, from Liverpool and Manchester, from Hull, Halifax, and Leeds, indeed from all parts of Yorkshire and many other counties besides. Was this correspondence of no account? Or was it suggested that a second mail-coach should be established? Already the Post Office was paying many thousand pounds a year for an express service between London and Holyhead which it did not require. Could it in reason be expected to incur the further expense which a second mail-coach would involve? The thing was impossible, and the project could not be entertained.

Foster, though silenced for the time, was not convinced. In 1808 the subject was mooted again. Clancarty, who had recently been appointed joint postmaster-general with O'Neill, had arrived in London, prepared to argue the point with all the energy of his energetic nature. Foster was unable to come; but he had sent a memorandum which no one who was not thorough master of the subject could have produced. A meeting was appointed at Lord Hawksbury's office. Freeling poured out all the old objections, and proceeded to contend, as he had contended three years before, that the project was impracticable. But one was present there who did not believe in impracticabilities. This was the new Chief Secretary for Ireland, Sir Arthur Wellesley. Wellesley's opinion was emphatic—that all other considerations must be made subordinate to the one grand purpose of facilitating communication between the two capitals of London and Dublin. Freeling had encountered a stronger will than his own. What had been impossible before was possible now, and that very evening arrangements were begun to be devised for accelerating the Irish mails.

Even now, what little was done was done grudgingly. The mail-coach from London which ran through Oxford and Birmingham to Shrewsbury was extended from Shrewsbury to Holyhead, and was met at Llangollen by an express from Chester bringing the cross-post correspondence. Thus matters remained for nine years, when, under pressure which the Post Office could no longer resist, the Coventry route was adopted. The Post Office opposed the change to the last, even though a Parliamentary Committee had recommended it, and an address in its favour had been presented to the Prince Regent. At length Vansittart, the Chancellor of the Exchequer, brought his authority to bear, and in July 1817 a mail-coach by way of Coventry began to run, accomplishing the distance between London and Holyhead in thirty-eight hours.

But in order to facilitate communication between England and Ireland a good deal more was required than to set up an additional coach or to send an existing coach by another and shorter route. The roads of the country were still in a state to make rapid travelling impossible. Much, no doubt, had been done to improve them. Between the years 1760 and 1809 no less than 1514 Turnpike Acts had been passed, and under the turnpike system the roads were better than before. Still the making of them had been entrusted to incompetent hands, and they were constructed on false principles. For the bed or foundation of the roads improper or insufficient materials had been used. Little or no attention had been paid to drainage. Few roads were provided with side channels. Not seldom, indeed, the sides were encumbered with huge banks of mud which had accumulated to the height of six, seven, and even eight feet. Not only had convexity of surface, as a means of carrying off the water, been disregarded, but the road was frequently hollow in the middle and everywhere cut into deep ruts. High hedges and trees were still allowed to intercept the action of the sun and wind, the importance of a rapid evaporation of moisture being as yet unrecognised. Even the roads themselves had been laid out on no fixed principle. Their lines of direction were, almost without exception, identical with the footpaths of the aboriginal inhabitants of the country; and these, doubtless to avoid the bogs and marsh lands, and possibly also for purposes of observation, had invariably followed the hills.

Hence it came to pass that almost every road of any importance was both steep and crooked. Where there were no hills and the roads passed across wet and flat land, they were almost always below the level of the adjacent fields, the mud having been carried away by constant use. While such was the general state of the roads during the first twenty years of the present century, the road between Shrewsbury and Holyhead, over which a mail-coach had been travelling since the summer of 1808, was notoriously one of the worst in the kingdom. "To Kenneage,[88] six miles of narrow road; scarcely room for two carriages to pass, and much out of repair; in winter, the drivers say, the ruts are up to the bed of the coach." "From Kenneage to Capel Curig, road narrow and wants walling to prevent carriages falling down precipices 300 or 400 yards perpendicular." "From Capel Curig to Bangor, side of the road unguarded, and many accidents may happen to passengers by the coach running off the road as the mail passes here in the dark." Thus wrote the assistant superintendent of mail-coaches in 1808, and nothing had since been done to remedy defects.

The mail along this line, of road was now to be carried at a higher rate of speed than before, and, if only on this ground, it would have been necessary at least to remove actual causes of danger. Even before 1817, however, Parliamentary Commissioners had been appointed for the improvement of the Holyhead road; and these Commissioners had summoned to their aid the first of that line of illustrious men who, during the last eighty years, have transformed the face of England. This was Thomas Telford, who had already achieved distinction by the roads he had made in the Highlands of Scotland.

Telford commenced operations in the autumn of 1815; and now for the first time in England, or at all events for the first time since the ancient ways were laid down by the Romans, a road was to be constructed on scientific principles. "Every valley shall be exalted, and every mountain and hill shall be made low; and the crooked shall be made straight, and the rough places plain." This—we say it without irreverence—is what literally came to pass. Easy inclinations, ample breadth, perfect drainings, complete protection, and a smooth and hard surface—these were the distinguishing characteristics of the road which Telford now made between Holyhead and Shrewsbury. A road that had been one of the worst in the kingdom was now the very best. In summer it was not even dusty, and in winter was free from dirt. Frost and rain produced upon it but trifling and superficial effects. To crown all, the Menai Straits were spanned by a noble bridge, where before there had been only an inconvenient ferry.

While Telford was thus raising the business of road-making to the level of an art, John Loudon Macadam was demonstrating of what materials the surface of a road should be made. Macadam had travelled about the kingdom much as John Palmer had travelled about some thirty years before in pursuit of a different object, and, as the result of long observation, he had come to the conclusion that the surface of roads should be made of broken stones; and having in 1816 been appointed general surveyor of roads in the British district he proceeded to put his views into practice. With success to recommend it, the new system spread like wildfire, and "a macadamised road" soon became a household word.

Nor was it to the business of road-making alone that science now lent her aid. What force of traction or power is required to draw carriages over different kinds of road, in what line of direction the power can be best applied—what, in other words, is the proper angle for the traces, and what in the case of hills is the highest inclination up which horses can go at a trot and down which they can with safety be driven at full speed—these were some of the questions which now engaged the attention of the scientific world. Some thirty years before, Walsingham and Chesterfield when postmasters-general had dabbled in matters of the kind;[89] but now they were reduced to the form of mathematical problems and received a mathematical solution.

The excellence of the road constructed between Holyhead and Shrewsbury brought into bold relief the imperfections of the road between Shrewsbury and London. To this road, which, in comparison with the other, had at one time been pronounced good and was now pronounced execrable, Telford proceeded to apply the same principles as before. He raised the valleys, lowered or avoided the hills, and corrected deviations. To give only one instance—an instance taken from the second stage out of London—the old road from Barnet to South Minims ascended three steep and long hills; the new road avoided two of these hills altogether, and at the same time was shorter than the old one by more than 600 yards. And so it was in a greater or less degree all the way from London through St. Albans to Coventry, and thence through Birmingham and Wolverhampton to Shrewsbury.

It should also be mentioned that at this time, while the country roads were hollow in the centre instead of convex, the roads in and about London within a radius of about ten miles were the exact contrary. Here convexity, as a means of carrying off water, had been pushed to so absurd an extent that the road was in the form of a slanting roof, and a carriage, unless kept in the centre, was on a dangerous slope. This, which had been a prolific source of accidents, Telford now altered. The effect of his operations upon the first stage out of London, the Highgate Archway Road as it was called, is perhaps best described in the words of one of the principal mail-coach contractors. Before Telford took this road in hand, he wrote, "It was all we could do to walk up both sides of the archway with six horses, and now we can trot up with our heaviest loads with four."

The road from London to Shrewsbury, in continuation of the one from Shrewsbury to Holyhead, was completed in 1828, and, corresponding alterations having been made in the eight miles of road which connect Howth and Dublin, a line of communication was established between the capitals of England and Ireland such as, until the days of railways, could hardly have been improved. Some few years before, when the Post Office had received orders to accomplish the distance between London and Holyhead in thirty-eight hours, Hasker, the experienced superintendent of mail-coaches, while zealously applying himself to carry the orders into effect, had felt it incumbent upon him as a loyal servant to make a protest in writing against the "extraordinary expedition projected." It would, he urged—and no doubt rightly so as the road then was—be inhuman to horses and dangerous to life. This extraordinary expedition was at the rate of seven miles an hour. Along the Parliamentary Road the distance was accomplished, without hurt to horses and with perfect safety, at the rate of ten miles an hour, and the London and Holyhead coach soon became one of what were known as the "crack" coaches of the kingdom.

Meanwhile the Post Office had shewn its appreciation of Telford's achievement in a remarkable manner. It had imposed an additional charge of 1d. upon every letter carried over Conway Bridge, and a second penny for carriage over the Menai Straits.[90]

CHAPTER XVI
THE BEGINNING OF THE END 1817-1836

We must now go back a few years. On the cessation of hostilities with France the state of the finances occupied a large share of men's thoughts, and among the plans for relieving the burden upon the taxpayer none perhaps was more obvious than to abolish sinecures and useless offices.

On the 16th of February 1817 Mr. Lambton, member for the county of Durham, gave notice of motion for a return shewing the number of Boards which had been held by the postmasters-general during the last twenty years, and distinguishing the names of the places where such Boards had been held and the persons by whom they were attended. The Post Office was in a flutter. Just twenty years before, the Commissioners of Inquiry into Public Offices had recommended, and the recommendation had been approved by the House, that a Board should be held by the postmasters-general at least once a week; and from that date to the present not a single Board had been held. The position was no doubt embarrassing, and not the less so because the postmasters-general, Lords Chichester and Salisbury, were the one at Stanmer and the other at Hatfield. Nothing could be done without the concurrence of both, and at such distances, little as would be thought of them now, it was a tedious process eighty years ago to arrive at a common understanding.

Freeling, who regarded it as little short of an outrage that the two noble peers, his masters, should be thus called to account, appealed to the Chancellor of the Exchequer to have the terms of the motion altered; but Vansittart refused, and the return was granted and ordered to be laid on the table of the House. Of course it was necessary to admit that no Boards had been held; but the work of the Post Office, the return went on to state, did not lend itself to Boards. Boards could be held only at intervals, and the work of the Post Office was so continuous and pressing that, without detriment to the public interests, it could not be kept waiting for a single day. A daily transmission of papers to the postmasters-general was, therefore, necessary; and by such means the business was better conducted than it would be by any system of Boards. Such was the substance of the return which was now laid before the House. Eventually the matter was referred to a friendly Committee, and the appointment of second postmaster-general escaped for a time.

But it was for a time only. In May 1822, on the motion of Lord Normanby, an address to the throne was adopted in the following terms: "His Majesty's faithful Commons, relying upon His Majesty's gracious disposition expressed in answer to former addresses of that House to concur in all such measures of economy as the exigencies of the time require, and in such reductions in the civil department of the State as may be consistent with due consideration for the public service, humbly pray that His Majesty will be graciously pleased to give directions that the office of one of the postmasters-general may be abolished and the salary thereby saved to the revenue." It was Lord Salisbury, as the junior of the two postmasters-general, that was affected by the resolution of the House. Many men, incensed by such treatment, would have thrown up their appointments in disgust. Lord Salisbury did nothing of the kind. The very day he received official intimation that the address had been acceded to by the King he gave directions that his salary should be stopped;[91] but the appointment of postmaster-general he retained, and to the duties of it he gave at least as much attention as before. It was not until his death a year later that Lord Chichester was appointed sole postmaster-general, and the Post Office received the constitution under which it still remains.

Other economies followed. All periodical increases of salary were suspended and salaries were for the first time made subject to abatement in order to provide a superannuation fund.[92] The effect of these two measures was to reduce the Post Office servants to a state of destitution not very far short of that from which Pitt had rescued them some thirty years before. It must not be thought, however, that ministers imposed upon others conditions to which they were unwilling to submit themselves. On the contrary, they procured an Order in Council to be passed reducing their own salaries and those of all the great officers of State by 10 per cent, and the reduction was to continue for five years. The desire to be just and equal was present; the one thing wanting was a due sense of the difference between superfluity and need.

And now a blow which had long been impending fell. This was the transfer from the Post Office to the Admiralty of the packets stationed at Falmouth. The question had been discussed again and again during the war; but how it came to be revived at this particular time is not very clear. There had indeed been a mutiny among the seamen at Falmouth, and the packets had been temporarily removed to Plymouth; but many years had since elapsed, and now, so far as appeared, matters were perfectly quiet.

We only know that at the instance of Lord Liverpool a memorandum was prepared by Lord Melville, the First Lord of the Admiralty, and that after a sharp paper-warfare between him and Freeling the arguments in favour of the change prevailed. At Falmouth thirty packets were employed, nearly double the number at all the other stations put together; and these thirty packets with their crews of 600 seamen, whose deeds of daring had often shed lustre on the Post Office, were now made over to another department. Freeling was in despair. This little fleet had, next perhaps to the mail-coaches, been the object of his keenest solicitude; and it gave him little consolation that the packets at the other stations—at Dover and Harwich, at Weymouth, Milford, Holyhead, and Portpatrick, were to remain under the charge of the Post Office.

Some little comfort, however, was at hand. Steam packets being beyond the means of the captains to purchase, the Government provided them and purchased the sailing packets, which they replaced, at a valuation. Thus the Post Office became once more absolute owner of its own boats. This, though by no means reconciling Freeling to the loss of the Falmouth packets, was at all events some compensation. "The steam flotilla belonging to the Post Office," he was able to write in 1827, "consists of no less than nineteen vessels complete, to the aggregate amount of 4000 tons, with machinery equal on the whole to the power of 1540 horses."

Exaggerated opinions have been expressed as to the speed of the mail-coaches during the first two decades of the present century. In 1821 few mail-coaches travelled as much as eight miles an hour, and only one mail-coach attained to a speed of nine miles, and that for only part of the journey. The exact rates of travelling are shewn in the following table:—

1821.

Mail Coach from London to	Number of Miles.	Hour of Despatch.	Hour of Arrival.	Rate of Travelling per hour.	Remarks.
	M. F.			M.	
Berwick	341 6	8.0 p.m.	6.15 p.m.	7-13/16	The rates of
Berwick to					travelling
Edinburgh	59 4	—	2.55 a.m.	7-2/16	include
Birmingham	110 2	8.0 p.m.	10.0 a.m.	7-13/16	stoppages for
Bristol	122 4	"	"	8-10/16	change of

Carlisle by					horses, but
Manchester	311 4	"	1.30 p.m.	8-5/16	not stoppages
Carlisle by					for refresh-
Boroughbridge	302 6	"	1.40 p.m.	7-10/16	ment and for
Carlisle to					Post Office
Glasgow	103 2	—	4.50 a.m.	7-4/16	business.
Chester	191 0	8.0 p.m.	10.50 p.m.	7-8/16	
Chester to					
Holyhead	88 0	—	7.5 a.m.	7-7/16	
Dover	73 4	8.0 p.m.	6.45 a.m.	7	For a
Exeter	176 2	"	7.40 p.m.	7-11/16	considerable
Exeter by Bath	194 0	"	7.50 p.m.	8-7/16	part of the
Gloucester	111 0	"	10.0 a.m.	8-3/16	distance the
Holyhead	264 6	"	6.50 a.m.	7-15/16	London and
Leeds	196 0	"	11.25 p.m.	7-8/16	Bristol
Liverpool	207 4	"	12.10 a.m.	7-6/16	coach
Norwich by					travelled at
Ipswich	114 4	"	11.0 a.m.	7-14/16	the rate of
Ipswich to					nine miles an
Yarmouth	54 2	—	11.56 a.m.	7-15/16	hour.
Poole	117 4	8.0 p.m.	11.20 a.m.	7-14/16	
Portsmouth	72 6	"	6.45 a.m.	7-1/16	
Worcester	114 4	"	10.40 a.m.	8-7/16	

It was not until some fourteen or fifteen years later, when the main roads of the kingdom had passed under Telford's hands and vehicles of lighter build had been introduced, that mail-coaches attained the speed which is very commonly ascribed to an earlier period. In 1836 there were in England 104 mail-coaches, all drawn by four horses. Of these the fastest was the Liverpool and Preston coach, which travelled at the rate of ten miles and five furlongs an hour; and the slowest was the coach between Canterbury and Deal, which travelled at the rate of only six miles an hour. The average speed of all the mail-coaches in 1836, namely eight miles and seven furlongs an hour, was actually higher than the highest speed attained by any one mail-coach in 1821. It should be added that in 1821, as in 1836, the number of passengers by a mail-coach was limited to four inside and four out. On some mail-coaches, indeed, no more than three outside passengers were allowed.

But the mail-coach at the beginning of the present century did something more than carry mails and passengers. It was the great disseminator of news. In times of excitement men would stand waiting along the mail roads and learn the latest intelligence as shouted to them from the tops of the coaches. It may well be believed that this mode of communication did not tend to either accuracy or completeness of statement. We cannot, therefore, be surprised that on important occasions or occasions on which false or inexact intelligence might lead to mischief recourse should have been had to the expedient of printing hand-bills, and sending them to the postmasters with instructions to distribute them in their respective towns. The following are specimens of hand-bills which were so distributed:—

LONDON, *February 10, 1817.*

The statement in the morning papers that several persons have been arrested by warrants from the Secretary of State is true.

The meeting was held this morning at Spa Fields; but the arrests which have taken place and the precautions adopted by Government caused everything to end peaceably and the town is perfectly quiet.

17th November 1818.

Her Majesty the Queen expired at one o'clock this day.

The following hand-bill sent to the different ports where vessels from Jamaica were likely to arrive is interesting in so far as it shews the exceptional facilities which, even seventy or eighty years ago, the Post Office possessed for making inquiries:—

GENERAL POST OFFICE, *February 10th, 1821.*

Mr. Freeling requests the postmaster to make inquiries of the master of any ship arriving from Jamaica into the state of the Duke of Manchester's health, and inform him of the result by the first post.

Of the reason of this solicitude we are not aware.

Police notices, notices giving particulars of crimes which had been committed and offering rewards for the apprehension of the criminals, were similarly dealt with. These, like the hand-bills of which specimens have been given, were sent from Lombard Street under cover to the postmasters with instructions to circulate them in their respective towns. The propriety of this proceeding is not free from doubt. Of course, every department of the State is interested in the detection and punishment of crime; and yet it may be a question whether by taking an active part in the distribution of these documents the Post Office was not to some extent identifying itself with a class of business from which, for obvious reasons, it had better hold itself aloof.

While changes were taking place in other directions, the regulations for the transmission of newspapers through the post remained as they had been at the beginning of the century. Within the United Kingdom newspapers could not pass free except under the frank of either members of Parliament or of the clerks of the roads. To the Continent of Europe and to the colonies they could pass only at the letter rate of postage unless they were franked, in the case of the Continent, by the comptroller or clerks of the foreign department, and, in the case of the colonies, by Freeling. This privilege of franking was to the Post Office servants who possessed it a source of considerable profit. Freeling's share alone amounted to nearly £3000 a year; but he, unlike his subordinates, claimed to frank not newspapers alone but the *Edinburgh* and *Quarterly Reviews* and other publications of a like nature.

The West India merchants had long writhed under this exaction, and now at their instance Joseph Hume, the member for Montrose, brought the matter under the notice of the House of Commons. The practice had only to be made known in order to secure condemnation. A bill was brought in and passed extinguishing the privilege so far as the colonies were concerned, empowering the Treasury to grant compensation for the loss of it, and providing for the transmission of newspapers at easy rates. These rates were, from the United Kingdom to the colonies, 1-1/2d. and, from the colonies to the United Kingdom, 3d. for each newspaper, the reason for the difference of charge being that the paper would bear a stamp-duty in one direction and not in the other.

In the case of newspapers for the Continent the franking privilege remained untouched. It may seem strange that this should have been so; indeed, not more than two or three years had elapsed before members of Parliament were expressing surprise that the Act which had taken away the privilege in respect to one class of newspapers had not taken it away also in respect to the other. But the explanation, we think, is simple. Some nine or ten years before it had been rumoured that in the case of all Post Office servants the franking privilege was to be abolished, and those who would have been injured by its abolition proceeded to shew cause why in their own case an exception should be made. Only by those who franked to the Continent were even plausible reasons given; and there can be little doubt that, at all events to some extent, the same reasons operated now. These were that over a great part of the Continent, except for the arrangements made by the Post Office servants in Lombard Street, English newspapers could not circulate at all or could circulate only under most onerous conditions. In France their circulation was prohibited. To Holland they could not be sent unless ordered by some postmaster there. In Germany and Sweden, unless so ordered, they could not pass through the post except at the letter rate of postage. In Portugal the letter rate of postage was always charged. In Russia, besides being charged 7s. 6d. apiece, they were generally delayed and not seldom suppressed altogether. These obstacles had been overcome by the private arrangements made from Lombard Street, and, if these should be disallowed, the transmission of newspapers to the Continent, instead of being facilitated, would be rendered more difficult and costly. Thus in 1816 argued those who were interested in the maintenance of the privilege, and we can well understand that in 1825 much the same considerations prevailed.

The same Act of Parliament which imposed upon newspapers to the colonies a postage of 1-1/2d. allowed newspapers within the United Kingdom to pass through the post free from any postage at all. This was the effect of the Act, but it was accomplished in a roundabout manner. By a statute passed early in the century[93] a member of Parliament was required, in order to send his newspapers free, to sign his name on the outside in his own handwriting, and, in order to receive them free, to have them addressed to some place of which he had given previous notice in writing at the Post Office. By the present statute these provisions were repealed. A newspaper, to be exempt from postage, need no longer bear the signature of a member of Parliament and need no longer be addressed to a place of which previous notice had been given. In other words, newspapers might pass through the post free; and as a consequence the franking privilege possessed by the clerks of the roads was at an end.

This, it might naturally be supposed, was a signal epoch in the history of the Post Office. As a matter of fact, it was nothing of the kind. For many years past the law had been disregarded. It had indeed been insisted upon that a newspaper, in order to pass free, must bear a member's name, without which the full letter rate of postage would be charged; but by whom the name was written, whether it was written at all or only printed, and whether the use of it had been authorised, had long ceased to be considered material. So well was this understood that some of the largest news-vendors in the kingdom adopted a member's name without the slightest reference to the member himself, and had it printed on their newspaper-covers.

This laxity in the case of newspapers may appear all the more extraordinary in view of the stringency which was observed in other matters. The Chelsea pensioners had by statute enjoyed the privilege of sending and receiving letters at low rates of postage. Freeling never rested until the statute was repealed. At the close of hostilities with France letters which had been detained in Paris since the war broke out in 1803 were forwarded to London, and the merchants urged that they might be delivered free. The Treasury were in favour of granting the request; but Freeling energetically opposed it. The delivery of such letters free, he insisted, would be a plain breach of the law. On a dissolution of Parliament those who had been members lost their privilege in the matter of franking; and yet it might be supposed that a short period of grace would have been allowed, a period sufficient to admit of letters which were already in the post being delivered free. Nothing of the kind. These letters were surprised in course of transit and charged with postage.[94]

Lord Salisbury when at the Post Office contrasted the stringency of later years with the laxity which prevailed in his early manhood. "In the year 1778," he wrote, "and in many succeeding ones while I took the field with the militia it was the constant practice to write on all regimental papers the words, 'On His Majesty's service,' which insured a free delivery; but in process of time the Post Office became rather stricter and more attentive, and then such a superscription was charged except when addressed to peers and members of Parliament, and I have frequently paid for such letters overweight without getting any redress."

When such strictness was observed in other matters, one can only wonder at the liberties which were allowed to be taken with newspapers, and it appears all the more strange because the very act which in the case of newspapers was countenanced and encouraged was in the case of letters a highly penal offence. Was it not for forging a single frank, the frank of Sir William Garrow, that the clerical impostor, Halloran, was in 1818 sentenced to seven years' transportation? The plain truth would seem to be that vested interests were so deeply involved in the matter of newspapers that there was on the part of the Post Office the utmost indisposition to make them the subject of legislative enactment; and yet, without some concessions to the news-vendors, it would have been impossible to resist the pressure which would have been brought to bear. This, we doubt not, is the true explanation; and it will account for much that is otherwise dark and obscure. It will explain why that which was regarded as a heinous offence in the case of letters was sanctioned and encouraged in the case of newspapers; why, enormously as the circulation of newspapers within the United Kingdom increased during the first quarter of the present century, we look in vain for any legislative enactment regulating the conditions under which, except when sent or received by members of Parliament, they might pass through the post; and why in 1825, when at length they had conceded to them the right to pass free, the concession was enacted in an indirect and circuitous manner.

So far, therefore, as inland newspapers were concerned, the practical effect of the statute which now passed was little more than to make law correspond with usage. During many years newspapers had been passing through the post, as they were to pass for the future, free. The only difference was that, in order to secure exemption, it was no longer necessary to go through the farce of either writing or printing the name of some member of Parliament on the outside of the cover. The clerks of the roads were unaffected by the statute. The advantage which these officers had at one time derived from their franking privilege had already been lost to them through the action of the Post Office in evading the law; and we can well believe that even so they considered themselves fortunate in being permitted to escape with their newspaper-business. This business, long after they had begun to compete with the news-vendors on equal terms, was of large dimensions. During the year 1829, out of 11,862,706 newspapers despatched from London into the country, 1,207,794 or more than one-tenth of the whole number were despatched by the clerks of the roads.

But it was not only in respect to newspapers that the House of Commons began about this time to manifest in the proceedings of the Post Office an interest such as it had never taken before. Committee after Committee was appointed to report upon the communications of the country, upon roads, mail-coaches, and steam packets; but without any definite result. Obviously the House was not satisfied with things as they were, and yet did not well see how to improve them. Only one man appears to have had a clear perception of what he wanted, and to have been possessed of the requisite ability to carry his object. This was Sir Henry Parnell, chairman of the Select Committee on the Holyhead Road, a Committee the title of which only inadequately denotes either its scope or importance. Parnell, presuming on the authority which this position gave him, and convinced no doubt of the feasibility of his scheme of improvement, adopted towards the Post Office an air of superiority which was peculiarly galling to Freeling, who for the first time in his life found himself dictated to in respect to matters in which he had hitherto been regarded as supreme. The effect of this Committee was not only to keep the Post Office busily employed in the preparation of returns but to put it on the defensive.

Another inquiry which was going on contemporaneously contributed to the same result. Early in the reign of George the Fourth a Commission had been appointed to inquire into the state of the revenue, and this Commission, which began with the Post Office in 1823, did not report the result of its labours until 1829. Meanwhile the Post Office, which was practically on its trial, put forward as few proposals as possible; and even from those that were put forward the Treasury withheld assent on the pretext that the Commission had not yet reported. Hence followed the somewhat curious result that the very period during which the House of Commons began to manifest an interest in the Post Office was on the part of the Post Office itself a period of more than ordinary inaction.

And yet the period in question, though not remarkable for Post Office progress, is by no means an uninteresting one if only because within its limits the old and the new are brought together in striking contrast. In 1818 the express office in the Haymarket is closed, an office which had been established in 1797 for the purpose of facilitating the receipt and despatch of Government expresses. In 1821 gas, or oil-gas as it was then called, is introduced into the Post Office, and at once asserts its superiority over oil in point not only of illuminating power but of cheapness as well. In 1822 the Post Office, by virtue of a warrant under the royal sign-manual, is cleared of its irrecoverable debts. These have been accumulating during a period of 137 years—since 1685, when the Post Office was first taken out of farm, and now amount to £62,141.

About the same time Thomas Gray, writing from Brussels, advocates the introduction of steam engines on iron railways and predicts that, once established, they will absorb the carrying trade of the kingdom and displace mail-coaches. In 1823 Brunel, who has already achieved distinction, offers his services in the construction of a steam engine which shall prove as efficient and as safe at sea as when employed on land. The brilliant engineer receives no encouragement, and Gray receives not even the courtesy of an answer. In the same year passes away at Tunbridge Wells, James Sprange, the courtly old postmaster, who up to the date of his last illness might be seen pacing the Pantiles scrupulously dressed in the costume of the reign of George the Second, even to the long ruffles. In 1825 Glasgow is pleading, and pleading in vain, for a Post Office which shall not be kept at a shop. In 1828 the Roman Catholic peers are once more protesting against the outrage which precludes them, on the score of their religion, from exercising the privilege of franking. In 1829 Waghorn is vainly striving to induce the Post Office to co-operate in facilitating communication with the East.

The inferiority of sailing vessels to vessels propelled by steam has now been conclusively established, and steam packets are being placed on every station. Not the Holyhead Road alone but all the great roads of the kingdom have passed under Telford's hands and are beginning to assume the condition in which we see them to-day. And all this while postage remains at the ridiculously high level at which it was fixed in 1812. To Windsor the charge on a single letter is still 6d., to Birmingham 9d., and to Liverpool 11d. Letters are still held up to a strong light to see whether they contain an enclosure or not, and are to be charged as single or as double. The first general delivery in St. James' Square is not begun before twelve o'clock in the day or finished much before one. Offices for the receipt of general post letters are still kept separate and distinct from those for the receipt of letters for the twopenny post. By the twopenny post the postage is not necessarily 2d., but, according as it is a twopenny post letter, a general post letter, or a foreign letter, may be 3d., 2d., or nothing. On a letter for abroad the fee for registration is still one guinea.[95] An additional penny is still charged upon every letter that crosses the Conway or the Menai Bridge. Two hundred and seventy-five post towns still remain without a free delivery, and—what proves a constant source of contention between the Post Office and the inhabitants—even in those towns in which the letters are delivered free, the limits of the free delivery are not defined.

Twenty years before, the office in Gerrard Street, the headquarters of the twopenny post in Westminster, had been enlarged. Of this office, which ranked next in importance to the General Post Office in Lombard Street, the postmasters-general wrote in 1809—not, surely, without a touch of exaggeration: "The sorting office, where fourteen persons are generally employed at a time and nearly one-half of which is occupied by tables, is only seventeen feet long by thirteen wide"; and, again, "The letter-carriers' office, in which fifty persons are employed at a time and one-fourth of which is occupied by tables, is but eighteen feet by sixteen." Such were the conditions under which, until lately, the Post Office servants had been accustomed to work; and now on a site rich in historical associations is rapidly approaching completion a stately edifice which not only provides ample and even lavish accommodation for the present, but will, it is confidently predicted, suffice for all time.

The new Post Office in St. Martin's-le-Grand was opened on the 23rd of September 1829. Little more than sixty years have since elapsed, and the building has been shorn of its chief attraction, the central hall, and has otherwise been so altered internally that even the accomplished architect, were he to revisit us, would probably fail to recognise his own handiwork. Of the old Post Office in Lombard Street, with its courts and its alleys and its interesting associations, not a fragment remains. Part of the site was retained for Post Office purposes, and is now occupied by what is known as the

Lombard Street Branch Office; part was thrown into the street then forming, and to be called after the King, King William Street; and the remainder was sold, and has long been covered with banks and counting-houses.

It were much to be wished, if only for his own reputation and peace of mind, that Freeling had now retired. Full of years, recently created a baronet, of ample means, and enjoying the confidence of the Government as probably civil servant had never enjoyed it before, he could not have selected a better moment for relinquishing the duties of his arduous post. But a man who has been accustomed to exercise power is seldom willing to give it up. And in Freeling's case we suspect there was an additional reason. Of the large income which he derived from the Post Office, exceeding £4000 a year, considerably more than two-thirds was compensation for the loss of the franking privilege; and this compensation, according to a well-understood rule, was not to count for pension. As the fees which had been received for the exercise of the privilege must have ceased on retirement, so the compensation was to cease also.

That Freeling would have received a special pension is beyond doubt; but even a special pension, with the utmost goodwill on the part of the Government, could not have approached the amount of his official income. And of this Freeling must have been well aware, for grumblings were already to be heard. The Commissioners of Revenue Inquiry, indeed, had gone so far as to question his right to receive any fees at all, and, even assuming such right to exist, had impugned the conduct of the Government in fixing the amount of his compensation at close upon £3000 a year.

The removal into the new building was celebrated by two important steps in advance. Two branch offices were opened, one at Charing Cross and the other in Oxford Street, where letters were received without a fee until half-past six o'clock in the evening. Up to this time, except in Lombard Street, no office for the receipt of letters had been kept open later than five o'clock. A still more important step was the earlier delivery of letters in the morning. This was accomplished within the city by the employment of additional letter-carriers, and in the more distant parts by conveying the men to their walks in vehicles. A whole hour was thus gained. In the west end of London the delivery had not been completed until between twelve and one o'clock. It was now to be completed, except on Mondays, when the greater number of letters caused delay, between eleven and twelve.

It will be convenient here to notice, though not strictly in chronological order, a third step in advance which took place about a year later, a step regarded as of little moment at the time, and yet one which, in view of subsequent events, was of the highest importance. On the 11th of

November 1830 the first mail was sent by railway, this being the mail between Liverpool and Manchester. Except as the opening of a new era, the fact would hardly deserve to be recorded, for many years had yet to pass before railways became sufficiently general to afford to the Post Office any sensible relief. Meanwhile the roofs of the mail-coaches groaned under the weight of the mails. Time had been when no mail was allowed to be put on the roof or elsewhere than in the mail-box; but, as the correspondence increased, the Post Office was forced to countenance a practice of which it highly disapproved. What, except for the railways, would have happened on the introduction of penny postage is a question into which, happily, we need not inquire.

The new Post Office had not been long occupied before the Government changed hands, and Earl Grey came into power with the Duke of Richmond as postmaster-general. It is not often that a change of Government affects the proceedings of the Post Office. One postmaster-general may be more active than another, or he may take a more lively and personal interest in the questions with which he has to deal; but there must, from the nature of the case, be a continuity of policy which can seldom be broken. Nor was there in this respect any exception to rule in the present instance. And yet the peer who now assumed the direction of the Post Office adopted a mode of procedure so different from that of his immediate predecessors that it is impossible to pass over the occasion in silence.

Richmond on his appointment as postmaster-general declined to receive any salary; and having formed this determination on the ground that the office was notoriously a sinecure, he straightway proceeded to shew that a sinecure was the very thing which in his hands the office was not to be. He devoted himself heart and soul to his new duties. Early and late, at his private residence as well as the Post Office, he was in constant and personal communication with officers of all classes from the highest to the lowest. Nothing like it had been seen since the days of Walsingham. He frequented the sorting office, saw for himself how the work was done, and with many a kindly word encouraged the men to do their best. With his own hands he on one occasion opened a bag for the colonial office, and, in confirmation of the suspicion which had prompted the act, found it full of letters for bankers, army agents, and others, representing postage to the amount of £60.

Yet hard as he laboured, the Duke's repugnance to receive remuneration for his services could not be overcome. Learning that his salary remained undrawn, the Treasury addressed to him a letter of gentle remonstrance. To this letter he returned no reply. Fourteen months later the Treasury wrote again. To gratuitous service there were, in their Lordships' opinion, serious objections. The Lord Privy Seal had declined to receive the salary annexed to his office, and a Select Committee of the House of Commons had expressed disapproval of the step as being inconsistent with the wishes and the dignity of the country. Could that be right on the part of the postmaster-general which had been held to be wrong in the case of the Lord Privy Seal? Richmond now yielded, feeling that it would be indelicate, if not disrespectful to the House, to force gratuitous service where he was authoritatively informed gratuitous service would not be welcome; but while yielding he managed to draw as little of the arrears of salary as possible. His appointment as postmaster-general bore date the 14th of December 1830, and the views of the Committee were for the first time made known to him at the end of April. The end of April, he was pleased to say, was an inconvenient time to begin. It was a broken quarter. He would, in deference to the opinion of the Committee, draw salary from the 5th of July but not before.

Richmond had been only a short time at the Post Office when he had a most invidious task to perform. This was the carrying out of the arrangements consequent upon the consolidation of the Irish Post Office with the Post Office of Great Britain. The state of things arising from the maintenance within the United Kingdom of two independent Post Offices had long been felt to be intolerable. Until four or five years before, not only had the rates of postage in Ireland been different from those in England, but on a letter passing from one part of the kingdom to another both the English and the Irish rates had been charged. This had now been altered,[96] but the inconvenience of the dual control remained. A letter from Ireland might have miscarried or been delayed. The postmaster-general of England could not answer for its course except on this side of the Channel, and for further particulars the complainant had to be referred to Dublin. The English packets were timed to arrive in Ireland at a particular hour; but on the goodwill of the authorities in Dublin it depended whether the Irish posts corresponded or whether, as had not been unknown to be the case, their times were perversely fixed so as to keep the English mails waiting.

Nor was this all. The Revenue Inquiry Commissioners had recently reported upon the Irish Post Office, and the evidence, on which their report was based, revealed the existence of scandalous abuses such as no Government could suffer to continue. For nearly fifty years the Irish Post Office had been independent of the Post Office of Great Britain, and it was now determined that this independence should cease. In 1831 an Act was passed incorporating the two Post Offices into one, and Richmond's patent as postmaster-general of Great Britain had hardly been completed before another passed constituting him postmaster-general of the United Kingdom.

Upon Richmond as postmaster-general of Ireland as well as England and Scotland it now devolved to sweep out the Augean stable; and his stern sense of duty peculiarly qualified him for the task. Rosse and O'Neill had ceased to be postmasters-general of Ireland upon the Act of incorporation passing. Lees, their secretary, was removed from Dublin to Edinburgh. Only those who had performed their duties in person were retained. All others were summarily dismissed and pensions were refused to them. In the result the Irish establishment was reduced in point of numbers by one-half, and in point of cost by nearly £10,000 a year; and this after the salaries of those who were retained had been increased all round.

One important function had yet to be performed. This was to audit the Irish accounts, which had not been audited for fourteen years, and were known to be in a state of the utmost confusion. The receiver-general, who carried on the private business of banker and money-lender, had recently died, and speculation was high as to what further scandals the audit would reveal. All preparations had been made, and the persons selected for the task were on the point of starting for Dublin when intelligence reached London that the receiver-general's bond was not forthcoming. It had, shortly after his death, been surrendered under an instruction from Lees which, like the instruction which conferred upon his brother a valuable appointment, purported to have been given at a Board at which were present "the earls." The earls, as a matter of fact, had not been present and had never been consulted on the point. As it was felt that in the absence of the bond an audit would be of little use, the Government abandoned their intention, and the Irish Post Office accounts from 1817 to 1831 remain unaudited to the present day.

Lord Althorp was at this time Chancellor of the Exchequer, and the position which he assumed towards the Post Office was probably unique. Ordinarily, between the Treasury and the Post Office there is a certain amount of antagonism which, deplorable as it may be, is not difficult to understand. The Post Office wants to spend money; the Treasury wants to save it. The Post Office knows by experience that it must sow before it can reap; the Treasury, while ready enough to reap, has a rooted aversion to sowing, and resolutely shuts its eyes to the fact that between the two processes there is a direct and necessary connection. All this was reversed in Althorp's time. Often, during his tenure of office, might be witnessed the strange spectacle of a Chancellor of the Exchequer urging the Post Office to adopt some improvement, and the Post Office attempting to frighten him with the bogey of cost.

The first matter on which Althorp brought his authority to bear was the boundary of the general post delivery. The limits of this delivery were irregular and capricious in the extreme. Of two streets, possibly adjoining streets, one might receive its general post letters for the general post rate alone, while the other, though at no greater distance from St. Martin's-le-Grand, had to pay the twopenny rate as well.

The question now forced itself into prominence. Belgrave Square had been laid out, and the houses were being occupied as fast as they could be built. Those of the occupiers who were members of Parliament found to their chagrin that every letter they received cost them 2d., for the franking privilege did not clear the twopenny post; and, of course, by those who were not members of Parliament, 2d. had to be paid in addition to any other postage to which their letters might be liable. Althorp insisted that the general post limits should be not only extended but fixed on some definite principle. But what was the principle to be? Contiguity of building? This was held to be impracticable. A line drawn on such a basis would extend beyond Brentford on the west to Hampstead and Highgate on the north, and beyond Clapham on the south. A line drawn according to parishes would be little better. The parish of St. Pancras, which nearly touched Holborn in its southern extremity, extended as far as Finchley in the north, and the parish of Lambeth reached nearly to Croydon.

Another course would be to draw a circle of which the Post Office should be the centre, and let all letters within this circle be delivered free; but even with a radius of no more than three miles, the additional cost would be £25,000 a year. This was an outlay which the Post Office could not recommend, and, if it were incurred, the Government must take the responsibility. Althorp was not to be daunted, and after April 1831 the general post limits extended for a distance of three miles from St. Martin's-le-Grand. A little later, the threepenny post was extended to a radius of twelve miles. This, boon as it was considered to be sixty years ago, was shorter by some miles than the radius of the penny post when Queen Anne ascended the throne.

Althorp was hardly less determined on the subject of the packets. It had been a matter of principle with Freeling, that to all places beyond the sea to which there was regular communication the Post Office should carry its own mails. That they should be carried in vessels belonging to private persons, however respectable these persons might be, appeared to him to be unworthy of the English Government, and on this ground many an advantageous offer had been refused.

Althorp held a different opinion, and an opportunity soon offered of carrying his own view into effect. From Harwich the mails to Holland and to Hamburg were still carried by sailing packet, and the merchants of London, regarding this as an anachronism, urged that the sailing packets might be replaced by steam packets. The request was not unreasonable, but, unwilling that the Government should be at the cost of substituting one description of packet for the other, Althorp directed that the service should be put up to public competition. Here we see the first application of a principle which in the result has furnished us with a fleet of packets such as no other country in the world can produce. The tender of the General Steam Navigation Company was accepted, though saddled with the condition that its vessels should start from the Thames. This was a death-blow to Harwich. The sailing packets for Sweden were, indeed, still retained there; but in little more than eighteen months the Swedish Government contracted for the mails to be forwarded from Hull, and Harwich as a packet station was closed.

But of all the changes which Althorp introduced perhaps the most important, and certainly the one which excited most opposition at the Post Office, was the abolition of the newspaper privilege. The number of newspapers sent by post from London into the country had, within the last fifty or sixty years, increased enormously. In 1764 they averaged 3160 a day, in 1790 the daily average was 12,600, and in 1830 it had risen to 41,412. The rate of increase, moreover, was advancing. In 1829 the total number of such newspapers was 11,862,000, and in 1830 12,962,000; and more than one-tenth part of the whole number was supplied by the clerks of the roads.

The news-vendors now took the matter up in earnest. A general meeting was held to protest against the Post Office servants being any longer allowed to compete with the private dealers, and a petition to the same effect was presented to Parliament. This called forth a vigorous rejoinder from Freeling, and it is interesting to note by what arguments he defended his position. So far, he said, from the news-vendors having any ground of complaint against the Post Office servants, it is the Post Office servants who have reason to complain of the news vendors. For their own interest and advantage a few persons engaged in a trade of modern creation are endeavouring by clamour to deprive others of the remains of an old and long-established privilege, which they exercise not only under the sanction of immemorial usage, but by the direct authority of Acts of Parliament. It is not as though the public were interested in the question. The public have absolutely no interest in it, except indeed to this extent—that, if what remains of the privilege be withdrawn, they will be asked to compensate those whose incomes are reduced in consequence, and to provide higher salaries for their successors; and this "for the sole purpose of transferring their authorised official remuneration to the pockets of a few individuals who, having been admitted to a participation in what was originally an exclusive privilege, have now thought proper to set up a claim to the whole."

Such were Freeling's arguments, but Althorp was not convinced by them. By his direction the privilege was withdrawn as from the 5th of April 1834, and those whose incomes suffered were handsomely compensated. Thus ended a practice which had existed from the first establishment of the Post Office, and which, while the Post Office was still in its infancy, may perhaps have had this to justify it—that except for the franking privilege possessed by the clerks of the roads the provinces would probably have had to go without even the few copies of newspapers which at that time found their way there.

It may appear strange that, while Althorp was thus applying his sturdy common sense to the affairs of the Post Office, no steps were taken to correct what most needed correction—the exorbitant rates of postage. Our own belief is that in a very short time, had the Government of which he was a member remained in office, a reduction would have been made, and that it was to this result that he and Richmond, who worked hand in hand together, were preparing the way. As to Richmond's views on the matter there can be little doubt. Under previous Governments the Post Office had been accustomed in exceptional cases to appeal to the Chancellor of the Exchequer to mitigate the severity of its own rates by the exercise of a dispensing power; but Richmond set his face against the practice, insisting that the law should be obeyed until it was altered; and, after being released from the trammels of office, he was one of the first to propose an alteration.

But if such were indeed Althorp and Richmond's intention, we cannot regret that it was not carried into effect. The illustrious man who gave us penny postage had not yet directed his attention to the subject; and, as he tells us himself, it was with him a matter of long and careful consideration whether he should devote his energies to the reform of the Post Office or to the improvement of the printing machine. If in 1834 only a moderate reduction had been made in the extortionate rates of postage which were then in force, Rowland Hill might not have embarked upon his plan, and, even if he had done so, that plan might have failed to evoke from the public sufficient support to overcome opposition in high quarters. In proportion to the extent of the evil did men welcome the remedy.

Meanwhile, although the demand for cheap postage had not yet taken shape, profound dissatisfaction existed with the conduct of the Post Office. This, under the reformed Parliament, was perhaps to be expected in any case; but there were special circumstances which contributed to the result. Nearly five years had elapsed since the Royal Commission of Inquiry had reported upon the Post Office, and nothing had since been done to carry its recommendations into effect.

It is not difficult to understand this inaction. In Freeling's view the Post Office had been brought to a pitch of perfection such as it had never reached before, and he regarded it as little short of sacrilege that a body of outside novices should presume to lay its hands upon the sacred ark which he had now for more than a generation been moulding into form. Of the change of opinion which the labours of the Commission had wrought he appears to have been utterly unconscious. Hitherto the Post Office had been regarded as a marvellous mystery, which none but experts could understand. This mystery had now been invaded, and men were beginning to wonder, not, as in the past, at the things which the Post Office was able to do, but how it was that these things were not done better.

The Commission had also brought to light the existence of abuses, and these on one pretext or another had remained uncorrected. We will give a single instance. The Money Order Office had been established in 1792 with the object of facilitating the transmission of small sums from one part of the country to the other by means of orders drawn on the different postmasters. The plan was excellent and deserved success. The only objection to it was that the enterprise was a private one, undertaken by a few Post Office servants for their own benefit, and that to make it remunerative to the projectors required from the authorities an amount of favour which they had no right to bestow. Originally there had been no limit to the amount for which a money order might be drawn;[97] but long before 1829, in order to prevent interference with the banking interest, the limit had been fixed at £5:5s.; and the commission chargeable was at the rate of 8d. in the £1 on the sum remitted. Of this amount 3d. went to the postmaster who issued the order, 3d. to the postmaster who paid it, and the residue to the proprietors. [98]

Seeing that the postage on a single letter between two towns no farther apart than London and Bristol was at this time 10d., it will be obvious that in respect to orders for small sums the enterprise would have been conducted at a loss unless the correspondence on money order business had been exempt from postage. And such indeed was the case. All letters passing from London to the country were impressed with the official stamp, and those passing from the country to London were enclosed in printed covers addressed to the secretary, and bearing, immediately below the secretary's name, that of the proprietors, "Stow and Company." For correspondence between themselves on money order business the postmasters were supplied with franks sent down from London in blank. Strongly as the Commission of Inquiry had animadverted on this abuse, nothing had been done to correct it, and the franking privilege was, for money order purposes, being as freely used as ever.

The returns which the House of Commons called for about this time, and the returns which the Post Office furnished, shew, more forcibly perhaps than anything else, in what direction men's minds were tending, and how hollow was the foundation on which a part of the Post Office system rested. More than sixty years had elapsed since the Law Courts decided that inhabitants of post towns were entitled to a gratuitous delivery of their letters. The House now inquired at how many post towns a charge on delivery was still being made, and by what authority. The return furnished by the Post Office shewed the number of towns to be eighty-nine, and after giving as the authority for the charge "immemorial usage," went on to state that "the payment is not compulsory if the parties choose to object."

It was still the practice to hold up to a strong lamplight every letter that passed through the post in order to see whether it was a single or a double one; and the House called upon the Post Office to state by what authority this was done. The Post Office, having no authority to adduce, returned an evasive reply. The House next called for the number of persons who had been prosecuted in the course of the year for the illegal conveyance of letters. The Post Office return shewed that on this ground, during the last twelve months, as many as 341 prosecutions had taken place, many of them involving a large, and some of them a very large, number of persons, and that the cases were still more numerous in which, in order to avoid prosecution, the transgressors had submitted to fines. And how had the revenue been prospering meanwhile? A return called for by the House in April 1834 answers the question. During the last ten years, despite the increase of population, the net Post Office revenue had actually declined. In 1824 the receipts were £2,055,000 gross and £1,438,000 net, as against £1,391,000 net and £2,062,000 gross in 1833.

In 1834 Earl Grey was succeeded by Viscount Melbourne; and one of the first acts of the new Government was to appoint another Commission of Inquiry into the Post Office, with directions to ascertain and report how it was that the recommendations of the former Commission had not been carried out. These recommendations were now set down one by one, and the Post Office was called upon to explain, opposite to each, whether any and, if so, what steps had been taken to give effect to it. One or two of them had indeed been adopted—such, for instance, as the recommendation that Post Office servants should cease to deal in newspapers—but only under compulsion. Others affecting the internal administration of the Post Office were certainly not feasible. But there remained not a few which, while excellent in themselves, had been discarded on the merest pretext.

The Commissioners had recommended that the "early," that is the preferential, delivery of letters should be discontinued. The Post Office replied that it was impossible. The Commissioners had recommended that, instead of the receiving houses for general post letters being separate and distinct from those for the letters of the twopenny post, every receiving house should take in letters of both kinds. The Post Office replied that the existing arrangement was the best adapted not only to the convenience of the public but to the business of the department. The Commissioners had recommended that the letter-carriers, instead of being separated into general post, twopenny post, and foreign letter-carriers, should all form one corps and deliver letters of every description. The Post Office replied—a reply all the more extraordinary inasmuch as the very arrangement which the Commissioners recommended was already in force both in Edinburgh and Dublin—that "it would be productive of the greatest confusion and delay."

The last of the recommendations to which we shall refer was that "the total charge upon all letters should be expressed in one taxation." The Post Office replied that it was "not possible for country postmasters to know the precise line of demarcation between the general post and twopenny post deliveries." In other words, no postmaster could know what, in the case of letters for London—and, it might have been added, for any other town than his own—the proper charge should be. This was no pretext. It was, on the contrary, perfectly true; and perhaps no more striking testimony could be afforded to the unsoundness of the system then in vogue.

It is impossible to conceive that on Freeling's part there can have been anything in the shape of contumacy, still less of defiance; but we are by no means sure that the House of Commons did not incline to that view. Be that as it may, however, the Post Office was in bad odour, and an unfortunate series of incidents which occurred about this time little tended to remove the unfavourable impression which the unwillingness to carry out the Commissioners' recommendations had created. The House, at the instance of the Select Committee on Steam Navigation, had called for a return of the casualties which within a given period had happened to the Irish packets. The return furnished by the Post Office omitted two accidents in which one of the members of the Committee had himself assisted; and the Committee forthwith ordered the attendance of a witness from the Post Office to explain the omission. Another return contained obvious errors, and was sent back to the Post Office to be corrected.

But the two returns which excited most comment referred to the mileage allowance received by the mail-coach contractors, and to the Money Order Office. As regards the mileage allowance the only reply vouchsafed by the Post Office was that it "has not the means of furnishing any account of the amount paid." The return as regards the Money Order Office was still more unfortunate. The ground on which this office had been condemned by the Revenue Inquiry Commissioners was that it was carried on for the benefit of individuals, and yet in so far as its correspondence was exempt from postage, at the expense of the revenue. Several years had since passed, and the House, not doubting that the abuse had been corrected, called for a return shewing the amount of postage derived from letters containing money orders, and to what purpose it was applied. "The Money Order Office"—thus ran the return which the Post Office furnished—" is a private establishment, and the business is carried on by private capital under the sanction of the postmaster-general; but as no accounts connected in any degree with it are kept at the Post Office, no return can be made by the postmaster-general to the order of the House of Commons." The House was highly incensed, and ordered that, both as regards the Money Order Office and the mileage allowance, proper returns should be rendered at once.

The energy of the new Commission had now nearly brought the Post Office into trouble. The contract for the supply of mail-coaches was in the hands of Mr. Vidler of Millbank, who had held it for more than forty years, and little had been done during this period to improve the construction of the vehicles he supplied. Designed after the pattern in vogue at the end of the last century, they were, as compared with the stage-coaches, not only heavy and unsightly but inferior both in point of speed and accommodation. Moreover, the charge made for them, namely, 2-1/2d. a mile in England and 2d. a mile in Scotland, was considered to be high; and the Commissioners, altogether dissatisfied with the manner in which the contract had been performed, arranged with the Government not only that the service should be put up to public tender, but that Vidler should be excluded from the competition. This decision was arrived at in July 1835, and the contract expired on the 5th of January following. To invite tenders would occupy time, and, after that mail-coaches would have to be built sufficient in number to supply the whole of England and Scotland. A period of five or six months was obviously not enough for the purpose, and overtures were made to Vidler to continue his contract for half a year longer. Vidler, incensed at the treatment he had received, flatly refused. Not a day, not an hour, beyond the stipulated time would he extend his contract, and on the 5th of January 1836 all the mail-coaches in Great Britain would be withdrawn from the roads.

A man less loyal than Freeling or endued with less generous instincts might have felt a twinge of satisfaction at this result of interference with what he considered his own domain. But such emotion, if indeed he felt it, was not suffered to appear. With a difficulty to overcome, some of his old energy returned, and when the 5th of January arrived there was not a road in the kingdom from Wick to Penzance on which a new mail-coach was not running.

It was now that the mail-coaches reached their prime. Eight or nine miles an hour had hitherto been their highest speed, and now, with vehicles of lighter build, the speed was advanced to ten miles an hour and even more. Truth compels us to add that while the fastest mail-coach on the road, the coach between Liverpool and Preston, travelled at the rate of ten miles and five furlongs an hour, a private coach accomplished within the hour rather more than eleven miles. This was the coach between Edinburgh and Aberdeen, of which Captain Barclay of Ury was the proprietor. Besides coachman and guard it carried fifteen passengers, namely, four inside and eleven outside, while a mail-coach carried four in and four out or eight altogether. Nor would Captain Barclay admit that, in order to attain this high rate of speed, recourse need be had to anything like furious driving. Nothing more, he maintained, was necessary than to keep the horses at a "swinging trot."

Freeling's success in averting a breakdown with the mail-coaches did little or nothing to arrest the tide which had set in against him. After exercising an influence such as probably no civil servant had exercised before, he found himself discredited and the object of vehement and not over-scrupulous attack. Of the ministers under whose orders he had acted not a few had passed away, and none were in a position to share his responsibility, while their successors only knew him as identified with a system which had become unpopular. Owing to an unusually rapid succession of postmasters-general,[99] he was without even the solace and support which a chief of some years' standing might have given him. Single-handed, the old man had maintained a gallant defence; but his spirit was now broken. In the midst of his exertions to prevent any interruption of travelling facilities the House of Commons had called for a return which was calculated to wound him deeply. This return implied not only that he had been guilty of gross mismanagement, but that his salary was higher than he was entitled to receive, that he was drawing unauthorised emoluments, and that the Post Office was made subordinate to his personal interests.

To the outside world Freeling maintained much the same demeanour as before, and few would have suspected the weight that pressed at his heart; but in the solitude of his study he was an altered man. There he brooded over the past and contrasted it with the present. Notes jotted down haphazard on official papers that chanced to be on his table reveal the inner workings of his mind. We know few sadder records. He recalls the time when Governments consulted him and he stood high in favour with the public. He cannot forget how, in the course of debate in the House of Commons, his own proficiency and devotion to duty were urged as reasons for not retaining the second appointment of postmaster. In the recollection of those happy days he endeavours to find consolation for the calumny and detraction of the present. He repudiates as unfounded the charge that he has long ceased to consult the interests of the public, and affirms that in this cause he has of late years laboured even more abundantly than he did of old.

Then there is a break, after which he takes up his pen again. "Cheap postage,"—to this effect he writes. "What is this men are talking about? Can it be that all my life I have been in error? If I, then others—others whose behests I have been bound to obey. To make the Post Office revenue as productive as possible was long ago impressed upon me by successive ministers as a duty which I was under a solemn obligation to discharge. And not only long ago. Is it not within the last six months that the present Chancellor of the Exchequer[100] has charged me not to let the revenue go down? What! You, Freeling, brought up and educated as you have been, are you going to lend yourself to these extravagant schemes? You, with your four-horse mail-coaches too. Where else in the world does the merchant or manufacturer have the materials of his trade carried for him gratuitously or at so low a rate as to leave no margin of profit?"

Here the manuscript abruptly ends. It is dated the 24th of June 1836. Within sixteen days from that date Francis Freeling was no more.

We have done. From 1836 downwards the story of the Post Office is told, far better than we could tell it, in the Autobiography of Sir Rowland Hill and the reports which, since 1854, the department has issued annually. The story of the preceding period is less well known, if indeed it be known at all. To tell the earlier story—to trace the Post Office from its humble beginnings down to the time when the illustrious reformer took it in hand— this has been the extent of our object, and no one perhaps is more conscious than ourselves how imperfectly it has been accomplished.

APPENDIX

SUCCESSION OF POSTMASTERS-GENERAL
from 1660 to 1836

From 1660 to 1667 the Post Office was in farm, the farmers being—

1660 to 1663.
Henry Bishopp. Rent, £21,500.

Bishopp surrendered his patent, which was for seven years, in 1663.

1663 to 1667.
(Being residue of Bishopp's term.)
Daniel O'Neile. Rent, £21,500.

1667 to 1685.
Henry, Earl of Arlington.
Rent for later part of the term, £43,000.

Office managed, at first, by Sir John Bennet, Lord Arlington's brother, and afterwards by Colonel Roger Whitley.

1685 to 1689.
Lawrence Hyde, Earl of Rochester.
(For part of the time Lord Treasurer.)[101]

Office managed by Philip Frowde, Esq., under the title of Governor.

July 1689 to March 1690.
Colonel John Wildman.

1690 to 1708.
Sir Robert Cotton, Knight, and
Sir Thomas Frankland, Bart.

1708 to 1715.
Sir Thomas Frankland, Bart., and
Sir John Evelyn, Bart.

1715 to 1721.
Charles, Lord Cornwallis, and
James Craggs, Esq.

1721 to 1725.
Edward Carteret, Esq., and
Galfridus Walpole, Esq.

1725 to 1732.
Edward Carteret, Esq., and
Edward Harrison, Esq.

Christmas 1732.
Edward Carteret alone to Midsummer 1733.

1733 to 1739.
Edward Carteret, Esq., and
Thomas, Lord Lovell, afterwards Earl of Leicester.

1739 to 1744.
Thomas, Lord Lovell, and
Sir John Eyles, Bart.

1744 to 1745.
Thomas, Earl of Leicester (sometime Lord Lovell) alone.

1745 to 1758.
Thomas, Earl of Leicester, and
Sir Everard Fawkener, Knight.

1758 to 1759.
Thomas, Earl of Leicester, alone.

June 2, 1759 to November 27, 1762.
William, Earl of Bessborough, and
Hon. Robert Hampden.

November 27, 1762 to September 23, 1763.
John, Earl of Egmont, and
Hon. Robert Hampden.

September 23, 1763 to July 19, 1765.
Thomas, Lord Hyde, and
Hon. Robert Hampden.

July 19, 1765 to December 29, 1766.
William, Earl of Bessborough, and
Thomas, Lord Grantham.

December 29, 1766 to April 26, 1768.
Wills, Earl of Hillsborough, and
Francis, Lord Le Despencer.

April 26, 1768 to January 16, 1771.
John, Earl of Sandwich, and
Francis, Lord Le Despencer.

January 16, 1771 to December 11, 1781.
Francis, Lord Le Despencer, and
Right Hon. Henry Frederick Thynne, afterwards Carteret.

December 11, 1781 to January 24, 1782.
Right Hon. Henry Frederick Carteret (sometime Thynne) alone.

January 24 to April 25, 1782.
William, Viscount Barrington, and
Right Hon. Henry Frederick Carteret.

April 25, 1782 to May 1, 1783.
Charles, Earl of Tankerville, and
Right Hon. Henry Frederick Carteret.

May 1, 1783 to January 7, 1784.
Thomas, Lord Foley, and
Right Hon. Henry Frederick Carteret.

January 7, 1784 to September 19, 1786.
Charles, Earl of Tankerville, and
Right Hon. Henry Frederick Carteret. (Created Baron Carteret,
January 29, 1784.)

September 19 to December 10, 1786.
Thomas, Earl of Clarendon, and
Henry Frederick, Lord Carteret.

December 10, 1786 to July 6, 1787.
Henry Frederick, Lord Carteret, alone.

July 6, 1787 to September 19, 1789.
Henry Frederick, Lord Carteret, and
Thomas, Lord Walsingham.

September 19, 1789 to March 13, 1790.
Thomas, Lord Walsingham, and
John, Earl of Westmorland.

March 13, 1790 to July 28, 1794.
Thomas, Lord Walsingham, and
Philip, Earl of Chesterfield.

July 28, 1794 to March 1, 1798.
Philip, Earl of Chesterfield, and
George, Earl of Leicester.

March 1, 1798 to February 27, 1799.
George, Earl of Leicester, and
William, Lord Auckland.

February 27, 1799 to March 31, 1801.
William, Lord Auckland, and
George, Lord Gower.

March 31, 1801 to July 19, 1804.

William, Lord Auckland, and
Lord Charles Spencer.

July 19, 1804 to February 20, 1806.
Lord Charles Spencer and
James, Duke of Montrose.

February 20, 1806 to May 5, 1807.
Robert, Earl of Buckinghamshire, and
John Joshua, Earl of Carysfort.

May 5, 1807 to June 6, 1814.
John, Earl of Sandwich, and
Thomas, Earl of Chichester.

June 6 to September 30, 1814.
Thomas, Earl of Chichester, alone.

September 30, 1814 to April 6, 1816.
Thomas, Earl of Chichester, and
Richard, Earl of Clancarty.

April 6, 1816 to June 13, 1823.
Thomas, Earl of Chichester, and
James, Marquess of Salisbury.

Since Lord Salisbury's death on the 13th of June 1823, no second
Postmaster-General has been appointed.

June 13, 1823 to July 4, 1826.
Thomas, Earl of Chichester.

July 4, 1826 to September 17, 1827.
Lord Frederick Montague.

September 17, 1827 to December 14, 1830.
William, Duke of Manchester.

December 14, 1830 to July 5, 1834.
Charles, Duke of Richmond.

By his first patent, dated the 14th of December 1830, the Duke was appointed Postmaster-General of Great Britain; and by a second patent, dated the 14th of April 1831, he was appointed Postmaster-General of Great Britain and Ireland.

July 5 to December 31, 1834.
Francis Nathaniel, Marquess Conyngham.

December 31, 1834 to May 8, 1835.
William, Lord Maryborough.

May 8 to May 30, 1835.
Francis Nathaniel, Marquess Conyngham.

May 30, 1835, to September 15, 1841.
Thomas William, Earl of Lichfield.

SUCCESSION OF SECRETARIES TO THE POST OFFICE down to 1836

The appointment of Secretary was created by Treasury Warrant dated the 20th of June 1694.

1694 to 1700.
Name uncertain; but probably Willboyl.

[In 1694 the Postmasters-General urge the creation of the appointment of Secretary; in 1697 they speak of "having sent our Secretary down to Worcester"; and in October 1701, when reporting on a paper which had been referred to them as far back as June 1699, they explain that "by the death of our late Secretary ye paper has been mislaid and but very lately recovered." That there was a Secretary during this period is, therefore, beyond doubt.

During the same period the Post Office letter books are written in a handwriting as peculiar as it is good; and in the same handwriting, of the identity of which there can be no question, there is in the Frankland-Blaithwaite correspondence, until lately in the possession of Sir Thomas Phillipps, a letter from the General Post Office dated the 27th of May 1697, and docketed thus, the docket having obviously been written at the time of receipt:—"From Mr. Willboyl, Commissioner of the Post Office." Now, Commissioner of the Post Office he certainly was not, there being at that time no such appointment; but it is probable that he was Secretary, and that with this official title, which had been only recently given, Blaithwaite was not acquainted.]

1700 to 1714.
Benjamin Waterhouse.

1714 to 1715.
Henry Weston.

1715 to 1721.
James Craggs.

1721 to (about) 1730.
Joseph Godman.

(About) 1730 to 1737.
W. Rouse.

1737 to 1738.
Thomas Robinson.

September 1738 to July 1742.
John David Barbutt.

July 1742 to December 1762.
George Shelvocke.

December 1762 to July 1765.
Anthony Todd.

July 1765 to January 1768.
Henry Potts.

January 1768 to June 1798.
Anthony Todd (again).

June 1798 to July 1836.
Francis Freeling.

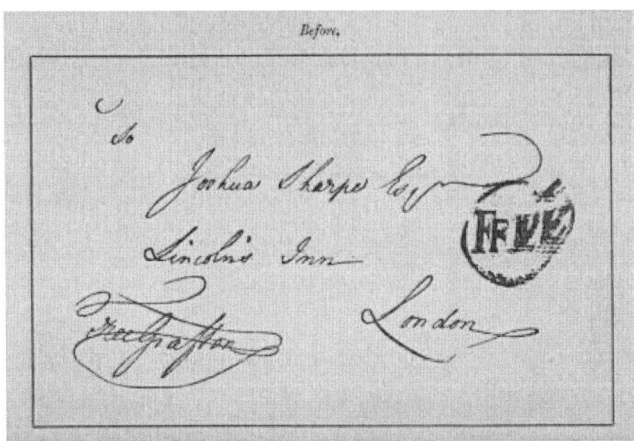

FACSIMILES of FRANKS written before and after 1784, when the obligation to date was imposed.

Before.
The Duke of Grafton, First Lord of the Treasury from 1766 to 1770, commonly called Junius Grafton from the attacks made upon him by Junius.

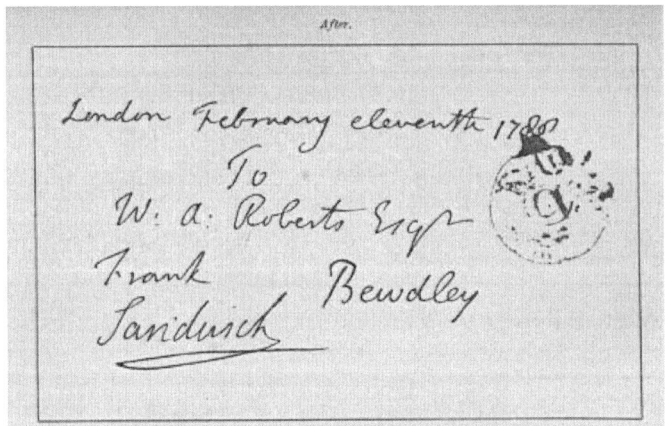

After.
The Earl of Sandwich, nicknamed by the satirists of the period Jemmy Twitcher. "See Jemmy Twitcher shambles—stop, stop, thief"—an allusion to his shambling gait.
Lord Sandwich was postmaster-general from 1768 to 1771, and afterwards First Lord of the Admiralty.

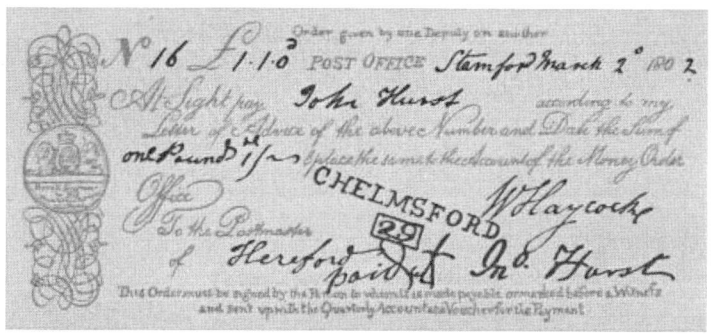

FACSIMILE of a PAID MONEY ORDER of the year 1802.

INDEX

Abdy, Sir Robert

Abercorn, James, Earl of, his unreasonable complaint

Absenteeism, in England,
in Ireland

Alien Office, assists the Post Office in procuring foreign newspapers

Allen, Ralph, postmaster of Bath, takes in farm the bye and cross-post letters,
conditions of his contract,
success of his enterprise,
is thwarted by the postmasters,
his contract renewed,
nature of his plan and his special qualifications for carrying it into effect,
his local knowledge,
his difficulties with the postmasters, *seq.*;
as a means of check lays down certain propositions,
instances of imposition practised by postmasters,
by post-boys,
by carriers and others concerned in the illegal conveyance of letters,
the liberality of his arrangements,
his course of procedure contrasted with that of the postmasters-general,
pays higher rent and increases the frequency of the post every seven years when his contract is renewed,
his injunction about the use of expresses,
his death,
his character,
is an object of jealousy to Palmer

Alphabet,
ingenious one in use at Belfast

Althorp, John Charles, Viscount, urges on Post Office improvements,
fixes the limits of the general post delivery,
throws the packet service open to public competition,
abolishes the newspaper privilege enjoyed by the clerks of the roads,
contemplates apparently a reduction of postage

America, posts set up in,
first postmaster of New York,
and of Virginia and Maryland,
establishment of what was virtually a penny post between England and
America,
American posts become self-supporting,
postmasters ejected from their offices

Amsterdam, practice at, on arrival of the mails

Anne, Queen, treatment of letters for, when in residence at Newmarket

Antelope packet, Captain Curtis, gallant action with privateer

Apertures, introduction of, on the outside of post offices

Argyll, John, Duke of

Arlington, Henry Bennet, Earl of, appointed postmaster-general

Armit, secretary to the Post Office in Ireland, displaced by Lees

Ashburnham manuscripts

Ashurst, Mr. Justice, his judgment touching the free delivery of letters

Aston, Mr. Justice, his judgment touching the free delivery of letters

Attorneys, their provisional resolution to withhold postage on writs,
hold appointments in the Dublin Post Office

Auckland, William Lord, postmaster-general, his pleasantries

Auditors of the imprests, note

Austria, liberties taken with post-horses by travellers in, *note*

Aylsham, Norfolk, post established to in 1733

Baker, Sir George, physician to George the Third

Bank of England notes, robbery of, from mail evokes important legal decision,
origin of cutting bank notes when sent by post,
contemplated reduction of postage on letters containing second halves of bank notes

Bankers' franks, meaning of term, *note*

Barbutt, John David, secretary to the Post Office

Barclay, Captain, of Ury, high speed of his coach

Barclay's plot, expresses sent on discovery of

Barham, Edmund, packet agent at Dover, terms of his agreement with Walcot, secretary to the Post Office in Ireland

Barlow, clerk in the secretary's office, modifies the practice of the Dead Letter Office

Barnstaple, private post set up to Exeter in 1633

Bath asserts its right to a free delivery,
right admitted and letter-carrier appointed,
slowness of post between Bath and London,
amount of toll between the same towns,
Post Office Establishment at Bath and amount of the postmaster's salary in 1792

Beccaria, Bonesana, his essay on Crimes and Punishments

Belfast, ingenious "alphabet" in use at,
peculiar usage of delivery

Belgrave Square, included in the limits of the general post delivery

Bell, Colonel, comptroller of the Inland Office, particulars of charge against, *note*

Bells, letters collected by ringing of, introduction of system, and its termination, *note*;
bellmen in England and in Ireland paid on different principle,

Bernard, Sir Robert

Besant's patent coaches

Bethnal Green, a second penny on penny post letters improperly charged at

Bianconi, Charles, his enterprise

Bigg, Stephen, his enterprise as a farmer of the posts

Billingsley, Henry, a broker, carries letters of foreign merchants, and is consigned to prison

Bills of exchange and of lading to and from foreign parts exempt from postage until 1801, exemption then withdrawn

Birmingham, one of many towns in which a free delivery of letters had ceased,
free delivery restored and letter-carrier appointed,
salary of postmaster in 1792,
penny post opened at

Bishopp, Henry, farmer of the posts,

"Black-box"; the box in which the correspondence of the Secretary of State for Scotland was carried

Blaithwaite, William, Secretary of War, remonstrated with on his abuse of the franking privilege

Blome's *Britannia*

Bonnor, Charles, deputy comptroller-general of the Post Office, his conduct in the matter of the king's coach,
delays replies to the postmaster-general's inquiries,
practises deception,
his base ingratitude,
is suspended by Palmer,
suspension removed by the postmasters-general,
his treachery,
receives the reward of infamy

Boulton and Watt build the first steamboats used by the Post Office

Bourne, Frederick, clerk in the foreign department of the Post Office; suggests the establishment of a Ship Letter Office

Bournemouth, mode of receiving its letters in 1854, *note*

Bowen, passenger by packet; brings news of the victory at Oudenarde

Boyle, Henry, Secretary of State, charges the packet agent at Harwich with receiving a bribe

Bracken, Henry, author of *The Gentleman's Pocket Farrier*, his device to obtain exemption from postage

Braithwaite, Daniel, clerk to the postmasters-general, his honesty of purpose

Brighton, salary of the postmaster of, in 1792

Brill, The,

Bristol, course of post between Bristol and Exeter in 1660,
and in 1696,
salary of the postmaster of, in 1690,
and in 1792,
first mail-coach starts from Bristol,
penny post opened there,
revision of postmaster's salary in 1686, Appendix, *note*

Brown, sub-agent of packets at Ostend, his clandestine letter

Brunel, Sir Marc Isambard, offers to construct a steam engine for the Post Office packets

Buckingham, George Villiers, Duke of, letter endorsed by, in 1627

Buckingham, George Villiers, Duke of, son of the preceding, tedious course of letter addressed to, in 1666, .

Buckingham, George Grenville Nugent Temple, Marquis of, Lord Lieutenant of Ireland, deprecates reduction of packet establishment at Holyhead

Burlamachi, Philip, is appointed Master of the Posts,
his title contested,
is consigned to prison

Bye-letters, probable meaning of the term in Queen Elizabeth's reign,
its certain meaning in 1690 and after,
postage upon bye-letters intercepted, *note*;
Bye-Letter Office

Bye-nights

Byng, Sir George,

Cadogan, Brigadier-General, packet detained for

Camden, John Jeffreys, Earl, promotes Palmer's plan,
gives to Pitt Palmer's version of his differences with the postmasters-general

Candles, inordinate supply of, to Post Office servants

Canning, George, charges the Post Office with forestalling his intelligence

Carlisle, salary of postmaster of, in 1792

Carriers allowed to carry letters under restrictions,
restrictions more clearly defined

Carteret, Edward, postmaster-general from 1721 to 1739. *See* Postmasters-General, Part IV.

Carteret, Henry Frederick, Lord, postmaster-general from January 1771 to September 1789. *See* Postmasters-General, Parts V. and VI.

Carts, first employment of, in London for bringing letters to the General Post Office

Castello, a prisoner on board packet

Chalmers, George, his suggestions,
excites Palmer's jealousy

Channel Islands without an official post in 1792,
official post provided,
rates of postage

Charing Cross, opening of branch office at

Charlemont, Lord, his misunderstanding as to packet charges

Charles, Archduke,

Chelsea pensioners, their privilege of sending and receiving letters at low rates of postage withdrawn

Chenal, captain of packet, rebuked by the postmasters-general, *note*

Chepstow, the inhabitants of, though under no obligation, continue to pay pence on the delivery of their letters

Chester, in 1720 the only town outside London with two Post Offices, salary of postmaster in 1792

Chesterfield, Philip, Earl of, postmaster-general from March 1790 to March 1798. *See* Postmasters-General, Part VII.

Chichester, Thomas, Earl of, postmaster-general from May 1807 to July 1826. *See* Postmasters-General, Part VIII.

Christmas boxes, intercepted

Clancarty, Richard, Earl of, postmaster-general of Ireland from 1807 to 1809; and of England from September 1814 to April 1816. [This latter appointment he did not take up.] His decision of character, instance of, advocates facilities of communication between England and Ireland

Clarendon, Thomas, Earl of, postmaster-general from September to December 1786,

Clerks of the roads, their duties,
their salaries,
are allowed to frank newspapers,
their franking privilege invaded,
mischief resulting from a reduction of their emoluments,
their financial troubles,
extent of their newspaper business after newspapers become exempt from postage

Clermont, William Henry, Earl of, deputy postmaster-general of Ireland

Clies, Francis, captain of packet, his audacious smuggling,
his attention to religious observances,
strikes his colours

Coals supplied to Post Office servants in profligate profusion

Cobbett, William, inveighs against the early or preferential delivery,
and against the treatment of foreign newspapers

Coke, Sir John, his indignant protest against the claim of the foreign merchants to have a post of their own

Colours, special colours assigned to the Post Office boat employed in the Pool,
the colours of the packets altered at the Union with Scotland

Comer, postmaster of Tunbridge Wells in 1725

Common Council of London, The, sets up a post of their own to Scotland

Compensation for losses by the penny post,
when ceased to be given

Conspiracies against the State, to check these the original object of the Post Office monopoly,
danger chiefly apprehended from the Continent,
Coke's opinion on the subject,
the same opinion expressed in the Act of 1657

Constables, the duty of, in certain cases, to seize horses for the service of the posts,

Convention posts, establishment of,
their failure and the reason,
are gradually absorbed

Conway Bridge, additional rate of postage on letters passing over

Conyngham, Francis Nathaniel, Marquess of, postmaster-general from July 1834 to January 1835, and again from May 8 to May 30, 1835, *note*

Cornwall, its posts improved in 1704

Cornwallis, Charles, Lord, postmaster-general from 1715 to 1721. *See* Postmasters-General, Part III.

Cotton, Sir Robert, postmaster-general from 1690 to 1708. *See* Postmasters-General, Part I.

Counsel in Post Office cases required to give receipts for their fees

Country letter, meaning of term

Courier newspaper, sum paid by the, for early intelligence from the Post Office

Couriers originally employed to carry letters on affairs of State

Court, The, at one time the centre of all the posts,
a trace of the old state of things to be found in an existing statute

Court letters, definition of, in 1706, *note*;
mails detained for the Court letters,
these letters, unlike others, delivered the moment they arrived

Court-post, his duties,
duties performed by deputy

Coventry, Sir Thomas, Attorney-General, afterwards Lord Keeper, holds
De Quester's appointment to be valid,
cajoles Stanhope into surrendering his patent

Craggs, James, postmaster-general from 1715 to 1721. *See* Postmasters-
General, Part III.

Crichton, Doctor, refuses to pay his fare by packet

Cromwell, Thomas, Brian Tuke's letter to, on the paucity of the posts

Crosby, Brass

Cross-posts, first post of the kind set up,
cross-post letters, definition of the term

Croydon, postmistress of, Auckland's pleasantry on her marriage for the
third time

Culverden, captain of packet boat, engages in smuggling

Culvert, member of Parliament, expostulated with as to the irregular use
of his frank, *note*

Curtis, Alderman,

Customs, Commissioners of, lodge a complaint against the captain of the
Expedition packet,
represent that smuggling is carried on by packet from Ostend,
take proceedings against some of the Harwich packets,
are charged by the postmasters-general with unhandsome conduct,
seize the Dover mail-coach

Dacre, Lord, superscription on Protector Somerset's letter addressed to

Dartmouth, William, Lord, his attention called to the late arrival at the Post
Office of the Court letters

Dashwood, Francis, postmaster-general of Jamaica, exaction from, as a condition of his appointment

Davy, Mrs., her account of the condition of Penzance before 1784

Day, John, sent from London in 1733 to establish a post at Aylsham in Norfolk, his instructions

Dead letters, treatment of, a source of perplexity to Allen, irregular payments claimed under cover of, Dead Letter Office, returned letters charged with postage

Decypherer, the chief

De Joncourt, express clerk

Delivery, claim made by several towns to have their letters delivered free resisted by the Post Office and question tried at law, claim allowed by the Courts, decision carried out grudgingly, hour of delivery of foreign letters in 1790, early, that is preferential, delivery, hour of delivery in St. James's Square between 1820 and 1830, in the country, limits of free delivery not defined, morning delivery in London accelerated, limits of general post delivery fixed at three miles, recommendation of Royal Commission to abolish early or preferential delivery not carried out

Delivery penny, meaning of term

Denmark, Frederick the Second, King of, his letter of complaint to Queen Elizabeth, *note*

De Quester, Matthew, appointed postmaster for foreign parts out of the King's dominions, his appointment offends Lord Stanhope, is superseded by the Privy Council, is restored at the instance of Sir John Coke, assigns his patent

Derby, salary of the postmaster of, in 1792

Dereham, Sir Thomas, Court-post, his duties

Derrick, Samuel, Master of the Ceremonies at Bath, his account of Ralph Allen, *note*

Despatch of mails, hour of, in 1690,
and until 1784,
indignation caused by the change then made

Devonshire, William, Duke of, course of post between Chesterfield and Manchester altered in 1736 at the instance of

Directories,

Distances, inaccuracy of, as computed by the Post Office

Dockwra, William, establishes a penny post in London,
his right contested and case decided against him,
is granted a pension and, on the penny post being absorbed into the Post Office, is appointed comptroller,
is dismissed,
provision made by, for the care of general post letters,
contrast between Dockwra and Povey

Donlevy, William

Double letter, definition of

Dover, a packet station,
packets to Flanders provided by the packet agent,
engage in smuggling,
and bring news clandestinely,
the Dover mail-coach seized by the Customs

Drink and feast money,

Dublin, Post Office establishment at, in 1690,
penny post proposed at, in 1703,
and opened in 1773,

the clerks at the castle surrender their franking privilege,
the roof of the Dublin Post Office falls in,
office in Dublin styled British Mail Office, account of,
abuses

Dummer, Edmund, Surveyor of the Navy, builds packets for the Harwich station,
also for the West India service,
undertakes this service himself,
his miscalculations,
ill-fortune attends him,
his bankruptcy and death

Early, *i.e.* preferential, delivery,

Eastbourne, mode of receiving its letters in 1792

East India Company, send to the Post Office letters received at the India House,
object to the provisions of the Ship Letter Act,
procure its alteration,
their generosity,
unhandsome return contemplated by the Post Office

East Indies, rates of postage to the, in 1815

Edinburgh, post to, set up by the city of London,
Post Office establishment at, in 1707,
horse-post between Edinburgh and Glasgow refused by the Treasury,
course of post between London and Edinburgh accelerated in 1758,
and increased in frequency in 1765,
Edinburgh Post Office falls into decay,
penny post established at

Eldon, John, Lord, reluctantly assents to the giving of repressive powers

Elections, Parliamentary, Post Office servants prohibited from intermeddling in,
and from voting at

Ellenborough, Edward, Lord

Evelyn, Sir John, postmaster-general from 1708 to 1715. *See* Postmasters-General, Part II.

Exeter, private post set up between, and Barnstaple in 1633,
course of post between Exeter and Bristol in 1660,
in 1696,
salary of postmaster in 1792

Expresses,
when to be sent from Dover,
employment of, becomes more general about the middle of the eighteenth century,
is jealously restricted,
their number reduced on the establishment of mail-coaches,
fees on expresses,
express sent daily to and from Ireland after the Union

Express clerks

Express office, Haymarket

Eyles, Sir John, postmaster-general from 1739 to 1744

Falmouth, packet station opened at, in 1689,
closed and reopened,
packet regulations,
systematic smuggling,
packet agent also victualler

Fares, by packet to Holland before and after 1689,
by steam packet and by sailing packet, comparative statement

Farmers of the Post Office, their popularity and the reason of it,
are ruined by increase of postage and converted into managers,
as managers prove useless

Farra, John, is supplied with a special travelling order, *note*

Faversham, marriage of the postmistress

Fees, exacted from postmasters,
received by the chief sorter on the occasion of royal birthdays,
on expresses,
on the registration of foreign letters

Ferrers, Countess

Fielding, Henry, his tribute to Ralph Allen

"Fifth-clause" posts,

Firearms, worthless quality of those originally supplied to mail guards

Fire of London, intelligence of, takes five days to reach Worthing

Flemings, resort to London, where they introduce the manufacture of wool
into cloth,
instance of value set upon cloth made in London, *note*

Flying coach,

Flying packet, meaning of the term,

Flying-post, *note*

Foreign bottoms, employment of, by the Post Office illegal

Foreign merchants claim to set up a post of their own to the Continent,
claim conceded by the Privy Council,
and repudiated by Coke

Foster, John, Chancellor of the Irish Exchequer, his efforts to improve
communication with Ireland

France, Post Office treaty with, imperfectly observed,
a new one made and its onerous conditions,
postage on letters from, increased,
improvement of communication with, deprecated by merchants of London

Franking, abuses of, in 1711, and means taken to check them,
effect of franking upon the Post Office revenue,

becomes the subject of Parliamentary enactment,
conditions altered,
franking in Ireland,
of newspapers inland,
franking privilege possessed by the clerks at Dublin Castle surrendered,
franks to be dated and are otherwise restricted,
further restrictions imposed,
franks do not clear either the penny, the twopenny, or the convention posts,
franking privilege withdrawn in the case of newspapers to and from the Colonies,
privilege remains in the case of newspapers to and from the Continent,
and in the case of newspapers circulating within the United Kingdom gradually disappears,
franked letters charged immediately on dissolution of Parliament,
franking privilege withheld from Roman Catholic Peers,
abuse of franking in the case of the Money Order Office,
specimens of franks, Appendix

Frankland, Sir Thomas, postmaster-general from 1690 to 1715. *See* Postmasters-General, Part I.

Frankland, William, son of the preceding, Comptroller of the Inland Office, in attendance upon the Queen at Newmarket

Franklin, Benjamin, his dismissal,
amicable relations with, not suspended

Free delivery. *See* Delivery

Freeling, Sir Francis, appointed surveyor,
appointed joint secretary with Todd,
devises new arrangements for the sorting of the American and West Indian mails,
his project for guarding the horse and cross-posts,
becomes sole secretary,
his craze for high rates of postage,
his zeal in repressing illicit correspondence,
is checked by Auckland,
procures additional measures of repression,
recommends increase of postage rates,
his estimate of Cobbett,

his emoluments from franking newspapers,
his indignation at criticisms in the *Times* newspaper,
brings an action,
contemplates a high-handed proceeding towards the town of Olney in Buckinghamshire,
procures a charge to be made on returned letters,
his contention with the India House in the matter of ship letters,
urges a technical adherence to the provisions of the statute,
his elation at the increase of the Post Office revenue,
contrast between Freeling and Lees,
his difference with Lees,
his claim for the Post Office in the matter of steam vessels,
opposes improvement of communication with Ireland,
his interview with Sir Arthur Wellesley,
attempts to get terms of a hostile motion altered,
his dismay at the transfer of the Falmouth packets from the Post Office to the Admiralty,
his strictness in Post Office matters,
is irritated by Sir Henry Parnell's assumption of superiority,
the probable reason for not resigning on the opening of the new Post Office in St. Martin's-le-Grand,
his view that the packet service should not be thrown open to public competition opposed by Althorp,
defends the newspaper privilege enjoyed by the clerks of the roads,
his attitude towards the Royal Commission,
averts a breakdown with the mail-coaches,
becomes the object of vehement attack,
broods over the past,
his death

Frizell, William

Frowde, Ashburnham, comptroller of foreign office

Furness, Sir Harry

Gardner, penny postman, murder of, *note*

Garrow, Sir William, his frank forged

Gas, introduction of, into the Post Office

General Steam Navigation Company undertakes first packet contract

George the Third, when at Cheltenham or at Weymouth is attended by a
mail-coach,
his illness and distribution of a prayer for his recovery,
his interest in his coach,
objects to roof-loading,
attends trial trip,
distributes largesse among mail guards and coachmen

Gerrard Street, crowded condition of Post Office in

Glasgow petitions for a horse-post to Edinburgh,
and for a post office which shall not be kept at a shop

Gloucester protests against certain houses being excluded from the free
delivery,
salary of postmaster in 1792

Godolphin, Sidney Godolphin, Earl of, his rebuke to the postmaster-
general,
insists upon communication with the army in Flanders being improved,
his instruction about extraordinary payments,
directs that in Post Office cases Counsel shall give receipts for their fees,

Grafton, Augustus Henry, Duke of, specimen of his frank, Appendix

Grand mail

Grand Post Nights,

Granville, Lord, urges improvement of the Cornish posts

Gratuities, on delivery of letters,
legality of, questioned in the case of towns,
question decided in favour of the public,
still being charged

Gray, Thomas, his prediction that mail-coaches would be displaced by
railways

Grey, Charles, Earl,

Grosvenor, Sir Richard, member for Chester, expostulated with as to the irregular use of his frank

Groyne, The,

Guide to accompany post-horses when two are taken

Guildhall Library, letter preserved in, showing tardy course of post in 1666

Halfpenny carriage set up by Povey

Halloran, a clerical impostor

Hamburg, practice at, on arrival of the mails

Hamilton, Andrew, acts as Neale's agent for setting up posts in North America,
his suggestions for improving the posts,
acquires Neale's patent,
dies and the patent is surrendered to the Crown

Hamilton, John, son of the preceding, appointed deputy postmaster-general of America

Harley, Robert, afterwards Earl of Oxford, raises the rates of postage,
attempts to trace the writer of an anonymous letter

Harwich, a packet station,
number and strength of its packets,
packet regulations,
a hot-bed of smuggling,
its exorbitant charges,
is closed as a packet station

Hasker, Thomas, chief superintendent of mail-coaches, his pithy instructions,
is complimented by the King,
will not suffer even the King to detain the mail-coach,

enters a protest against the speed of the Holyhead mail

Hayman, Peter, first postmaster of Virginia and Maryland

Heath, Sir Robert, Solicitor-General

Hickes, Prideaux's servant, imprisonment of

Highwaymen, rewards for apprehension of,
refrain from attacks upon mail-coaches,
confine their attention to horse and cross-posts,
instances of the recovery of mail bags stolen by

Hill, Sir Rowland, *note,*

Hippisley, Sir John

Hiver, Richard

Holt, Sir John, Chief Justice, his opinion respecting compensation for losses
by post, *note*

Holyhead, packet service at beginning of eighteenth century performed
with regularity,
contemplated reduction of the packet establishment deprecated by the
Lord Lieutenant of Ireland,
conditions of passage between Holyhead and Dublin in 1813

Hompesch, Baron, packet detained for

Horn, when to be blown,
a man on horseback blowing a post-horn assigned as a device for Post
Office colours, *note*

Horses, to be kept in readiness for affairs of State,
two to be kept at every post-house,
use of, obtained under false pretences,
overridden, overladen, and not always paid for,
charge for post-horses in 1603,
in 1635,
in 1660,
not to be supplied except at post-houses,

to be attended by a guide when two are hired,
not to be let when the post is expected,
not to be taken without the consent of the owners,
only indirectly a source of revenue,
monopoly of letting horses continued to the Post Office by the Act of 1711,
control exercised by the Post Office over horses for travellers merely
nominal, exception given,
charges for post-horses increased by the erection of milestones,
monopoly of letting post-horses withdrawn

Horse and cross-posts, project for checking robberies of,
authority withheld,
eventually given

Hostages taken on capture of a packet,
instance of inhuman treatment of

Houses numbered,
their not being so a hindrance to the Post Office,

Hume, David

Hume, Joseph

Hungerford selected to try the question of free delivery,
question decided in favour of the public and a letter-carrier appointed,

Illicit conveyance of letters, between town and town and between the
country and London,
is stimulated by increase in the rates of postage,
becomes less after the introduction of mail-coaches,
prosecutions for,
return to the House of Commons

Impressment, persons employed on the packets exempt from,
specimen of protection order, *note*

Instructions to the sorting office communicated by word of mouth

Insurance an essential condition of Dockwra's penny post,
this condition abandoned

Invoices to and from abroad exempt from postage until 1801, exemption then withdrawn

Ipswich asserts its right to a free delivery,
right admitted and letter-carrier appointed

Ireland, tardiness of post to, before 1635,
postage to,
method of Post Office business in 1690,
abuse of franking in 1773,
clerks at the castle surrender their franking privilege,
posts to and within Ireland improved,
Penny Post Office opened in Dublin,
the roof of the Dublin Post Office falls in,
the Irish Post Office separated from that of England,
effects of the separation in the case of correspondence by the Milford Haven and Waterford route,
between the Irish and English Post Offices differences in point of law, and of practice,
office in Dublin styled British Mail Office, account of,
and improper use made of it,
Clancarty's energy and decision of character,
Lees, secretary to the Post Office in Ireland, his mode of conducting business,
Lees contrasted with Freeling,
the postmasters-general absentees,
absence also of the subordinates and other abuses,
the express clerks and clerks of the roads deal in newspapers and are given undue advantages,
account of the alphabet,
ingenious one in use at Belfast,
arrangement in favour of soldiers' wives,
peculiar mode of delivery at Belfast,
mail-coach contracts in Ireland different from those in England,
Charles Bianconi,
arrangement between Ireland and Great Britain in the matter of the packets,
Lees is dissatisfied with it,
and sets it aside,
Freeling's indignation,
sailing packets replaced by steam packets,

effect upon the number of passengers carried by the Post Office,
Irish traffic diverted from Holyhead to Liverpool,
and Liverpool made a packet station,
except in the matter of the packets, indisposition of the British Post Office
to improve communication with Ireland,
such improvement urged by Foster, Chancellor of the Irish Exchequer,
and resisted by Freeling,
Freeling forced to give way,
the Irish Post Office consolidated with the Post Office of Great Britain,
and the Dublin establishment reformed,
the auditing of the Irish accounts rendered futile

Iron mail-cart stopped and rifled of its contents

Isle of Wight, its Post Office establishment in 1792

Jackson, a passenger by packet without a pass

Jacob, Giles, *note*

Jamaica, Post Office establishment in, and sea rates fixed,
duration of voyage to and fro in 1798,
House of Assembly vote sum of money in recognition of the gallant
defence of the *Antelope* packet

James, Duke of York, afterwards James II., opposes introduction of the
penny post,
wrests it out of Dockwra's hands,
suffers the clerks of the roads to retain their newspaper privilege

Jamineau, Isaac, purveyor of newspapers to the clerks of the roads

Jeffreys, Sir George, afterwards Lord, inflicts exorbitant fine upon Edmund
Prideaux, son of the Master of the Posts

Johnson, Edward, letter-carrier, improves the penny post,
is appointed deputy comptroller

Johnson, Dr. Samuel, *note*

Jones, distiller of Old Street, St. Luke's, his action against the Post Office

Kent, post through the county of, more carefully nursed than any other

Kenyon, Lloyd, Lord, when Attorney-General, gives receipts for fees in Post Office cases

King's coach, deception practised on Walsingham in the matter of the

King's messengers, their complaint against the Post Office on the erection of milestones

Lambton, John George, moves for a return of the number of Post Office Boards

Lancashire, the badness of its posts in 1699

Le Despencer, Francis, Lord, postmaster-general from 1766 to 1781,

Leeds, salary of postmaster in 1792

Lees, Sir John, secretary to the Post Office in Ireland, his testimony to the abuse of franking,
having been transferred to the War Office, recapitulates conditions on which he accepts reappointment to the Post Office,
recapitulation gives offence to Carteret,
and leads to Carteret's exposure

Lees, Sir Edward Smith, son of the preceding, also secretary to the Post Office in Ireland, his method of conducting business,
deals in newspapers,
his instruction respecting the alphabet,
his difference with Freeling,
becomes a director of the Dublin Steam Packet Company,
is transferred to Edinburgh,
his unauthorised surrender of the receiver-general's bond

Leet, express clerk

Leicester, the Corporation of, binds itself to keep post-horses for the use of the Sovereign, salary of postmaster at, in 1792

Leicester, George, Earl of, postmaster-general from 1794 to 1799

Letter-carriers, their pay in 1690,
as late as 1772, none employed except in London, Edinburgh, and Dublin,
are appointed at certain other towns,
in London their interests suffer from the earlier closing of the Post Office,
are put into uniform,
the sufferings of some of their number during the winter of 1794-95,
select their walks according to seniority,
deliver letters according to classes, one class for general post letters,
another for penny or twopenny letters, and a third for foreign letters

Letters, on affairs of State originally sent by courier,
particulars of, when sent by post, to be carefully recorded,
letters on other than the affairs of State received at the post-houses,
not, without the authority of the Master of the Posts, to be collected,
carried, or delivered,
notice that none are to be sent except through the post served on the
merchants of London,
letters detected in being illicitly conveyed to be sent to the Privy Council,
and their bearers apprehended,
what letters excepted from monopoly,
are given precedence over travellers,
circulate mainly through London,
their mode of distribution,
clandestine conveyance of,
number of penny post letters for the suburbs of London at the end of the
seventeenth century,
letters for America and Jamaica charged with postage, although there was
no packet service,
clandestine conveyance of, stimulated by increase of postage,
definition of single and double letter,
Allen's injunction to check illegal conveyance of,
are examined by means of a strong light, ,
penalty for opening letters,
letters containing patterns or samples, whether to be charged as single or
double letters,
right to make, on the delivery of letters, any charge beyond the postage
contested,
memorials for and against the earlier delivery of foreign letters in London,

average number of letters for each foreign mail in 1790,
treatment of dead and missent letters before and after 1793,
return of the number of letters passing through the London Post Office submitted to the postmasters-general daily,
made penal not only to carry letters, but to send them otherwise than through the post,
on the delivery of letters, despite the decision of the Courts, a charge beyond the postage continues to be made,
owing to the complication of rates, not possible to express the total charge upon a letter in one taxation

Lewis XIV. assembles a squadron before Dunkirk,
his delay in refusing to sign the preliminaries of peace

Lichfield, Thomas William, Earl of, appointed postmaster-general May 1835, *note*

Lincolnshire, the paucity of its posts before 1705

Liverpool, salary of postmaster in 1792,
penny post established at,
is opened as a packet station

Liverpool, Robert, Earl of, mediates between Freeling and Lees,
transfers the Falmouth packets from the Post Office to the Admiralty

Lloyds supplied by the Post Office with ship news

Loppinott, Colonel

Losses by post, compensation for,
when ceased to be given

Lovell, Mary, receiver in St. James's Street, Lord Abercorn's complaint against

Lovell, Thomas, Lord, afterwards Earl of Leicester, postmaster-general from 1733 to 1759,
receives a threatening letter, *note*;
his loose notions about smuggling

Lowndes, William, Secretary to the Treasury, takes charge of the Post

Office Bill of 1711,
overbears Swift, the solicitor to the Post Office,
confounds gross and net revenue, (*note*)

Macadam, John Loudon, introduces new method of road-making

Macaulay, Lord, his account of the fine inflicted upon Edmund Prideaux,
son of the Master of the Posts,
his statement that a part of the Post Office revenue was derived from
post-horses questioned,

Mackerness, Thomas, postmaster of Chipping Norton

Macky, John, packet agent at Dover, proceeds to Flanders,
receives a remarkable caution,
having become contractor for the Dover and Ostend packet service, his
boats engage in illicit operations,
and bring news clandestinely,
is commissioned to settle posts for the army, his excellent arrangements

Maddison, George

Magistrates, the duty of, in certain cases, to seize horses for the service of
the posts,
are enjoined to see that horses are procured at the post-houses alone

Maidstone, excellency of the delivery at, in the seventeenth century,
amount of the postmaster's salary

Mails, hour of despatch of the, from the General Post Office in 1690,
after 1784,
cost of conveyance of, before and after the introduction of mail-coaches,
are exempt from toll in Great Britain but not in Ireland,
exemption withdrawn in Scotland

Mail bags, curious instances of recovery of

Mail-carts, mail-cart made of iron rifled of its contents,
first used in London to bring letters to the General Post Office

Mail-coaches, begin to run,

rapid extension of the system,
system deprecated by some of the leading merchants,
their effect upon expresses,
upon the illicit conveyance of letters,
a mail-coach in attendance upon the King when at Cheltenham,
are put off the road by Palmer,
number of, in 1792,
model of mail-coach preserved at the Post Office,
mail-coaches of new pattern supplied,
number of passengers by, restricted,
roof-loading, and objections to it,
roof not always safe,
mileage allowance in the case of mail-coaches,
their freedom from attacks by highwaymen,
become liable to a duty of one penny a mile,
are diverted from the direct route for a consideration,
number of, in 1811,
their unpopularity with road trustees,
question considered of withdrawing their exemption from toll,
mail-coaches withdrawn instead,
in Scotland, are made liable to toll,
and their number is reduced,
speed of mail-coaches,
the mail-coach the great disseminator of news,
supply of mail-coaches thrown open to public competition, immediate
result

Mail guards, not originally Post Office servants,
their little excesses,
their wages,
treatment of their wages a cause of difference between Walsingham and
Palmer,
their position one of responsibility,
their fees,
specimens of instructions to,
carry parcels and game, and suffer to be carried excess-passengers,

Main, George, deputy-postmaster of Edinburgh

Maîtres de poste in Canada

Managers, sometime farmers, of the Post Office

Manchester, its Post Office establishment in 1792,
establishment increased and Penny Post Office opened

Manley, Captain John, Post Office farmed by

Manley, Isaac, deputy-postmaster of Dublin, *note*

Mansfield, William, Earl of, his opinion upon compensation for losses by
the post, *note*;
his judgment as to the duty of the Post Office in the matter of delivering
letters

Marlborough, John Churchill, Duke of, interests himself in the post with
Flanders,

Maryborough, William, Lord, postmaster-general from December 31, 1834
to May 8, 1835, *note*

Master of the Posts, his duties,
no one not authorised by, allowed to collect, carry, or deliver letters,
his salary and emoluments

Melbourne, William, Viscount

Melville, Robert, Viscount, advocates transfer of the Falmouth packets to
the Admiralty

Menai Straits, additional rate of postage imposed on letters crossing the

Merchants' accounts to and from abroad exempt from postage until 1801,
exemption then withdrawn

Merchant adventurers. *See* Foreign Merchants

Methuen, Sir Paul, ambassador to Portugal, calls attention to the irregular
proceedings of the packets

Mileage allowance, in case of mail-coaches,
higher in Ireland than in England,
flippant return to the House of Commons on the subject of

Miles, difference between measured and computed miles

Milestones, erection of,
their effect upon the charge for post-horses

Milford Haven and Waterford, packet service between

Missent letters, treatment of, before and after 1793

Money Order Office,
the subject of a flippant return to the House of Commons,
facsimile of a money order issued in 1802, Appendix

Monopoly of the Post Office, origin of, in the matter of letters and of
post-horses,
confined in the first instance to the county of Kent,
confirmed by Act of Parliament,
withdrawn as regards post-horses

Mountstuart, John, Viscount, *note*

Murray, Robert, reputed to have been the first to suggest the penny post

Neale, Thomas, obtains grants for setting up posts in North America,
his pecuniary difficulties,
offers to surrender his patent,
patent passes on his death to Andrew Hamilton

Newcastle, Thomas Holles Pelham, Duke of, his orders about the packets
countermanded by Pelham,
sends to the Post Office to inquire the price of corn

Newcastle, salary of the postmaster in 1792

News, hunger after,
the postmasters-general the great purveyors of,
news disseminated by the mail-coaches

Newspapers, franking of, by the clerks of the roads,
are received from abroad by Post Office servants in advance of the general

public,
conditions of franking newspapers altered, effect of alteration,
copies of, supplied to Post Office servants,
newspaper office established,
number and weight of newspapers passing through the Post Office in
1788, *note*;
treatment of foreign newspapers,
newspaper agency at the Post Office largely developed,
London newspapers supplied by the Post Office with early intelligence
from abroad,
newspapers, though franked, not exempt from postage by the penny,
twopenny, and convention posts,
postage on newspapers for the East Indies reduced below the letter rate,
improper dealing with newspapers in Ireland,
on newspapers to and from the Colonies special rates established and
franking privilege withdrawn,
this privilege retained in the case of newspapers for the Continent,
newspapers circulating within the United Kingdom exempted from
postage,
extent of newspaper business conducted by the clerks of the roads in 1829,
in 1830,
newspaper business finally withdrawn

Newton, Sir Isaac

New Year's gifts, extortion of

Nicholas, Sir Edward

Nodin, passenger on board the *Antelope* packet, his gallantry

Normanby, Henry Constantine, Viscount, proposes abolition of the office
of second postmaster-general

North, Frederick, Lord,
receives singular reply from the Post Office

Northampton, Countess of

Northey, Sir Edward

Northumberland, Hugh, Earl of, Lord Lieutenant of Ireland

Nottingham, salary of postmaster in 1792

Ogilby, John, calls attention to the difference between measured and computed miles, *note*

Oldfield, Thomas, postmaster of York

Oldmixon

Old Street, St Luke's, a second penny charged on penny post letters addressed to

Oliphant, Robert, deputy postmaster-general for Scotland

Olney, Buckinghamshire, attempts to improve its post and the consequence

O'Neile, Daniel, farmer of the posts,

O'Neill, Charles Henry St. John, Earl, postmaster-general of Ireland from 1807 to 1831, *seq.*

Onslow, Denzil

Opening of letters, during the Commonwealth,
under James II.,
practice systematically carried on under Walpole's administration,
continued, as regards foreign letters, until 1844, *note*

Ordnance, Board of

Ormonde, James, Duke of

Oxenbridge, Clement, reduces postage,
receives an appointment under the Post Office

Oxford Street, branch post office opened in

Packets (sailing), packet establishment in 1690,

are forbidden to carry merchandise in times of war,
regulations for control of,
carry their own surgeon,
are not, without a pass, to carry passengers,
or goods,
fares are not sufficiently made known and inconvenience arises, instances given,
curious assortment of goods sent free by packet,
packets bring both passengers and goods without passes,
engage in smuggling,
are forbidden to give chase,
are not entitled to the prizes they take,
agreement with prizes honourably observed as a rule, exceptions given,
are victualled at Falmouth and at Harwich on different principles,
objections to both systems,
copy of letter-bill by the *Prince* packet,
transport recruits with disastrous results,
must be of English build,
engage with privateers,
are placed on a peace footing,
colours altered on Union with Scotland,
sufficiency of the burthen and crew of the Falmouth packets questioned by the merchants,
the packets generally meet with a series of disasters,
wholesale smuggling on the part of the Harwich packets,
inordinate growth of the packet expenditure,
and the reason,
packets established between Milford Haven and Waterford,
representation by the merchants as to the number of packets captured,
their gallant actions with privateers,
probable explanation of these actions occurring only when passengers were on board,
mode of procuring packets for the East Indies and the Cape in 1815, and their cost,
arrangement in the matter of packets between Great Britain and Ireland,
steps taken by the Dublin Post Office to set the arrangement aside,
sailing packets replaced by steam packets between Holyhead and Dublin,
between Milford Haven and Waterford,
between Portpatrick and Donaghadee,
the Falmouth packets transferred to the Admiralty

Packets (steam), between Holyhe ad and Dublin, charges by, as compared

with sailing packets,
number of passengers before the introduction of steam, *note*;
and after,
number of steam packets possessed by the Post Office in 1827,
packet service thrown open to public competition,
Irish steam packets, defective return to the House of Commons in the
matter of

Pajot, director of the French posts, his obstinacy,
his unreasonableness

Palmer, John, his activity,
general sketch of his plan,
his plan is brought to the notice of Pitt,
and is tried on the Bath road,
extends his plan,
induces Pitt to raise the rates of postage,
alleges obstruction,
alters the length of the stages,
his plan is opposed by the merchants,
opposition dies away,
procures appointment of his nominees,
conditions of his own appointment,
his jealousy of Allen,
expedites the morning delivery in London, and introduces an improved
method of business,
imposes upon Walsingham in the matter of the King's coach,
his treatment of official papers,
pays an unexpected visit to Walsingham at Old Windsor,
betrays his jealousy,
establishes, but without the necessary authority, a newspaper office,
and a mail guards' fund,
is called to account by Walsingham,
takes umbrage at a rebuke administered to his deputy, Bonnor,
disobeys orders,
becomes aggressive and defiant,
and appeals to Pitt,
is charged by Bonnor with promoting a public meeting antagonistic to the
postmasters-general,
suspends Bonnor,
is suspended himself,
is dismissed,

receives a pension and, later on, a Parliamentary grant,
general result of his plan,

Palmerston, Henry John, Viscount, his humorous reply to Freeling

Parkin, Anthony, solicitor to the Post Office

Parnell, Sir Henry

Pascoe, John, boatswain of the *Antelope* packet, his gallant resistance to the attack of a privateer

Patterns and samples, letters containing, and being less than one ounce in weight, whether to be charged single or double,
question tried at law,
settled by Act of Parliament,
concessions in favour of

Pay. *See* Wages

Pelham, Henry, countermands Newcastle's orders about the packets

Pennant, Thomas

Penny post, its introduction by Dockwra,
general plan of,
carries up to one pound in weight,
includes a system of insurance,
days on which it does not go,
increases number of country letters,
is absorbed into the General Post Office,
establishment of, in 1690,
stimulates the clandestine conveyance of letters into London,
on its acquisition by the State its general conditions remain unchanged,
number of penny post letters for the suburbs at the end of the seventeenth century,
its contemplated extension to Dublin in 1703,
affects the number of ship letters,
is without legal sanction,
legal sanction given,
its limits restricted to ten miles,
the charge of a second penny on all letters delivered outside the bills of

mortality made legal,

weight carried by the penny post reduced from one pound to four ounces,

compensation for losses by the, when ceased to be given, *note*;

attempts made by the Post Office to charge a second penny within the bills of mortality,

principal officers of the penny post absentees,

stagnation of the penny post,

the post is improved by Johnson, a letter-carrier,

financial result,

prepayment, hitherto optional, made compulsory,

restriction on limits withdrawn,

the charge of a second penny, heretofore confined to letters delivered at places outside the bills of mortality, imposed upon letters coming therefrom,

the penny post converted into a twopenny post,

and the twopenny post into a threepenny one, . *See* twopenny and threepenny posts

Penzance, its post before and after 1784

Pepys, Samuel, *note*

Perceval Spencer,

Percival, Joseph, a passenger by packet without a pass

Pickwick, "Mr. Pickwick's coach,"

Pitt, William, his attention is called to Palmer's plan,

sweeps away frivolous objections and desires that it may be tried,

raises the postage rates,

relaxes the restrictions upon franking,

dismisses Tankerville,

settles conditions of Palmer's appointment,

his knowledge of abuses at the Post Office and his unwillingness to expose them,

suppresses report of Royal Commission,

authorises increase of salary to the clerks of the roads,

declares Palmer's proceedings to be irregular,

turns a deaf ear to the postmaster-general's request for an interview,

interview at length granted,

a second interview,

acquiesces in Palmer's dismissal and grants him a pension,
makes to Post Office servants a periodical grant pending a revision of the establishment,
promotes plan for improving the penny post,
disallows practice of charging returned letters,
modifies arrangements for dealing with ship letters,
his precepts in this matter afterwards disregarded

Plymouth, salary of the postmaster in 1792

Political Register, its criticisms on Post Office practice

Pope, Alexander, his lines on Ralph Allen

Portage

Portland, William Henry, Duke of

Portland Packet, Captain Taylor, its gallant action with privateer

Postage, introduction of,
settled by Act of Parliament,
original meaning of term, *note*;
rates of postage in 1635,
in 1657 and 1660,
in 1711,
in 1765,
in 1784,
in 1797,
in 1801,
in 1805,
in 1812,
device resorted to in order to evade high rates of,
rates lapse through effluxion of time,
rates of postage between London and the Channel Islands and within the islands themselves,
from Portugal and America,
financial result of increase of rates,
bewildering complications,
extraordinary toleration of the public, explanation suggested,
an additional rate imposed in Scotland on withdrawal of exemption from toll,

and on letters passing over the Menai Straits or Conway Bridge,
rates of postage to the East Indies in 1815,
instances of exorbitant rates

"Poste for the Pacquet," 5 *note*

Post-boys

Post-coaches

Post-haste

Post-horn. *See* Horn

Post-horses. *See* Horses

Post-houses, to have horses in readiness,
horses not to be let except at,
pay of keepers of, in arrear

Postilions

Postmarks, introduction of

Postmasters, their duties in 1690,
their salaries,
their grievances,
their contingent advantages,
intercept postage on bye-letters,
their correspondence exempt from postage,
their moderation on the erection of milestones,
are enjoined to frequent the local markets and report the price of corn,
salaries of certain postmasters in Scotland in 1707,
in England in 1792

Postmasters-General (I.) [Cotton and Frankland, 1690 to 1708], their
simple-mindedness,
their accessibility,
their concern about the illicit correspondence,
their powerlessness to check it,
let the posts out to farm,
refuse to sublet the penny post,

their difference with Pajot, minister of the French posts,
remonstrate with captains of packets at Falmouth,
and at Harwich,
chuckle over the capture of a prize,
their rebuke to the captain of a Falmouth packet, *note*;
instance of their rough-and-ready justice,
take vigorous measures to protect the packets from Flemish privateers,
their admonition to the packet agent at Dover,
act as purveyors of news to the Court, instances given,
advocate cheap postage to America,
become, at the Union with Scotland, responsible for the Scotch posts,
their inaction, explanation suggested,
action forced upon them,
are contrasted with their successors,

Postmasters-General (II.) [Frankland and Evelyn, 1708 to 1715], their
interview with Godolphin,
their instruction about expresses from Dover,
treat personally with Povey,
Frankland ceases to be a member of Parliament,
concern themselves only slightly about travellers,
take measures to check the abuse of franking,
in vain urge the appointment of surveyors,
negotiate new treaty with France,
quit office on accession of George the First

Postmasters-General (III.) [Cornwallis and Craggs, 1715 to 1721], are
amazed at the absence of check in the Post Office,
note how little the increase in the rates of postage has added to the
revenue,
and how largely it has stimulated the abuse of franking,
their dispute with the merchants,
convict Lowndes of a ludicrous error,
their harsh treatment of their secretary

Postmasters-General (IV.) [Edward Carteret and Walpole, 1721 to 1725],
their kindness to subordinates,
their interview with Abercorn, .
[From 1725 to 1733 Carteret had for his colleague Edward Harrison, and
from 1733 to 1739 Lord Lovell.]
Carteret establishes a post to Aylsham

Postmasters-General (V.) [Henry Frederick, Lord Carteret and, for the second time, Tankerville, 1784 to 1786], collect opinions on Palmer's plan and submit them to Pitt,
entertain doubts as to its feasibility,
their differences between themselves,
their open rupture,
Tankerville is dismissed by Pitt,
his ungovernable temper

Postmasters-General (VI.) [Carteret and Walsingham, 1787 to 1789],
Walsingham's industry and thoroughness,
questions Carteret's right to sign first,
his preponderating influence,
his habit of annotating and execrable handwriting,
reduces packet establishment at Falmouth,
is dissuaded from carrying out a similar reduction at Holyhead,
is powerless to control the correspondence by the Milford packets,
in conjunction with Carteret procures increase of salary for the clerks of the roads,
is imposed upon in the matter of the King's coach,
calls for the surveyors' journals,
his correspondence with Chalmers,
receives an unexpected visit from Palmer,
detects Palmer's jealousy and endeavours to allay it,
calls Palmer to account for acting without authority,
exposes Bonnor's attempt at deception,
Carteret's dismissal,
Walsingham inquires into the solicitor's accounts

Postmasters-General (VII.) [Walsingham and Chesterfield, 1790 to 1794],
Chesterfield's playful allusions to Palmer,
Palmer sets the postmasters-general at defiance,
they seek in vain an interview with Pitt,
receive assurances from Bonnor of Palmer's disloyalty,
remove Bonnor's suspension and suspend Palmer,
Chesterfield's letter,
Walsingham's interview with Pitt,
feel confident of their own dismissal,
are furnished with evidence by Bonnor,
have a second interview with Pitt and dismiss Palmer,
contrast Palmer's reticence in official matters with Freeling's wealth of

explanation,
Walsingham attempts to improve communication with France,
and to reduce postage on letters containing the second halves of bank notes,
give attention to coach-building

Postmasters-General (VIII.) [Chichester and Salisbury, 1816 to 1823], are called upon for a return of the number of Post Office Boards,
address to the Throne praying that one of the two offices of postmaster-general be abolished,
Salisbury stops his own salary, and on his death Chichester becomes postmaster-general sole,
Salisbury's testimony to increase of stringency in Post Office matters

Post Office, origin of its monopoly,
monopoly confined in the first instance to the county of Kent,
a Post Office opened in the city of London,
dispute for its possession,
becomes the subject of Parliamentary enactment,
its position in 1680,
is the only receptacle for letters in London,
description of it,
relations between the Post Office and the Treasury,
the Post Office becomes unpopular and the reasons, seq.;
its retrogression,
assumes a new character,
loses monopoly of letting post-horses,
Post Office buildings in Edinburgh and Dublin fall into decay,
indignation caused by the earlier closing of the Post Office in London,
this office enlarged,
state of the Post Office as between the years 1695 and 1813 compared,
the Post Office disseminates news,
and police notices,
becomes object of interest to the House of Commons,
is cleared of more than a century of debt,
a new post office opened in St. Martin's-le-Grand

Post-runners

Posts, paucity of, in time of Henry the Eighth,
their close connection with the Sovereign,
instructions for the regulation of,

designed not only to carry the letters of the Sovereign, but for the use of
persons travelling on the Sovereign's concerns,
posts originally maintained at loss to the Crown,
at the beginning of the seventeenth century only four in number,
of these the post to Dover the most important, precautions taken lest this
post should be used for designs against the State,
decadence of the posts,
improved by Witherings,
to be self-supporting,
thrown open to the public,
let out to farm,
rent paid in 1650,
in 1653,
in 1660,
in 1667,
in 1657 become the subject of Parliamentary enactment,
their inadequacy to meet public demands,
even where they existed, their existence not generally known,
at what intervals they left London in 1680,
regarded as vehicles for the propagation of treason,
again let out to farm,
resumed by the State,
as late as 1728, not of general concern

Povey, Charles, sets up a halfpenny post,
contrast between him and Dockwra,
his insolence,
is proceeded against and cast in damages

Prideaux, Edmund, takes part with Burlamachi against Warwick,
rescues the mail from Warwick's servants,
brings the imprisonment of his own servant before the House of
Commons,
becomes Master of the Posts,
his activity,
suppresses unauthorised post to Scotland,
makes profit out of the posts and is called upon to pay rent,
is dismissed,
retains an interest in the posts,
Oldmixon's estimate of his character,
destination of a part of his wealth

Prideaux, Edmund, son of the preceding

Prior, Matthew, negotiates Post Office treaty with France

Prior Park

Prizes, practice observed on capture of

Prosecutions, for the illicit conveyance of letters,
measures taken to secure their publicity,
return to the House of Commons on the subject of

Protection order, specimen of, *note*

Quartering of soldiers, a grievance to postmasters

Quash, Ralph Allen's predecessor as postmaster of Bath

Queen's letters, meaning of term in 1706, *note*

Queen's servants not exempt from fare by packet

Queensberry, James, Duke of

Raikes, a diamond merchant, suggests the giving of receipts for registered
letters, *note*

Railways, prediction concerning,
first mail sent by railway

Ramsgate, cost of Post Office at, in 1792

Randolph, Thomas, Master of the Posts to Queen Elizabeth

Receiving offices, first opened in London,
generally kept at public-houses,
to remain open on six nights a week instead of three,
letter-boxes at, to be closed and fixed,
receiving offices for twopenny post letters separate and distinct from

offices for letters by the general post,

Recruits, exemption of, from fare by packet,
disputes with officers in charge of,
packets employed for transport of

Registration, exorbitant fees for, of foreign letters,
amount of these fees in 1783 and 1784,
receipts for foreign registered letters begin to be given, *note*

Returned Letters. *See* Dead letters

Revenue of the Post Office, surrendered by the Crown to the public, in part, in 1711,
and wholly, in exchange for a Civil List, in 1760,
amount of, from 1635 to 1694,
in 1710 and 1721,
in 1787 as compared with 1784,
in 1796 and 1806,
in 1824 and 1833

Richmond, Charles, Duke of, postmaster-general from December 1830 to July 1834, declines to receive salary,
his industry,
becomes postmaster-general of Ireland as well as Great Britain, and reforms the Dublin establishment,
contemplates, apparently, a reduction of postage

Ripon, Post Office at, refused in 1713,
in possession of one in 1792

Roads, condition of, in 1691,
during the first two decades of the nineteenth century,
begin to be constructed on scientific principles,
Macadam's plan for dealing with the surface of,
difference between roads in the country and roads in the neighbourhood of London

Rochester, Lawrence Hyde, Earl of, postmaster-general from 1685 to 1689, *note*, , Appendix *note*

Rogers, captain of packet, engages in smuggling

Roof-loading of mail-coaches,

Rosencrantz, the Danish envoy, to be specially accommodated on board Harwich packet

Rosse, Laurence, Earl of, postmaster-general of Ireland from 1809 to 1831,

Rotterdam, practice at, on arrival of the mails

Royal boroughs of Scotland

Royal Commission of Inquiry into the Post Office in 1787,
in 1823,
recommendations of this last Commission not carried into effect,
another Commission appointed to ascertain the reason,
this Commission procures the contract for mail-coaches to be thrown open to public competition

Runners

Rye-House Plot, the cause of a Post Office proclamation

Sailors on board the packets, their conditions of service,
receive pensions for wounds,
their wages withheld,
their wages increased

St. John, Henry, afterwards Viscount Bolingbroke

St. Leonards, Shoreditch, a second penny on penny post letters improperly charged at

St. Martin's-le-Grand, opening of Post Office at

Salaries. *See* Wages

Salisbury, James, Marquess of, postmaster-general from 1816 to 1823. *See* Postmasters-General, Part VIII.

Samples. *See* Patterns

Sampson, captain of packet

Sandwich, John, Earl of, postmaster-general from 1768 to 1771,
specimen of his frank, Appendix

Sandwich, John, Earl of, son of the preceding, postmaster-general from
1807 to 1814

Sandwich, Kent, asserts its right to a free delivery,
right admitted and letter-carrier appointed,

Scotland, tardiness of communication with, before 1635,
communication expedited by Witherings,
postage to Scotland,
post to Edinburgh set up by the City of London,
extent of correspondence with Scotland in 1690,
Scotch posts placed under the postmasters-general of England,
salaries of Scotch postmasters,
course of post between London and Edinburgh accelerated in 1758,
in 1765 posts to and within Scotland increased in frequency,
Post Office in Edinburgh no longer habitable,
internal administration of Scotch Post Office revised by Palmer,
penny post established in Edinburgh,
postage rates within Scotland raised,
wholesale prosecutions for illicit correspondence,
exemption from toll withdrawn and an additional postage rate imposed,
unhandsome conduct of the road trustees,
roads discoached

Search, powers of, refused by the House of Commons

Sebright, Sir John, his letter accidentally opened

Secretary of State, clerks in the office of, compensated for the loss of the
newspaper privilege

Secretary of the Post Office, appointment of, created in 1694

Secret Office,

Sharpus, postmaster of New York

Sheffield, salary of postmaster in 1792

Shelburne, William, Earl of

Ship letters, origin of ship letter money,
by means of the penny post evade full postage,
number of, in 1686,
pence paid upon, without legal sanction,
legal sanction given,
ship letter office established,
rates on, increased and restrictions imposed,
restrictions modified,
made compulsory upon private ships to carry mails

Ship news supplied by the Post Office to Lloyds

Shipwrecked seamen pass free by packet

Shrewsbury, curious reply to petition from, for earlier post

Single letter, definition of

Smart and bounty money

Smuggling, on board the packets at Falmouth,
at Harwich,
at Dover,
in the Dover mail-coach

Soldiers' wives, when travelling supplied with money through the
medium of the Post Office

Solicitor to the Post Office, appointment of, created in 1703,
an absentee and his duties performed by deputy,
his accounts inspected by Walsingham's direction

Somerset, Protector, superscription of his letter to Lord Dacre

Sorters, pay of, in 1690

Southampton, salary of postmaster in 1792

Speed of post in Queen Elizabeth's time,
in time of James the First,
at the end of the seventeenth century,
between London and Falmouth and London and Harwich, at the
beginning of the eighteenth century,
under Allen's contract,
in 1765,
after 1784,
speed of Holyhead mail-coach before and after Telford's improvement of
the road,
of mail-coaches generally in 1821 and 1836,

Spencer, Lord Charles, postmaster-general from 1801 to 1806

Spitalfields, a second penny improperly charged on penny post letters
addressed to

Sprange, James, postmaster of Tunbridge Wells

Spring Rice, Thomas, Chancellor of the Exchequer

Stage, inconvenience resulting from term not being defined,
term dropped as unit of charge

Stanhope of Harrington, John, Lord, Master of the Posts,
resents what he conceives to be an invasion of his patent,
dies and is succeeded as Master of the Posts by his son

Stanhope of Harrington, Charles, Lord, Master of the Posts, son of the
preceding, vigorously asserts his rights,
vacillating decisions of the Privy Council,
surrenders his patent,
alleges cajolery

Stanhope, Arthur, comptroller of the foreign department, his emoluments
from franking,
supplies newspapers with summaries of foreign intelligence

Stanhope, James, Secretary of State

Stanwix, Colonel

State letters, *note*

Staunton, John, postmaster of Isleworth; appointed comptroller of the bye and cross-roads

Steam packets, first employment of, by the Post Office

Stock Exchange, The, outwits the Post Office

Stockdale, a highwayman, execution of, *note*

Stokes, William

Stone, George, Receiver-General, a defaulter

Stowmarket, its position and its trade unknown to Allen

Strangers' post. *See* Foreign merchants

Sudbury, duties and salary of postmaster in 1690

Sunderland, Charles, Earl of

Surveyors, appointment of, refused by the Treasury,
afterwards sanctioned,
their original functions,
their functions and emoluments after 1786,
their journals,
cease to hold postmasterships in addition to their appointments as surveyors

Swift, Richard, solicitor to the Post Office, prepares Post Office bill of 1711, is overborne by Lowndes, secretary to the Treasury

Tankerville, Charles, Earl of, postmaster-general from April 1782 to May 1783, and again from January 1784 to September 1786. *See* Postmasters-General, Part V.

Telford, Thomas, takes in hand the road between Holyhead and Shrewsbury,

between Shrewsbury and London,
other roads

Thanet, Elizabeth, Countess Dowager of, undertakes to establish a penny post in Dublin

"Thorough poste," 5 *note*

Thrale, Mrs., *note*

Threepenny post,

Thurloe, John, secretary, assumes direction of the Post Office in 1655, intercepts letters

Thurlow, Edward, Attorney-General, afterwards Lord Chancellor; his opinion as to the duty of the Post Office in the matter of delivering letters,

Thynne, Henry Frederick, afterwards Carteret. *See* Postmasters-General, Parts V. and VI.

Timepieces, mode of regulating mail-guards'

Times newspaper, its priority of intelligence,
its criticisms on Post Office procedure,
proceedings against, taken by Freeling

Tinware, supply of, to the postmasters-general

Todd, Anthony, secretary to the Post Office; his correspondence with Benjamin Franklin,
his indifference,
comments upon Tankerville's temper,
his compromising position in respect to the packets,
his emoluments,
his remark upon Bonnor's dilatory replies,
devotes himself to social amenities,
unknown to the postmasters-general, retains his shares in the packets,
his death

Toll, mail-coaches exempt from, in England and Scotland but not in Ireland, exemption withdrawn in Scotland

Townshend, Horatio, Lord

Townshend, Charles, deprecates alarm because a letter is sent by express

Travellers, obtain use of post-horses under false pretences,
are not to be supplied with horses except at the post-houses,
paucity of travellers,
are not to be supplied with horses when the post is expected,
have to pay more for horses after the erection of milestones,
their restriction to post-houses for a supply of horses withdrawn

Treasury, its relations to the Post Office,
refuses the appointment of surveyors,
refuses a horse-post between Edinburgh and Glasgow,
experience of its ways a bar to the suggestion of improvements,
extorts blackmail

Treves, Peregrine, the recipient of Carteret's bounty

Tring, the postmaster of, opens a letter addressed to Sir John Sebright

Tuke, Sir Brian, Master of the Posts to Henry the Eighth, his letter to
Thomas Cromwell,
his duties,
explanation suggested of statement in his letter

Tunbridge, salary of postmaster in 1792

Tunbridge Wells, old-fashioned postmaster of, in 1823

Turnpikes, condition of the trusts at the beginning of the nineteenth
century,
number of Turnpike Acts passed between 1760 and 1809

Twopenny post, a second penny charged by Dockwra on delivery of letters
in the outskirts of London,
this second penny not legally sanctioned until 1730,
the twopenny post thus established in one direction established also in the
other,
the penny post converted into a twopenny post,

and the twopenny post into a threepenny one,
the revenue of the twopenny post as compared with that of the penny post,
the crowded condition of the twopenny Post Office in Westminster

Tyrconnel, Richard Talbot, Earl of, opens the mails at Dublin Castle

Uniform, letter-carriers put into

Urin, captain of packet, makes wrong port

Vanderpoel, packet agent at the Brill

Vansittart, Nicholas, Chancellor of the Exchequer, insists upon mail-coaches being withdrawn from the roads,
raises the rates of postage,
changes the route of the Holyhead coach,
refuses to get the terms of a hostile motion altered

Van Vrybergh, Envoy Extraordinary from the States-General

Venetian Ambassador, the, protests against the opening of his letters

Vidler, his contract for the supply of mail-coaches terminated

Village posts. *See* Convention posts

Viner, Sir Robert

Wade, General

Wages and salaries, of Post Office servants in 1690,
of seamen on board the packets,
of certain postmasters in England, and in Scotland,
of mail-guards

Waghorn, Thomas

Wainwright, postmistress of Ferrybridge, her original mode of supplying an omission

Walcot, John, secretary to the Post Office in Ireland, terms of his agreement with Barham, packet agent at Dover

Walpole, Sir Robert, maintains an office for the opening of letters

Walpole, Galfridus, postmaster-general from 1721 to 1725. *See* Postmasters-General, Part IV.

Walpole, Horace, precautions taken by, to secure his correspondence against inspection

Walsingham, Thomas, Lord, postmaster-general from July 1787 to July 1794. *See* Postmasters-General, Parts VI. and VII.

Warwick, Robert, Earl of, acquires Witherings's patent and claims possession of the letter office,
attempts to obtain it by force,
continues to assert his claim

Warwick, course of post to, altered in 1695

Waterhouse, Benjamin, Secretary to the Post Office, *note*

Watson, Sir Charles

Way letter, meaning of term

Weights to be attached to sea-borne mails

Wellesley, Sir Arthur, sets aside objections to improving communication with Ireland

West Indies, packets to the, established,
amount of correspondence in 1705,
service discontinued in 1711,
resumed in 1745,
improved arrangements for disposing of the West Indian mails

Westmorland, John, Earl of, postmaster-general from September 1789 to March 1790

Weston, Henry, secretary to the Post Office, harsh treatment of

Weston brothers, trial of

Wetherall, Robert, master of ship *Albinia*, proceedings against, for refusing
to take mails on board, *note*

Weymouth, constituted a packet station

Whinnery, Thomas, postmaster of Belfast, his revolving "alphabet,"
his mode of delivery

Whitworth, Richard

Wildman, Colonel John, postmaster-general from July 1689 to March 1690

Willatt, Dame, postmistress of Manchester in 1792,
granted a pension

Willes, Doctor, Dean of Lincoln, afterwards Bishop of St. Davids; the "chief
Decypherer,"

Willes, Mr. Justice, his judgment upon the question of free delivery

William III., confers a pension upon Dockwra,
refuses to exempt postmasters from the quartering of soldiers,
is unwilling to prosecute for the illegal conveyance of letters,
his opinion as to the requirements of a mail packet,
the soundness of that opinion confirmed

Williamson, Peter, sets up an office for the delivery of letters in Edinburgh

Willimott, Receiver-General, *note*

Wilson, mail-coach contractor, his exorbitant bill for horsing the King's
coach

Witherings, Thomas, succeeds De Quester as foreign postmaster,
is commissioned to examine into the inland posts,
suggests a scheme of reorganisation,
introduces postage,

contemplates posts being self-supporting,
but not, apparently, a source of revenue,
becomes postmaster for both inland and foreign letters,
his appointment is sequestered,
assigns his patent

Wolters, Dirick, a suspected person, to be searched for at Harwich

Worthing, course of post from London to, in 1666

Wren, Sir Christopher, surveys the Post Office premises in Lombard Street

York, salary of postmaster in 1792,   .

FOOTNOTES:

[1] 9 April, 17 Elizabeth.—Further att the same Common Hall [of the town of Leicester] it was for dyuers cawses thought good and mete for the service of the Prince to have at the chargies of the Towne certen poste horses kepte, whearevppon theare was appoynted foure to be kepte, which, thees persouns vnderwritten have vndertaken to kepe, and to serve from tyme to tyme so oft as nede shalle requier, for and dureinge the space of one wholle yeare nexte after the date hereof, viz. Mr. Roberte Eyricke, one; Fraunces Norris, chamberlayn, twoe; Thomas Tyars, one. For the which theyre is allowed vnto them of the towne for euerie horse thurtie-three shillinges and foure pence, that is to say for foure horses vili. xiiis. iiiid. Provyded always that if theye the said Robert Eyricke, Frauncis Norrys, and Thomas Tyars doe not kepe good and able horses for that purpose and to be readie vppon one half howres warnynge to forfitt, lose, and paye for euerie tyme to the Chamber of the Towne of Leycester the somme of fyve shillinges. For the payement of the said xxli. nobles it is further agreed vppon, in the manner and forme followinge, That is to saye, the Mayor and euerie of his bretherene called the xxiiii. to paye iis. a pece, and euerie of the xlviii. xiid. a pece, and the Resydue that shalbe then lackinge to be levied of the commonaltie and inhabitantes of the said towne and the liberties thereof.—Appendix to the Eighth Report of the Royal Commission on Historical Manuscripts, p. 425.

[2] The two posts were, at first, distinguished by different names. The travellers' post was called "The thorough poste," and the letter post was called "The Poste for the Pacquet."

[3] Austria, in the infancy of her post office, appears to have had much the same experience. "The postmasters," writes M. Læper, Director of Posts at Markirch, "were in no way protected from the most outrageous behaviour on the part of travellers, and were unable to prevent them from overloading the horses and vehicles with unreasonably heavy things, chests, boxes, and similar articles, by which the conveyance of the same was delayed. They could not hinder many travellers from riding heavily-laden horses at full speed over hill and dale without drawing rein, so that the animals were crippled, disabled, or even ridden to death, and in consequence the postmasters were frequently unable to carry out the service for want of

horses. The worst treatment, however, which the postmasters experienced was at the hands of cavaliers and couriers, who often demanded more horses than they needed, took them by force, overloaded the coaches with two or three servants, and with an immoderate quantity of luggage, and paid an arbitrary sum, just whatever they pleased, often not half what was due." — L'Union Postale of October 1, 1885.

[4] An amusing illustration of the value which, at the end of the sixteenth century, was set upon cloth made in London is afforded by a letter from Frederick the Second of Denmark to Queen Elizabeth. This letter, dated the 14th of June 1585, is thus summarised in the 46th Annual Report of the Deputy Keeper of the Public Records, Appendix ii., page 28. "Has for some years past had cloth prepared in London of different colours and after a particular pattern, for his use in hunting both in summer and winter. Hears now that certain German merchants, having found this out, have had similar cloth manufactured, which they sell everywhere, outside his Court and family, to many inquisitive and foolish imitators, at a very dear rate. It is no concern of his what anybody may wear, but still, as this cloth was made of a special kind and colour for himself, he takes it ill that it should be sold to others, and begs her therefore (on the application of his agent, Thomas Thenneker) strictly to prohibit the sale."

[5] The Proclamation enjoined that on letters "to Plymouth, Exeter, and with the two other places in that road," Witherings should "take the like port that now is paid, as near as possibly he can."

[6] *Her Majesty's Mails*, by William Lewins, p. 19.

[7] The term "postage," in the sense of a charge upon a letter, is comparatively modern. The Act of 1764 is the first so to use it. The term is indeed used in the Act of 1660, but there it signifies the hire of a horse for travelling. "Each horse's hire or postage."

[8] Lord Macaulay's words are: — "The revenue of this establishment was not derived solely from the charge for the transmission of letters. The Post Office alone was entitled to furnish post-horses; and, from the care with which this monopoly was guarded, we may infer that it was found profitable."

[9] Curiously enough, the Post Office Report for 1854 gives the year as 1683; but this is an error.

[10] Here also the Post Office Report for 1854 is in error. It says that at first there was no limit to the weight of a packet.

[11] The exact date of incorporation is uncertain. The decision in the Court of King's Bench was given in Michaelmas term 1682; but the first

public advertisement of the penny post does not appear to have been issued by the Postmaster-General until the 11th of March 1684/5.

[12] In the reigns of Charles II. and James II. the practice of billeting, illegal as it then was, was necessarily resorted to in order to provide quarters for the troops they maintained in time of peace; and even billeting in private houses was not unknown. An Act of 1689, the second Mutiny Act, as it is called, while forbidding billeting in private houses, authorised it at "inns, livery stables, ale houses, victualling houses, and all houses selling brandy, strong waters, cyder or metheglin, by retaile, to be dranke in their houses."

[13] In the agreement with Ralph Allen, dated thirty years later, bye-letters are defined to be "letters not going or coming from, to, or through London."

[14] Occasionally, even after William's accession, the postmasters-general addressed the King direct. The remonstrance against quartering soldiers upon postmasters was so addressed. This document is dated the 1st of February 1692/3.

[15] In the case of Grimsby it is the more surprising that this should have been so, because out of the only five towns in the kingdom which the Act of 1660 mentions by name Grimsby is one. According to this Act the post was to go there once a week.

[16] 1661. Feb. 3rd. Robert Reade to Charles Spellman. "Att the right honourable my Lord Townshend's in the Old Palace Yard, Westminster." The writer says that he has as yet received no command from Mr. Spellman or from Lord Townshend, "nor do I wonder at it, because the flying post lay drunke last Friday at Fakenham (being the day that he should have binn at Thetford to take those letters then there which he should bring hether on Saterday), and had not changed his quarter yesterday as I am informed by one of Scott's men who saw him pittyfully drunke. The cuntry complaines of him."—Historical Manuscripts Commission, Eleventh Report, Appendix, Part iv. p. 25.

[17] The Forty-Sixth Annual Report of the Deputy-Keeper of the Public Records, Appendix ii. p. 69.

[18] *Clarendon's Life*, vol. i. p. 135.

[19] Writing in 1709, Mr. Manley, the postmaster-general's deputy in Dublin, says, "There are not less than a thousand more houses now than there were at my first coming here [*i.e.* in 1703]. Besides, there are many new streets now laid out and buildings erecting every day."

[20] "To divers Masters of Shipps for 60447 letters by them brought from forreigne parts this year at one penny each according to the usage—£251:17:3."—Extract from writ of Privy Seal for passing the accounts of "our Right Trusty and Right well-beloved Couzen and Councellor Lawrence Earle of Rochester, Late our High Treasurer of England."

[21] "This is to give notice that Lancellot Plumer and William Barret are appointed by the Postmaster-General of England to receive all such letters and pacquets from masters of ships and vessels, mariners and passengers as shall be by them hereafter brought in any ships or vessels into the Port of London, to the end the same may be delivered with speed and safety according to their respective directions and the laws of this kingdom; and that all masters of ships or vessels and all mariners and passengers may the better take notice thereof, the Right Honourable the Lords of the Admiralty have directed that the boat employed in this service do carry colours, in which there is to be represented a man on horseback blowing a post horn."—*London Gazette*, No. 3247, from Monday 21st December to Thursday 24th December 1696.

[22] Equal, at the then rate of exchange, to £2437:10s.

[23] "It being a certain maxim," he wrote to the postmasters-general on the 15th of February 1707, "that as Trade is the producer of correspondence, so trade is governed and influenced by the certainty and quickness of correspondence."

[24] In 1706, Court or State letters, for at this time the terms were used indiscriminately, were defined to be letters directed to "the Queen, His Royal Highness the Prince, the Lord High Treasurer, and the two principal Secretarys of State and their clarks." Sometimes, but more rarely, they were called "Queen's letters."

[25] Here is one among many similar complaints addressed by the postmasters-general to the packet agent at Harwich: "We admire to find the two Bags with the States letters brought over by the Prince and Dispatch which arrived at Harwich June 21st at 7 in the morning should not be dispatcht till 10 the same day; as also at the comeing in of the Mayls, one of which being dispatcht at 12 arrived here at 11 at night, yet the other came not till 7 next morning."

[26] The following is a specimen of the protection order given:—

To all Commanders and Officers of our Shipps, Pressmasters and others whome it may concerne.

James R.

You are not to imprest into our service any of the six persons hereunder named belonging to the Jane of Dover, whereof Richard Moone is master, the said vessell being employed in our service as a pacquett boate at Dover. Given at our Court at Whitehall the 6th of October 1688.

By His Majesty's Command.

Pepys.

1. Anth. Deleau.
2. Jasper Moore.
3. David Williams.
4. Pet. Foster.
5. Dennis Matthew.
6. Wm. Ambross.

[27] Equal to £562:10s.

[28] This captain had long been noted for his truculent conduct. Here is a letter which the postmasters-general had written to him two or three years before:—

GENERAL POST OFFICE, *May 13, 1704.*

Captain Chenal—We received the mail from Portugal brought over by you in the *Mansbridge* packet boat which arriv'd here on Wednesday last. We yesterday received your letter and journal of the said voyage, with the certificate from the sailors who remained in the service the last voyage. We are concern'd to find such differences among persons imploy'd under us, but do think the best way to compose them is to advise every one to mind their proper business and duty. We do think you may keep all your officers and sailors to strict duty without so rugged a treatment as is complain'd of. As we are desirous of good discipline, so are we of good agreement, to which we would have our agent and yourself to contribute your endeavours.

We herewith send you a specimen of a method to keep an abstract of your journal by which you would save yourself and us much trouble by observing.—We are, your loving friends,

R. COTTON.
T. FRANKLAND.

[29] The packet agent at Falmouth.

[30] The provision is as follows: "And for the better management of the Post Office, be it enacted that the postmaster-general shall observe such orders and instructions concerning the settlement of Posts and stages upon

the several roads, Cross roads, and Byeways within the United Kingdom and other Her Majesty's Dominions, as Her Majesty shall from time to time give in that behalf." —1 Vic. cap. xxxiii. sec. 8.

[31] The victory at Oudenarde. Who Mr. Bowen was we are not informed.

[32] Mr. (afterwards Sir John) Evelyn had recently succeeded Sir Robert Cotton as postmaster-general.

[33] This is an allusion to the period antecedent to 1657.

[34] These runners or post-boys carried the mail through the whole journey, resting by the way. It was not, according to common repute, until about the year 1750 that the mail began to be carried from stage to stage by different post-boys.

[35] In London the practice continued until the end of 1846; and in Dublin, which was the last town in the United Kingdom to give it up, until September 1859.

[36] Even the notice to the public announcing the change was as unapologetic as it well could be:—"These are to give notice that by the Act of Parliament for establishing a General Post Office all letters and packets directed to and sent from places distant ten miles or above from the said office in London, which before the second of this instant June were received and delivered by the officers of the penny post, are now subjected to the same rates of postage as general post letters; and that for the accommodation of the inhabitants of such places their letters will be conveyed with the same regularity and dispatch as formerly, being first taxed with the rates and stamped with the mark of the General Post Office; and that all parcels will likewise be taxed at the rate of 2s. per ounce, as the said Act directs."

[37] Chamberlayne's *State of England*, 1710.

[38] The following letter affords an instance of the exertion of authority referred to in the text:—

To the DEPUTYS between LONDON and TINMOUTH.

GENERAL POST OFFICE,
April 6, 1708.

Gentlemen—The bearer hereof, Mr. John Farra, being directed by order of the Lord High Treasurer to proceed to Tinmouth on the publick affairs of the Government, I am ordered by the postmasters-general to require you to furnish the said gentleman with a single horse [*i.e.* a horse without a guide] if required through your several stages, he being well acquainted with the roads and coming recommended by such authority, which by their order is signified by, Gentlemen, your most humble servant,

B. WATERHOUSE,
Secretary.

[39] In documents intended for the public eye it was the practice of the postmasters-general—and it was by them that these warrants were prepared—to speak of an existing abuse as an abuse that was past. This was, of course, to avoid giving offence.

[40] "And whereas divers deputy postmasters do collect great quantities of post letters called by or way letters and, by clandestine and private agreements amongst themselves, do convey the same post in their respective mails, or by bags, according to their several directions, without accounting for the same or endorsing the same on their bills, to the great detriment of Her Majesty's revenues."—9 Anne, cap. x. sec. 18.

[41] The leases of seven out of the nine branches were cancelled in 1716; and those of the other two the postmasters-general expressed their intention of cancelling with as little delay as possible. And yet as regards one of the number, viz. the Chichester branch, there is reason to doubt whether it did not survive until the year 1769.

[42] Here are two letters they wrote:—

To Mr. CULVERT.

Nov. 1, 1714.

Sir—As the three inclosed letters are directed to you in several places we have reason to think that some persons have presumed to take the liberty of your name. This practice is so great an abuse upon this office, and so very prejudicial to His Majesty's revenue, that we must desire you'll be pleased to send such letters inclosed that don't belong to you to the office to be charged; and we are very well assured you'll discourage the like practice for the future.

—We are, sir, your most humble servants,

T. Frankland.
J. Evelyn.

To Sir RICHARD GROSVENOR, Bart.

April 29, 1715.

Sir—Having observed a letter directed to the Rev. Mr. Harwood at Billingsgate that arrived here yesterday in an Irish mail frank't with your name in Ireland, and knowing that you are in England, we have reason to think that somebody in that kingdom has taken the liberty of signing your name to the prejudice of His Majesty's revenue, which is a practice that we are convinced you will discourage, and it is in order thereunto that you have this trouble from your most humble servants,

CORNWALLIS.
JAMES CRAGGS.

[43] A strongly-worded petition on the subject was presented to Parliament only a year or two after the Restoration. This petition, after calling the charge an "abuse and extortion," goes on to say that "it cannot be imagined the Parliament should either so far forget themselves, or the countrey for which they served, or the necessary and convenient correspondence, as well as the trade of His Majesties dominions, as to put them upon worse and harder tearms than foreigners, or foreign trade, to the prejudice of the kingdom...."

[44] Historical Manuscripts Commission, Appendix to Eleventh Report, Part iv. pp. 233, 234.

[45] *British Curiosities in Art and Nature, likewise an Account of the Posts, Markets, and Fair-Towns*, 1728.

[46] The book was afterwards published—*The Gentleman's Pocket-Farrier*, by Doctor Henry Bracken of Lancaster, 1735.

[47] Lord Sandwich was postmaster-general in 1768.

[48] This, although unknown probably to the postmasters until now, was no new discovery. As far back as 1674 John Ogilby had called attention to the erroneous reckonings in vogue. Ogilby had been commissioned by Charles the Second to survey and measure the principal roads of England, and having performed his task he published the result of his labours in a large folio volume. In the preface to an abridgment of this work, published in 1711, he thus wrote: "The distances are all along reckoned in measur'd miles and furlongs, beginning from the Standard in Cornhil, so that the reader must not be surprized when he finds the number of miles set down here exceed the common computation. For example, from London to York are computed but 150 miles, whereas by measure the distance is 192 miles. And computation being very uncertain, it must be granted that no exactness could be observed but [by] adhering constantly to the standard-mile of 1760 yards, which contains eight furlongs."

[49] This explains why in the Road Books of the time the distance between two places is stated differently in two parallel columns under the initials C and M, the one being the computed and the other the measured distance.

[50] 26 Geo. II. cap. xiii. sec. 7.

[51] The box into which the letters fell was at this time an open one, *i.e.* without a cover and movable. It was not until 1792 that the letter-box was closed, fixed, and locked.

[52] Among these robberies there was, so far as we are aware, only one which possessed any feature of interest; and in this case the interest was of a psychological nature. Gardner, a postman, was stopped by three highwaymen on Winchmore Hill, and, on his refusing to give up his letters, they murdered him. Atrocities of this kind had been frequent, and executions had failed to check them. But the resources of civilisation were not exhausted. Lord Lovell—or the Earl of Leicester, as he had now become—waited upon the King and procured His Majesty's assent that, after execution, the highwaymen's bodies should be hung in chains. To be hanged was one thing; after hanging, to have one's body suspended in chains was another. This was an indignity to which no respectable criminal should be called upon to submit. Such would seem to be the idea conveyed in the following letter which Leicester received:—

To the Right Hon. the EARL OF LEICESTER,
at HOLKHAM, NORFOLK.

THURSDAY, *Oct. 1753.*

My Lord—I find that it was by your orders that Mr. Stockdale was hung in chains. Now, if you don't order him to be taken down, I will set fire to your house and blow your brains out the first opportunity.

Stockdale was clerk to a proctor in Doctors Commons.

[53] Elsewhere we have expressed a desire to avoid, as far as possible, the use of technical terms, and the propriety of this course will probably not be disputed when we state that the charge against Bell was that having "crowned the advanced letters" he failed to account for the proceeds. An "advanced" letter was one on which the postage had been advanced, a letter which, having been undercharged in the country, was surcharged in London. To "crown" a letter was to impress it with the stamp of the Crown, denoting that the surcharge had been made. Virtually, therefore, the charge against Bell was that he had embezzled the surcharges.

[54] Of Allen's personal appearance the only account, so far as we are aware, is to be found in the correspondence of Samuel Derrick, Master of the Ceremonies at Bath. Derrick writes, under date May 10, 1763: "I have had an opportunity of visiting Mr. Allen in the train of the French Ambassador. He is a very grave, well-looking old man, plain in his dress, resembling that of a Quaker, and courteous in his behaviour. I suppose he cannot be much under seventy." — Vol. ii. p. 94.

[55] 1: *The Present State of Great Britain and Ireland*, published in 1742, states that at that time compensation was still given for losses sustained in the penny post. The words are: "If a parcel happen to miscarry, the value thereof is to be made good by the office, provided the things were securely inclosed and fast sealed up under the impression of some remarkable seal." This is an error; and that an error should be made on the point serves to confirm the view that little was known of the Post Office and its doings even 150 years ago. That compensation was not at that time given for losses is beyond all question. It happens that in that very year, 1742, a Mr. Vavasour appealed to Whitehall to grant him compensation for the loss of bank notes to the amount of £20 which had been stolen from a letter in its transit through the post; and the postmasters-general, after stating that no precedent existed for granting compensation, implored the Treasury not to create one. "All persons," they write under date the 4th of August 1742, "that for their own convenience send notes or bills of value by the post inclosed in letters do so at their own risque without any foundation that we know of for recovery of this office in case they should be stolen or lost by robbery or other accidents. And this we take to be not only reasonable but just in all construction of law." Again, in 1778 an action for compensation was brought against the Post Office, and Lord Mansfield, after delivering the unanimous opinion of the Court of King's Bench that the postmasters-general were not responsible for losses sustained in their department, proceeded to observe that no similar action had been brought since the year 1699. Giles Jacob, in his *Law Dictionary*, published in the last century, gives this account of the matter: "It was determined so long ago as 13 Will. III., in the case of *Lane* v. *Cotton*, by three judges of the Court of King's Bench, though contrary to Lord Chief Justice Holt's opinion, that no action could be maintained against the postmasters-general for the loss of bills or articles sent in letters by the post."

[56] The reason for the provision was thus given in the preamble: "Whereas many heavy and bulky packets and parcels are now sent and conveyed by such carriage which by their bulk and weight greatly retard the speedy delivery thereof...." — 5 Geo. III. cap. xxv. sec. 14.

[57] For what constituency Richard Hiver sat we have been unable to discover. His name does not appear in the return of members of Parliament presented to the House of Commons in 1878.

[58] "Whereas the several streets, lanes, squares, yards, courts, alleys, passages and places within the city of London and the liberties thereof are in general ill-paved and cleansed and not duly enlightened, and are also greatly obstructed by posts and annoyed by signs, spouts, and gutters projecting into and over the same, whereby and by sundry other encroachments and annoyances they are rendered incommodious and in some parts dangerous not only to the inhabitants but to all others passing through the same or resorting thereto...."

[59] Thus, Mrs. Thrale to Doctor Johnson. Writing from Bath on the 4th of July 1784, she says: "I write by the coach the more speedily and effectually to prevent your coming hither." —Hayward's *Autobiography of Mrs. Piozzi*, vol. i. p. 241.

[60] Thus, the Act 20 Geo. III. cap. li. sec. 2—an Act passed four years before the mails were carried by coach:—

"That every person who shall keep any four-wheeled chaise or other machine commonly called a diligence or post-coach, or by what name soever such carriages now are or hereafter shall be called or known...."

That the term post-coach, as distinguished from mail-coach, was in vogue as late as 1827 appears from evidence taken in that year before the Commissioners of Revenue Inquiry—"(Q.) Are you acquainted with the post-coaches? (A.) Not any very great deal. (Q.) Comparing them with mail-coaches, which do you think are the best formed? (A.) Decidedly the mail-coaches, I think." —Appendix to Eighteenth Report, p. 443.

[61] A foreign registered letter *outwards* would be a letter registered as far as Dover or Harwich or Falmouth for transmission abroad, and possibly on board ship. A foreign registered letter *inwards* would not be the exact converse, for there would be no registration from the port of arrival to London. The fee of 5s. covered the registration of a letter only from London to its destination.

[62] *i.e.* boats. At Liverpool packets, in the sense of boats commissioned by Government to carry letters, did not at this time exist.

[63] The King's physician.

[64] The Post Office accounts for the year 1749 were not passed until 1784; and then only through the exertions of Lord Mountstuart, who had succeeded Mr. Aislabie as one of the auditors of His Majesty's imprests.

[65] A letter to a member of Parliament on mail-coaches, by Thomas Pennant, Esq., 1792.

[66] At this time the number of newspapers passing through the London office averaged 80,000 a week, of which 78,000 were from London to the country and 2000 from the country to London. Mixed, that is wet and dry together, they were computed to weigh sixteen to the pound.

[67] How Carteret managed to retain his appointment for more than eighteen years is not the least perplexing of Post Office problems. Meanwhile the joint postmaster-generalship had undergone the following changes:—

Lord Le Despencer	} From Jan. 16, 1771,
Right Hon. Henry F. Thynne (afterwards Carteret)	} to Dec. 11, 1781.
Right Hon. Henry F. Carteret (sometime Thynne)	{ From Dec. 11, 1781,
	{ to Jan. 24, 1782.
Right Hon. Henry F. Carteret	} From Jan. 24, 1782,
Viscount Barrington	} to April 25, 1782.
Right Hon. Henry F. Carteret	} From April 25, 1782,
Earl of Tankerville	} to May 1, 1783.
Right Hon. Henry F. Carteret	} From May 1, 1783,
Lord Foley	} to Jan. 7, 1784.
Right Hon. Henry F. Carteret, created Lord	}
Carteret Jan. 29, 1784	} From Jan. 7, 1784,
Earl of Tankerville (a second time)	} to Sept. 19, 1786.
Lord Carteret	} From Sept. 19, 1786,
Earl of Clarendon	} to Dec. 10, 1786.
Lord Carteret	{ From Dec. 10, 1786,
	{ to July 6, 1787.
Lord Carteret	} From July 6, 1787,
Lord Walsingham	} to Sept. 19, 1789.

[68] Sir Rowland Hill, in his *Autobiography* (vol. ii. p. 28), does not hesitate to write as follows: "Incredible as it may appear to my readers, it is nevertheless true that so late as 1844 a system, dating from some far distant time, was in full operation, under which clerks from the foreign office used to attend on the arrival of mails from abroad, to open the letters addressed to certain ministers resident in England, and make from them such extracts as they deemed useful for the service of Government."

[69] Even in such a detail as the manner of dismissal, Pitt shewed his usual consideration for Palmer. By the minister's direction Palmer was not to be dismissed in so many words. The postmasters-general were simply to make out another nominal list of the establishment, and from this list Palmer's name was to be excluded.

[70] Later on, Mr. Pickwick would seem to have extended his operations. "(Q.) Are you in the habit of working coaches to any great distance from London? (A.) I work them half-way to Bristol. With Mr. Pickwick of Bath I work to Newbury."—Evidence of Mr. William Home, taken on the 2nd of March 1819 before the Select Committee on the Highways of the Kingdom.

[71] The packet agency had been removed from Harwich to Yarmouth during the war. Yarmouth, by road, is 124 miles from London.

[72] Mrs. Davy was born in 1760.

[73] As late as 1854 Bournemouth received its letters from Poole by donkey and cart.

[74] This was a commission of three halfpence on every dozen newspapers, besides one newspaper in every quire.

[75] From this time the expression "banker's frank" passed into a by-word, and was used to denote any frank, whether given by a banker or not, which was in excess of the prescribed number.

[76] This is Godolphin's letter:—

Treasury Chambers, *June 8, 1703.*

Gentlemen—My Lord Treasurer hath commanded me to signify to you his Lordship's direction that whenever your Sollicitor shall pay any fees to any Serjeant or Councellor at law, or give any sum or sums of money for coppys to any Clerk or Clerks or Officers in any Court or Courts of Record at Westminster, he shall take a ticket subscribed with the hand and name of the same Serjeant or Councellor or from the Clerk or Officer testifying how much he hath received for his fee or hath been paid by him for coppys, and at what time and how often, according to the statute in the third year of the reign of King James the First, made and provided in that behalf, and His Lordship directs you to take care that what money shall be hereafter expended for law charges relating to the Revenue under your management, the same be so expressed in the Bill of Incidents, that it may appear to His Lordship that the above-mentioned directions have been duly comply'd with.—I am, gentlemen, your most humble servant,

William Lowndes.

Sir Robert Cotton, Knight, and
Sir Thomas Frankland, Bart.

[77] 42 George III. cap. lxxxi. (June 20, 1802).

[78] This experience is not to be compared with that of Inspector Dicker, who in 1839 wrote to the Secretary of the Post Office as follows:—

"Honoured Sir ... On arriving at Caxton, in the course of conversation with the landlord of the Crown Public-House respecting the loss of the above-mentioned bag, he informed me he had found a mail bag secreted under an oak floor between the joists that supported the floor in one of the upper rooms of his house, and that the letters it contained were of very ancient date, as far back as the year 1702. I requested to be allowed to see them, and, on his producing them, discovered it to be a London bag labelled Tuxford. I desired to be allowed to take two of the letters with me and a bit of the bag, which I gave to Mr. Peacock the solicitor. The only intelligence I could gain as to the probable cause of the bag being found there was that a post-rider was robbed and murdered about the date of the above-mentioned letters." The two letters are still with the official papers. One of them is undecipherable. The other is nearly as legible as on the day it was written. In it the writer announces to his uncle the death of his mother from "the Small Pox and purples," and states that this disease is devastating the town of Kirtlington.

[79] *Weekly Political Register*, Nos. 25 and 26, 21st and 28th Dec. 1805.

[80] What we have here called "franked" newspapers went free in both directions; but of course it was only newspapers outwards that bore a signature on the superscription. On those inwards a signature was immaterial, as they would in any case go, without being charged, direct from the port of arrival to Lombard Street. Abroad, special arrangements for their transit and delivery were made from London. Thus, the London Office by means of its private agency could get an English newspaper delivered in Paris for 2d. By post, the charge between Calais and Paris would have been from 3s. to 4s.

[97] At the outset in 1792 the limit had indeed been fixed at £5:5s.; but even in the first year this limit was largely exceeded. During the three months ending the 10th of October 1800, 697 money orders were issued, viz. 220 in London and 477 in the country, representing an aggregate amount of £8863, or at the rate of more than £12 apiece.

[98] Among the records of the Post Office is still preserved a money order drawn by one postmaster upon another at the beginning of the century. A facsimile of it is given in the Appendix. see facsimile

[99] Five within a single year. The Duke of Richmond ceased to be postmaster-general in July 1834; and he was followed by Lord Conyngham, Lord Maryborough, Lord Conyngham a second time, and Lord Lichfield, the last of whom was appointed in May 1835.

[100] The Right Hon. Thomas Spring Rice.

[101] The concentration of the offices of Lord Treasurer and Postmaster-General in one person served to facilitate the transaction of Post Office business in a manner which those who have had experience of the present system will not be slow to understand. Take, for instance, the question of increasing a Post Office servant's salary. At the present time the Postmaster-General may be thoroughly convinced himself that an increase is called for, but—what is a very different matter—he has also to convince the Treasury. In 1686 the Postmaster-General's own conviction was enough. The following will serve as an illustration. Thomas Cale, Postmaster of Bristol, applies for an increase of salary, and Frowde, the Governor, satisfies Rochester that an increase will be proper. Forthwith issues a document, of which the operative part is as follows:—"You are therefore of opinion that the said salary (£50) is very small considering the expense the petitioner is att, and his extraordinary trouble, Bristoll being a greate Citty, but you say that you doe not think all the things he setts downe in the aforesaid accompt ought to be allowed him, the example being of very ill consequence, for (as you informe me) you doe not allow either candles, packthread, wax, ink, penns or paper to any of the Postmasters, nor office-rent, nor returnes of mony, you are therefore of opinion that tenn pounds per annum to his former salary of £50 will be a reasonable allowance, and the petitioner will be therewith satisfied, these are therefore to pray and require you" to raise his salary from £50 to £60 accordingly.

Rochester.

Whitehall Treasury Chambers, *Dec. 13, 1686.*

[81] One of the first, if not the very first, against whom proceedings were taken under this provision of the statute was Robert Wetherall, master of the ship *Albinia*, from Gravesend to the Cape of Good Hope. Wetherall had at the last moment refused to take the mails on board, consisting of 173 letters. On the advice of the law officers the Post Office contemplated proceeding against him by indictment; but the Government decided to proceed by information, with a view apparently to give to the case greater importance and notoriety.

[82] Clancarty was afterwards appointed joint postmaster-general of England. This appointment he held from 30th September 1814 to 6th April 1816, but he never took it up. Between the dates mentioned he was employed on missions abroad.

[83] At one time the express newspapers went all the way from London to Dublin post free; but this, at the date of the advertisement, had been stopped, and as far as Holyhead their carriage was now being provided for under an arrangement with the London agents. From Holyhead to Dublin, however, they still went in the mail free of postage, and on arrival in Dublin such of them as were destined for the country were franked by the clerks of the roads.

[84] In 1823 the Irish mail-coaches travelled daily a distance of 1450 miles at a cost to the Post Office of more than £30,000 a year, while in England the cost over the same number of miles would have been only £7500. From this, however, it is not to be understood that in one country the cost was four times as heavy as in the other, because the Irish mile was longer than the English one by about two furlongs, and in England the contractors did not, as they did in Ireland, provide the coaches.

[85] The exact number of passengers in the year 1814 was 14,577, made up as follows: Cabin passengers, 12,142; passengers' servants, 1136; hold passengers, 1299.

[86] The following are copies of the advertisements referred to:—

"The Howth Royal Mail-Coach sets out every evening at seven o'clock from the Cork Coach Office, 12 Dawson Street, where passengers and luggage will be booked, and arrives at Howth at a quarter after eight, when the packet will immediately sail (independently of the tide) with the Irish mails and passengers for Holyhead. From the admirable construction of these vessels for fast sailing and excellent accommodation the passage from the pier at Howth to Holyhead will on the average be performed in one-third less time than by the *Pigeon House*. Besides, as no more than eight or ten passengers will be admitted into any one of these packets, the public, on the score of expedition and comfort, will soon experience the advantage of going to Holyhead by Howth.

"Passengers by the mail-coach have a preference as to berths in the packets.

"*July 21, 1813.*"

"Howth Royal Mail-Coach, well guarded, sets out from the Cork Coach Office, No. 12 Dawson Street, at seven o'clock every evening with mails and passengers to His Majesty's express packets at Howth, from whence one of these excellent vessels sails at half after eight o'clock every night for Holyhead.

"*July 31, 1813.*"

[87] By the Post Office packets the number of passengers between Holyhead and Dublin during the years 1818-20 was as follows:—

Year.	Number of Passengers.
1818	13,128
1819	12,956
1820	7,468

Private steam packets began to ply in July 1819.

[88] *i.e.* Kinniogga, the old name for Cernioge.

[89] "God knows whether we are to remain postmen or not, or whether all the lights which philosophy is now throwing upon coach-making are not to be left by us as an official legacy to some more pliant successors." — Chesterfield to Walsingham, 22nd April 1792.

[90] The postage between Liverpool and Dublin by way of Holyhead was 13d., as thus made up:—

Inland postage to Holyhead	9d.
For the Conway Bridge	1d.
For the Menai Bridge	1d.
Sea postage	2d.
	—
	13d.
	—

[91] The official intimation was received at the Post Office on the 28th of May. On the same day Lord Salisbury wrote to the receiver-general as follows:—

General Post Office, *May 28, 1822.*

Sir—I have received instructions from the Lords Commissioners of His Majesty's Treasury to acquaint you that on the 5th of July next you are to retain in your hands the salary of £2500 hitherto paid to me as joint postmaster-general.—I am, etc.,

Salisbury.

R. Willimott, Esq., Receiver-General.

[92] The sums abated were afterwards returned. It was not until 1834 that abatements towards superannuation were imposed by statute.

[93] 42 George III. cap. lxiii. sec. 10.

[94] This is the circular which was issued to postmasters on the occasion of a dissolution:—

"The Parliament is dissolved. The franks of this evening are necessarily charged with postage, and you will immediately charge all letters and packets excepting the letters franked by such public officers as are by law at all times exempted from postage. Full instructions will be sent to-morrow."

[95] Since 1814 receipts had been given for registered letters. In that year Mr. H. M. Raikes, of 4 Portman Square, represented that he frequently sent valuable parcels of diamonds between this country and Holland, and that these parcels he insured, but that, to be certain of recovering his insurance should any casualty happen, "the London merchant ought to have some proof in his possession of his having delivered such a packet into the charge of the Post Office." If, he added, the clerks would give a receipt, the merchant would gladly give them for their trouble an additional guinea. The suggestion to charge a second guinea was not adopted; but from that time a receipt had been given for a registered letter in the following form:—

Foreign Post Office.

LONDON 181

It is hereby certified that .... has registered at this office a sealed packet said to contain .... addressed to .... which will be forwarded to .... by the mail of this evening; but for its safe conveyance this office is not responsible.

(*Signature*) ....

[96] 7 and 8 George IV. cap. xxi.